'2

Wk 24.

GRAND PRIX PRIX
REQUIEM

By the same author
POWER AND GLORY Vols 1 and 2
CAR ENGINES (with Dr Lionel J. Stretton)

Patrick Stephens Limited, a member of the Haynes Publishing Group, has published authoritative, quality books for enthusiasts for a quarter of a century. During that time the company has established a reputation as one of the world's leading publishers of books on aviation, maritime, military, model-making, motor cycling, motoring, motor racing, railway and railway modelling subjects. Readers or authors with suggestions for books they would like to see published are invited to write to: The Editorial Director, Patrick Stephens Limited, Sparkford, Nr Yeovil, Somerset, BA22 7JJ.

GRAND PRIX REQUIEM

A celebration of motor racing greats who paid speed's ultimate price

William Court

Foreword by Nigel Roebuck, Grand Prix Editor of *Autosport*

Patrick Stephens Limited

First published in 1992

British Library Cataloguing-in-Publication Data:
A catalogue record for this book is available from the British Library.

ISBN 1-85260-386-0

Jacket illustrations:
Front *(top left, clockwise) Early Dynasts, Antonio Ascari with Alberto; Mad Ronald, Ronnie Peterson; Sun of a gun from Arizona, Jim Bryan; Master Car Controller, Jochen Rindt; The Incomparable, Jim Clark; Mad Ronald's Friend, Mike Hailwood; Bella Figura, Dr Giuseppe Farina; Ferrari's New Wonderman, Gilles Villeneuve; and (foreground) A Man With the Devil to Pay, Luigi Musso.*
Back *(top left, clockwise) Mr Monaco, Graham Hill; Expatriate Englishman, Loraine Barrow; Complete Man and Maestro, Sir Henry Segrave; Meteor and Meteorite, Frank Lockhart and Black Hawk Stutz; Monzanapolis 1958; The Irrepressible, Bernd Rosemeyer; and (foreground) Larger Than Life, Cav. Giuseppe Campari.*

Patrick Stephens Limited is a member of the
Haynes Publishing Group P.L.C., Sparkford,
Nr Yeovil, Somerset, BA22 7JJ.

Typeset by Wyvern Typesetting Ltd, Bristol
Printed in Great Britain by Redwood Press Ltd, Melksham, Wilts.

FOR JANE

'For he shall carry nothing away with him when he dieth: neither shall his pomp follow him. For while he lived, he counted himself an happy man: and so long as thou doest well unto thy self, men will speak good of thee.'

—Psalm 49: 17–18

* * *

'A direct relation with the reading public could be established by anyone prepared to be moving and memorable.'

—*Graeme Wright (Ed. of* Wisden*) from* The Independent on Sunday *(15 December 1991) on the death of John Arlott (he had died on 14 December 1991) who wrote:*

'Cricket is a game; its purpose is enjoyment, not a form of nationalist propaganda.'

* * *

'The Corrida accepts that death must be accepted as a part of life'.

* * *

'We have made a covenant with death, and with hell are we at agreement;'
—Isaiah 28:15

* * *

'Dead—For My Life—Even So:—My Tale Is Told.'

Contents

Preface

In writing this book I took for my text the second of the five epigraphs on page 7 and what better inspiration could any sports, writer have than from the late John Arlott? So, 'Give Them Something Different!' became not so much my watchword as my words to watch for. Hence, in particular, the style and approach of Parts 3, 4, 18 and, almost as an afterthought, 19, though I hope this will not make the other parts seem to be lagging behind.

This book is concerned with the action and interaction of individual attitudes to life, competition, risk and death; in which all these elements remain as constant as the pole star, with only the actual degrees of risk as variables. Thus, the fact that this book has a mainstream background of motor racing is little more than coincidence and, given risk as its subject, its relevant attitudes would remain the same whatever the human activity involved.

Similarly, the reader, no less than the writer, of these pages, will be struck at the end of their tale by the incidence and coincidence of one or another or even all of four elements: Foreboding, Luck, Superstition and Coincidence. The tales of men like Loraine Barrow, Marcel Renault, Eliot and Louis Zborowski, both Ascaris, Bernd Rosemeyer, Richard Seaman, Eugenio Castellotti, Luigi Musso, Peter Collins, Wolfgang von Trips, Jochen Rindt, Pedro Rodriguez, Wilbur Shaw, Bill Vukovich I, Jim Bryan, Jimmy Murphy and Frank Lockhart bear this out, and maybe you, my readers, will find out more examples of your own.

So, Good Reading!

Acknowledgments

The problem is really where to start, for I have been simply inundated with interested and, above all, friendly helpers, on whose time and patience I have incessantly trespassed during the two years it has taken me to put this book together. As always, my sources have been myriad, and by no means all (at first sight anyway) have too discernible a connection with motor racing; although my indulgent readers must be getting used to that by now!

So, let me start with the archival matter which has loomed large in these pages with close on 80 very varied individuals to be researched. I have found the backbone of this work in the memory of Peter Blair-Richley and in his library, which seems to grow another room every time I visit him! Running Peter an increasingly close second are David Venables, Dr Paul Sheldon and his associates, and Nigel Roebuck who have constantly had to endure and answer my tide of queries on so many things that I simply did not know about—and they always did; Cyril Posthumus and Doug Nye when I have been really stumped; and Eoin Young, not least when I have needed some well-aimed shooting down of some of my flights of fancy. Where would I be without such friends?

Next come the periodicals: chiefly *Motor Sport*, *L'Équipe*, *Autosport*, and *Autocar & Motor* whose Managing Director, Simon Taylor, generously allowed me the run of their libraries when my own shelves were found wanting. Alan Henry, Maurice Hamilton, David Tremayne, Norman Howell of *The Times*, and, of course, DSJ. Also my own professional body in Chancery Lane for copying to me the Report of Loraine Barrow's case (see pages 65 to 67).

Then there are books. I started to compile a bibliography of the works I had consulted, and I soon came to the conclusion, that it would need a small volume itself to include all my sources, so I have listed just the main titles and a few extras in the Bibliography at the back of this book.

But books and records cannot always give you all the answers and angles that you need and I have often had to look for the precious 'one off' help of many others. To mention just a few: John Cooper, with whom I spent a very pleasant half hour recently clearing up a question about Sommer's last race from 1950; Esmond Lewis-Evans, an elder brother of Stuart, who provided the sort of family background that you just do not find in records; that most cultured of Grand Prix Drivers, Tony Brooks, for clarifying much about the Vanwall of 1957/8 and the unhappy death of Stuart Lewis-Evans; Eric Thompson for his memorial of Raymond Sommer in 1950 again; David Venables for so many things like directing me to a French account of Sommer's last

15

race at Cadours, helping some of my thoughts over 'The Chipmunk Theory' (see pages 40/41), telling me of some otherwise long lost memories of the young Mike Hawthorn at Goodwood, and also his account of a meeting with Pierre Levegh in 1949 (see page 299); my old friend Michael Dowler for refreshing my memory of the story of the Seller and the Buyer that appears at the beginning of the Introduction, and the story of Harry Schell and 'Schellsley Walsh'; Ken and Norah Tyrrell for some moving memories of François Cevert; Martyn Flower for some helpful additional details of Dario Resta; David Hayhoe for finding me some obscure dates of death and birth; Mrs P. Hatfield, the Archivist of Eton College for details of the early life of Count Louis Zborowski; Mrs Eileen Measures for information on the life and times of Sir Henry ['Tim'] Birkin; Eoin Young for similar help about Bruce 'Whoosh-Bonk' McLaren; Nigel Roebuck for the charming and touching vignette of Chris Amon and Lorenzo Bandini on the morning of his death; David Tremayne for shedding new light on the tragedy of Seppi Siffert; René Dreyfus for all the pleasures of *Le Chanteclair* (his restaurant in New York) and, more recently, his book *My Two Lives*; the staff of Queens Club for sparing the time to seek out details of the velocity of a rackets ball for me; to John and Adèle Sebert for their memoir of Gilles Villeneuve (see page 314) from 1978/9 and just countless others with whom I could fill half of this book.

Let me close this all too brief Harvest Festival of Thanksgiving with one further 'source' that I most particularly want to acknowledge, even though its author may have no interest or connection with motor racing, let alone with me. At least, however, the imprint of his publishers proclaims him to be an Oxford man! While working out the format of this book I chanced to read a review of Mr Philip Furia's highly entertaining book, *The Poets of Tin Pan Alley*, whose period coincided perfectly with the twenties and thirties and whose heroes form a central part of this book. For me and, I hope, for my readers, the transatlantic mix that has resulted was as irresistible as the Tragi-Comic Opera pieces on Campari and his contemporaries.

Thank goodness that photography is easier to catalogue, although the problem of finding 'fresh' subjects becomes increasingly more difficult as the years go by. I am, as always, chiefly in Geoffrey Goddard's debt. There are, however, others whose help it is a pleasure to acknowledge. Neil Eason-Gibson has contributed some rare prints, and also Michael Hewett, whose book on the Monaco Grand Prix is beautifully illustrated by many of his own shots.

Another most welcome newcomer to my photographic pages has been Bob Tronolone from Burbank, California, who was introduced to me by Nigel Roebuck. Our communication by letter and telephone has been a source of great pleasure and help during this book's lengthy gestation. Apart from being a most delightful correspondent, he is also a remarkably good photographer.

Finally, but in no way least, come Haynes' publishing staff, without whose endeavours none of this could come into being. My particular thanks to Darryl Reach, Editorial Director of the Book Trade Division, his Editorial Department Manager Alison Roelich, Editor Flora Myer, Editorial Secretary Carole Turk, and to John Hardaker who did such a first-class job copy editing the book. They are a very happy team to work with.

Foreword

When first William Court asked me to write a Foreword for this book, I was pleased to agree, for he is a friend of many years' standing. It was only later I began to wonder at my decision: on the face of it, was not a book about dead racing drivers perhaps a touch morbid?

Such thoughts quickly withered. Even before reading the first part of the manuscript, I had recovered my senses, sure in my own mind that—in Court's hands—this would be no work of maudlin sentimentality, no ghoulish study. He *appreciates* racing drivers, I believe, as I do myself. As human beings, some may be splendid, others despicable, but as racing drivers they put something in our lives we cannot put there ourselves.

Grand Prix Requiem therefore celebrates the lives of a widely disparate group of men, all of whom chased something they considered worthwhile, and ultimately died in that pursuit. Some were great and some were not, but common to each was the simple desire to drive a racing car faster than anyone else. At the highest level, they had—and will always have— an audacity and resolution beyond normal understanding. If you think this folly, chances are you never saw the majesty of an Ascari, a Clark or a Villeneuve.

William Court has always earned his living in more ordered a world than full-time motor racing journalism, so that when he writes of this greatest of all sports, his spur is enthusiasm, the pure love of it. This brings a freshness of approach, and also a degree of lateral thinking perhaps denied those of us too closely involved. Thus, racing drivers of very different cut, nationality and time, are frequently compared in ways at once whimsical and wise.

Striking, too, is the relative absence here of men from the modern era, which says everything about the comparative safety of motor racing in the 80s and 90s. If, by its very nature, it can never be safe in any workaday sense, it was more perilous by far even a decade ago, to say nothing of the days before seat belts, roll-over bars, crash barriers, even helmets. Common to all those in this book is that they measured the risks of the time, and found them worth the running. For that, and much else besides, we should honour them.

NIGEL ROEBUCK
Grand Prix Editor of *Autosport*

Introduction

'. . . And summer's lease hath all too short a date.'—William Shakespeare
(Sonnet 18)

One might well think that men who choose to live by the daily risk of their lives would be the first to share Bacon's thought that death was the least of all evils, were it not for the widely held belief that death only happens to 'the other chap'—like those little bells of hell that go:

'Ting-a-ling-a-ling for you, but not for me.'

For some, like the dashing Marquis of Portago, this comforting thought was enough to allay death's flip side—fear: 'I don't believe a racing driver is necessarily a brave man, as much as a man who isn't afraid.' For others, like Napoleon's Marshal, Jean Lannes, whom he called 'The Bravest of the Brave', it was a case of: 'No-one but a swine or a coward ever boasts that he is never afraid.' So, perhaps the dashing Marquis, who was neither, was slightly over-stating his case.

Death we seek to postpone or conveniently forget; fear we fight to conquer, and certainty we would fain achieve. Yet, what control do we really have over any of them? I recall a pit lane dialogue of many years ago between the new and the former owner of a somewhat fractious and uncertain Grand Prix car that had just changed hands:

The buyer (anxiously crowding the seller): 'But are you certain it's the Mag.?'
The seller (casually and not really wanting to prolong the dialogue): 'Dear Boy, nothing in this life is certain!'

No man may choose the time of his birth. A few may choose that of their death, though none can know its very hour, with the possible exception of a deliberately planned suicide or of Thrasyllus, astrologer to the Emperor Tiberius, who the ancients said had foretold his own precisely. That improbable fable apart, does not the only real certainty for any of us lie with Horatius:

'To every man upon this earth,
Death cometh soon or late.'

The advent of middle age, coupled with three close brushes with the Old Reaper when I chanced to be drafting the 'risk element' chapters for Volume 2 of *Power and Glory*, set me thinking about these ultimates against a growing background of the distressing fatal accidents in the 50s, 60s and 70s. More recently, these were poignantly brought back to me by the moving writing of Ian Fraser in *Supercar Classics* about Grand Prix racing in those 50s and 60s, which he described as 'A heavyweight affair', before adding:

'And if we glorify the cars of that period without thinking of the price, we do so at our peril. . . . Human tragedy surrounds all. It's that side, the darker side, that deserves more of our thoughts. None of the events and none of the cars would be famous if it were not for the drivers who originally made them so.'

What he says is just as true of every other decade of that Grand Prix racing which some call 'the greatest sport known to man'.

Notwithstanding Fraser's fine writing, when Patrick Stephens Limited first asked me to do a 'reading book' to bridge the gap between the appearance of Volume 2 of *Power and Glory* and the commissioning of Volume 3, I turned *Requiem* down flat, and it was only by long and laboursome petition that my old friend Darryl Reach prevailed upon me to think about writing a book that had death as its apparent main theme. I remembered that in the aftermath of Vol. 1's first appearance it had actually occurred to me that the book should have included some form of valedictory for the brave departed of its years. So, while Vol. 2 was approaching proof stage I added, as one of four tail-pieces, a set of 30 captioned photographs of chosen Grand Prix drivers who had been killed during that volume's period.

Their recollection proved a sobering and salutary exercise in facing up anew to the price of speed, and it also convinced me that there was at least one book to be written as a celebratory thanksgiving for the lives of so many brave and gifted men from the present time back to that day in 1897 when the first true Grand Prix driver, Émile Levassor, had given up his own life. So, in the end, I found myself saying: 'Oh, whyever not?' After all, death is one of the only two certainties in life, whatever that old songster, Gus Kahn, may have said about the rich and the poor and—God Bless you for the thought Mr Kahn—that:

'In the meantime
In between time
Ain't we had fun!'

The next task was to settle on a framework for the book before starting to flesh it out to meet the publisher's Procrustean demand for 100,000 words and 80 pictures. As the work progressed it seemed more and more like I was putting together my own guest list for a rather special party complete with all its tally of social problems: who was going to sit with whom; who drank this and who that; who could not stand whom and such like; and, last, what was I to do about the last minute additions that I had embarrassingly forgotten all about.

At first for its framework my mind turned to the Noah's Ark of Jean-Marie Balestre's two-by-two Grand Prix grid formations. This worked out well enough as a starting point while I busied myself fulfilling every writer's first essential: to get on and write!—it's surprising the number of would-be writers who fall down on that first basic essential! So, to the fitting and tuneful background of Haydn's six last Masses, the racer's requiem began slowly to take shape as my carefully paired characters took their appointed places and the processor clicked, buzzed and bleeped merrily away, interrupted occasionally by cries of anguish when some of my pearls mysteriously deserted the disk or the VDU screen for limbo, leaving me wishing for the safe old certainties of the typewriter, or even grubby old-fashioned pen and ink!

The 'Ark' formula worked out well enough until I found that, in my overpowering zeal to get writing, I had created yet another Frankenstein's monster in the shape of enough material and characters for two books of my Requiem rather than the required single volume of Brief Lives! So it was time to exercise the salutary disciplines of blue pencil and cutting room scissors!

As this involved the drastic shortening of most of the 'Lives', I decided to re-plan the whole of the work and, while I was at it, to cast around for some fresh ideas and angles. This coincided with Jane and I taking a couple of weeks holiday in Madeira, where we chanced upon a recently re-issued paperback edition of Rose Macaulay's 1946 book, *They Came to Portugal*, a charming set of rather longer pieces about the English in Portugal down the centuries. I had also thrown into our holiday book bag an old travelling friend and earlier testament to English eccentricity: John Aubrey's *Brief Lives* from the mid-to-late seventeenth century. Apart from the sheer entertainment value of two such total departures from the mainstream of motor racing, these delightful works told me exactly how I should best set out the revised framework of this book, though obviously not its content.

So, out of the window went the systems of Noah and M. Balestre, and in came a new *modus operandi* involving the reshaping of my pairs of characters into a series of blocks of inter-connecting individuals. I then turned my thoughts to the centrepoint and slant of each block, which I set up to vary with each group of my 77 characters. The effect that I most passionately sought to avoid was of just one more 'Grand Prix Fact Book', built to the straight, historical and deadly dull 'Generations of Methuselah' matrix. At the same time, though, every movement has to start somewhere and every book has to have a beginning, and it seemed pointless to me to start anywhere else but with the first Grand Prix driver, who was also the first such driver to die from racing. Thus Émile Levassor. Yet, behind every great man there is often to be found a significant woman, and who more so than that widowed Madame Sarazin who melted the 'Frowning Providence' that was M. Émile and, no less importantly, rescued for him the vital Daimler patents that had otherwise died with her first husband.

Down the years Grand Prix racing has grafted on to its collective soul a pot-pourri of noise, colour, drama, pathos, cost, characters, showbiz, spectacle, razzamatazz, magic, superstition, a foreboding that is sometimes close to necromancy, lucky charms, romance, sex and silken favours, music, atmosphere, pageantry and, at the end, death. How to single out and apportion these elements is a matter of individual choice and, for sure, there is plenty of that. Inevitably, in the decades from 1895 these particular waters have been victim to over-fishing. So, to avoid excessive repetition, new approaches, angles and slants had to be found, to lighten the ever increasing stodge of 'the usual', and better to refresh the jaded palate with new delicacies.

Now, I know only too well that this broad brush philosophy may be anathema to those who see it as an indulgent and sinister departure from 'the mainstream'. None the less I cherish the hope that it has not involved too much straying from the straight and narrow, while still holding fast to that old and so true saying: 'What can they know of (in this context) motors that only motors know?'

I come back, then, to my introductory idea of throwing a party for my favourite guests and, clinging to the hope that I shall not find, in Bruce McLaren's graphic expression, that 'Whoosh-Bonk', I have asked far too many people and put together such a good party that there are no convenient 'drop outs'! So, who would be a host or, for that matter, an author?

Now a quick look at the characters that you, as readers, are going to meet on the way—most, I suspect, as old friends, but I hope there will be some who are new to you or who demonstrate a different side to themselves. The Grand Prix world is 'full of folks', and it is only from the starting grid that we can properly take our view of it.

First must come the fastest starter of them all—in his outward show at least, a supremely relaxed Alberto Ascari, though no longer in an old world populated by lurking black cats.

Then, after him, the great car controllers, companions of Helius whose daily task it was to drive all-mighty Zeus's train of horses across the sky: Pietro Bordino, Bernd Rosemeyer, Mike Hawthorn, Jochen Rindt, Ronnie Peterson and Gilles Villeneuve; and, with them, some great drivers who were also fliers: Georges Boillot, Robert Benoist, Wilbur Shaw and Graham Hill.

Some men from over the sea: David Bruce-Brown, Dario Resta, Jimmy Murphy, Frank Lockhart, Bill Vukovich I, Rex Mays, Ralph Hepburn and Jim Bryan.

The drivers who were also watermen: Henry Segrave and Didier Pironi.

The aristocrats: Counts Eliot and Louis Zborowski, Stanislas Czaykowski and Godin de Beaufort, the Marquis de Portago, Baron von Trips and Sir Henry Birkin Bart.

The firebrands: Cesare Giuppone, Paul Zuccarelli, Raymond Sommer, Harry Schell, Eugenio Castellotti, Luigi Musso, Jean Behra and Patrick Depailler.

The quiet men: Baconin Borzacchini, Jean-Pierre Wimille, Peter Collins, Bruce McLaren and the incomparable Jim Clark.

The desperately unlucky: Loraine Barrow, Marcel Renault, Mike Spence and Tom Pryce.

Some others of whom we have perhaps lost sight: Stuart Lewis-Evans, Lorenzo Bandini, Jo Schlesser, Piers Courage, Roger Williamson, Joakim Bonnier and Mark Donohue.

Some brothers and comrades in arms: André Boillot, Ricardo and Pedro Rodriguez and Jo Siffert.

Two golden lads: Peter Revson and François Cevert, and two victims of unguarded moments: Mike Hailwood and Elio de Angelis.

The brave handicapped: Alan Stacey, Archie Scott-Brown and Gunnar Nilsson.

The men of pride: Antonio Ascari, Achille Varzi, Luigi Fagioli and Giuseppe Farina.

The good who died young: Guy Moll, Richard Seaman and Carlos Pace.

Two Beaux Gendarmes of France: Pierre Levegh and Louis Rosier.

The larger than life: Giuseppe Campari.

And, finally, an oddly assorted trio: one man who somehow survived, Niki Lauda; others who gave up life for country; and bringing up the rear at the back of them all—the first great racing driver to be recognized as such—Émile Levassor, and his remarkable lady.

For each and every one of them it was a case of 'so little time' as death's greed consumed their summer's leases with all too short a date, begging the inevitable question: 'Why did they do it?'

The ancient Greeks and Romans had all the artistic flair and learning in the world, yet they still managed to hand down two chill, dark and unedifying sayings: that it was better not to have been born at all, and that no man might be counted happy until he was dead. Old fashioned and thousands of years out of date? Not a bit of it, for within a week of drafting this page I was being told of the view of a very distinguished Grand Prix writer who still believes that even the greatest of drivers can only demonstrate their truest greatness by first dying, for all the world like some ancient sacred king! For myself, I cannot subscribe to such views, be they those of classical antiquity or the world of today. The greatest of mountaineers must surely be those who reach the top first and get back again, just as the greatest Grand Prix driver needs also to be a survivor.

Yet none of these reflections answer the age-old question: 'Why?' So, to conclude, here are a few random thoughts from the worlds of both fiction and fact.

Kipling's fictional character, Jack Barratt, who went to Quetta simply 'because they told him to'.

George Mallory wanted to climb Everest simply because it was there.

The American novelist, John P. Marquand, in his haunting and appropriately named book, *So Little Time*, contains this dialogue between two ex-World War I fliers who are talking of risky activities (in this case show jumping):

'Some day you'll break your goddamn neck,' Jeffrey said.

'Some day, maybe,' Minot answered.

'What do you do it for?' Jeffrey asked.

'Because I've always done it,' Minot said. 'You used to do it once.'

'I had to do it,' Jeffrey said, 'in the Squadron, in the War.'

'I'll tell you something,' Minot said, 'there's just a moment in it— it's like flying. You do everything you can. You get the pace, you steady him and there's nothing more you can do. You've shot the works and there it is. That's the part that's worth waiting for.'

'You sound like *Death in the Afternoon*,' Jeffrey said.

Minot sat silently and nodded: 'That boy Hemingway knows how to say it exactly right. What's the matter with it? Why be afraid of dying?'

'Reflex,' Jeffrey said, 'that's all.'

'Well,' Minot said, 'there are worse things.'

It could just as well have been Nick Brittan, Patrick Depailler's sometime manager, speaking of his risk-laden charge:

'No. No. Patrick loved life. But what he did—he accepted the inevitability of death.'

Or Sir Henry Birkin in 1932 in *Full Throttle* as he 'considered motor racing provided the energy . . . adventures and risks most like those of the battlefield . . . the promise of a great future and . . . the same chance of unexpected disaster, the same need for perfect nerves . . . the peculiar delight of being responsible for your own calamities . . . a state of independence few individuals enjoyed during the war.'

Or Dick Seaman in the Spring of 1934: 'But, you see, Mother, I am utterly unfitted for an indoor life in offices and chambers. . . . So why waste time at my present age [21]? Motor racing, apart from being an occupation and a career in itself, combines so many of the things I enjoy and like best, and I always feel in such wonderful health, with a full zest of life.'

Or the typically French attitudes of Louis Renault to his brother as he lets in his clutch at Versailles en route for Bordeaux in 1903: 'Right, Marcel. Good Luck, the factory relies on you', and André Boillot, collapsing over the wheel at the end of the fraught Targa Florio of 1919, with a loud cry of: 'C'est pour la France!'

In their different ways both novelist and racing driver are telling us precisely 'why' in all these extracts from the saga of their Great Game.

One last thought, I have deliberately excluded the morbid, the obsessional and the sensational from this book, which I hope will be seen for what it is from first to last: an expression of pride and gratitude for the brave examples of its many men of stamp who, like the hands of a clock, have gone on their way to join 'the choir of those immortal dead who live again in minds made better by their presence.' In that way, as I firmly believe, their loss can never go unremembered or their honour unsung, for to think and speak of our dear dead departed must be the surest way of having them live again.

STOP PRESS

This book was literally on its way to the press when I chanced on Mr Jack Tatham's letter in the August 1992 issue of *Motor Sport*. Headed 'More on Benoist', it enlarges considerably on *Requiem's* references to the Resistance work of Benoist, Grover-Williams, Wimille and their wives.

The title of the book by Mr M. R. D. Foot on which Mr Tatham's letter is based is *SOE in France*. Readers of *Requiem* are warmly recommended to add to their knowledge of these great men by reading Mr Foot's book, which can be obtained from most large public libraries even though it was published in 1956.

I am particularly grateful both to Mr Tatham himself as well as to Mr Simon Arron, Editor of *Motor Sport* and his editorial staff in progressing this last minute note.

PART 1

A PROLOGUE OF HEROES AND HIGHLIGHTS

Chapter 1

The Young Meteorites

Frank Lockhart

(Born 1902 in California: Died 25 April 1928 attempting World LSR at Daytona Beach, Fla)

Bernd Rosemeyer

(Born 14 October 1909 at Lingen an der Ems, Germany: Died 28 January 1938 while attacking World Class Record on Frankfurt-Darmstadt autobahn)

'To send us out, at this time o'year,
to sail upon the sea . . .'
The Ballad of Sir Patrick Spens

These two men, who were my earliest racing heroes, were separated in their deaths by the ten years between 1928 and 1938. Although my draconian private school of the thirties was in no way orientated towards motor racing it did at least boast a few books on the subject, mostly those of Segrave and Campbell, although I could never greatly enthuse over the 'Camion' approach of the Land Speed Record battalions of the late 20s and 30s. However, Lockhart's Black Hawk Stutz from 1928 and its manifestly German derivatives of the next decade were a very different story. Of the two, Lockhart's achievement was perhaps the greater for he could put his cars together just as superbly as he drove them. Indeed, one of the special 3-litre class record cars which Mercedes-Benz brought to Dessau in 1939 bore a considerable resemblance to Lockhart's 1928 challenger.

For Frank Lockhart speed represented an eternal quest and continuous voyage into the unknown. For Rosemeyer it was mostly fun, though mixed with a sudden seriousness that could surface surprisingly quickly, as his newly married wife, the German airwoman Elly Beinhorn, found out during practice at Pescara in 1936, when she was sternly reproved for complaining about their accommodation: 'Can't you understand that I am here to work?' was all the sympathy she got!

The earliest Land Speed Record was set at 39.2 mph in 1898 by the electrically powered projectile of the Comte de Chasseloup-Laubat. The magic century was surpassed six years later by Rigolly's Gobron-

Brillie at 103 mph, but it then took another 23 years for Segrave's 1,000 hp Sunbeam to achieve the double ton—on 29 March 1927 at Daytona Beach.

The years 1927/28 saw a rare flurry of record work at Daytona: Segrave and Campbell from England; the Americans, Ray Keech and Lee Bible, with White's giant Triplex Special; and Lockhart's brilliantly conceived little Black Hawk Stutz. His tiny machine was quite unlike any record car then seen and, in hindsight, a clear forerunner of the 3-litre class record car used by Caracciola in 1938. Campbell himself enthused over Lockhart's car: 'a picture . . . low and narrow, most marvellously streamlined, and with the wheels hidden by special fairings. . . . Its appearance may be conveyed by saying that it looked more nearly a scientific instrument than any car ever constructed for the record,' before adding on a more sombre note, '. . . one could only wish Lockhart the best of good fortune.' And, for sure, he was going to need every one of Campbell's good wishes, and a good few more besides.

His test runs were carried out in February 1928 in highly adverse weather conditions, as blighted as those of the unhappy Sir Patrick Spens—rain, poor visibility and crosswinds—so that it was no surprise when Lockhart soon lost control of his lightweight car and was very lucky to sustain only slight injury from his first accident. After some weeks' delay for repairs, Lockhart found that Keech had set a new target of 207.5 mph, which he immediately challenged. After several runs around the 200 mph mark, Lockhart crashed fatally when a tyre burst; the cause of the lightweight record car died with him that day and was not revived for a decade.

The power base of all the record cars from the mid-twenties was increasingly that of sheer engine capacity (and, with it, more and more weight) coupled with a very gradual move toward improved aerodynamics. There were, however, two significant exceptions to this burgeoning cult of the mechanical dinosaur: Lockhart's Stutz and, ten years later, the first 'Stromlienwagen' of Mercedes-Benz and Auto-Union. These advanced concepts depended on aerodynamics, lightness and relatively small, highly concentrated power units. That both projects culminated in the tragic deaths of their two principal actors was largely due to the needlessly dangerous venues chosen for their high endeavours. Neither the Frankfurt-Darmstadt autobahn nor the wind-swept sands of Daytona were remotely safe enough or suitable for the speed and lightness of these advanced cars. This was clearly recognized by the leading record breaker of those twenties and thirties, Sir Malcolm Campbell, when he moved to the Bonneville Salt Flats of Utah for his final record attempts in 1935 and became the first man to top 300 mph on land.

Although they came from different continents and vastly differing backgrounds, Lockhart and Rosemeyer were very much cast in the same mould. Both were young, both swiftly became national heroes and both had shown their worlds just how good they were from Day One. The first time Lockhart raced in Indy's famed 500 in 1926 he scored a decisive Rookie's win, and in 1927 he also set a new record by leading for the first 90 laps of the race, which was not to be bettered until 1990 by Emerson Fittipaldi. The first time Rosemeyer took part in a true road race for Grand Prix cars, he challenged, led and almost defeated the great Caracciola on the Nürburgring in his all-conquering year of 1935. Lockhart was also a wonderfully gifted mechanic and engineer so that, after Indy, Miller immediately offered him a car for the rest of the 1926 season; and, in his turn, after early 1935, Rosemeyer would have no more need to beg a drive from Auto-Union. Both Harry Armenius Miller and Dr Ferdinand Porsche knew top liners when they saw them.

Bernd Rosemeyer became the great racing driver he was not least for being in the right place at the right time, just when Auto-Union were looking out for some likely young men to back up Stuck and Varzi in 1935. In those days it was fashionable for such drivers to be recruited from motor cycle racing in the way of both Varzi and Nuvolari in the twenties, and Rosemeyer was no exception. After two training seasons on two wheels with NSU and DKW, he showed immediate promise in trials for Auto-Union during the autumn of 1934 when he also greatly alarmed his team manager, Willi Walb, by doing a 'Depailler' (see page 281) and getting a place in the German 4-man-bob team for the 1936 Olympics at Garmisch-Partenkirchen! After an agonizing period of waiting during that winter he was entered for Avus in May 1935, when he burst a tyre. However, his luck held and on 16 June he started in the 11-lap Eifelrennen, and from that day he never looked back until it all ended on 28 January 1938.

Like two other supremos of road and track, Georges Boillot and Jim Clark, Rosemeyer only ever raced Grand Prix cars for one marque — Auto-Union from 1935 through 1937. He won his first Grand Prix in late 1935; the supreme title for Grand Prix racing in the thirties was the European Championship and Rosemeyer won it hands down in 1936. In 1937 he found himself with indifferent back-up drivers and opposed by the formidable W125 Mercedes-Benz led by Caracciola, Lang and von Brauchitsch. Yet, he was still able to win 4 Grands Prix that year besides setting some formidable class records in the autumn. A meteorite by any standard but, at the end of the day, still a mere mortal of whom too much was being asked.

Almost from the beginning of the 750 kg formula of 1934/37 the German teams and, to a much lesser extent, their Italian rivals set about attacking the existing class speed records with their new Grand Prix cars, usually running with enclosed rather than open wheels. By January of 1937 Caracciola had achieved a speed of 225 mph on the Frankfurt autobahn with a special V-12 Mercedes, which was also raced in the 'formule libre' Avusrennen of that year. In October of 1937 Rosemeyer returned fresh from his thrilling victory at Donington to take part in the Frankfurt 'Rekordwoche' with a similarly streamlined Auto-Union.

The German autobahn was a very different proposition from Daytona beach of the previous decade, but, in its way, it was no less hazardous. At that time few men had ever driven at over 200 mph anywhere, and fewer still on an ordinary road that was normally used as a public highway. Caracciola described that autobahn at high speed as 'coming to look like a tunnel', interspersed as it was by bridges over the road at intervals of about 1 km. Thus a driver travelling at over 200 mph had to set his sights something like two bridges ahead on a record run and these bridges, combined with the banks and woods at either side of the road, explained Rudi's tunnel vision very clearly.

A stretch of 20 kms of specially surfaced road was set aside for the record runs, and even more was actually closed off. At the start, where the cars accelerated before reaching top gear, there was a left hand curve. Then there was a rise and then a dip, followed by the long, level six-mile straight, which contained the measured mile and kilometre. Thereafter there came a noticeable right hand curve, followed by two more rises on a 6 km straight and a final right hand curve.

The highest speed achieved during that October Week was Rosemeyer's new average of 252.5 mph at a time when Campbell's record of 301.29 mph from 1935 had still to be raised by George Eyston's 'Thunderbolt' to 312.9 mph that November. Nor was he the only challenger. Britain's John Cobb had gone out to observe the Week with his engineer-designer Reid Railton, as had the inevitable Dr Porsche, with a watching brief over both his design and his gallant and brilliant German protégé. By contrast Mercedes were in constant difficulties throughout the Week with their body shapes, and eventually had to give up and go back to base camp.

Three months later, at the end of January 1938, Caracciola was back with the Big Twelve in a new body and this time it was his turn to send Auto-Union's record flying with a superb run at 270.4 mph, a mere 40 mph less than Eyston's new world record. Rosemeyer described his experience of his record work in these graphic words:

> The most intense concentration is required to hold the car in the middle of the road. The side-blasts of air felt when going through bridges demand instant reactions, and after a few minutes the driver's nervous energy is exhausted. The strain of a Ten Mile attempt is therefore greater than that of a Grand Prix, even though it lasts only about two minutes and forty seconds.

It is history that Rosemeyer went out almost immediately after Caracciola had set his new record—but with a distinct difference, for the wind was now getting up and there were still traces of frost on the road. A few minutes later he was dead, having lost control of his car in circumstances that have never been really explained.

For so many of his admirers, especially those who had actually seen him drive, this writer not least, it was as if a great light had gone out of our lives, and it is in no way surprising that those who remember that unbelievable day still hold it in treasured annual memory. Let John Dugdale, who observed and reported on 'The Week' in 1937 have the last word on this indelible personality:

> ... soon after dawn one morning, there was a fanfare from a musical trumpet horn and past us hissed a special streamlined Horch. The figure at the wheel was familiar with his Tyrolean hat ... the irrepressible Bernd ... a bundle of nervous energy ... self-conscious but preoccupied ... (talking) ... to Dr Porsche ... [and] ... wandering over to the Mercedes camp to make some crack. ... One day to create a diversion he bought a toy car into which he jammed a fire-cracker. It certainly livened things up when he let it off among the unsuspecting bystanders. Rosemeyer was a true star. He knew his worth and, like a latter-day boxing champion, felt he was 'The Greatest'.

And so he was.

By contrast, Lockhart himself was forever seeking new ways of developing his engines to give more power and his cars more speed than the hierarchic Miller was willing to approve. In the way of another autocrat called Enzo Ferrari, Miller would not tolerate design changes being made to his cars by anyone but himself. So, after his great Indy win of 1926, Lockhart had to go his own way, and he teamed up with another genius of a mechanic and organizer of victory—Ernie Olson—and, with a greatly modified and improved Miller 91, Lockhart achieved a two-way average of 164.85 mph against a heavy crosswind and a best speed of 171.02 mph at Muroc Dry Lake in California's Mojave Desert. And this with an unstreamlined, open wheel, track racing car of only 1.5 litres!

At the beginning of 1926 the LSR had stood at the 152.3 mph of Segrave's 300 bhp 4-litre Sunbeam, which was simply a 1925 Grand Prix car fitted with two of the current 2-litre Grand Prix engines married to a common crankshaft, a type that continued to be raced on road and track for some years. Like Lockhart's Miller it was an open wheel, unstreamlined racing car.

By early 1927 Campbell's 'Blue Bird' had raised the LSR to 174.2 mph at Daytona beach, and within a very short time Segrave had broken the 200 mph barrier for the first time. Ranged against them was the lone-star, single-short Derringer approach of Frank Lockhart. He reasoned that, with a slightly larger engine, racing over a longer and straighter run than Muroc could provide, a new record at around 225 mph should be well within his grasp. Engine displacement was doubled to 3-litres by building a 30-degree U-16 engine in which two Miller crankshafts were geared together in a common crankcase. Lockhart had originally intended to have an all-enveloping streamlined body, but he was talked out of this in favour of minimizing frontal area, although this added considerably to both cost and complexity.

Black Hawk was probably the first car in the USA to have had the benefit of serious wind tunnel testing, the sealing off of the underside of the car and the elimination of the radiator in favour of a tank for ice and water in the nose of the car. However, much of this good thinking was vitiated by an excessively large fuel tank when only minimal amounts of fuel had to be carried on short runs unlikely to exceed 10 or 15 miles at a stretch. Thus, the tanks for fuel and water/ice could well have been reversed to give additional weight over the rear wheels for better traction.

Others also said that the worm drive to the rear axle made the car fatally unstable, because, whenever the driver lifted his foot the gear-set was so inefficient that it would lock up the rear axle of so light a car. All of which was borne out by Griffith Borgeson's comment that the officials who had examined the evidence of the accident before the tide came in had said that 'in braking at the end of the third run Frank had locked his rear wheels for nearly a hundred feet and that a clam shell had cut into the casing of the tyre that blew', although the clam shell had no connection with the locking up of the rear wheels.

In truth, Lockhart had been incredibly lucky to have walked away from that first accident with so little damage to himself. Indeed only the prompt action of sponsor Fred Moscovics, then President of Stutz, saved Lockhart from almost certain drowning. By mid-April Lockhart was back at the beach and on the 25th he made 'his first sally', a warm-up run to the south. The beach was perfect and he returned north a little faster. Then south again with the supercharger's wail announcing that he was getting down to business. The pragmatic Lockhart was perennially short of the money he needed to fund his ambitious projects and, on this occasion, he had switched from Firestone to a less well known tyre supplier who was offering better terms. It proved a penny-wise-pound-foolish choice and, just when he was about to enter the traps, a spray of sand shot from his right tyre, which exploded at an estimated 225 mph as car and driver went smashing, tumbling, thudding down the beach, and that was the end.

Witnesses' impressions were that he was going at over 200 mph when he crashed, and still accelerating hard, and his third run had been clocked at 198.29 mph. Like Rosemeyer, 'Lucky Lockhart', the beau ideal, the all-American kid, was dead when they reached him. Like Rosemeyer, again, it was a case of 'who knows what wonders he would have accomplished had he lived?' More recently, writers researching his story have often 'been handed a rod, valve or a piston and been told in reverent tones: "this belonged to Frank Lockhart!" and then [after explanations] it was returned carefully to the shelf, as if it were a precious icon of a god.'

In the same way, my father and I successively owned between 1938 and the mid-fifties a Horch-bodied, twin-cylinder, two-stroke-powered DKW which, years later—and long after I had parted with it—I learnt that Rosemeyer had used as his personal transport when he had been in England for the 1937 Donington Grand Prix. With that knowledge a whole wilderness of wild horses would not have dragged that car from me and I can still remember the little plaque on the car's dashboard:

> Fahr sie nicht mid wilden Pferden
> Dürch das Weltgetümmel;
> Besser mal zu spät auf erden
> Als zu früh im Himmel!

It could have been an epitaph for both Bernd Rosemeyer and Frank Lockhart and it was, no less, the end of a small boy's dream world.

* * *

Chapter 2

The 'Wild Boar of the Ardennes'

Raymond Sommer (the man they called 'Coeur de Lion')

(Born 31 August 1906: Died 10 September 1950 driving a 1100 cc Cooper in the Grand Prix de Cadours)

If you heaped up all the Guts, Courage, Dash, 'Avoir-du-Cran' and Elan that go to make up a great fighting man you would get some idea of the qualities of the great racing driver and outstanding individual that was Raymond Sommer. It would also show you why another great fighter called Seppi Siffert (see page 253) learnt so much from Sommer and thought so highly of him.

Sommer came from a well-to-do French manufacturing family and, like so many of his great contemporaries, he failed to reach the top until after World War II. The basic reason for this was the stranglehold established by the 'axis' powers of Italy and Germany on the top rungs of the Grand Prix ladder and, in some cases, by the strong national feelings of some French drivers who preferred to stay clear of any 'axis' involvement during the thirties.

Like his great exemplar, Nuvolari, Sommer was always a tremendous trier, for whom no cause could ever be totally lost and whose whole philosophy was to drive anything on four wheels for as long as it was capable of movement, and beyond, even if it meant working a car with a nearly blocked fuel line on the starter, yard by yard, from the few drops of fuel that the carburetter could muster. On that occasion he restarted from the pits seven laps and one hour behind the lead which he had had to concede. Another time he had to siphon petrol from one car to another by suction and swallowed a generous helping of fuel in the process. Yet, while Sommer undoubtedly made his cars work very hard for him—and sometimes too hard—he always put just as much effort into the job himself and, inevitably, made more fastest race laps than he ever won races.

In the 30s, before his Talbot days, Sommer had been a great Alfa Romeo man, winning the 24 hr races of 1932 and 1933 with his own cars, co-driven in 1932 by Luigi Chinetti and, in 1933, by his idol, Nuvolari. They put up a race record that stood for four years till 1937, and Nuvolari fought a thrilling last lap duel with Chinetti right down to the wire. As they went on to the last lap, Nuvolari, with fading brakes and a leaking petrol tank, led by a matter of yards till Chinetti caught him through the Esses. Nuvolari then returned the compliment on the Mulsanne straight and led till his weary brakes forced him to slow a little earlier than Chinetti and lose him his precious lead again. Nuvolari now knew that if he could not get past before they reached the next succession of slow bends, Chinetti must win. Being Nuvolari, he squeezed past and managed to hold on through the bends, when a crash seemed inevitable, to finish a few vital seconds ahead. As the Duke of Wellington might have said on such an occasion: 'By God! I don't think it would have been done if I had not been there!' — and, for once, perhaps even Sommer would have had to accept that.

Three little touches of Sommer's influence on the racing world should not be overlooked.

He followed so many of his countrymen into working with the French Resistance during World War II, which was to leave behind it a bitter legacy of revengefulness to be vented on collaborator and former foes alike. Two remarkable men of those years would have had good cause to be grateful for Sommer's interventions on their behalf in the suspicion-charged atmosphere of the so-called 'Peace', when his efforts, coupled with those of the highly influential Charles Faroux, secured the release from French custody of the ageing and ailing Dr Ferdinand Porsche. Like H. J. Aldington of Frazer Nash-BMW, Sommer was also able similarly to help Dr Rudolf Ühlenhaut of Mercedes-Benz. The subsequent influence of these two great engineers was to be felt throughout the world for many years thereafter. Sommer was also the first non-Italian to drive for Ferrari in a Grand Prix car of his own — that of Italy at Turin in 1948, when he finished third, behind Villoresi (Maserati) and the inevitable Wimille (Alfa-Romeo). In addition, Ferrari himself has told how it was Sommer who first encouraged him to build the big unblown engines in place of the blown V-12 125s.

Finally, three of his more remarkable 'records'. The first was in the otherwise obscure Marseilles Grand Prix of 1932 on the featureless Miramas autodrome with its wide radius and slightly banked turns. Sommer, with only a Monza Alfa, won from Nuvolari's monoposto and Guy Moll's Bugatti. On that occasion it is thought that, just for once, Lady Luck had ridden at Sommer's side and allowed the Alfa pit men to hoodwink themselves into a fatal miscalculation of the true position!

Fourteen years later, in 1946, the 158 Alfas emerged from wartime hibernation for their first taste of active duty on the hilly little circuit of the Grand Prix of St Cloud, where Sommer's Maserati shared the front row of the grid with Wimille's 158, and Nuvolari's Maserati the next row with Farina's Alfa. The result was a minor sensation with Sommer winning from Chiron's Talbot and Arialdo Ruggieri's Maserati. While no one deserved the break more, Sommer's hour of glory had to last him a long time. Until the Belgian Grand Prix of 1950, to be precise.

In practice, Sommer, with not the fastest of Lago-Talbots, had equalled Villoresi's time with a two-stage blown 1.5-litre Ferrari and, in the race, he passed Villoresi on the fifth lap and then shook the Alfa pits rigid by assuming the lead from all four of their cars when they made their first fuel stops. Needless to say, this goaded the perhaps easy going Alfa drivers to put their best feet forward until Sommer's valiant car gave out after 20 of the 35 laps, when he lay third, still ahead of one Alfa! As for Sommer, he had done everything and more than could have been expected of him even to the point of shocking team manager Guidotti into trying to persuade both himself and the race organizers that there had been a wholesale mistake (like Miramas all over again?) and that Sommer must already have been a whole lap behind the Alfas when they made their first fuel stops!

Above all, Sommer's love of motor racing was total, and it was thus not a surprise to find him taking part in three of the racing classes of Silverstone's International Trophy meeting on 26 August 1950 in 3 different types of car. Starting at the bottom there was the over 2-litre class for sports cars where he was driving the lead car for Aston-Martin supported by Reg Parnell and Eric Thompson. Before the start Sommer had told the team manager, John Wyer, not to trouble him with pit signals; it would be quite enough if he just went fast! For once he must have allowed his natural self-confidence to get the better of him as he gradually found his team being swallowed up by a burly stranger in the shape of Duncan Hamilton, driving of all things a Silverstone Healey. Not surprisingly, Duncan was absolutely thrilled to find that he could outpace the great Frenchman coming into Stowe Corner and beat the elegant Aston-Martins—including Sommer's—by a couple of lengths, 'drifting through the bends at high velocity and topping the ton on the straights!' At least that was how Gregor Grant described it in the first ever issue of *Autosport* when Sommer assured Gregor that his three greatest joys of 1950 were leading the Alfas at Spa, his invitation to drive the V-16 BRM and racing a Cooper 500/1100.

Sommer's 'conversion' to Coopering had taken place earlier in the 1950 season at the Aix-les-Bains meeting the weekend after Monaco with his great friend, the exuberant Harry Schell, playing the unlikely part of the vicar! That day he was starting in pole position in a works F2 V-12 2-litre Ferrari. Next to him was Harry Schell's diminutive 1100 cc twin-cylindered Cooper and, although Sommer eventually won the race, it was Harry who stole the show by leading off the grid and holding station until his clutch burnt out.

After that it was inevitable that Sommer would jump on the works Cooper bandwagon which he did in John Cooper's special lightweight in the Zandvoort 500 on 23 July. Soon he was leading the race by a country mile until he missed a gear, over-revved and dropped a valve, leaving the race to the popular 'Curly' Dryden, still remembered for his keeping of the attractive George Inn at Dorchester-on-Thames until his death at the wheel of a Cooper in 1951.

Sommer came out again in John Cooper's car at Silverstone when he was foiled by Stirling Moss's acquisition of a 'double-knocker' Norton engine, an advantage that not even Sommer's skills could overcome. He finished second, 8 seconds behind Moss, after 'throwing caution to the winds and indulging in a display of pace forcing that made the spectators 'hold their breath'!

The sequel to these stirring events was pure bathos. After myriad alarms, one BRM had at last emerged from its tent to give battle on that same day and although it did not arrive until early on the morning of a damp race day, it had at least managed to last out its practice period of three laps when it had sounded pretty good. Its sudden and unexpected arrival had caught me sleeping at the switch with only half a printable exposure in my Leica and no time to change the spool and record the happy scene. Come the start of Sommer's heat, it was a sadly different story with the wretched driver left on the line fishing for ratios and watching the field receding into the distance. Third time decidedly not so lucky for M. Sommer.

Although Ferrari reputedly had a 4½-litre car that could have been placed at Sommer's disposal for the coming Italian Grand Prix, this did not materialize, and he was left with his ageing Talbot from Spa to combat the Alfas of Farina, Fangio, Fagioli, Taruffi and Sanesi and the Ferraris of Ascari and Serafini. By the 48th lap (of 80) Sommer had fought his way up to fourth when gearbox trouble ended his last Grand Prix drive. How he must have wished it had been a Ferrari, if not an Alfa.

And so to Cadours, a little town some 35 kms to the North West of Toulouse, which did not even rank a mention in the *Guide Michelin*. Time was when any group of local enthusiasts could conjure up a race meeting almost anywhere, almost overnight and run a race or a series of races. Typical examples of such local enterprise were the races at Brignoles (see pages 269/270) and La Châtre (see pages 285/289) mentioned in this book. Of course, the races were often for amateurs hoping to make a reputation, but occasionally a big name would join in the fun as well. Just such a race was the second Circuit de Cadours held over a tight little 2.5 mile course on 10 September 1950 and no less of a big name was that of France's leading driver, Raymond Sommer, down to drive John Cooper's little car with the bigger 1100 cc engine.

Because of the tightness of the circuit, the racing was split into two heats and a *repêchage* of ten laps each and a final of 15. Sommer retired with ignition trouble on the second lap of his heat, before winning the *repêchage* with great ease and then storming into an equally convincing lead in the final, until he left the road on a fast bend and was fatally injured in the ensuing crash on the fifth lap.

Sommer had always been a particular favourite of mine since I first read of the way of his racing in the 1935 Donington Grand Prix and, like so many others, I can still recall with total clarity where and when I read the news of his death the following day. For French motor racing it was a tragedy on the levels of Alberto Ascari and Jim Clark, as the whole racing world mourned the loss of a great friend and a bold competitor. Perhaps the heaviest blow was that of the Coopers now having to face their first racing fatality. Eric Brandon, one of the greatest of the early Coopermen, had been testing the car at Silverstone, just before its departure for Cadours in the Schells' truck, when it had caught fire. Brandon had managed to put the fire out, but, after Sommer's crash he 'always wished I'd let the bloody thing burn!' Yet would it have made any difference, for death has an uncomfortable habit of lurking in wait for his victims as he had for that Major Peter Braid who survived a crash landing on the guardroom roof at Blandford Camp circuit in a Mark III Cooper in August 1949. Earlier that day the well-known amateur driver, Gordon Woods, had been killed there, while the Major had merely fallen to the ground bruised and shaken. As Doug Nye puts it in his *Cooper Cars*: 'Some people have no real luck. The unfortunate Major was to die in 1955 in the Barnes railway accident . . .' in the manner of the Somerset Maugham character, who sought to evade death by travelling from one place to another, yet still finding 'the last enemy' patiently waiting for him.

As for Sommer, his admirers were left with the moving epitaph of his friend Rodney Walkerley—then 'Grande Vitesse' of *The Motor*:

> Whether his list of successes is short or long Sommer will be remembered for the quality of his make-up, which seemed to combine so well the gaiety of the Gaul with the determination of the Saxon. In any case, success is not necessarily a criterion and those who knew him will miss his bright example of how one should really go motor racing.

* * *

INTERLUDE
Jean-Pierre Wimille, Sommer and the Chipmunk Theory

That France's two greatest champions of the day should both have lost their lives in light racing cars within 19 months was a fearful blow which left a void that would not be fully filled until the arrival of Depailler, Pironi and Prost in the 80s. In the meantime the world was left to wonder at the passing of these two great men.

At much the same time I had a friend who had learnt to fly in Chipmunks before cleaving the skies in Gloster Meteor jets. Today he is content to reminisce about the fun of the old Chipmunk days, which reminded me powerfully of the Cooper 500 and 1100 cc cars of the same period, save that the Chipmunks seemed a darn sight safer. To my surprise my friend told me not to be so sure, for those innocent looking little planes harboured hidden dangers. The catch, as he explained, was when the 'jet jockeys' came down to earth for an afternoon's light relief with the little planes, for all the world like a

Grand Prix ace of the day turning to a Cooper or a small Gordini for the same reason. Needless to say, my mind immediately flew to the fate of Sommer at Cadours and Wimille (see pages 218/21) in the Argentine.

Neither accident has ever been satisfactorily explained, and I wondered if it might lie in my friend's 'Chipmunk Theory' with its emphasis on the hazard implicit in switching suddenly to a car that was very different from the big, conventional Grand Prix machines and, for a fateful second, forgetting that for all its smallness and simplicity, it, too, was fallible and able to catch even the greatest and most experienced of drivers napping with its switch from light hearted playmate to lethal she-devil.

Not for nothing does one often find the warning legend on small aircraft 'This Aeroplane Bites!' Indeed, the *Flight Safety Review* publications of the fifties show that the incidence of Chipmunk accidents became a matter of lively concern to those responsible for training aircrews on them in those years.

Chapter 3

Two Freak Accidents

Jochen Rindt

*(Born 18 April 1942: Died 5 September 1970 in a practice accident at Monza before
the Italian Grand Prix)*

Ronnie Peterson

*(Born 14 February 1944: Died 11 September 1978 in an accident during the early
stages of the Italian Grand Prix at Monza)*

Like Sommer, both Jochen Rindt and Ronnie Peterson died in freak
accidents and, by sombre coincidence, both happened at Monza.
Both men were also fast, spectacular drivers and master car controllers, though they did not always excel at the essential business of
actually winning the races. Thus Rindt drove in Grands Prix for more
than five years before winning the famous Race of Jenks's Beard at
Watkins Glen at the end of 1969 (the story is that Rindt took so long to
win his first Grand Prix that Jenks said that he would shave off his
famous beard if Rindt ever accomplished this seeming impossible!)
and, for all his brilliance, Peterson was in his fourth Grand Prix season
before he won the first of his ten.

A useful way of summarizing the achievements of racing drivers is to
adopt a framework of First, Best/Worst and Last. My sequence for
Jochen goes: First—Watkins, 1969; Best—Monte Carlo, 1970; Last
when he beat Ickx to the line at Hockenheim by split seconds in
August of that year. Yet it might just as well have been his drive in the
wet at Spa with the lumpish, tail-heavy Cooper-Maserati from 1966 or
his fantastic hand-to-hand fight with Stewart at Silverstone in 1969.

Expressed as a bald statistic, a tally of only five Grand Prix wins in
seven seasons from a driver of true world championship stature might
seem a poor one unless, that is, you had seen him drive, when it became
a case of: 'It's not what you do, but the way that you do it!' just as it was
with Villeneuve. And it was the same with his lifestyle: colourful
clothes, beautiful wife, Swiss chateau and everything that went with it.

The legend of Jenks's Beard actually happens to be true, and even if
it were not, would still be alive with artistic truth, the tribute of one
great artist to another, and if ever there was a driver who deserved to
win a Grand Prix it was surely Jochen Rindt.

Having once overcome the hump of winning, it then seemed as if he
would never be a loser again as he went on from success to success
through the central part of 1970. For some unaccountable reason I
could not get to Monaco in 1970, which fell at a time when Jochen was
having nothing but trouble with Chapman's new wonder, the Lotus 72.

At the same time Jack Brabham was at the height of his final season's early 'Sunset Touch' with his first non-space-frame Grand Prix car, the BT 33 that had been very much the flavour of the second quarter as March gave way to May.

Viewed in that light, not too many people were giving Jochen much hope in his ageing Lotus 49 in which he had only managed to qualify eighth, two whole seconds slower than polestar Stewart in his new March 701. And not even Jochen thought much of his chances until mid-race when the walls of the top men were beginning to tumble and he was suddenly able to make up time on Jack Brabham, who still led, and Chris Amon with another works March. With 20 laps to go Amon was out and Rindt was second, but still 14 seemingly unbridgeable seconds behind Brabham, always a notoriously difficult man to pass especially when he was on a high. So, the chips were down and guts, courage, dash and bags of luck besides were at a premium.

Although the gods had some pretty nasty traits, they did love a hero fighting the odds and even gave him a helping hand from time to time, particularly if he was their special favourite, and this was how it panned out for Rindt on the last four laps. At the last corner, trying to overtake Courage, Brabham made a rare mistake which let Rindt sprint through the gap and win by a short head. The lap times tell the story: Jochen had qualified for the race in 1-25.9: his last two laps were covered in 1-23.3. and 1-23.2!

Over the last two, or more, decades it has become increasingly fashionable to refer to the driver as the mere function of his car. That day no-one could have had any doubt about who was wearing the trousers, calling the shots and dictating the function of the car.

After that, Chapman got the 72 properly into its stride and there was simply no holding Jochen, who won four more Grands Prix on the run, before faltering on his own home ground in Austria. I have always cherished his remark about the 72 being so simple that a monkey could have done it all for him! And, as the tide of victory rolled on, it seemed as if nothing could stop him. Paradoxically, though, this worried him a lot: 'Things are going well', he was heard to say, 'almost too well . . .'

And so they were, for the gods are also known to be mean and jealous and they were not long in gathering the gallant soul of Jochen Rindt into their midst. In an odd sort of way he had perhaps accepted it himself, for he was already saying that he did not want to race any more, and in an interview from 1970 he had spoken of his worries: 'Yes, I get scared, we all get scared, but I get scared that something will happen with the car. It's the cars that break, not the drivers.' And then, again paradoxically: 'I am always frightened of something breaking, but while I am frightened, I do not think it will happen. I know I am driving too good a car.'

Perhaps that time he was not for, by some accounts, his Lotus certainly did break in practice at the Parabolica on 5 September 1970. Other accounts tell a different story of his losing control at high speed through using little or no 'wing'. Whichever it was, for many motor racing was never to be the same again.

* * *

Ronnie Peterson opened his Grand Prix career in the year that Jochen Rindt died after winning the renowned Formula 3 race at Monaco in 1969. He was, in every sense, the inheritor of Grand Prix racing's Crown of Speed and, if I missed out on Rindt in 1970, Peterson's drive in 1971 most surely made up for it. Peterson in the dry, driving down from Casino Square to the seafront, carving his way through the established names like there was no tomorrow, was as much of a sight for sore eyes as 'shooting' him through the camera lens in the wet on full opposite lock past the Hotel de Paris had been in practice.

The 701 March from 1970 had been a clumsy old ship of the line: the 711 that replaced it for 1971, with its frontally mounted, oval-shaped, luncheon tray for a spoiler might have looked odd but how Ronnie could make it go! Neither in terms of car nor driver could anyone have foreseen how well he and his flame-coloured March were going to run through 1971. Yet, somehow, those Men of March had transformed their dull, plebeian journeyman of a car into something altogether different, and rounded up a rare kind of driver to race it.

At the age of 26 Ronnie Peterson had come relatively late to Formula 1 after acquiring a whole bundle of experience in go-karts (European champion) before getting into Formula 3, Formula 2 and long-distance sports car racing. After a dull 1970 he ended the 1971 season with four seconds, one third, one fourth and one fifth to place him second in the title rankings behind world champion Stewart, who is said to have called him a 'seat-of-the-pants driver', while adding 'but then I'm one myself'. While Ronnie had not actually won a race, he had at least finished second in the Italian Grand Prix, only 1/100th of a second behind the winner, Peter Gethin, in the famous 'four-horse' finish of that year. He had also attracted some favourable comment from Stirling Moss.

Regrettably, the 721 March for 1972 was as bad as the 711 had been good and, much to the chagrin of Max Mosley and Robin Herd, Peterson, not surprisingly, signed a 2-year contract with Team Lotus beside Emerson Fittipaldi for 1973/74. At the end of those years he could look back on a record of seven wins, two seconds, two thirds, one fourth and one sixth, yet still be left with the feeling that things could have been better both for him personally and Team Lotus.

Alan Rees, who had first seen Ronnie drive at Albi in 1969, suddenly found all the hopes and expectations he had cherished for him materialize, although there were still times when the new 'Special Relationship' that Chapman had hoped to rekindle from Clark-Hill days felt uneasy. 'Joint No. 1' status has never been an easy horse to ride, especially when the newcomer was thought to be the faster man and consistently able to prove it—save, frustratingly, under the chequered flag. This seemed to be increasingly his lot in 1973 as if it were a re-run of Jochen Rindt's pre-1969 period.

And then the magic thing happened: appropriately enough on the speed circuit of Paul Ricard. For much of the race Scheckter had made the running in real style by leading off the grid and staying there for 43 of the 54 laps with neither of the Lotus drivers able to get by. Then Fittipaldi decided it was time to put the heavy boot in and closed up on Scheckter, who manfully held on to his line and attacked the corner come hell, high water—or Fittipaldi! It was a perfect recipe for disaster and ended both their races on the spot, but it also gave the persevering Peterson his first Grand Prix win after 39 tries and a good few near misses. For once the waiting game had paid off as Ronnie romped home easily from François Cevert; Chapman performed his victory leap and bluff, old, battle-scarred Denny Hulme told 'Baby Bear' after the race: 'I was trying to get up there to tell you, kid! That Fittipaldi always pulls those tricks!' Which could be the secret of Emerson's continued and long-lived success into the nineties! At the race's end the happiest man at Ricard was probably Mike Hailwood for the way in which his good friend, 'Mad Ronald', had at last achieved that first win that is traditionally the sweetest, before going on to win nine more—all but one for Team Lotus.

After a relatively poor showing of the 77 in the opening Grand Prix of 1976 Ronnie returned to March before passing on to Team Tyrrell for 1977. Although 1976 and March had given him one more win (at Monza), these were neither fruitful nor happy years for Ronnie who finally returned to Chapman/Lotus for 1978, though on rather different terms.

The new deal was that while he was to be, technically, equal No. 1, Mario Andretti was to have the right to win whenever and wherever possible, to enable him to be the more sure of winning the world championship. It was a strange compact, but somehow it worked, basically because of Ronnie's total integrity. No naughty tricks from Gentleman Ronnie. Not like wicked old Nuvolari pretending, with the guile of Nelson at Copenhagen, not to have seen any signals to slow down! As the season progressed there was little doubt that Ronnie was the quicker of Chapman's twins, but orders were orders and Mario ran out the titular champion for 1978 with six wins, one second, one fourth, and one sixth compared to Ronnie's two wins, four seconds, one third and one fourth: Team Orders complied with to a 'T'! Reutemann had scored four wins for Ferrari, and Lauda two for Brabham, but then Ronnie had missed the last three races of that tragic year and had previously opted out of another year with Team Lotus in favour of going to McLaren, whose great days were then still a long way into the future.

The whole of the 1978 Monza meeting was a succession of disasters for Ronnie after his splendid win in Austria and his split second finish behind Andretti, to orders, at Zandvoort. He started by blowing the engine of his 79 in the first practice and, in the afternoon, he had to fall back on his spare 78 as his 79 was still unready. It was much the same during untimed practice on the Saturday, when his 79 was still in trouble with overheating brakes and a leaking gearbox, all of which pushed him down to fifth on the grid, narrowly ahead of Alan Jones's Williams-Ford. Then, during Sunday morning's warming up, his 79's rear brakes failed completely and he was fortunate that there were four layers of catch-fencing to protect him from seriously hitting the barriers behind. Even then the malign gremlins of Monza were by no means through playing havoc with its hapless drivers. First, the start was given much too soon and then, as the closely grouped cars arrived at the point where the road narrows past the entrance to the old banked circuit, they started spinning off in all directions. James Hunt has described in *Autosport* how 'as we approached the funnel where the tracks divided, Patrese, with nowhere to go, barged over, pushing me into Ronnie . . . [adding] . . . by some miracle I wasn't hit again, [before] arriving on the scene to find Ronnie's Lotus ablaze, with one marshal already on hand . . . using short blasts of foam to knock down the flames [before wrenching] . . . the steering wheel clear . . . [and] . . . picking Ronnie up by the epaulettes of his uniform and dragging him clear of the car.' James was 'appalled at how long it took the other marshals to arrive, and it seemed an eternity before the ambulance reached us.'

Besides being a most gifted driver, Ronnie was also one of nature's best loved folk heroes, and blame was not long in being planted squarely and, almost certainly, unfairly on the shoulders of the young and brash Riccardo Patrese, who had already, in one and a half short seasons, acquired a somewhat controversial reputation as 'the wild man of motor racing'—inviting the journalistic question: 'Saint or sinner . . . Dr Jekyll or Mr Hyde?'

At the time I thought this view, expressed by Chris Hickley in *Autosport* to be trite and straining for effect, but this was as nothing compared to the witch hunt that was then orchestrated by a clique of disaffected drivers into a wholly unofficial, self-appointed Kangaroo Court that succeeded in getting Patrese banned from the ensuing US Grand Prix. Their arguments could best be compared to a bunch of bully-boy school prefects deciding that one of their juniors was getting too big for his boots and needed taking down a few pegs; that 'something' needed to be done about Patrese—and quickly—and that 'they' were the only people prepared to take the bull by the horns and do it. The fact that this ignored the enquiries that had already been made by both the Italian authorities and the CSI, under the newly appointed President Balestre, and that neither body had put any specific blame on Patrese, mattered not a scrap. Not surprisingly, a ripple of apprehension ran through the Grand Prix world at what the future might bring.

Inevitably Ferrari disagreed with everyone and everything: perhaps because he was Ferrari, perhaps not. He claimed that the drivers' action was unjustified because Patrese's driving was not the only cause of the accident. Despite all that was being said about his being unacceptably difficult to pass, a wheel banger, a practice shunter and such like, he had still managed to lead the South African Grand Prix perfectly safely, and by the length of a street, in an Arrows that was by no means the fastest car on the road, before his engine blew!

The end-product was a great deal of hot air and ill will, with Patrese getting barred from the next race before being grudgingly allowed to race in the Canadian Grand Prix where he regained a modicum of respectability from an uneventful fourth place.

But, of course, none of it could ever bring poor Ronnie Peterson back to life, as yet another hero took his place in the Vale of Memory.

Chapter 4
Blues in the Night

Alberto Ascari (the man who was two men)
(Born 13 July 1918: Died 26 May 1955 at Monza while sampling a sports Ferrari)

Johnny Mercer's mournful lyric about the unpitying nature of women

> a woman's a two-face
> a worrisome thing who'll leave ya t'sing
> the blues in the night

only tells half the truth, for men can be no less two-faced.

For all his phlegmatic outward appearance (see page 86) Antonio Ascari had been a deeply emotional and temperamental man whose apparent sunshine could cloak a surprisingly darker side. His son, Alberto, inherited all these unwelcome characteristics and a few more besides, like superstition, numerology and even a touch of necromancy. Things are rarely what they seem and it was thus hard to believe that this calm, composed, self-contained man, so confidently encapsulated in his single-seat racing car, might hide a nature that could be metamorphosed, almost on the instant, into near hysteria at the sight of a common-or-garden black cat.

While down-to-earth characters like Lady Macbeth might have had no truck with 'the eye of childhood that feared the painted devil', if half the stories associated with Alberto's superstition are true, you could be pardoned for wondering how he ever risked crossing a road or driving a car of any sort, let alone become the fastest Grand Prix driver of his time. A divided personality if ever there was one, with melancholy lurking in every pore—at least, until it was time to imitate the action of the tiger on the circuit. Then a completely different Alberto stood revealed and it would be God help anyone, the formidable Fangio or the bristling Farina included, who durst come between him and his chosen objective.

After a promising career racing motor cycles from 1936 Alberto graduated to four wheels and, in 1940, he took part in his first important race: the makeshift Mille Miglia over ten laps of the 100-mile Cremona circuit, along the same classic roads as his father before him and in front of the great Nuvolari who was present as a spectator. Alberto retired with a broken valve after just one lap—well in the lead in his class.

He got in two more races, before Italy became disastrously engulfed in World War II, with a real single seater racing car—a 1.5 litre, 6-cylinder Maserati that he and Taruffi had bought. This time he finished one race, in ninth and third in class, demonstrating thus early 'an easy style, controlled, without cunning, reflexes apparent—all qualities not easy to find in a man as young as Ascari.' Fired with this early success he descended on Palermo to contest the Targa Florio, downgraded since 1937 to a race for 1.5-litre voiturettes. Unfortunately over-enthusiasm got the better of him and he crashed out of a race that was won by the man who was to play such a formative part in the rest of his life—Luigi Villoresi, who took Alberto into business partnership and also introduced him to his future wife, Mietta Tavola.

By the end of World War II Alberto was 27 and seemingly settling down to the same quiet prosperous life that his father had enjoyed when he was not motor racing—until he went to a race where Villoresi was driving and found himself almost subconsciously sliding into the cockpit of Gigi's car and thinking: 'this is the life for me'. And so a further partnership was forged between the two friends, who were already in business together, with Alberto at first content to follow in his friend's wheeltracks while learning from his wealth of talent and experience.

The name Ascari first reappeared in a French race programme when Alberto took the wheel of a 4CLT Maserati entered by the Scuderia Ambrosiana in the Marne Grand Prix at Rheims in July 1947. It gave him a good race without his ever actually holding the lead before he retired. At Nice a couple of weeks later he managed to finish fourth, having held both second and third for much of the race. After another appearance at Comminges in August he confirmed his fast-growing promise in the Italian Grand Prix at Milan by achieving third fastest race lap and attracting this tribute from that shrewdest judge of racing talent, the late John Eason Gibson:

> Ascari (behind Trossi, Varzi and Sanesi) meanwhile was astonishing the crowd and the experts . . . and there were many excited spectators to be heard comparing him with his famous father and hailing him as a Nuovo astro del firmamento automobilistico Italiano.

His second season opened slowly and disappointingly until a bright, spanking new red 4CLT/48 Maserati was ready for him at San Remo where he won convincingly from Gigi, in a similar car, and Farina, who retired after a typically spirited fighting drive. The 158 Alfas were out at Berne and the best that the Maserati duo could achieve was third (Gigi) and fifth (Alberto), split by Sanesi's 158.

The ensuing French Grand Prix at Rheims was an odd kind of race, with Alberto being retained for the first and only time by his father's old firm and Gigi sharing what was now styled his 'San Remo' Maserati with Nuvolari, on a surprise visit. The great man claimed to have left his Ferrari at the frontier and come on a busman's holiday, assuring T. G. Moore of *Motor Sport* that he was going to drive till he died adding: 'and I'm not dead yet!' In the race he drove a few characteristically quick laps and, with that, vanished quietly from the

Grands Prix, although he went on driving in isolated sports car events and attending some of the races.

In early 1949 Alberto made the first of several trips down Argentina way with Gigi and Farina, all with Maseratis. Alberto won the first race from Gigi, retired in the second and third and took third place in the last before the flying circus moved on to Brazil. Here Gigi won both races, at Rio de Janeiro and Sao Paulo, while Alberto crashed in Rio on the dicey Gavea circuit, known as 'the Devil's Trampoline'. The man who was so soon to become the fourth member of their circus, Juan Manuel Fangio, had also won one of the four Argentine races and taken second in another before going on to Europe, where he won at San Remo, Pau and Perpignan, while Alberto was recovering from his brush with the Devil at Gavea.

Alfa-Romeo went into a year-long seclusion for 1949, which left competition between the big unblown Talbots, the 4CLT/48 and other assorted Maseratis and some much improved versions of the V-12 125 Ferraris from the end of 1948. The duo had abandoned Maserati on their return to Europe for Ferrari and, by the Italian Grand Prix they had appeared in a pair of two-stage supercharged cars. While Alberto won comfortably enough, it was quite clear that even these new cars would be no match for the 158s when they took to the warpath again in 1950.

By then Ferrari had seen the warning lights and heeded the message of, amongst others, Raymond Sommer (see page 9) to leave the blower movement to Alfa-Romeo and Maserati in favour of the big unblown cars of up to 4.5-litres. This proved an increasingly wise move, and by September Alberto, in a full 4.5 375 Ferrari, was able to challenge Fangio at Monza for all he was worth. Fangio had had to make a very special effort to retain pole position in his 158, but in the race itself, with the Alfas having to make two fuel stops to Alberto's one, victory should have been in Alberto's pocket if his car had not expired.

The stage was now set for the elemental, hand-to-hand, eyeball-to-eyeball confrontations of 1951, the like of which were not to be seen on the Grand Prix circuits for many years to come, as Alberto, with the staunchest support from the mighty Gonzalez, fought out his great struggle with Fangio and Farina for a World Championship that, for once, seemed really worthy of its name. Of course Alberto and Juan Manuel were the top men in the top cars aiming at the top of the tree, yet if the 'third man', who was actually the first to best the Alfas, had had a Grand Prix Ferrari for the whole of 1951, it was very possible that he might have emerged from his relative obscurity to full Championship at the expense of the two leading contenders.

However, history cannot be written backwards and it was Fangio and Alberto who, between them, ruled the rankings from 1951 through to 1957.

The Grand Slam of all the European Majors in a single season is now unlikely to be repeated and has only ever been achieved by three drivers: Felice Nazzaro with three wins from 1907. Robert Benoist with four from Delage in 1927 and Alberto with six from Ferrari in 1952, with an extra three from the first races of 1953 thrown in for good measure. Jim Clark might have won more races in a single season in both 1963 (7) and 1965 (6), but Alberto's record for the number of wins in a row remains in his safe keeping, and while Mike Hawthorn finally broke Alberto's record at Rheims in 1953, he continued, however ruefully, to respect his team leader as 'that bloody Ascari', who was 'spot on all the time' without variation.

In the way of Napoleon, Ascari passionately clung to his luck and his star, and there was something chillingly prophetic about the way he told Fangio, on the eve of that 1955 Monaco Grand Prix which was to be his last race, that he believed his Luck had left him, for all the world like King Richard II bidding his courtiers 'sit on the ground and tell sad stories of the death of Kings' or Napoleon himself telling his oldest friend, Marshal Marmont: 'My game is going wrong—the Star is setting.'

Yet, despite a poor season in 1954, Alberto had shown that he could still play the Master Driver as he fought off the challenges of Fangio, his old friend and mentor, Luigi Villoresi, in a sunset touch, and the rising Stirling Moss at Monza in the autumn with the 625 Ferrari which Enzo had let him have in the continued absence of the Lancia D50. He continued his fighting form at Barcelona when it at last went into action, driving like the true champion he was, into pole position and leading for the nine laps that the car lasted. Come the new year and he was once again fighting the good fight with the Mercedes and Ferraris of Fangio, Moss and Gonzalez until he crashed out after 21 laps in the torrid heat. Back in Europe he won at both Turin and Naples and dominated at Pau until a split fuel pipe lost him his lead in the closing stages. No doubt about it, Alberto was still a mighty force to be reckoned with as he approached the opening European Grande Epreuve at Monaco.

The race pattern there was a simple one. Fangio and Ascari tied for fastest practice lap with Moss 0.1 sec slower. Fangio led from the grid to lap 49 before retiring to leave Moss ahead of Ascari from laps 50 to 80. On that lap it all began to go wrong. Given today's pit to driver communication systems, it might have been very different. As it was, with 20 laps to go, Moss suddenly lost his comfortable lead of over a minute, as he was completing lap 81 when his car expired in a great cloud of smoke. Out on the circuit, though he little knew it, Ascari was now poised to take the lead and run through to a win he could never have expected. Then, for whatsoever reason— and many have been advanced—Ascari lost control at the chicane and both he and his car took a nose dive into the harbour before ever he could inherit Moss's lead.

Was it brake failure, a broken steering arm, a skid on an oil slick or the effect of emerging from the darkness of the tunnel into the shimmering blinding light of the harbour complex—those and more? You can really take your pick, though they all travel by the same road to the same inevitable end, be it the harbour at Monaco or the equally inexplicable crash at Monza four days later? Either way, Alberto's name had been on the bullet from the minute he accepted the invitation to try out Ferrari's new 750 sports racing car on that fatal afternoon of 26 May 1955.

Coincidence is the child of both superstition and premonition and Kevin Desmond's book on the Ascaris, father and son, is steeped in references to both elements which he singles out as one of his 'outside interests'. Desmond also quotes from an obituary of Alberto written by the renowned motor journalist, Giovanni Canestrini, for whom Alberto united the 'vehement style of Bordino', 'the competitive spirit of Nuvolari', 'the meticulousness of Varzi', 'the optimism and exuberance of Rosemeyer' and 'the power, tenacity and seriousness of Caracciola'. Not a bad set of credentials to be going on with!

Though he spoke little English, Alberto greatly enjoyed his visits to England where, he averred, even the black cats seemed to bring him luck! He often wished he could have stayed longer to enjoy its lifestyle in the way that he enjoyed his golf with Dr Farina and those Royal Belgian 'tifosi', King Baudouin and ex-King Leopold.

Superstitious or no, Alberto ranked with the very greatest of drivers, his only one weakness consisting of an occasional inability to snatch victory from defeat when the chips were down, in the way that Graham Hill was able to achieve. Thus he drove some mildly unworthy races in mid-1954 in that amiable workhorse, the 250F Maserati, particularly when the young Stirling Moss could show him just how to do it with a similar car.

As many of these pages show, a surprising number of these Very Greats met inexplicable deaths, and Alberto's like Jim Clark's was all of a piece. Though barely recovered from the shock of his accident at Monaco only four days earlier, needs must that he should go out for a drive in the new Ferrari at Monza—and not wearing his own personal blue helmet, but a white one borrowed from Castellotti. After that both his death and its apparent inexplicability seemed no coincidence, for Death has an uncanny habit of letting his victim off the hook one day and then catching up with him on the next.

However, at the end of his road, it is to 1952/53 that one returns, when there was simply no holding Alberto as he piled victory so effortlessly upon victory until it became an almost inexorable habit, which his great friend, Luigi Villoresi, put so succinctly: 'One of the secrets of a good start was to be considered Number One.'

Whatever the Commendatore might say about his wonderful cars, Alberto's success just cannot have all been down to the 500 Ferrari.

Chapter 5

The Shepherd of the Hills

Jim Clark

(Born 4 March 1936 at Kilmandy, Fifeshire, Scotland: Died 7 April 1968 at Hockenheim, Germany, during a Formula 2 race)

With some drivers I have often felt that the mad fellow was bound to write himself off sooner or later, but with the likes of Alberto or Jim Clark—and for that matter, Bruce McLaren (see pages 222/5)—just no way. Men of their stamp always seemed so safe as to be wholly immune from serious accident, let alone death.

Barry Gill's experience was so typical of the way different people learnt of the unbelievable on that day in April 1968:

> I was in Mombasa for the East African Safari when I spotted his name on a paper in the lobby. I bought it and said to my wife: 'Jimmy's won'. I had assumed that that was what had earned the headlines. I walked away and looked at the paper. I couldn't believe it.

In my own case I was having an Easter family holiday in Cornwall and had asked one of the children to go out for some morning papers. Children can often be horribly matter-of-fact, and their return with the bald statement: 'Dad, I suppose you know Jim Clark's been killed' was typical of my own rejection of The Impossible—almost as if it were some cruel practical joke. It seemed no more credible just 20 days later as we all stood in silence before the start of Silverstone's International Trophy while a Scottish piper played the mournful lament 'Crimond' at the circuit where Clark had begun his major motor racing career.

In a wholly different way Clark had become almost as much of a household word as his great predecessor, Stirling Moss:

> It was strange to pull into a tiny drug-store in an out of the way village and see youngsters recognize Jim Clark. It was gratifying to see the way he accepted their recognition. Nothing seemed too much trouble for Jimmy out there—breakfast radio shows; speeches at parties; a highland fling for some ambitious photographer—even a flight in the nose of an insect-spraying plane just to please the pilot.
>
> Of course, he took a keen interest in the farming and proved he was an expert in more than one conversation . . . My best remembered morning is a visit . . . to a training stable where 'trotting' horses were kept. The challenge had to come. The owner provided silks, goggles, breeches and all for Jimmy. And all in good part he not only put them on but risked his

neck on a rapid circuit behind the flying hooves of a horse aptly named 'Regal Scot' . . .

From a memoir in Barry Gill's book *The Men* of a trip to the Tasman Series of 1977–78. Thousands upon thousands of Clark's friends and fans must have similar memories.

'Semper Augustus' was an expression generally associated with a modest man who was one of the greatest Roman Emperors. Clark was equally modest and it is the word 'Incomparable' that always springs to my mind when speaking, thinking or writing of him. That is just what he was and has remained, and when the sheer quality and quantity of a man's achievement make him such a household name, it becomes increasingly difficult to find adequate words to describe, let alone explain, his excellence.

With Clark it is best to start with simple statistics while adding that, for once, they tell no lies. Clark raced in Formula 1 through eight full years and one Grand Prix in early 1968. During this time his record was:

	MAJORS (first to sixth)	OTHERS (first to third)
First	25	14
Second	1	7
Third	6	1
Fourth	4	—
Fifth	2	—

GP fastest race laps:	28
GP pole positions:	33

Percentage of GPs won   34.72
[compared to Ascari's 68.42 and Fangio's 43.13].

If anything, these bald figures understate his case, for they do not tell of the many races that he dominated without actually winning because The Incomparable could so often be an astonishingly unlucky driver through minor car failures. Those who know about racing tyres say that his were more uniformly and evenly worn than those of his rivals, highlighting that supremely delicate touch and sense of balance that has ever been the hallmark of the greatest drivers—and particularly of The Incomparable himself.

Despite his apparent mildness of manner he had all the zest for and the habit of victory that one associates with Ascari; the supremacy of speed and the ability to turn it on when it most mattered, that one associates with Fangio and Moss, coupled with that equally uncanny ability to know just how fast—or slowly—he had to drive to win, as well as make a sick car a winner and fight rearguard actions.

One thinks of the British and French Grands Prix that he won in

1965 with cars that were either ailing or just not as good as their best opposition: of the American Grand Prix of 1966 when he became the only man ever to win a Grand Prix under the dubious power of the H-16 BRM engine and of much of his driving in 1966/67 with cars that were outclassed in both power and speed.

His versatility, too, was a byword, whether the car was a bog-standard saloon, an out-and-out sports car, a Grand Prix or Indy car and, by 1968, an Indy Turbo car. Whichever side the coin of championship might come down, it almost invariably had Jim Clark's head on it. Like his great predecessor in championship, Jean-Pierre Wimille (see page 220), he died inexplicably in an accident (generally thought to have been caused by a punctured tyre deflating) in an unnecessary minor event when an ever-expanding world seemed absolutely at his feet.

Those who have hailed Chapman's Lotus 25 as the cornerstone of succeeding ages in Grand Prix racing design would do well to reflect on the possibility that its most outstanding virtue was, in reality, a driver called Jim Clark. What more can one thoroughly inadequate writer say about the man who was and has remained simply 'The Incomparable'?

For me he has still to be the most perfect, complete, versatile and gentlemanly of drivers. Given, say, another five years, to what heights might he not have sent his tally of 25 Major Grands Prix, soaring higher and higher and leaving even Alain Prost and Ayrton Senna in faint pursuit and, unlike Senna, a modest Scot, who had 'borne his faculties so meek and been so clear in his great office'. It is almost superfluous to add that, like all the other drivers in this section, he was also a master car controller.

Chapter 6

A Farewell to . . .

John Michael 'Mike' Hawthorn

(Born 10 April 1929: Died 22 January 1959 in a road accident on the Guildford by-pass)

Gilles Villeneuve

(Born 18 February 1950 at Richelieu, Montreal: Died 8 May 1982 in a practice accident at Zolder in Belgium

The poisoned chalice of Mike Hawthorn

Towards the end of the fifties Rob Walker took delivery of a light-weight 300SL Mercedes from the factory and, by evil mischance, he happened to be driving it on a typically bleak, wet and cold day in late January, 1959, along the windswept Hog's Back and down to the Guildford by-pass. Who, then, should he see first in his driving mirror and, then, at his offside in the dual carriageway, but Mike Hawthorn in a fast moving Jaguar. It did not take Walker long to work out that this was no ordinary Jaguar, but Hawthorn's production racer, and, in a flash, they were booting it along, neck and neck, at around the 100 mark.

Like so many other things in life—or death—it all went right till it all went wrong. Thus they got through the first bend after the straight safely enough before Walker decided that discretion was the better part of valour and conceded a car's length to Hawthorn. After all, he reasoned, Hawthorn was the reigning world champion and one of the fastest drivers in the world as well as one of the most accident free. Walker's own account from *Supercar Classic* in August, 1988, goes on:

> Just as I did this the tail of his car broke away at about 5 degrees. I thought 'Oh, that's Mike playing the fool' but then it broke away further and the back wheel hit the kerb. The car spun around completely and . . . shot off the road backwards, knocking off his back bumper, and just missed a lorry . . . he went on to the grass on the far side and . . . the Jaguar hit a tree . . . I stopped absolutely opposite his car . . . planning on telling Mike that he had been bloody silly . . . I looked in the back and he was lying on the seat just as if he'd gone to have a kip . . . within about 20 secs his eyes glazed over and he died.

The Coroner's Court found that their speeds had been around the 80 mark, although one suspects that they could well have been higher. However, a wise Coroner will sometimes soft pedal a fatal incident when no useful purpose would be served by making things look worse, and a sensible verdict of simple Accidental Death was recorded.

In retrospect it was a thousand pities that Walker's friend, Rudi Ühlenhaut of Mercedes, had ever offered him that poisoned chalice of a lightweight, or, for that matter, that Mike Hawthorn had chosen to go riding out on so bleak and wintry a day. That is, unless you happen to be a fatalist and believe that your time is numbered from Day One.

Choose how, 22 January has remained yet another of those days I go on remembering to this day, like that of another fearless and intrepid young driver called Rosemeyer, who had died equally needlessly in the same month 21 years before.

A little dog's day: a memoir of Gilles

They thought 'twas the Devil was holding a revel,
For the town never knew such a hullabaloo
As that little dog raised . . . —*Rupert Brooke: The Little Dog's Day*

During just over his three last seasons Gilles was to win five more Major Grands Prix as well as the then significant Race of Champions at Brands Hatch; perhaps not the greatest of records, but with Gilles, it was rarely what he did so much as The Way That He Did It. His distinguished biographer, Gerald Donaldson, has written such a wonderfully memorable account of part of a 'Villeneuve Lap' on his home ground that its very least excision, let along paraphrase, would be both travesty and insult. So, here follows his text and, with it, the best memoir I can give of this remarkable driver who was cast in the true mould of Nuvolari and Rosemeyer:

> His reputation had preceded him and now his countrymen saw it first-hand.
>
> Gilles came howling down the pit straight, foot-to-the-floor in fifth with the 500 prancing horses in the Flat-12 behind his back singing a siren song of 11,300 rpm. He gave a quick glance at the pit board held out by the Ferrari crew but had to file it away for future reflection at an easier place on the circuit, because the first turn was looming up between the guard rails like a speeded up movie.
>
> The flattened S-section began with a gradual right-hander, then quickly tightened into a kink in the opposite direction just beyond the overhead pedestrian bridge. For spectators, this was one of the most thrilling places to watch their heroes at work, because the middle of the 'S' featured a bump in the pavement that picked the car up and hurled it sideways. More timid types lifted off briefly, but the bravest (and quickest) did not. Gilles did not disappoint.
>
> Moving at something like 265 kph, Gilles came flying around the right-hander on full opposite lock. Instead of detecting the telltale engine note of a cautionary right foot being exercised, the fans noted that Gilles never wavered. Rather, the engine revs soared as his T3 achieved a momentary liftoff on the bump, lurching sideways at least two meters, with the fat rear Michelins pawing aimlessly in the air before regaining traction with puffs of blue smoke erupting from the tyres.
>
> From their vantage points on the surrounding hillocks fans gasped in

amazement at the terrifying spectacle. As they looked down into the beehive of activity in the Villeneuve cockpit they saw the steering wheel being yanked vigorously right and left as Gilles grabbed handfuls of lock, in opposition to the directions his car threatened to go. The sound and fury of it all shook the ground and was over in little more than the blink of an eye. Until the next lap.

Thank you, Gerald Donaldson, for this precious memorial of a great driver and master car controller from an old-timer with the memory of a fast wearing out sponge, which can happily still give him instant recall of the sight and sound of Rosemeyer himself at Donington in 1937, beautifully evoked in an all-too-short BBC2 clip of that great driver doing his own 'Villeneuve' more than 40 years before, demonstrating that there really were other heroes.

Chapter 7

The Double Widow and the 'Frowning Providence'

Louise Sarazin and
Émile Levassor

(Born 27th May, 1841: Died 14 April 1897 as a result of a previous motoring accident)

In the beginning there was Benz and the Power was with Benz, and without Benz there was not anything mechanical made that did not run with power by Benz. Yet Benz was to be swiftly dethroned by upstart rivals like Daimler, Peugeot and Panhard. The four-stroke Daimler engines which powered so many of the early cars had been imported into France by Edouard Sarazin, a Belgian businessman to whom Daimler had granted certain commercial concessions. Sarazin chanced to be a friend of Émile Levassor who had joined Panhard, and they soon reached an agreement that Levassor's firm should build and market their Daimler engines in France.

By December 1887 Sarazin was a very sick man and he died that Christmas Eve. The Levassor-Sarazin connection was a very close one and one account tells of a touching scene, worthy of Victorian melodrama, of Sarazin expiring in the arms of his wife and clasping the hand of M. Levassor.

Levassor managed to survive the setback of Sarazin's death after which his rights in those Daimler patents passed, in the short term, to his widow. Fortunately she had already impressed Daimler as a lady of both charm and business acumen and, soon enough, she had overcome the dour exterior of M. Levassor sufficiently for them to have achieved the remarkable Spring Double of marriage to her 'Frowning Providence' on 17 May 1890, and the return to her of M. Sarazin's Daimler concessions.

So, although Peugeot had in a sense beaten Levassor to the beginnings of motor sport by running one of their cars with the racing cyclists in Paris–Brest–Paris of 1891, it was the dogged Levassor and his Mechanical System that was to prevail. Thus, by the end of 1891, Panhard were building their cars to what came to be recognized as the 'Système Levassor'. Its precept involved the vertical placement of the engine at the front of the car, a frame of armoured wood,

Lenkensperger steering, and transmission via a cone clutch and a series of sliding pinions upon a shaft, with final drive by chains.

Now, in themselves, none of these constructional elements contained anything radically new. Levassor's novelty lay rather in their combination for the first time: a trend which Mercedes were to exploit further in 1901. In a word, the genius of Levassor and Daimler/Maybach lay in the way that they were both able, successively, to assemble their various components into a viable mechanical package which produced first the embryo, and then the actuality of a vehicle that had, on the instant, become a car in its own right rather than just a horseless carriage.

While the primordial country ramble from Paris to Rouen in 1894 was the first motor trial en masse, the honour of running the world's first recognizable Grande Épreuve rested with the Automobile Club de France's 1895 race from Paris to Bordeaux and back again. Oddly enough, and with true perverse Gallic logic, it was 'won' by the man who actually finished second! For all his Providence and System, M. Levassor had failed to heed the regulations that required a minimum of four seats, whereas his own speedster boasted only two! Yet it mattered little enough, for today who remembers the technical winner, Rigoulot, whose Peugeot finished second on the road, nearly six hours behind Émile Levassor the all-conquering hero? Such can be the whirligigs of fame!

Levassor's car was nothing short of a slow moving bed of pain. Its twin-cylinder engine of 1206 cc (80×120 mm) rated 4 hp. In top gear (of three) it could reach 18.5 mph at 750 rpm and its running average of 15 mph through the 732-mile race meant that it must have travelled at rather more than its quoted top speed for much of the race. And what a handful it must have been even for its iron-willed driver. Its total loss lubrication system demanded constant attention, and its lack of a radiator obliged the driver to stop roughly every 100 kms to top up its cooling water. To add to the joys—or, more likely, hardships—of the new sport, the car, with its wheelbase of just over 5 ft 7 ins, was mounted on solid tyres and its fully elliptic springs lacked any form of damping, while its direct tiller steering, with no castor angle, made every obstacle on the road a source of constant hazard and discomfort. As a final touch, much of the journey was through the night when its primitive carriage lamps could only be kept alight with the greatest difficulty because the vibrations of the engine and the jolting of a virtually unsprung car on the harsh roads frequently split the soldered seams of the lamps. Viewed against this massive background of sheer physical discomfort, Levassor's effort must continue to stagger belief even after nearly a century.

Levassor had set off from the Place de L'Étoile at 1213 hrs on 11 June and reached Bordeaux at 1040 hrs on 12 June. There he paused to sign on and swallow a glass of champagne before the return journey. A relief driver had been laid on for him at Ruffec on the way down, but Levassor made such good time that the reserve was still asleep in his bed when Levassor came by at 0330 hrs! On the way back he thought it wiser to give the reserve another miss in case he was unable to sustain his master's winning pace! Levassor only made one stop of any length (some 22 mins) and reached the Porte Maillot on Wednesday 13 June after 48 hours 47½ mins at the tiller.

The Grand Épreuve for 1896 was from Paris to Marseilles and back: 1,062.5 miles, but now spread over 12 days between 24 September and 3 October. Contrary to popular belief, the weather in Southern France at that time of the year can be capricious, bleak and inclement. The appalling conditions encountered in 1896 played absolute havoc with the drivers and the dubious stability of their cars, as trees were uprooted by the roadside and a howling Mistral whipped up the pitiless rain.

Levassor made a cracking start to be nearly two hours ahead as he battled on towards Orange; but there his luck ran out for, in the prevailing murk, he either hit a dog or thought he had while swerving to avoid it. Whichever it was, his high, short-wheelbased car turned over and threw him out. Characteristically he was soon up and away, driving on as far as Avignon, some 31 kms away, before handing over to his co-driver for the rest of an ill-starred race, which turned out to have been his last.

Émile never really recovered from that accident, although he seemed well enough outwardly and continued to attend assiduously to his business until, one day, he felt unwell and went home early. Madame Sarazin-Levassor chanced to be out and when she returned it was to find her husband dead in bed.

As is so often the case, this was not the only account of this remarkable man's death and H. O. Duncan in *The World on Wheels* has him dying while sketching out a design for a new car in his office.

Ten years after his epic drive, his monument was unveiled at the Porte Maillot. In the meantime his wife had become a widow again and the great house of Panhard-Levassor had gradually declined. Unlike their Peugeot and Renault contemporaries, Panhard never returned to the Grand Prix scene after 1908. For the mighty Levassor himself it seemed an off-beat end to a remarkable career that was, none-the-less, somehow in keeping with the character of this outwardly dour and self-contained man.

Levassor and Gottlieb Daimler had been close friends and, by a strange coincidence, Daimler's seventh and last child had been born on the very day that Levassor had died, 14 April 1897. Daimler had the little girl christened Émilie after his friend, although he himself did not survive very long either. Like Levassor he had a tumble from a car, in which he was actually being driven, at the end of 1899, and although he lived on until 4 March of the new century, he never really recovered from the shock of his accident.

Chapter 8

The Count's Cuff-links (1)

Count Eliot Zborowski

(Died 1 April 1903 in a racing accident on La Turbie hill climb)

By contrast with Panhard, Mercedes went from strength to strength from 1901 with their new technology cars that were to be campaigned with such enthusiasm and panache by their wealthy sporting patrons, including Count Eliot Zborowski. He had been born in America of a wealthy Polish family before becoming a naturalized Englishman and marrying one of the daughters of an American millionaire. He was very much the all-round sportsman of his day, riding to hounds from Melton Mowbray and maintaining houses both there and in London, while spending much of his time in Paris, where he inevitably caught the motor racing bug just when Mercedes were launching into their Maybach-inspired range of cars—the '35', the '60', and the '90'. One of the Count's English friends was the pioneer motorist, E. M. C. Instone, who accompanied him on several foreign trips in a 28 hp Canstatt Daimler, similar to the one which a well-known German driver, Wilhelm Bauer, had crashed fatally on La Turbie Hill in 1900. The accident was horribly similar to the one which was to end the Count's life at the same spot just three years later. In the meantime he was to become a notable Mercedes driver.

By 1902 the new Mercedes had become a 40 hp racer of 6795 cc capable of scaring the racing daylights out of the French pundits of Panhard and Mors on anything but the fastest of French roads. Thus the great race of the year from Paris to Vienna became the catalyst not just for the cars and driving of the remarkable Renault brothers, Marcel and Louis, but also for that of Mercedes and Count Eliot.

Of the four '40' Mercedes in Paris–Vienna, the Count's had a new kind of radiator with an integral header tank. It was also the only one to finish well, taking second place in the Heavy Car category and fourth overall, although many said that he had been 'robbed' of victory in the Heavy Class and, perhaps even in the overall reckoning, by an unnecessary technical delay, although perusal of Rose's *Record of Motor Racing* shows that while this might have been the case in the Heavy Class, the right to overall victory rested clearly enough with the astonishing Marcel Renault from the Light Car Class.

Whichever way you look at it, the heroes of the race were Marcel and Count Eliot, both of whom were presented with enormous garlands at the finish and, in a humorous tailpiece, Rose tells how the Count solved the problem of coping with his unwieldy decoration by wearing it round his waist like a gigantic floral cummerbund! Another fourth was Count Eliot's lot in the Circuit des Ardennes, widely welcomed as the first long-distance race to be run round a closed circuit and without time-wasting controls. Although again outclassed on sheer power, his '40' put up an excellent showing over the long and mostly straight roads of the 53-mile triangular circuit against the opposition of the bigger Mors and Panhards of Gabriel, Vanderbilt and Jarrott.

The annual Nice Week of 1903 included the traditional Battle of the Flowers in which many dignitaries, motor and otherwise, took part. In beautiful spring weather on 1 April a long column of cars were driven up the Grande Corniche to the well-known beauty spots or up to La Turbie itself for the annual hill climb. The hill top is a typical example of a French 'Village Perché' and had been the finishing point of a three-day race from Marseilles in late January, 1897. The first two days were a pretty leisurely affair, and the main interest lay in the third day's 'mountain race' from the outskirts of Nice up 16.6 kms of the Grande Corniche to La Turbie at 480 metres above sea level.

On that first climb the competitors met with snow at the summit and heavy rain as they descended to the warmth and comfort of Monte Carlo. By 1903 the climb had become almost as hardy an annual as its flowers, with not even Bauer's death in 1900 breaking the succession. Count Eliot's fatal accident was to change that happy pattern from 1 April 1903 as the sober tones of *The Autocar* warned:

> There is no doubt that with the high powers of modern racing cars (1903), La Turbie is not a suitable hill. It is not steep enough to reduce the speed of the motors sufficiently to make the very sharp bends safe, and while racing must always be dangerous, it appears that La Turbie is unduly so.

The racing started at 0900 hrs on 1 April with the cars being sent up at three-minute intervals, led by the five '60' Mercedes, first Wilhelm Werner and, fifth, Count Eliot starting at 0912 hrs. By 1903 the distance had been marginally reduced to about 15.3 kms but, for some reason, the Count was anything but his usual charming, cool and laid-back self as he took his seat in his brand new, pale blue racer on that bright spring morning. Some said that he had not had time to accustom himself to the performance of his new car or to the hill; others that he was just in a nervous and tense mood; others again that the cause of it lay in a fortune teller's malign prophecy from the previous year. As it was, the Count jumped his start by several seconds and shot off at a pace 'viewed with apprehension by all spectators at the start'.

His passenger, the Baron Pallange, who survived the accident, said that the Count had . . .

> . . . manifested nervousness and impatience and was determined at all hazards to win [and] started like a rocket . . . the speed was too great. Count Zborowski realised the danger, tried to block the wheels but was

unable to do so and in a flash we were in front of the rocks . . . going at
about 90 kph . . . the automobile struck the rocks with a frightful crash
. . . I was flung out and rendered unconscious.

In all of which the Count was unluckier than the Baron, for he, too,
.was flung out, but was killed immediately on impact.

After that tragic interlude the Nice Festival went on, but the hill
climb was shelved for six years. That great sportsman of the age,
Baron de Caters, himself a great Mercedes enthusiast, sorted out the
bereaved Countess's legal and other problems arising out of the
accident, including Canstatt's bill for an outstanding balance on the
'60' of 21,000 francs. One Baron Pallu de la Barrière, bought the
ultimately rebuilt '60', while another, the injured Pallange,
approached Consul Jellinek, the father of the fair and eponymous
Mercedes, to sell him the 'great Daimler', which was presumably the
28 hp car he had driven about Europe with Mr Instone. Pallange
wanted the car for hiring out and, as he charmingly put it, to:

> . . . earn in this way until I am completely recovered and at the same time
> make some publicity for you [the publicity seeking Jellinek] . . . [and, as
> a final touch] Permit me to ask if you could possibly let me have an
> engine for the car if I pay it off in monthly instalments!

Consul Jellinek's reaction to this example of 'live now and pay later!'
is not recorded and the 'Tropea Augusti', transposed down the centuries into 'La Turbie', continued blandly to look down on the follies
and foibles of mankind from the lofty eminence of its perch at the top
of La Turbie as it had done since it had been dedicated to the Emperor
Augustus himself in BC 6 to celebrate his subjugation of the Gallic and
Germanic tribes.

Chapter 9

The Dog and the Dust Cloud

Loraine Barrow
(Died 13 June 1903 in hospital following an accident in the Paris–Madrid race on 26 May 1903)

Marcel Renault
(Born 14 May 1872: Died 26 May 1903 in an accident in the same race)

Three years before these unhappy events, that same Consul Jellinek had placed an order for 36 of the new '35' Mercedes, the first of which was ultimately delivered to Loraine Barrow in the veriest nick of time for him to start in the first Grand Prix of Pau, in February of 1901, though, sadly, with little success.

Claude Loraine Barrow was an expatriate Englishman married to a French lady, Valerie Marie, who had long been resident in Biarritz. He was also something of an amateur of motor racing, besides being on friendly terms with the wealthy and well-connected Jellinek family, which doubtless accounted for two significant events in his life in 1901/02: his being invited to drive the first car to race under the name of Mercedes by the Daimler works and then to stand Godfather to Jellinek's son, Guy Jellinek Mercedes, who had been born on 10 April 1902.

A little earlier, in November and December of 1900, he had entered into two life insurance arrangements, describing his occupation in his Proposal as 'driving motor cars', although he had also informally told the insurers that he 'sometimes took part in motor races'. The Policy had a value of £2,000, which was a tidy sum in those days, so that it was no surprise to find the insurers hedging their bet by re-insuring their risk for the entire sum with another company. They described their risk to the re-insurers as death 'arising solely and directly from accidental injuries received from an accident to a motor car in which (he, Barrow) shall be riding at the time of the accident'. The original insurers hedged their bet rather more cannily by describing Barrow's occupation to the re-insurers as 'Gentleman', thereby covering a multitude of sins, and they were equally careful not to tell the re-insurers that Barrow had proposed to his own insurers that his occupation was that of 'driving motor cars', still less that he sometimes drove them in races.

When Barrow's Will came to be proved after his death on 13 June 1903 his estate was valued at £7,390 gross and £7,106 net, again quite a tidy sum. His wife was his sole executrix and beneficiary and his insurers paid out their policy meekly enough, but then had the neck to pursue a claim against the re-insurers on their contract of re-insurance.

Now until recently I had accepted the legend which appears in several references that (1) the original insurers had declined to pay out on Barrow's policy on the ground that he had failed to disclose his racing activities in his proposal, in which he had simply described his occupation as 'Gentleman'; (2) his estate had then sued arguing that motor racing was a fitting activity for an English gentleman with no further qualification: and that (3) the trial judge had found on this basis so that the original insurers had been obliged to pay out.

I could, however, find no authority or reported case for all this, so in a fit of legal diligence I spent an idle afternoon in a London law library where I succeeded in tracking down a case of 'Equitable Life Assurance Co. v. General Accident Assurance Co. Ltd' in the *Scots Law Times* of 22 October 1904, which gave me the true answer. What really happened was that Barrow's insurers *had* paid out his estate in full, but, very properly, failed in their action against the re-insurers, for their having been so blatantly economical with the truth to them. No mention, be it noted, in any of the reports of what might or might not have been an Occupation for a Gentleman!

Of course, such a disaster as that of Paris–Madrid just had to happen sooner or later and the fatal day turned out to be the hot Sunday of 24 May 1903, when all the world and his wife, to say nothing of the young W. F. Bradley covering the race on his bicycle, were out by the side of the classic N10 from Paris to Bordeaux, over which so much motor racing history had already been made in the years from 1895. All the motoring might of Europe was gathered together, with the sorrowful exception of Count Eliot Zborowski and his Mercedes, and lots were drawn for starting positions. These were every bit as important in those far off days as today's grid positions because of the hazards caused when overtaking 'blind' through the storm of dust raised by the car ahead, so that drivers had often to navigate by reference to tree tops! In today's world a good grid spot is just as necessary to enable overtaking to be attempted at all on the small, constricting circuits now in use. The other great hazard lay in safety standards and crowd control, which were often marginal in the extreme and are best likened to some of the special sections of today's road rallies.

The two principal actors were that same Claude Loraine Barrow and Marcel Renault, button-maker and draper turned brilliantly successful racing driver and company director, who had drawn starting numbers 5 (Barrow's 45 hp de Dietrich) and 63 (Marcel Renault's 30 hp Renault). The cars were to be started at one-minute intervals, which meant that Barrow would have a virtually clear run, whereas Marcel would have something between 39 and 47 cars (for accounts vary) ahead of him. But this was nothing to the problems of the actual winner, Fernand Gabriel, with one of the wind-cheating 70 hp Mors way back on No. 168 who had, somehow, contrived to be the third driver to reach Bordeaux, after driving in a semi-permanent dust cloud for most of the way in what has rightly been described as 'one of the most wonderful feats of skill and courage . . . recorded in the annals of motor racing': a feat that was, in a sense, the flip side to Levassor's achievement from 1895.

Like Charles Jarrott, Barrow had gone over to de Dietrich, whose new cars had been designed by a wayward Italo-Alsatian genius called Ettore Bugatti. He had planned to fit his new cars with 80 hp engines, but the weight limit of 1000 kg made this impossible, so he had to be content with a smaller and near-untried 45 hp unit. Jarrott himself had drawn starting place No. 1 and, after considerable difficulty, he had eventually got his car to the start at Versailles and it was just as well that Barrow had promised to keep dinner for him on that memorable evening before the race.

Although the car had eventually run well enough on its short journey, Jarrott arrived full of gloom as 'Barrow expressed his delight that I had at last got to the start safely' and adding, while raising his glass: 'Whatever is the matter with you? Are we not all here? Let us eat, drink and be merry, for tomorrow we die!' Small wonder that those words came back to haunt Jarrott 'with horrible distinctness' within 24 hours.

Coincidentally Marcel Renault had been harbouring similar forebodings and for rather longer. In May 1903, when the Renault works were being threatened by the possibility of strikes, Marcel had been heard to tell some of his workers that they would be doing him a good turn by striking as it would give him every reason to abandon the race—and that from the overall winner of the previous year's classic! At that point the remarkable combination that the two brothers Louis and Marcel, had worked up between them in the years 1900/02 seemed almost unstoppable—not least from the way in which they seemed able to 'cover' for one another in their close-knit double act. To what new heights might they then aspire, whether in commerce or in competition, now that they had won 1902's premier race and doubled their factory area in readiness for a scheduled production of 1000 cars for 1903?

Yet, for all their cars' promise, Marcel was still uneasy and, like Count Eliot, far from his normal self at the start of Paris–Madrid, in sharp contrast to brother Louis who had his plan of campaign all carefully mapped out in his head. He had drawn starting position No. 3 and intended, very simply, to run the opposition into the ground over the fast, straight sections between Versailles and Chartres. And, with the memory of 1902 in mind, he never doubted that he and Marcel would succeed triumphantly with their faster and more powerful 30 hp cars.

Yet Marcel still persisted before the start: 'I'm worried, Louis; I don't feel very confident. Too many fast cars and too many opponents.'

'Nonsense,' replied Louis forthrightly, 'it's only a matter of taking the lead as soon as possible, in order to keep clear of the cloud of dust

. . . then we shall be sitting pretty.'

Finally, as Jarrott's car departed, there was a brief, touching and sadly final interchange between the two brothers: 'Right Marcel, good luck, the factory relies on you,' and a quick whispered: 'Good luck, Louis, good luck,' from Marcel, as Louis let in his clutch at precisely 0347 hrs.

For all his expressed uncertainty, Marcel must have been pressing on in true Renault style to have been lying fifth on the road by the time he reached Poitiers, with only Théry, Baras, Jarrott and Louis in front of him. As Marcel had started 47th, 45th or 39th—depending on which account you accept—this meant that he had overhauled all but four of the cars that had started ahead of him in the 334 kms from the start and it seemed logical to suppose that he would have caught at least three of the remaining four over the 200-odd kms to Bordeaux.

So he sped on towards his fate at Couhé-Verac in pursuit of the dust cloud that would envelop his next target—the 40 hp Decauville of that Leon Théry, who was to succeed the Renaults to the crown of French motor racing in 1904/05. Théry had started fourth, but by the time Marcel caught up with him he could see little or nothing of the way ahead, as he drove on into the impenetrable, just as another hard driving Frenchman, Didier Pironi, was to do in rain-enveloped conditions 79 years later. Then, of a sudden, he got a glimpse of Théry's car pulling over to the right, for Théry had seen something that neither Marcel nor his mechanic, Vauthier, had—a man at the side of the road waving a flag to warn drivers of an impending dangerous corner. All too late Marcel finally saw it as well, but he was going too fast to take the bend and his car left the road, rolled over and over, while ejecting both driver and mechanic, and finished up in a ditch pointing back in the direction of Paris.

Marcel died aged 32. He had been highly regarded as a good employer, a sound businessman and a bold and skilful race driver. After studying at the Lycée Janson de Sully, he had worked first in his father's business where, in a few short years, he had left his own mark on the relation of capital to labour, which was to consolidate the Billancourt enterprise.

Like Loraine Barrow, Marcel also left a legal problem behind him. Not content with being a fearless driver, he had also been a great ladies' man and the mistress who survived him, Suzanne Davenay, was also the heiress named in his will to his one-third share in the business; and, what was worse, she was now asking to be paid out in cash! This could have spelt financial ruin for the rising firm.

Yet again Louis was equal to the challenge and successfully persuaded Suzanne to accept a substantial annuity and a new car every year in full and final settlement. Louis faithfully executed his part of the bargain throughout his life, and after his death, those who succeeded him did likewise until Suzanne's death in 1953. Louis' action was a happy contrast to his extreme reluctance to pay for Marcel's mechanic, who survived Couhé-Verac, to have a month's convalescence after his accident, which did him little credit.

Now, what of Loraine Barrow whom we left waiting his signal to start fifth at Versailles? The reports say nothing about his progress during the race, although he had obviously never been a leader any more than he had in any of his other races from 1900. None the less, and in spite of incipient fever making him long to escape from the inferno of dust and noise in which he was encompassed, he had driven fast and well as far as Libourne, about 38 kms from Bordeaux, before death caught up with him.

Libourne is the centre for the delectable 'right bank' wines of Pomerol and St Emilion and its name is claimed to be derived from an English knight, Sir Roger de Leyburne, the Steward of the future King Edward I. This Sir Roger hit upon a novel kind of memorial for himself in the centuries' old Kentish church where was was commemorated by having a recess built into a wall to contain a shrine for the lodgement of the hearts of his family. After his own death in 1271 his heart was duly enshrined, though it is unlikely that the practice survived him.

For Barrow, disaster took the form of yet another errant dog, which either got enmeshed in his exposed steering or made him swerve to avoid it. Whatever the cause, it produced one of the most horrendous racing accidents in history when the car hit a tree at very high speed and disintegrated in all directions.

Barrow's mechanic, an old family servant called Pierre Rodez, was killed instantly, while Barrow himself was thrown clear and finally came to rest in a ditch at the side of the road some 20 yards away. Thereafter he lingered on in hospital at Libourne until he died on Sunday 13 June.

Barrow was highly regarded as 'one of the most enthusiastic automobilists in the South of France, highly esteemed in automobile circles, where his sad end has called forth a general expression of sympathy and regret . . . [for] . . . a keen sportsman and a thorough Gentleman.' Many years later, his Godson, Guy Jellinek Mercedes, wrote of his father's old friend:

> If there is nowhere a memorial to my Godfather, Claude Loraine Barrow, at least I keep in my collection one of his christening presents: a gilded silver bowl with a saucer and spoon.

We shall never know if Marcel Renault could have caught up with his brother on elapsed time. As it was, Louis lived on until 24 October 1944 when he died at the age of 67 in Fresnes Prison after spending the last months of his life under arrest awaiting trial for treason. His death was said to have been due to cerebral haemorrhage resulting from blows received in prison on the night 3/4 October.

With foreknowledge, Louis would surely have preferred to meet his end fighting the good fight alongside his dear brother to being cruelly and wantonly done to death in the anonymous darkness of a prison cell far from his loved ones.

Chapter 10
The Hazards of Practice

Giosue (aka Cesare) Guippone (also spelt Giuppone)
(Died 16 September 1910 in an accident practising for Coupe de l'Auto, Boulogne)

Paolo (Paul) Zuccarelli
(Born 1885: Died 19 June 1913 in an accident on N154 between Thomer and Tivoli, practising for the French Grand Prix at Amiens)

That witty and perceptive historian of motor racing, Kent Karslake, to whom we must now sadly refer as 'the late', opened his erudite book *Racing Voiturettes* with this passage:

> In a sense . . . the racing voiturette is as old as motor racing. The 4 hp Panhard . . . with which . . . Levassor won the first real motor race in 1895 . . . (would not have been) regarded as a small car. On the contrary it was . . . the record coach of automobilism; there was no need to excuse it, on the score of size, for its average speed over 700 odd miles of 15 miles an hour.

By the earliest part of the twentieth century the Grande Épreuve was the preserve of the big 35 to 70 hp racers, and the voiturette movement was being spearheaded by the miniscule 1.75/3.5 hp de Dion engined Renaults, which gradually grew into the 8 hp of Paris–Berlin, the 16 hp of Paris–Vienna and the 30 hp of Paris–Madrid. By 1903 the erstwhile voiturette of the Renault brothers had grown into a mini-Heavy Category car, called for convenience's sake, a Light Car and the true voiturette had thus to be born all over again.

That marvellously progressive series of Circuit des Ardennes races from 1902 to 1907 had included a class for voiturettes up to 1906 when these cars were given a race and Trophy of their very own, called the Coupe de l'Auto. From that time the Coupe swiftly grew into a hotly contested major event, second only in importance to the Grand Prix itself during the years to 1913. Indeed, in the years 1909/11 it was at least the equal (in Europe anyway) of the very ersatz and inferior Grands Prix that were actually run. The simple reason for this lay with the French manufacturers who, in a sulky fit of *amour*-[not very] *propre*, had thrown their Grand Prix to the dogs after their defeat of 1907 and downright whitewashing in 1908.

This shifted the whole weight and emphasis of French motor racing from the great monsters of the Heroic Age to the wiry, spindly, miniscules of the voiturette and even cycle-car classes. The importance and impact of this early example of class evolution can best be likened, historically, to the effect of the reversal in Formula 1 engine placement from front to rear that took place between 1957 and 1960. The most successful and competitively prolific of this new breed of automotive, 4-wheeled stick insect were undoubtedly the Lion-Peugeot (or just plain Peugeot) racers of 1906/13 and their drivers, the most successful of whom were Jules Goux, Cesare Guippone, Georges Boillot and Paul Zuccarelli.

Peugeot had produced some new V4 cars for 1910 to be driven by their two most forceful drivers, Guippone and Boillot, leaving the faithful Goux to soldier on with a V-twin. Because of the regulations that then governed engine capacity, all three cars had exceedingly long strokes, which made them unwieldy and also diminished their drivers' forward visibility. Both these factors could well have contributed to Guippone's fatal accident during an unofficial practice run before the 1910 Coupe when he had to brake sharply to avoid some cyclists who had emerged unexpectedly on to the circuit near the site of his later memorial on the road from Desvres to Boulogne. As a result, his high, unwieldy car became terminally unstable and turned turtle with fatal consequences for its driver.

At least that was how an old inhabitant of the nearby town of Desvres, who claimed to have been an eye-witness, described it to me over 25 years ago. Be that as it may, the accident deprived Peugeot of a highly successful and spirited driver and could also have had some bearing on the ensuing history of the high speed racing engine, for Guippone's death left a vacant space chez Peugeot that was soon to be filled by Paolo Zuccarelli, who had just left their keenest rivals at Hispano-Suiza.

* * *

The mysterious story of 'Les Charlatans' and the evolution of their new cars from 1912 has been told by many people including this writer. Undoubtedly the best and most authoritative of these accounts, and the nearest to the solution of their mystery, is that of Griffith Borgeson, which is to be found in the first part of his book, *The Classic Twin-Cam Engine* fittingly entitled 'The Charlatan Cycle'. As that 'Cycle' is only peripheral to the theme of this book, I shall not enlarge upon it here save to encourage anyone who has not already done so to beg, borrow or buy a copy of it without delay.

As to Guippone, what more is there to say, save to echo Fortinbras, Hamlet's named successor, as he bids four captains:

> Bear Hamlet, like a soldier, to the stage;
> For he was likely, had he been put on,
> To have proved most royally: . . .

Shakespeare never wrote a sequel to Hamlet so we have no means of knowing what became of Fortinbras, but there is an eerie similarity about the ends of the dashing young men of Peugeot: Cesare Guippone from 1900 to 1910, and his replacement, Paul Zuccarelli, from 1910 to 1913.

Around 1908 Marc Birkigt of Hispano-Suiza had sent his technical assistant, one Pilliverdier, to Northern Italy to look into the possibility of setting up a factory there. By one of those long chances, when Pilliverdier put his car into a garage for servicing, the work was carried out—and very well too—by a young Italian mechanic from Brescia, then called Paolo Zuccarelli. He and Pilliverdier hit it off at once, and Zuccarelli was promptly snapped up by Hispanos and taken on to their strength at Barcelona. He proved an apt pupil, and when Hispanos decided to go racing he was an obvious choice both as mechanic and test driver, along with his discoverer, Pilliverdier—now changed to Pilliverde as Paolo had become Paul.

Zuccarelli was an instant success for Hispano-Suiza, taking sixth in the Coupe of 1909 and winning it for them the next year in what was described as 'a very rational and pleasing looking Hispano'. He also won the Ostend race that year from Boillot himself. After that Zuccarelli drove one more voiturette race for Peugeot in the 'all-comers' event at Le Mans in 1912 which he won by almost an hour. On the other hand he had very little luck with the bigger L76 Grand Prix cars, being eliminated in the French Grand Prix of 1912 by ignition trouble and the Indy 500 of 1913 by carburetter trouble when lying second and after setting a new lap record.

So, at the end of his brief day, where did the young Zuccarelli fit in? Was he just a good young motor mechanic with a winning smile, who was no more than a competent racing driver, good enough to win just one major race by default when his most formidable rival Guippone had failed to survive a last practice session? For sure he had broken the Indy lap record and beaten the best of the Peugeot drivers a couple of times, but was that enough? And what of the part he may have played in the creation and evolution of the high speed racing engine? Was he in reality a gifted engineer-driver like, say, Bruce McLaren, or just a third stringer brought in to replace Guippone in the Peugeot team?

What a lot the Grands Prix and other races of 1913/14 might have told us if only a deaf old French farmer and his deaf old French horse had not chosen to emerge from the same sort of hidden track (as the cyclists had for Guippone near Desvres) on the long arrow-straight of RN154 between the villages of Thomer and Tivoli on that hot, sunny day of 19 June 1913, just 23 days before the French Grand Prix at nearby Amiens, when Zuccarelli and his mechanic Fanelli were both killed outright.

It is a question that I ask myself every time I have driven down that long stretch of Route Nationale during the last 30 and more years. I dislike vacuums, as much as does Nature, and have thus long since thrown my own hat into the ring, along with Fortinbras, as a pro-Zuccarelli man, whether as driver, evolver, or mechanic, not least because after his death nothing ever went so well again with the racing

Peugeots. Perhaps, too, Zuccarelli was gifted with a lucky streak—at least until that fatal day in June 1913.

As it is—and not for the only time in these pages—one is left with an elusive memory of a world in which all four of its 'Charlatans' were born, by bizarre coincidence, in the same *annus mirabilis* of 1885, and achieved their greatest fame in 1912/14 before being scattered to the four winds of fate: Zuccarelli (1913) and Boillot by violent death (1916); Ernest Henry by death in obscurity in 1950 and, finally, the quiet dapper meticulous Jules Goux, with or without his bottles of Indy bubbly, in 1965. This age-old alcoholic canard keeps cropping up in new guises, putting me in mind of Tom Lehrer's jingle:

> These are the only ones of which the news has come to Harvard,
> But there still may be others that haven't been discavard!

For example, the up-to-the-minute Rich Taylor version of Indy, from 1991 has 'Goux and his roving mechanic keeping themselves hydrated by downing a pint of champagne at each of his six pit stops, plus more in the Victory Circle'. The other side of the coin is represented by Goux's own account of 'How I Won Indy' published in *The Motor* of 17 June 1913, in which he said that he had a gallon of water poured over him at every pit stop and that he was dry as a bone again after another five minutes on the road; nothing about Dom Perignon and his Méthode Champenoise though!

Yet, in this remarkable pantheon of mechanical achievement, historical accuracy, no less than justice, demands that a proper place should be accorded to M. Henry. Boillot, who had entered the Peugeot works at Beaulieu in the Pays de Montbéliard and later gone into their drawing office before becoming involved in racing, might have been the cheer-leader who won the races and jollied everyone along; Zuccarelli might equally have been the man with bright mechanical ideas, and Jules Goux the age-long voice of calm and reason. Yet nothing could have been achieved without someone to put it all together on to paper. A long memoir published in *The Motor*, without a by-line, immediately after Boillot's death, sets this out clearly enough that this 'purely technical work [was] entrusted to Henry, a Swiss engineer who had made a speciality of high efficiency motors' and with no reference to Boillot, Zuccarelli or Goux.

Leaving aside the possibility of yet another 'Fifth Man', the identity of the 'Master Charlatan' is likely to remain as lasting a mystery as 'The Man in the Iron Mask', but *The Motor's* conclusion makes its point clearly enough.

Chapter 11

The End of the Beginning — 1912/14

Georges Boillot

(Born 1885: Died 20 May 1916 in aerial combat in the area of Verdun)

G eorges Boillot was the third and unquestionably the greatest of the voiturette drivers described in this section. He cast much the longest shadow for the way in which he came to epitomize all that was most glorious and flamboyant in French motor racing during the years leading up to World War I, when its military watchwords were 'Cran' and 'Elan'. Boillots's air of swaggering braggadoccio fitted perfectly into that age: big, broad and bristlingly bewhiskered, he knew that he was The Greatest—like Cassius Clay in his best days—and he made sure that everyone else knew it as well. Like the way he would stop his car opposite a Café in the Avenue de la Grande Armée by spinning it round in its length and, when war came, saying that he would win either a military or a wooden cross. A malign fate saw that he got both.

His active career lasted from May 1908 through to July 1914, and always with Peugeot. In the years to 1912 Jules Goux had been the more consistently successful of the two, but once Boillot got into his Grand Prix stride the tables were turned. Thus he won the French Grands Prix of 1912/13 and the significant Coupe de l'Auto of 1913 before dominating the Indy 500 of 1914, which he would surely have won but for tyre troubles. As it was, he put in a new single lap record of 99.85 mph, which was not bettered until 1919 by René Thomas with a straight-eight 5-litre Ballot.

With his return from Indianapolis in 1914 the stage became set for the greatest drive of his life—against no less than five of Mercedes' new 4.5-litre racers at Lyons on 4 July 1914. Once again tyres could have been a deciding factor, although the relative ease with which Max Sailer had led the opening laps pointed to more fundamental causes. Choose how, it enabled Boillot to put on one of the most sustained defences by any sportsman of his title, against a fittingly regal backdrop. Sailer went out after five of 20 laps, and thereafter Boillot was able to hang on to an increasingly tenuous lead until lap 17 when Lautenschlager at last overhauled him on elapsed time. Even then, Boillot gamely continued the fight, with a car that was literally near to falling apart, until his engine finally failed on the last lap of all, leaving the triple Mercedes victors to reap the glory of their first Grand Slam.

When war came a few weeks later, the *New York Times* reported that the first official act of France's newly appointed Generalissimo,

General (later Marshal) Joseph Jacques-Césaire Joffre, was 'the appointment as his private chauffeur of Georges Boillot, the greatest motor driver in France, and the three [sic] times winner of the Grand Prix', which, of course, was not strictly correct. Unlike his German opposite number, the younger Moltke, who never went to his Field Armies' Headquarters, let alone the front, Joffre, for all his girth and years (62), was in constant and energetic contact with his commanders from his Headquarters at Vitry-le-François on the Marne, about half way between Paris and Nancy, which enabled him to be in roughly equal distance (about 80–90 miles) of the HQ of each of his five armies. And it was Le Grand Georges who was the General's connecting link between them all: 'With Boillot driving his car Gen. Joffre frequently covers 70 miles an hour over the roads of France, and since the beginning of hostilities has covered thousands of miles', added the *New York Times* on 20 September 1914.

Later Boillot enlisted as a fighter pilot to fight Germans with all the 'Cran' and 'Elan' of his great racing days.

At least that is one version. However, after his death the *New York Times* version is strongly refuted both in *The Motor* of June 1916 and by an article by a French correspondent. According to them the story of Boillot and Joffre is totally incorrect and that Boillot, along with his Lyons team-mates, Goux and Rigal, joined the Motor Service of the French Army, by whom Boillot was employed on special missions travelling from the front to Bordeaux and Paris with urgent despatches until the front stabilized, after which Boillot sought transfer to the French Air Force.

Like so many of his racing contemporaries, he had already obtained his Pilot's Certificate (in 1911), and by the beginning of 1916 he was flying his Nieuport single-seater scout plane on patrol duty over hard-pressed Verdun. Early in April 1916 he was commended by his CO for bringing down a larger and more powerful twin-engined German plane under heavy fire, his own aircraft having crash-landed, riddled with bullets and wrecked beyond repair. For this feat he was immediately decorated with the Legion d'Honneur.

His end came shortly after at around 0600 hrs on 20 May 1916. As if to mirror his fight at Lyons, he now found himself opposed by five German Fokker planes, one of which shot him through the heart at 9,000 ft. His plane came to earth in a tree some distance from where he had fallen and he was buried the following day at Vadelaincourt some four to five miles behind Verdun, where a contemporary observer reported that 'as the little company moved away from the crowded graveyard German shells began to rain down around it!

Boillot was unlucky in being fatally wounded in the affray, else he might have been able to emulate the US flier, Gardner Fiske, who was reputedly the only World War I ace to fall out of a plane, catch hold of the rear struts and clamber back aboard. Fiske had a touching belief in the hereafter which he ascribed to knowing 'The Bishop' who is up there, and if there are any good clubs, he'll get me in!' Georges Boillot was not so lucky, or perhaps he did not know the right Bishop.

Georges' last racing victory had been at Boulogne in September 1913, and he had been commemorated after World War I by the Coupe Boillot, established in the twenties, and the erection of a memorial to him in the area of the start near to the Église St Martin. Back in October 1916, Jules Goux had opened a fund and formed a committee for a memorial to his great friend. Sadly it was no longer to be seen when I first visited the circuit after the last war, when I was told that it had not survived destruction during World War II 'par les sales Boches', which was how the French thought of them in those far off days. Personally I have always thought it a very good reason for someone to put up another one, not least to keep Guippone company.

One last thought that is common to both Guippone and Boillot. While drafting this 'Life' I chanced on the *Times* obituary of Harry Rée DSO, OBE, who was parachuted into France for SOE work under the codename 'Cesar', and who I had the privilege of meeting after the war in 1946. One of the highlights of his brave career was the way in which he was able to persuade the officials running the Peugeot plant at Sochaux, Montbéliard, to allow their armaments manufacturing equipment to be internally sabotaged in return for an agreement with the RAF not to bomb the plant from above, which 'became a classic ploy in the annals of subversion'. Rée's subversive Peugeot work inevitably blew his cover, and he ultimately had to escape to Switzerland after a hand-to-hand encounter in which he was seriously wounded.

Rée never forgot the peasants to whom he owed his life. For his work he was awarded the DSO and the Croix de Guerre and, like Georges Boillot, he was to become a legend in his lifetime in the parts of France in which he operated.

Chapter 12

'Cav.' & 'Trov.': The Cavalier and the Troubadour

Cavaliere Giuseppe Campari
(Born 1892: Died 10 September 1933 in the Monza Grand Prix)

Baconin Mario Umberto Borzacchini (aka Mikhail Bakunin)
(Died 10 September 1933 in the Monza Grand Prix)

Cav., Trov., Pag. and Trav. are the abbreviations of four of the best-known Italian operas—*Cavalleria Rusticana, Il Trovatore, I Pagliacci* and *La Traviata*—and in the early thirties it was equally well known that the melodious Campari had set his sights on an operatic career once he had chosen the day to hang up his goggles and windcap; although it was generally thought that his singing was not on a par with his driving!

'Il Negher', or 'Blackie', as he was nick-named for the darkness of his countenance, was a great big larger-than-life extrovert character; while little Borzacchini, his companion in death no less than life, was slightly built like a troubadour, and shy into the bargain. Their contrast called so easily to mind the meeting between Sydney Greenstreet and Peter Lorre in a railway compartment in Warner's film of *The Mask of Dimitrios*—or even the current-day British music hall duo of 'Little and Large'.

Campari was born in 1892, and by the outbreak of World War I he had become a well-established car tester, even aspiring to a drive in the 1914 Targa Florio in an Alfa-Romeo which failed to finish. His first important win was at Mugello in 1920 and, thereafter, he became a highly successful long-distance racer, mostly for Alfa-Romeo for whom he won the Mille Miglia of 1928/29, followed by third in 1930 and second in 1931. During the same period he was also placed second in the Ulster TT races of 1929 and 1930 and took two more second places in 1930/31 in the Irish Grand Prix for Maserati. In between times he had taken third in the Targa Florio of 1921, and won again at Mugello as well as a non-classified fifth in the 'Gran Premio Gentlemen' later in the year. Two interesting oddities have survived from this colourful event: first, the broad brush definition of the word 'Gentlemen' to include the Baroness Marie-Antonietta d'Avanzo, who actually finished third; and, second, the anonymous Fiat riding mechanic who took over the wheel from his 'Gentleman', Carlo Niccolini, when his clothes caught fire during a pit stop, and then succeeded in completing two laps at speeds not too far short of the great Bordino himself before officialdom woke up and called him in.

With Campari, though, all things were possible!

And they needed to be, for Il Negher had a pretty thin time with Alfa-Romeo as long as Fiat stayed on top of the Grand Prix world. At the end of 1923 his luck changed when he was called upon to test the new Jano-designed blown straight-eight P2 Alfa-Romeos for the French Grand Prix of 1924. This design and its derivatives marked the effective end of the line for Fiat and became, all at once, the benchmark of the Grand Prix car for the next ten years. The French race was run over a shortened version of the 1914 classic, and its sheer quality more than made up for a smaller entry. Of the actual 20 who started, only Count Louis Zborowski's somewhat hopeful entry of an Indy Miller on the rugged Lyons circuit struck an odd note, but, of course, the Count was a notorious and charming eccentric.

Campari's win in the Grand Prix was slightly lucky for being scored at the expense of Antonio Ascari, who had led for rather more of the race, but it had been a thrillingly close encounter, with only 66 seconds separating Campari from Divo's V-12 Delage after seven hours hard racing, and on a par with its great precursor from 1914.

Although Campari drove very successfully for another nine years, Lyons represented both the turning and the crowning point in his career. Not even his second French Grand Prix victory nine years later at Montlhéry was quite on that first level of achievement. In the meantime Lyons was followed by the triumphal months of 1924/25 before that bitter day on which all his success was to be overshadowed by the tragedy of Antonio Ascari.

Even before his victory at Montlhéry, Campari had been poised for his much publicized retirement from racing to devote himself more to his twin joys of music and good living, and as he approached 40 he felt he had earned them both. By that time he had become very much the senior citizen—the last of the pre-World War I veterans still actively racing in Grandes Épreuves. The young Giovanni Lurani, still happily with us, tells some delightful tales of 'the good old Campari' singing the Barnaba aria from *Gioconda* on the way to the start of a race, or 'being absolutely unbeatable in disposing of dozen after dozen of snails' at the *Escargot* restaurant prior to his win at Montlhéry. Not long after, Lurani was writing sadly of how 'a few minutes before his last fatal run, Campari had stopped and talked with me; his jovial face lit up with a smile as he recalled those gargantuan snail luncheons' in much the same way as the French drivers had rejoiced at the prospect of their fishy fare during the Great Savannah race meetings of 1908/11 (see page 91).

Campari's has to be one of the harder acts to follow, especially for a retiring subject like Baconin Mario Umberto Borzacchini. He had started out on motor bikes before graduating to Salmson cycle-cars in 1925 along with Fagioli, both men following the example of Robert Benoist before them in 1922/23. At the end of his Salmson years he went on to Maserati for whom he won his first important Grand Prix at Tripoli in 1930 after placing second there in 1929. Although the circuit was completely altered for 1933, this was by no means Borzacchini's last visit to Tripoli.

In the meantime he had emulated Chiron from 1929 in trying his hand at Indy in the 1930 500 with a 4-litre twin-eight Maserati. The big car lasted for only seven laps and had lost much of its punch through having to be raced without its superchargers which were now banned by the new Indy regulations—a great disappointment after Chiron's placing seventh in 1929 in a 1.5-litre Delage from 1927. The next Maserati invasion, by Cotton Henning and Wilbur Shaw in 1939, would be a very different story.

Borzacchini was now about to make his final move—to Alfa-Romeo—to be with his close friends, Compari and, most especially, Nuvolari. During these years he became one of the most enduring of those 'Eternal Seconds', taking no less than a dozen such placings in 1931/33. He did, however, have one great day of glory in winning the Mille Miglia of 1932 at a new record speed of 68.28 mph, which was the first record run to last for more than one year. However, it is not for his racing records that he has become chiefly remembered.

The Tripoli Grand Prix had been a dead letter since Borzacchini himself had won it in 1930 but, from 1933, it was to be lavishly revived as one of Il Duce's new show pieces and placed, initially, under the military command of the 'Sawdust Caesar's' Governor of Tripoli, General (later Marshal) Badoglio, who was to head the first post-war Italian government after the overthrow of 'Caesar' on 25 July 1943. At that time it seemed possible that the Allies might gain the whole of Italy almost without a blow, until the Germans decided otherwise. Thereafter, a long and grim struggle all the way up Italy largely under the able leadership of General (later Field Marshal) Albert Kesselring, who proved himself as adept a commander on land as he had been in the air; a versatility you might have expected to find in so able a Latin scholar.

The new Melaha circuit was 8.4 miles long and built for high outright top speeds. The centre-point was its ornate grandstand and pits that stood shimmering in the brilliant sunlight like a set piece straight from the pages of Chesterton's Lepanto:

White founts falling in the courts of the sun
And the Soldan of Byzantium is smiling as they run

As part of the great Libyan revival it had been decided to hold an immense nationwide lottery for which literally millions of tickets were to be available. This led to the notorious 'Tripoli Fix', a somewhat apocryphal account of which was attributed to Alfred Neubauer by his 1958 publishers, T. L. Martens of Munich, in his book *Manner, Frauen und Motoren*. Despite the flaw in Don Alfredo's 'Gospel', it does still manage to contain some grains of truth and even a sensible conclusion. More recently the diligent enquiries of Dr Paul Sheldon and his team of researchers have enabled something approaching accuracy to come to the surface, though at the expense of the colourful account in 'The Neubauer Version'! A letter from the Doctor to *Autosport*, published on 2 May 1991, makes all this very clear.

Dr Sheldon has been kind enough to make available to me copies of the relevant extracts from *Motori, Aero, Cicli et Sports* dated 6 and 22 May 1933, and from *Auto Italiana* for 20 May 1933, as well as the full starting grid for the race and its results. Between them these sources clarify several points of confusion:

1. The 'deal' was between Varzi, Nuvolari and Borzacchini.
2. There were not one but three ticket holders involved.
3. The total winnings distributed were Lire 5,400,000 split equally six ways between the three drivers and three ticket holders.
4. The race and its split-second finish between Varzi and Nuvolari was almost certainly genuine.
5. Such 'fix' as there may have been was between the six parties involved so that it hardly mattered whether it was Varzi or Nuvolari who won the race anyway, although there must have been some sort of agreement to include Borzacchini in the act as he both failed to complete the race and played little part in it.
6. That Louis Chiron did not even start in the race and it was very unlikely that Neubauer was anywhere near Tripoli at the time.

With the probable exception of Borzacchini, none of the drivers involved was exactly short of the world's goods, so for the 'Eternal Second' it was a windfall beyond his wildest dreams, a real fairy tale of a 'victory', calling for very little effort on his part. Though little good it did for either him or Campari, for whom the grim reaper was patiently biding his time till Monza's Black Day on 10 September.

Yet the conclusion of what is now clearly Don Alfredo's *spurious* Gospel may, none the less, have some validity when it states 'that, technicalities aside, any chance to increase the earnings from such a dangerous profession is worth taking. Good luck to them!' And it also had the blessing of the great journalist, Canestrini, who found that, after all the hue and cry, everything had been perfectly legal as well as a stimulation to motor racing. So, what had all the fuss been about anyway?

That fateful September morning of long ago 1933 had produced a spirited race between Fagioli and Chiron, now driving for Alfa-Romeo, and Taruffi and Nuvolari, recently switched to Maserati, all of whom led the race at different stages before victory finally fell to Fagioli.

The afternoon's programme followed a traditional end-of-season Monza pattern of eliminating heats according to engine size, with a combined final for the fastest in each class. In the first heat, Czaykowski's 4.9-litre Bugatti had the better of Trossi's 'Ferrari' Duesenberg clearly enough, although opinion is divided over the responsibility of the Duesie for spilling the oil on the South Curve where the multiple accidents took place in the second heat. The start of that heat was certainly delayed for some mopping up operations and, to make matters worse, it had also started to rain. All of which gave Campari plenty of time to receive the more than usually tumultuous applause that invariably greeted him as he had now announced that this was to be his last race.

It is melancholy history that it turned out to be just that, as both Campari and Borzacchini crashed fatally at the South Curve on the first lap of the second heat, while two other drivers, Count Carlo Castelbarco and Nando Barbieri, also crashed at the same spot and survived. Yet another example of W. S. Gilbert's bitter sweet couplet:

> See how the Fates their gifts allot
> Where A is happy, B is not.

'What,' ask the authors, editor and translator of *The History of The Scuderia Ferrari*, 'caused such a disastrous series of accidents?' They sought to answer as follows:

> Whether or not there was a major oil spillage, other factors must be considered, such as a section of track coated with oily residue and rubber dust laid down by the full Grand Prix field racing round there on the combined road and track circuit earlier in the morning; the intense rivalry between the drivers, especially between Campari and Borzacchini in Ferrari, Alfa and Maserati respectively, and, above all, it was a dull, cold day when the hard narrow track tyres of the day would not have generated much grip in the second corner of the race.

... before they noted, with somewhat grim irrelevance, that 10 September had also been a fatal day for Wolfgang von Trips in 1961 and Ronnie Peterson in 1978 (see pages 273/5 and 42/7).

Such is the sad story of Campari and Borzacchini, likened in these pages to a pair of British comedians called Little and Large and two film actors called Greenstreet and Lorre: two men who brought so much fun, joy and excitement—to say nothing of a piquant touch of piracy in times when people did not get themselves quite so worked up about mischievous goings-on as they seem to nowadays.

Two vignettes remain in the frame.

First, of 'Little' Baconin, who had had to change his name from that of a Russian revolutionary, Mikhail Bakunin, to his better known Mario Umberto to please the Fascists, dancing his jig—or should it have been a gopak?—of joy behind the locked door of his hotel room to the accompaniment of a big fan swirling bundle upon bundle of Lire 1000 notes in the air.

Finally, and writ rather more 'Large', was the bluff form of the seemingly eternal and indestructible 'Il Negher', falling like some much loved racehorse at his last jump of all. Campari who, in both career and outlook, so truly spanned the great historical gulf between the emergence of the vintage era of Grand Prix racing in 1912 and its glorious finale in 1933. The last survivor of that happy band, Campari was a man who, like his close friend Nuvolari, elevated the everyday performance of his chosen walk of life to the level of legend.

A whole microcosm of these vignettes spring effortlessly to mind: from the Great Lyons Sausage that was presented to him across the bonnet of his victorious car in 1924—and how, one suspects, he greatly enjoyed it!—through to the sight of him riding the wind, somehow perched on, rather than actually sitting in, his biposto Maserati, for all the world like the incarnation of Monsieur Bibendum, riding to his last win. Campari the gastronome cooking delicacies wearing a convict's striped pyjama suit; Campari playing Falstaff to Nuvolari's Puck in the Grand Challenge Bicycle Race at Monza only a few days before his death, with Nuvolari every inch the professional on a drop-handlebar lightweight racer, and Campari in plus-fours riding an old style sit-up-and-beg push-bike, unable to bend low because of his bulk. The 'Race' was over three laps of the full circuit, which both riders took fairly easily until the last sprint when Tazio put in a special home run to win by about ten yards. Campari was only too happy to pay the wager of their dinner afterwards, though even Tazio had to confess that the final burst had fair taken the wind out of him!

Finally, there has to be Campari the would-be opera buff and bon viveur, whose retirement was somehow symbolic, as if he had instinctively realized that there would be increasingly little place for a man of his character in the new firmament and style of racing that began in 1934; just as it ultimately was to be for his contemporary rival, Luigi Fagioli, who had been so much disaffected by his exclusion from 'the cut' in the Tripoli Plot.

Chapter 13

'Pag.': Heart-break, Triumph and Despair

Antonio Ascari

(Born 15 September 1988: Died 26 July 1925 when leading the French Grand Prix at Monthléry)

Soon after the end of World War I Campari met Antonio Ascari, who had then recently acquired the Alfa-Romeo agency in Milan's Via Castelvetro. His agency enabled him to embark on a career in motor racing, which he did with a Grand Prix Fiat from 1914 in the Targa Florio of 1919. The venture was not a success — Antonio crashed on the first lap. From 1920 he changed his car, if not his fortunes, for a series of Alfa-Romeos, the marque with which he was to be associated until the end of his days. But, change though he might, success of any kind continued to give him the slip and, in the depths of despair with tears in his eyes he implored his ever-present mechanic, Giulio Ramponi, to find himself another driver 'because if you stay with me, you'll never have the satisfaction of winning a race! All I've done is to make a reputation as the idiot that won't give up!'

He might just as well have been Canio talking, the broken hearted clown in *I Pagliacci*, and if he had been gifted with the voice, even of Campari, he would surely have thrown in the clown's famous sobbing lament — the 'Vesti la Giubba' forever associated with the great Caruso. Little did he know how dramatically his life was about to change, so that by 1925 he would be hailed like Caruso: 'no singer of our time . . . has ever made a more triumphant re-entree at the opera'. On that occasion, in 1914, Caruso was doing Pag. at Covent Garden and receiving eight solo calls, to say nothing of a fee of £500 a night. For a few fleeting months in 1924/25, Antonio's fame, if not necessarily his fortunes, was to reach those levels.

In the meantime, placing fourth in the 1922 Targa Florio was a useful start. The next year he improved his Targa place to second before winning the Circuit of Cremona in May and taking third at Mugello in June. At last his name was beginning to mean something, and at least to earn him a start in the Italian Grand Prix with Campari and his old friend Ugo Sivocci in the new straight-six P1 Alfa-Romeos. When Antonio had first met Campari he had scored few marks for telling the great man that he could drive as well as he! A terse 'Maybe!' through gritted teeth was all the answer he got from 'Il Negher' that day. Now, times had changed for the better, though tragedy continued to hover with Sivocci crashing fatally in his new Alfa in practice and the whole team being withdrawn. However, as 1923 gave way to 1924 Antonio's long apprenticeship was at last at an end as he took a well-earned place beside Campari and the great veteran, Louis Wagner, in the new straight-eight P2 Alfa-Romeo that Jano had designed to replace the disaster of 1923.

The leading Alfa-Romeo drivers of the mid-twenties were described by Sammy Davis as 'extraordinarily friendly, big, brown men', a picture that is well borne out by their group photographs as they look out on their expanding world with all the assured presence and confidence of the bluff, successful North Country businessmen that they all were. But it had not been always like that. Antonio Ascari had been born in a small village called Bonferraro di Sorga not far from Nuvolari's home, but four years before the birth of the Maestro. A mischievous attempt to set fire to his sleeping teacher's beard earned Antonio instant dismissal from school and a real taste of fire raising, working for the local blacksmith! Much of his work was welding cycle tubes, which soon brought him into contact with two local cycle racing heroes, Giuseppe and Arturo Nuvolari, and he may even have passed their young brother, Tazio, in the local towns and villages where he plied his next trade of servicing agricultural machinery. This pastoral life ended soon enough, at the turn of the century, when the family decided to seek richer bread in the smoke and grime of Milan, leaving the more rural Nuvolaris far behind—at least for the time being.

Antonio worked hard, and gradually began to prosper, and one wonders if that sleepy old Tuscan schoolmaster ever gave his pyromaniac pupil a thought then or later when Antonio's name had become an Italian household word. Then, five months before the Armistice, on 13 June 1918, Antonio and his wife Elisa had a son born to them—Alberto, who would also become a great name not just in Italy but all over the racing world.

The first of the new P2 Alfas was tested by Antonio and Campari before it made its debut on the Circuit of Cremona on 6 June 1924. Antonio drove the new car, backed by the RLS models of Campari and Enzo Ferrari, with Nuvolari also on the grid in a Chiribiri. All three of them retired, leaving Antonio to race away from a patchy field and win by 54 minutes at an average speed of 98.31 mph, a fastest lap of 100.85 mph and a timed speed of 121.16 mph through the 6-mile straight. Such was the quality of Antonio and his P2 that would now spearhead the opposition that Fiat, Sunbeam, Delage and Bugatti would have to contend with at Lyons.

Along with Pietro Bordino and Campari, the two brightest stars in the race were Henry Segrave of Sunbeam and Antonio himself. Segrave lost out because of a disastrous change to new magnetos at the last minute, but in all other respects it was Antonio who had the rawest deal after leading the race on 17 of its 35 laps. On lap 32 he was overtaken by Campari and then by Divo's Delage as he and Ramponi struggled to get their ailing car going again. Picture the sorry scene as the car shed tears of hot water from its block and tail-pipe; Antonio wept at the bitterness of his failure, while history does not relate what solace there was for the faithful Ramponi.

'Oh! Oh! Antonio!'—now about to enjoy his brief days of sheerest triumph at Monza in October 1924, and Spa in June 1925, before it all ended 22 laps into the French Grand Prix at Montlhéry. This meant that he had driven 1,170.1 racing miles in two long, full races and a third that had been cruelly cut short, without his ever having been seriously challenged, let alone headed. If ever there was one, this was a true realization of the Nelson touch that called not just for victory but sheer annihilation.

Yet, beneath the glittering tide of adulation, Antonio retained a touch of the man of sorrow and despair from his earlier days, that left him worried, brooding, superstitious and even strangely at odds with his well-trusted mechanic and friend, Giulio Ramponi. So much so that, as they worked together on the car before the fatal French Grand Prix, Ramponi asked Antonio outright: 'Look, what's the matter? Don't you trust me or something?' Such a rebuke, coming from Giulio, shook Antonio and all seemed well enough between them at 0800 hrs the following morning when Antonio swept straight into his accustomed lead. Then, on lap 23, he made a small and fatal error, clipping a fencing post and muffing his over-correction of the skidding car before it became hopelessly entangled with the paling fencing at the side of the road, after which the car finally overturned. Antonio's injuries were terrible, and he died in the ambulance on the way to hospital.

At the end of such a day what were all his brilliant achievements worth as the great Garibaldino lay dead in Linas, with the bark of the other two P2s stilled at the pits? Two great French sportsmen and gentlemen, Robert Benoist and Louis Wagner of Delage, drove to the fatal spot at the end of the race to leave their victor's garlands as a last gesture of respect to a great driver who had been their friend and most worthy opponent.

Four days later, what must have seemed like all Italy had assembled to pay their last respects to Antonio at Milan's Monumental Cemetery, and perhaps none more than a wide-dewy-eyed little six-year-old, holding Ramponi's hand and little thinking that he would first become the heir to his father's greatness and, shortly after, die of it.

For all the inexplicability of his fatal accident, Antonio had achieved a rare measure of driving perfection in his last races calling to mind such older artists as Felice Nazzaro, Georges Boillot, Henry Segrave (known in Spain as 'El Maestro Completo') and Italy's own Bordino. Antonio was soon to be succeeded by a pair of very different Maestri: Tazio Nuvolari and Achille Varzi.

Chapter 14

'Trav.': Perfection Led Astray

Achille Varzi

(Born 8 August 1904 at Galliate: Died 30 June 1948 at Berne practising for the Swiss Grand Prix)

Nuvolari was an elemental phenomenon, unfettered by the bonds of the natural. Varzi represented natural skill exalted to the point of classical perfection. As W. F. Bradley described them:

> Varzi had created his own driving style of which he was to remain the inimitable protagonist; until the last . . . methodical, cold-blooded, precise, comparable to the best Swiss watch, whereas Nuvolari could be likened jokingly to a cuckoo clock, liable to strike at the most unexpected moment and full of surprises.

In the famous Monaco Grand Prix of 1933 he had played cat-and-mouse successfully with the Campionissimo himself, he who men were beginning to call 'Maestro'—including even Varzi himself, when he was quite sure that Nuvolari was not in earshot! Varzi was the complete opposite to both the Ascaris, the supreme example of a driver who preferred to stalk his prey from behind; and many of his greatest races were won in this way. An outstanding and typical example was the Monza Grand Prix of 1930 where he hunted down his old friend and motor cycling rival, Arcangeli, after plug trouble had lost him nearly two minutes at the pits. He rejoined the race 'in an ice-cold fury . . . [as he] made up the time in 60 tempestuous miles . . . [catching] the astonished Arcangeli on the last corner of the last lap to win' by a fifth of a second. In another age it might have been Fangio's classic pursuit of Hawthorn and Collins on the Ring in 1957. But, then, Fangio had learned much from listening to both Varzi and Wimille in the Argentine in the late forties.

This trait in Varzi's character has been well described by Ferrari himself: '. . . intelligent, calculating, grim when necessary, ferocious in exploiting the first weakness, mistake or mishap of his adversaries'; which is, of course, what motor racing is all about. Yet elsewhere Ferrari speaks of Varzi in the same breath as Marchese Antonio Brivio as 'possessing the same gentlemanly chivalry at the wheel as Nazzaro and Minoia' and, no less, Varzi's great friend Louis Chiron.

In an article written many years ago, Cyril Posthumus also speaks of Varzi's 'gentlemanly charm and sardonic sense of humour . . . [and his] . . . calculated, machine-like perfection, following his own wheel tracks to the inch for lap after lap; when at bay he was magnificent, driving with grim, ice-cold ferocity, immensely fast but never making a mistake.'—at least until the one that was his first and his last.

Varzi inherited the precision as well as the immaculate turn-out of the great Felice Nazzaro, while engrafting on to it a grimness and fixity of purpose that were all of his own making, a legacy that he was to pass on to Juan Manuel Fangio. His style, no less than his name, lived on in the Argentine after his death, and it was a most moving tribute to his great memory for the Argentine A.C. to name their 1949 armada into Europe the 'Squadra Achille Varzi'.

Varzi was also one of the very few drivers who could make any sense out of the big rear-engined Auto-Unions of 1935/37. Most of the drivers brought up on front-engined configurations were much troubled by Dr Porsche's new racers, but Varzi and, significantly, another ex-racing motor cyclist called Rosemeyer, took to it all like ducks to water.

Like his great friend and rival of the period, Louis Chiron, Varzi had a sharp eye and a long pocket for all the best things in life, be they cars, women, food, wine or clothes. And, as the son of a wealthy manufacturer, he could indulge these pleasures as the fancy took him. Above all else, though, he was a man of pride. As with Farina and Fagioli, Face was all important to him and, with it, a pride that was to be his undoing just when he was at the very pinnacle of his frame and abilities in early 1936.

There has probably never been a more perfect driver than Varzi, but not even Perfection can be a complete armour against Fate, and in the heat of the early North African summer of 1936 Varzi's Achillean immunity began to desert him. Shortly after the fateful Tripoli Grand Prix, his Auto-Union had crashed at Tunis, owing, it was said, to a fierce wind blowing his car off course. During a terrifying series of end-over-end somersaults Varzi was thrown out of his car, miraculously emerging physically unscathed. Varzi was not in the habit of having accidents and this one, severe as it was, must have been a doubly shattering experience, especially coming so soon after his Tripoli Experience.

By 1936 Varzi had accumulated an enviable record at Tripoli: a split-second win in the famous Lottery year, a second win in 1934, second to Caracciola in 1935 and another split-second win in 1936. Yet, things were very far from green in Marshal Balbo's garden as the celebration dinner on the evening of the race progressed. By 1936 General Badoglio had been replaced by Mussolini's dashing aeronaut and air ace, Marshal Italo Balbo and, at the height of the party, as the popular and charming host, Balbo called upon his assembled guests to drink the health of Hans Stuck as the real winner of the race. Now, neither Varzi nor Stuck knew at the time that the result of the race, with Varzi 'winning', had been a Berlin-Rome Axis 'Fix' and, embarrassing as the disclosure must have been for Stuck, it was nothing short of hell and mortification for Varzi and his 'Pride'. Galling in particular because Varzi, had he been given an inkling of the mischief that was afoot, would have had merely to speed up and make sure Stuck was left well and truly standing.

On this occasion the 'Wrath of Achilles' reached truly Homeric proportions at the affront to Varzi's pride and his standing as a driver. He stalked angrily from the glittering scene and, although he continued to take good places for Auto-Union during the rest of the year, he gradually became a changed man. Had that well-meaning lady who was then his light of love, Ilsa Pietsch, been able to follow the excellent advice of Cole Porter and brushed up her Shakespeare, she would have learnt that 'not poppy nor mandragora nor all the drowsy syrups of the world' could have lulled Varzi's broken pride to the sweet sleep of yesternight. Instead, and no doubt with the very best of intentions, she turned him to drugs. It was a simply classic case of the wrong person being in the wrong place at the wrongest possible time.

A bluff, down-to-earth extrovert like Campari would have thumped Marshal Balbo, and perhaps Stuck and Dr Feuereisen as well, before going out on the town for the father and mother of a bender—returning the following morning with a hangover to match and nothing more. Sadly neither Varzi nor Ilsa Pietsch were made like that. At the end of the day it would not be the last of Varzi as a leading driver, for the silent man of Galliate was eventually cured of his addiction and married his Norma Colombo on 27 July 1940.

Thereafter, the peace found him back in the groove in July 1946, attended as ever by the faithful Bignami, with his master's eternal cigarette at the ready, on the grid of the first major post-war race, the Grand Prix des Nations at Geneva with a two-stage blown Alfa from Tripoli 1940 at his disposal. Quite a come-back for a supposedly sick and forgotten man!

By the end of 1946 he had chalked up one win and one second, and in 1947 he went on to one more win and four seconds, including the Swiss Grand Prix where he was seen to be wearing his best creased suiting, for all the world as if he were attending a smart garden party. While the years had not changed him too much, Old Father Time never stands quite still and some felt that the old master was no longer using quite all the revs that his car had to give.

At Berne the next year Time stopped altogether for Achille Varzi when he ran off the road practising in heavy rain, and overturned. Louis Chiron chanced to be following him and stopped at once, but this time Varzi was beyond human aid, and all Chiron could do was cradle his old friend in his arms and ease his passing from one world into another.

Alfa-Romeo made the usual polite proposal to withdraw their cars from the race, but Norma Varzi would have none of it, as Varzi would surely himself have wished, and took a leaf out of Cleopatra's book:

... and then, what's brave, what's noble
Lets do it after the high Roman fashion,
And make death proud of us.

so that Alfa-Romeo raced their remaining cars to victory with an old friend, Count Trossi, winning by a wheel from Alfa's real team leader, Jean-Pierre Wimille.

Just four small thoughts and a tailpiece to finish.

That in the thirties (and probably 1933) Earl Howe found that he could improve his practice times by as much as ten seconds a lap by following Varzi's wheeltracks.

That one of the Italian four-man Bob-Sleigh teams for the 1935/36 Olympic Games at Garmisch-Partenkirchen comprised Taruffi, Trossi, Cortese and Varzi.

That Caracciola was known to shake at the sight of Varzi in his driving mirrors, and . . .

That it was the loss of the whole racing world that there had been no woman like Baby Hoffman in Varzi's life back in the early summer of 1936 when he most needed one. Caracciola should have been so lucky.

But, what a fearful loss it had been of a great talent, and what might a combination of the impetuous fire of the young Rosemeyer and the mature icy coolness of Varzi have been able to achieve for Auto-Union during the remainder of 1936 and, more especially, through 1937 when Rosemeyer had to go it alone. In tandem theirs could well have been a near unstoppable double act to make even Caracciola in his mighty W125 blench at what he might see in those driving mirrors!

However, human beings are as they are, with all the faults of their virtues. Thus Varzi remained a man cast most truly in the mould of his Achillean Christian name—described by Homer as 'the perfect ideal of a Greek hero right down to the human touch of his bad temper, strong, brave, amorous, straightforward, doomed!'

PART 4

DAMN YANKEES AND TIN PAN ALLEY

'Give my regards to Broadway
Remember me to Herald Square'—*George M. Cohan*

Chapter 15

The Legacy of the Generals

David Bruce-Brown

(Died 4 October 1912 at Milwaukee in a practice accident before the US Grand Prize)

'And with the pedal
I love to meddle'
'I Love a Piano' by Irving Berlin

The European Grand Prix drivers who contested the early races on Long Island greatly disliked the circuit, and were correspondingly delighted to have the venue for the American Grand Prize of 1908 shifted to the picturesque Georgian city of Savannah. It had been founded and colonized in 1733 by an eccentric British General, James Oglethorpe, as a place for the refuge of British debtors and persecuted German Protestants—an odd combination if ever there was one. There was, however, nothing odd or eccentric about the way the General laid out his city, which he did in true military style on the pattern of a grid iron, and the next century saw it expanded until two dozen squares had been constructed covering an area of more than two square miles.

The next Generals to be concerned with Savannah were the no less colourful William Tecumseh Sherman and the future President, Ulysses S. Grant, from the Civil War. Sherman and his Dashing Yankee Boys of song fame reached the Savannah coast in double-quick time but without tearing the heart out of General Oglethorpe's lovely old city, which was thus spared the fate of Atlanta. Not the least of Savannah's joys for the European racers of 1908/11 were its local delicacies such as roast oysters, catfish and chocolate mud pie, all of which would have greatly rejoiced the heart and stomach of its founder, who was a worthy trencherman of the eighteenth century and a boon companion of Dr Johnson and his dining circle, when he could spare time from colonizing the New World or pursuing the rebellious Jacobites, in the Old, though in as gentle a way as he could manage.

Savannah was thus lucky in its Generals, not least because Sherman and Grant had established a very sensible working relationship, Grant standing by Sherman when he was thought to be crazy and Sherman during Grant's heavier addictions to Bourbon.

Forty-seven years after Sherman and one-hundred-and-seventy-seven after Oglethorpe, whatever the fears and anxieties of his well-to-do parents, 20-year-old David Bruce-Brown was gridding up for the second US Grand Prize to be held at Savannah in a 12.5-litre Benz of the type that his team-mate, the seasoned Victor Hemery, had raced with such telling effect in 1908 to win the race from St Petersburg to Moscow and then to take second in both the French Grand Prix and the US Grand Prize.

The 1910 race was to be over 415.2 miles (24 laps), and after 23 the issue lay between the two Benz of Hemery and Bruce-Brown, the Fiats of Wagner, de Palma and Nazzaro all having dropped out. Hemery had lost the 1908 race to Wagner's Fiat by just 56 seconds in over six hours racing. It was closer still in 1910 when the leaders went into their last lap with Bruce-Brown holding a 79 second lead on elapsed time. Hemery once again showed why he was regarded as one of the fastest drivers of his day with an ultra fast last lap that brought him within 1.42 seconds of Bruce-Brown at the finish. Like the true sportsman he was, Hemery was the first to pledge the young victor in a Coupe à Champagne, then very properly reserved strictly for drinking! And what a win it was to celebrate for the youngest man ever then to have won a Grand Prix as the question was being repeatedly asked: where had this young meteor come from and what might he do next?

Bruce-Brown had been born in 1890 and had much the same background as a speed hungry young Englishman of the future — Richard Seaman in the thirties. His first blushing tryst with the Goddess of Speed had been on 23 March 1908 at Daytona Beach in a 90 hp Fiat which he drove at 108 mph at a time when the Land Speed Record stood at the 121.57 mph of Marriott's Steamer.

By 1909 he had made a name for himself, winning the speed trials at Ormonde Beach and Long Island and also the Fort George Hill Climb, before he and his big Benz faced up to the challenge of the mighty Giant's Despair hill climb at Wilkes-Barre, Pennsylvania:

> From his flying start he flicked his gears with precision, ran in third up to the Devils' Elbow, took that risky corner in neutral, shifted into second and in a staccato roar charged to the summit . . . [in] . . . 1:31.60 . . . [and] . . . a full mile of cheers greeted the new record breaker . . . the Benz was best by five full seconds: Peter Helck, *Great Auto Races*

Such was the young cyclone who was soon to descend on Savannah.

Some, though by no means all, of Europe's best were out again for Savannah's third and last Grand Prize in 1911; notably a team of S74 Fiats led again by Louis Wagner, along with two Americans, one a Yale man called Caleb Bragg and the other Bruce-Brown himself now swapping horses. Race day was 30 November and 'one of the coldest ever witnessed', wrote my friend, the distinguished heart surgeon, Dr J. D. Quattlebaum, in his delightful book *The Great Savannah Races*. The Doctor was a great Savannahaian, whom I later had the pleasure of meeting on a trip to England, which he made not least so that he could be photographed by the statue of William Harvey, discoverer of the circulation of the blood, in his native Folkestone. In his book the Doctor tells how 'a number of negro waiters . . . did a land office business selling straight whisky without a chaser for 50 cents a drink' — and that at a time when Prohibition was a lively issue. Although Hemery set another fastest lap at a sizzling 81.6 mph he had to retire with valve trouble, which enabled Bruce-Brown to win a second successive Grand Prize, by 2 mins 4 secs from Hearne's Benz.

He had not been so lucky in the first 500 at Indy earlier in the year where he could only place third with a Savannah Fiat, as a result of ignition delays just when he was mounting his challenge for the lead. At Indy in 1912 a switch from Fiat to National brought him piston failure after an initially lively set-to with the leaders. These two 500s had been purely domestic events with no European challenge; but, after Indy, Brown set his course for an Old World that was all agog to see if America's new meteor could win a third Grand Prix Major on the trot in the revived French Grand Prix at Dieppe.

This was to be a long race spread over two full days, twice the length of its 1907/08 predecessors. Apart from the intriguing challenge of the 3-litre voiturettes, the main race lay between the 7.6-litre Peugeots, all set to achieve new mechanical horizons, and the great S74 Fiats with their mighty towering 14-litre engines that stood almost as high as a man. More fatally, they retained their allegiance to fixed wheels with detachable rims in preference to the detachable Rudge-Whitworth wheels of Peugeot, and in refuelling from equally primitive ten-gallon churns rather than Peugeot's more progressive pressure feed.

Despite these handicaps Bruce-Brown still led on elapsed time throughout the first day, and put in the fastest lap of the whole event on the eighth. So, had the race been just over the normal length of previous years, Brown would have pulled off his hat-trick of Majors, on both sides of the Atlantic between 1910 and 1912, by the narrow margin of 123 seconds. Sadly for him there had to be a second day. The cars were to be started at the intervals and in the order in which they had finished on the first day, so that the actual duel on the road between the two leaders could be clearly observed during the opening laps. After two laps Bruce-Brown still clung to the sliver of a lead at 11 secs before trouble struck in the open country on the run into the town of Eu, which had been much patronized by Queen Victoria in the early years of her reign. Either a fuel pipe split or Bruce-Brown's fuel tank was damaged in a collision with another of those wandering dogs. The former is the normally accepted version, but the knowledgeable M. Adriano Cimarosti in his recent *History of Motor Racing* favours the canine incident. Either way, it little mattered, save perhaps to the dog, for Bruce-Brown had to resort to wayside refuelling which wa banned by the regulations and earned him disqualification. Not tha this in any way inhibited him from pressing on with all his renowned courage and dash for the sheer joy of driving and putting in anothe fastest lap of the day, just one second faster than Boillot's!

An unhappy chance shifted the venue of the 1912 American Grand Prize from Savannah to Milwaukee, now having become a domestic event again in all but name, though including four S74 Fiats, including Bruce-Brown's. On the day before the race, and at the end of pre-race testing, starter Fred Wagner (no relation of Louis) warned Bruce Brown about the dangerous state of his worn tyres; but careless, care free youth knew better and unkind fate accomplished the rest for both driver and, what was more reprehensible, his mechanic, Scudalari.

Although, in the end, Bruce-Brown had narrowly failed to carry of Europe's 1912 Major, he had, none the less, scared the living daylights out of Peugeot's New Model cars and their vainglorious leader Georges Boillot, who very fairly made no bones about the death blow his 'Charlatans' would have suffered had they failed to win that day.

How well the great artist, Peter Helck, described Bruce-Brown in his book *The Checkered Flag*:

> Big in stature, strong in heart and hands, with the requisite competitive spirit and a passion for thundering speed, he was the ideal racing man in any period. For many close followers of the sport, he was supreme.

And, remember, he was only 22 when he died.

L. Scott Bailey wound up an article in *Automobile Quarterly* about him in 1966:

> The David Bruce-Brown story had the romance of a novel. For the historians, however, it presents a dilemma—the plague of facts recorded and unrecorded

adding, in a footnote, that his researches had failed to disclose any records at Yale of his ever having been a student there, and that while the *Social Register* for the years 1907/13 might list a Mrs George Bruce-Brown and her two children, William and David L., as living at 189 East 59th Street, New York City, Bruce-Brown's obituary listed him as having an address in Brooklyn.

Elsewhere (see page 208) this book contains a reference to Segrave having actually met William ('Bill') Brown when he was in America in 1918, but there the trail dries up, leading Mr Bailey to conclude that Brown's was 'a story yet to be plumbed', and leaving us to wonder where, given time, the meteorite might ultimately have come to rest perhaps to find an answer in Alexander Pope's couplet

> Or driven by strong benevolence of Soul
> Will fly, like Oglethorpe, from pole to pole.

Chapter 16

The Mighty Atom

James Anthony (Jimmy) Murphy

(Born 1894: Died 15 September 1924 at Syracuse Speedway)

'Anything You Can Do, I Can Do Better'
— *Irving Berlin: 'Annie Get Your Gun'*

Every inch is packed with dynamite' was what Mary Martin, the lady with 'the voice of brass', used to belt out night after night during the long runs of *South Pacific* through the forties and fifties, and it was much the same for an equally hard working trouper from the twenties called Jimmy Murphy. He only stood at 5 ft 7 ins, but Helck, in his tribute to Bruce-Brown, might just as well have been writing about Jimmy Murphy: the next American driver to triumph in both the New and the Old Worlds; that same Murphy, who tipped the scales at just 145 lbs, and whose every inch was packed with liberal doses of Miss Martin's dynamite.

Murphy was born in San Francisco in 1894, orphaned by its great earthquake and brought up by relations near Los Angeles, Judge and Mrs Martin O'Donnell. LA was one of the earliest hot beds of dirt, track and board racing, and pint-sized lightweights like Murphy were much in demand as riding mechanics. By sheer coincidence of name Murphy's first big opening was to ride with one Eddie O'Donnell in two winning races at Corona and Ascot, California in 1916. After that he had a score to settle with the Kaiser in Europe before returning to ride in Duesenbergs with Eddie Rickenbacker, Tommy Milton and O'Donnell again. His first actual drive was almost his last when he crashed Fred Duesenberg's car and injured his mechanic. At first not even Tommy Milton's intercessions could melt Fred's stony heart, but the luck of the O'Donnells, mixed up with the charm of the Irish, told in the end, when Eddie broke his arm and Jimmy got his second chance. This was at the Beverly Hills board track: the date, Leap Year's Day 1920, and the distance 250 miles. Again, the Luck of the Irish rode with him as his engine coughed and spluttered its last drop of fuel on the parade lap just after he had won the race from pole position.

His American season for 1921 was not so bright, with only 14th in the 500 and crashing into the north west wall after 107 laps on Memorial Day. Some two months later he was leading the four-in-hand Duesenberg outfit in their first European foray at Le Mans in the French Grand Prix revived from Lyons, 1914. Just how Murphy got through that race one will never know. He was already suffering from

95

a burnt hand before he succeeded in breaking two ribs in a practice accident, and on race day he had to be carefully strapped up and literally lifted into a car that would feel more like a mediaeval instrument of torture for the ensuing four-and-a-half hours.

The main trouble was caused by the wholly inadequate surfacing of the roads, which Murphy and Ernie Olson, his renowned mechanic, sought to mitigate by fitting a protective mesh screen. Their ordeal lasted precisely 4 hrs 7 mins and 11.4 secs, and Murphy averaged 78.10 mph to win by just under a quarter of an hour. He had also made fastest race lap at 83.40 mph and led the race on 21 of its 30 laps. In every sense of the word it was a wonderful achievement as his car and its stricken driver battled indomitably to the finish with a radiator that had been severely damaged by the sharp flying missiles, which caused the Americans to call the race a 'stone throwing contest'. However, what did any of that matter beside winning? In just a few short years the shy boy from California had become a man with a consuming passion for victory and the means to achieve it, to all of which his gallant car still bears witness as it stands on muted guard in the Indy Speedway Museum, as much an object of admiration for the immaculacy of its turn-out as it had been on the starting line at Le Mans.

In no way so admirable was the ill-mannered and unsporting way in which the American's French hosts had proposed the health of Jules Goux first and foremost when he had only finished third in what was supposed to be a Victory Banquet in their guests' honour! Little wonder that both Murphy and his Team Manager, George Robertson, left the room.

As for Murphy, he simply went from strength to strength, with fastest qualifying speed at Indy in 1922, before winning the race at a new record speed of 94.48 mph, nearly 5 mph faster than Tommy Milton's record 89.62 mph from 1921. In the same year he also won his first AAA National title, and a second was to follow, albeit posthumously, in 1924. In between those races he made a very sporting appearance in the Italian Grand Prix at Monza in 1923 with a 2-litre unsupercharged straight-eight Miller. Being Murphy he had to try all he knew, but he could never place higher than fourth until Bordino, leading the race despite having only one usable arm, had to retire with 'driver exhaustion' just after half distance. Although neither he nor Olson were competing with broken arms like Bordino, their drive was still a very exhausting experience, with their basic stopping power restricted for much of the race to the handbrake! Oh, shades of those Duesies and their hydraulic brakes from 1921! Murphy had been joined in Harry Miller's Italian Symphony by Count Louis Zborowski, with another works Miller, but he did not follow the Count to Spain for its Grand Prix a month later, even though Miller Automobiles had posted him as an entrant (see page 263).

By 1924 Jimmy Murphy was 30 and was achieving both wealth and fortune to say nothing of having a dance — 'The Jimmy Murphy

Trot'—named after him and, inevitably, his mind began to turn more and more towards retirement and a settled family life. Yet none of it seemed to diminish his competitive urge throughout the year, qualifying fastest again for the 500 and only losing out on outright victory due to a late tyre burst, which left him third. By September he had done enough to secure his second AAA title, but he still insisted on honouring a commitment to run at a 150-mile dirt race at Syracuse on 15 September. As the race neared its end, Murphy made his anticipated bid for victory only to get caught out on an oil slick. His car slid into the wooden inside railing, which cracked and split, transfixing the hapless driver like a lance. Forty-six years later, another posthumous champion, Jochen Rindt, was to die in a not dissimilar accident at Monza.

By any standards, Murphy's had been a most remarkable career including a board track career of 18 wins in over 2,900 miles on eight tracks. It is also worth mentioning that it was he who suggested the original concept of the FWD racer to Harry Miller, and that the famous Milton/Murphy 'feud' was finally resolved by Milton himself making the funeral arrangements after Murphy's death.

Shy during his school days, quiet and reserved with the world at large, there are few memorials to highlight his total acceptance and practice of the saying that not even the best was good enough. Murphy had been so utterly determined in everything that he did, right down to his insistence on keeping the commitment that cost him his life: his epitaph to the world remained Irving Berlin's—'I Can Do Anything Better Than You', save perhaps when he had to drive a Miller at Monza.

Chapter 17

The Mad Mullah

Pietro Bordino

(Born 26 November 1887 in Turin: Died 15 April 1928 practising for the Grand Prix of Alessandria, Northern Italy)

'Pack up all my
care and woe
Here I go—'
—'Bye-Bye Blackbird'—Mort Dixon, 1926

In the early/mid-twenties Henry Segrave thought Bordino the greatest and fastest driver in the world. He was born on 22 November 1887 and, in 1900, aged 13, he was chosen to be riding mechanic to the legendary Vincenzo Lancia, who was generally reckoned the fastest in his day, if not always the most successful or lucky driver in the years 1904/08. During this time he had also ridden with the great Felice Nazzaro and, in the autumn of 1908, he crossed the Atlantic for the first time to ride beside Ralph de Palma in his Fiat at Savannah in the US Grand Prize. In that race de Palma showed that he had inherited all Lancia's speed and ill luck by making fastest race lap, though only able to finish down in ninth after he had led the opening stages. The same year Bordino also won his first speed event—the 10 km Château Thierry hill climb—and, of course, in a red Fiat.

After his Savannah interlude Bordino went on taking part in domestic Italian events on both four and two wheels, chiefly with Lancia cars or Motosacoche bikes before switching to the big 1200 cc Harley-Davidsons until he got his chance to enter serious Grand Prix racing after World War I.

The 3-litre Grand Prix Fiat of 1921 was said to be so fast that 'no human driver could avail himself in the race of the speed possible with these machines'! To achieve such an Impossible was meat and drink to the fiery Bordino, who soon showed the Italian crowd at Brescia how it should be done. The only trouble was that the Fiats' tyres could not stand up to the 'inhuman' demands made by their drivers, Bordino and Louis Wagner, which gave the patient Ballots the win that they had been so patently unable to score over the American Duesenbergs earlier in the year at Le Mans.

In the twenties many of the fastest cars had the maddening habit of seeming to dodge each other in major races so that the Fiats, which raced at Brescia, had non-started at Le Mans and the Duesenbergs, who had won there, copped out on the Fiats at Brescia. My own bet would have been for the Duesies to have won again, but one will never know. However, Bordino's driving at Brescia had established him as the fastest driver in Europe, and so he continued throughout 1922/23, taking fastest race lap in each of the four Grands Prix in which he took part. Although the major races of those days were few and far between, he must surely have been the Ayrton Senna of his day.

Come 1924, the whole of the Grand Prix scene changed dramatically, with Fiat suddenly no longer the all-conquering, ever-victorious force of 1921/23. The cause for this lay in the mechanical brain drain of vital engineering personnel that was achieved on the backstairs by Alfa-Romeo, as a result, not least, of the machinations of Enzo Ferrari. Thus, in 1924, the rising men of Alfa-Romeo and Delage, as well as their old Sunbeam rivals, were able to topple the once mighty Fiats, so that Bordino's lead for Fiat on eight of the first eleven laps in the French Grand Prix of 1924 was, effectively, their last throw. After that 'The Red Devil', or 'El Diavolo Rosso' as he was known in Italy, quit the major racing scene at the age of 37: though not entirely, for there was another side to the Red Devil's talent.

The interchange of racing between Europe and America at Grand Prix level had been one of the great highlights of the years from 1912 to 1925; a commercial factor which Fiat were quick to spot in the early twenties as quickly as Peugeot had before and during World War I, when they had sent cohorts of their New Model racers over to bring their gospel to America from 1913. The possibilities of opening up even greater markets in the new land of post-war opportunity was just too good to miss. So, perhaps the American activities of the 'Mad Mullah', as American publicity hailed Bordino in America, were not quite so mad after all! The nick-name was thought to have been derived from that of a revolutionary Somali tribal leader.

Once again, there was nothing desperately new in the interchange of American and European drivers, and even cars for specific 'major' races. The novelty of the two Fiat/Bordino interventions lay in their campaigns being much more serious and sustained, and conducted during what was then the European close season. Bordino's attacks consisted of two such campaigns, the first in 1922 and the second in 1924/ 25. Unfortunately, both were a little too 'Johnny-Come-Lately' as the European effort in America had really peaked in 1913/19 and, by the time Bordino arrived on the scene, the state of American racing art had passed from Peugeot and Fiat to Duesenberg and Miller. None the less, Bordino persisted bravely with his two sterling attempts to reverse the tide before the two worlds finally parted company for close on 40 years.

In the meantime Bordino was hastening out to the West Coast with Al Jolson's song ringing in his ears:

> The sun-kissed mist says don't be late,
> That's why I can hardly wait,
> Open up that Golden Gate,
> California here I come!

And there he was, on 5 March 1922, all ready to race at Beverly Hills against the best America could throw at him: all 250 miles and 200 laps of it over unfamiliar, high-banked boards. This first race proved a little too much for the Fiat, which quit with engine trouble after 139 laps, though still being classified ninth. On 2 April, also at Beverly Hills, Bordino won a 25-mile sprint race at an average of 114.843 mph, which compared very well with the speeds of the leading Americans, who soon came to be known as 'The Black Devils' ('I Diavoli Neri') — Jimmy Murphy and Tommy Milton, who clocked 114.220 and 115.168 mph. In his next big race, the Fresno 150-miler, Bordino finished the full distance in fifth before going on to Cotati, some 80 miles north of San Francisco, where he first won a 50-mile sprint at 114.5 mph, before classifying ninth in its 100-mile race, though he only completed 72 of the 100 laps before he was 'flagged' due to 'motor trouble'. That was on 7 May and meant that he would be out of the running for the 1922 500.

The Red Devil was back on the coast again, at Culver City, for the 250-mile race on 14 December 1924, where he again completed the full distance, finishing eighth some 12 mins behind the winner and just 0.001 of a second behind the seventh man. He returned for a similar event on 1 March as a run-up to Indy, when he finished sixth before qualifying eighth for the 500 at 107.661 mph. But time had already passed him by and he could only manage tenth after running the full 500 miles distance at an average of 94.75 mph, compared to the winner, Peter de Paolo, whose 101.13 mph was a new record and the first race average to exceed 100 mph. Speeds had gone up considerably in the two years from 1923, when Bordino's 1925 average would have given him a comfortable margin of victory. This was reflected in the Mullah's 'take home pay' of just $1,400.

At the end of that 500, the man who the perennial W. F. Bradley described as 'probably the most able driver of the period', wept as he confessed to Bradley: 'At home I am supreme: here, I am like a child.' Such was the pace of change and, along with it, the new degrees of specialized sophistication being attained by the American engineers and designers during those few years, so rightly hailed as 'The Golden Age of the American Racing Car'. This sweeping process put an end to effective European efforts in American racing for decades to come, with the exception of the Vanderbilt Cup races on Long Island in 1936 (Alfa-Romeo and Bugatti) and 1937 (Alfa-Romeo, Auto-Union and Mercedes Benz) and those of Rex Mays's 8C Alfa-Romeo in 1937 and Wilbur Shaw's 'Boyle Special' Maserati in 1939/41. The same was true of the converse, for it would have been just as impossible for an American car and driver combination to have succeeded in Europe during those same years. The all-round abilities of men like Jimmy Murphy and David Bruce-Brown, no less than those of Jules Goux and Pietro Bordino, would not blossom again until the likes of Jim Clark and Graham Hill in the early/mid-sixties.

Although he was still only 38, Bordino's great years were now behind him and he might have been wiser to have recognized, like Bob Dylan, that 'the times they were a changing'. But a racer's blood has a habit of re-asserting itself, and so it was for Bordino as he sought to pull a few more small chestnuts from the smouldering ashes of a great career. In 1927 Monza staged its Milan Grand Prix as a kind of 'Digestivo' to follow the Italian Grand Prix itself, and to give Fiat the chance to demonstrate their remarkable and revolutionary 1.5-litre twin-six racer. The peerless Robert Benoist, who had swept up all the four Majors of the 1927 Grand Prix season for Delage, had also qualified his car for the Milan Grand Prix, but declined to come out and give battle, claiming to be tired. After 311 miles of driving in the wet this was probably very true although the claim that his fuel mixture was wrong was rather less so.

Nothing daunted, Bordino took the Fiat out for what was both his and Fiat's last great drive. He did it with all his legendary fire and panache, holding great slides in the wet with classic high Roman disdain, and putting in one astounding lap at 96.49 mph. His winning time was 19 mins 42.6 secs (94.57 mph), which was a faster race average than Benoist's fastest race lap of 94.31 mph. Bordino finished 41 secs ahead of Campari in a P2 Alfa-Romeo after less than 20 minutes of racing.

At the age of 40 Bordino was out again in the Circuit of Pozzo in early 1928 in a 35B Bugatti holding the lead until his engine died in mid-race, which was then won by Nuvolari in a 35C. Then, in April, while practising in his Bugatti for the Circuit of Alessandria, he lost control of his car—it was said to be the result of yet another Act of Dog—this time jamming his steering. His car overturned and fell into the river, where he died before help could reach him.

It seemed such an odd, inconclusive way for so great and decisive a driver to have ended his career and, while the Red Devil might have wept tears to Mr Bradley, I doubt if they had been anything but those of frustration, which might well have turned to tears of joy had he but enjoyed the advantage of a 91-inch straight-eight Miller to have raced in the States in the early twenties. In their way the Red Devil's endeavours on the unfamiliar American tracks—and, remember, with the wrong type of armament—were as praiseworthy as those of another gutsy European-based driver called Jack Brabham in the early 60s at Indy, before the arrival of Mickey Thompson and Colin Chapman in 1962/63. All praise, then, to the pioneering 'Mad Mullah' of those early roaring twenties for his sustained efforts through three seasons of campaigning.

'In London, he might be a clown,' wrote Lord Clark of the renowned art dealer, Lord Joe Duveen, 'in New York he was a King.' Turned inside out, the same was true of Pietro Bordino in the early twenties and, for certain sure, no other outsider could have mounted his sort of challenge to the Great American Racing Car during its Golden Age. One can only regret that the Fiats, led by Bordino, never made it to Le Mans to do battle with Jimmy Murphy and his cohorts in 1921.

Chapter 18

The Heavy Burden: a Tragedy of Three Novi Men and Their Cars

Ralph Hepburn
(Died 16 May 1948 in a practice accident at Indianapolis Speedway)

Rex Mays
(Born 1913: Died 1949 at Los Angeles Speedway)

Chester ('Chet') Miller
(Died 1953 at Indianapolis Speedway)

'There's no heavier burden than a great potential!'
Charles Schultz (Charlie 'Peanuts' Brown)

If you had to pick an approximate equivalent for the Novis of 1946 to 1953 it would have to be the V-16 BRM of 1950/54 as the car that, like the lady of one's dreams, was always going to do it good—tomorrow! In the same way 'the fabled Novi was a beautifully engineered, beautifully constructed "Bad Thing"!'

Literally translated, the Latin query *'quid novi?'* means 'what's new?'—and the bright new message for Indy in May 1941 was the first Novi engine, for which a chassis of sorts already existed.

The Ford V-8 engine had gone into production in 1932 and three years later a Ford employee, Lewis Welch, who was to play a crucial part in the creation and backing of the Novi engine, acquired a motor parts manufactory in Novi, Michigan. Another three years saw the replacement of the 'Junk Formula' by a transcontinental one for 3-litres blown, 4.5-litres unblown Grand Prix and Indy cars. This encouraged the construction of a new blown straight-eight engine that was the brainchild of Louie Meyer, the brothers Bud and Ed Winfield, Fred Offenhauser and Leo Goossen. It was called the 'Bowes Seal Fast' Special after its sponsor, Bob Bowes, and was debuted in competition with Mike Boyle's Special, the 3-litre 8CTF Maserati which Boyle himself, and Wilbur Shaw, had despatched the great mechanic and car builder, Cotton Henning, to obtain in person from the works at Bologna to be sure that they got a good one! In this they were unconsciously following the example of the British voiturette driver, Johnny Wakefield, who had made the same pilgrimage in 1937 and 1939, first for a new 6CM and then a 4CL. Whilst staying in the Belle

Vue Palace Hotel at Berne in 1939, he kindly went out of his way to explain to an enthusiastic small boy who all the drivers were—not that the boy needed any such instruction!—but the thought was kindly, and I naturally listened gratefully. Wakefield was one of those promising young British drivers who did not survive World War II, dying in a flying accident while serving in the Fleet Air Arm in April 1942.

The last 'pure' European Grand Prix car to race at Indy before the coming of the 'Junk Formula' in 1930 had been Louis Chiron's Delage, which took seventh place in 1929 and, like its competitors, had been built to the earlier Euro-Indy formula of 90/91 cubic inches for 1926/29. In 1930 two Maseratis had qualified for the 500, a 'one-off' works 4-litre V-16 sponsored by Alfieri Maserati himself and to be driven by Borzacchini (see pages 78/83) and a 2-litre straight-eight sponsored by plain 'Maserati' for a Sicilian driver, Letterio Cucinotta. The new formula forbade the use of superchargers, which put the Italian entries at a considerable disadvantage and, although Cucinotta's slower car eventually finished twelfth, it was 15 laps adrift. By contrast, Borzacchini's bigger car lasted just seven laps before retiring with magneto failure. After such a dismal showing no European chassis or engine, let alone a complete car, showed its face at Indy until 1937. By then several very interesting things had happened.

First, there was the fusion of the Euro-Indy formulae from 1938. Second, at the end of 1936, the old Vanderbilt Cup series had been revived from November 1916 over a twisty, dirt-surfaced circuit at Mineola, Long Island, that was graced and won by Nuvolari himself in a V-12 Ferrari Alfa-Romeo from Jean-Pierre Wimille in a 3.3-litre Type 59 Bugatti and Marchese Antonio Brivio in another works Alfa. He was followed by an assortment of other cars, European and native, including two of the four 4.5-litre V8RI Maseratis that were built at Bologna in 1935/36. They were driven by that doughty Maseratist, Philippe Etancelin, who finished eighth, and Raphael Bethenoud de Las Casas (aka-'Raph'), a well known amateur driver of the day, who was disqualified after a spin. Remarkably, all four of these unlucky cars reached America in time to take part in the next Vanderbuilt Cup race on 5 July 1937.

In that year the supercharger had been restored to favour and two blown European cars actually qualified at Indy—Babe Stapp, in the ex-Etancelin Maserati from 1936, and Rex Mays with an 8C 3.8-litre straight-eight Alfa-Romeo of the same year, now called a 'Bowes Seal Fast', and entered, not by Bob Bowes, but 'Bill White Cars'. Stapp converted his V8RI to LHD 2-seater to comply with 1937 Indy regulations and qualified 31st at 117.26 mph, retiring with clutch trouble after 35 laps. He later drove it as a proper single-seater in the Vanderbilt Cup, retiring this time with engine trouble. Wilbur Shaw drove a similar car in the Vanderbilt, finishing eighth. This car had previously been driven by Farina in the Modena Grand Prix of 1935, where it led briefly, and then in the Donington Grand Prix, where it led for much of the race before breaking a half-shaft. Count Trossi drove it twice in 1936, at Monaco and in the German Grand Prix where Seaman shared a fraught drive with him.

Neither of these cars achieved much in 1937/39, but Stapp did manage to place his 'Bill White' Alfa fifth at Indy in 1939, and Deacon Litz also qualified (in 31st spot) in the Farina/Shaw Maserati in 1939, with a reduced engine capacity of 3-litres.

In the meantime, however, the formidable Meyer-Winfield-Bowes-Boyle-Special ensemble had not been letting the grass grow under their feet. Louie Meyer himself had retired from racing immediately after his remarkable escape from death in 1939 when he was thrown out of his car on lap 198 while duelling for the lead with Shaw in the Boyle Maserati. Louie's departure left the main action open for an electric series of duels between the 'Big Six' of Shaw himself, Mauri Rose, Ralph Hepburn, Rex Mays, Chet Miller and Duke Nalon, and the great cars they drove: the Specials of 'Boyle Maserati', 'Bowes Seal Fast', Lou Moore and his 'Blue Crowns' and, above all, the Novis for ever associated with Lew Welch, Leo Goossen and the Winfields. Some of these great cars are now proud, silent exhibits at the Indianapolis Museum. No less miraculously, all four of those fragile and now much travelled V8RI Maseratis survive, and one is still active in British vintage racing! And how lucky we are to have had their story so lovingly told by DSJ in *Motor Sport* from January to March of 1990.

Now, to turn to the Novis themselves and the most recent book published about them by Dr George Peters and Henri Greutter— *Novi—The Legendary Indianapolis Race Car*:

> By 1938, virtually every piece of the jigsaw puzzle was ready for the birth of the Novi. It was now only a matter of time before all of the pieces would be in position for what would become the most legendary car and engine to appear at Indianapolis.

. . . and the most ill-fated in the 30-odd years to 1941. The way in which these new elements came together is reminiscent of the gathering together of 'Les Charlatans' when Indy was in the making 30 years before, but now with the new combination of the Winfields, Leo Goossen and Fred Offenhauser doubling for Ernest Henry and Paul Zuccarelli; Ralph Hepburn and Rex Mays for Georges Boillot and Jules Goux; and their new Mr Fixit, Lew Welch. In the meanwhile, biding their time patiently in the wings, playing the parts of Mercedes-men who were out of work for the duration of the war, stood Duke Nalon and Chet Miller waiting to exercise Don Lee's brilliant German escapee from middle Europe, the Mercedes W154, though sadly without Caracciola, Neubauer and their full supporting cast.

Mays and Hep were teamed up under Bob Bowes's 'Seal Fast' banner for both 1940 and 1941, Mays taking second place in both years and Hep fourth in 1941. Hep's 1941 car was an improved version of Welch's six-year-old fwd Miller-Ford chassis, but fitted with the new fwd supercharged dohc V-8 Novi engine designed by the 'New Charlatans', and the 500 of 1941 marked its first and only appearance before it went into wartime hibernation. This book is neither the time nor the place to review its technical features: that belongs properly to the Peters-Greutter book as the latest lineal successor, albeit on fewer fronts, to the superb work of Mr Griffith Borgeson (see page 336). The car was a classic makeshift example of putting a new and spirity wine into an out-of-date old bottle, and Hep did well both to qualify as well as he did (in 27th) and then to finish as high as fourth in the race. The same really went for Bud Winfield and the engine design staff, whose first rough drawings had not been completed before the late summer of 1940. Its speedy completion thus reflected the greatest credit on its designers and engineers as this extract from *Novi* shows, especially when you compare their facilities with those which, but for World War II, would have been at the disposal of Mercedes-Benz:

> Mercedes had a specialist for virtually every piece of the engine. Contrast this with the few individuals, with limited funding, who worked at developing the original Winfield V-8 from Bud's scratch paper designs into a very promising engine. Considering this . . . it is crystal clear that Ed and Bud Winfield, Leo Goossen, Fred Offenhauser, Lew Welch and a few other people performed a fantastic job with respect to the construction of the new V-8. Not to be overlooked is the contention that the Winfield engine still had untapped power.

In this context it is worth noting that Mercedes did not make their decision to build the two complete W165 cars for the Tripoli Grand Prix on 7 May 1939 until 18 November 1938 and then testing them at Hockenheim in April 1939, before taking first and second places at Tripoli.

So much for the backdrop. Now, let the players unfold their drama of those three mighty Speedmen who never won Indy.

First Ralph Hepburn. By 1948, at the age of 52, Hep had made all of 15 starts at Indy since his rookie drive in 1925, when he had placed 16th. From that same year he had also raced in at least 17 major long distance board track events with never a win in any of them. And, for so fast, courageous and gifted a driver, this had almost to be a record in itself when the best placings he could look back on were a pair of seconds, one on boards over 250 miles at Rockingham, Salem, back in 1925, and the other at Indy itself in 1937 when Wilbur Shaw had pipped him by just 2.16 secs at the end of four-and-a-half hours of hard racing. Looking ahead to 1991 this was about the same distance that was to separate fourth-time winner, Rick Mears, from Michael Andretti after a mere 2 hrs 50:00.791 secs of race driving.

Hep had started out as a racing motor cyclist before he was spotted as a likely lad by the veteran driver from Grands Prix, Board and Track, Earl Cooper. His outstanding ability was to go fast, and that remained with him throughout his career and made him one of the most colourful and daring of America's race drivers whatever the surface. Unlike some of his contemporaries he never made it to Europe, although his fwd Packard Special Miller from 1929 did, in the hands of James Stewart who also called himself 'Leon Duray'. At the time *Paris-Match* had infuriated Ettore Bugatti by stating that the Americans were far in advance of the French, whose 'cars of similar displacement were [in]capable of rivalling the speed of these Millers'. After two of these cars had spent some 30 years hibernating in the Bugatti works, the erudite Griffith Borgeson succeeded in getting both cars back to their homeland and seeing them beautifully restored. At one time, at least, the 'ex-Hepburn' car was on display in the Los Angeles County Museum.

The aftermath of World War II found Hep driving the first complete Novi at Indy in 1946 and setting a new lap record of 134.449 mph which stood for four years until Walt Faulkner pushed it marginally up to 136.013 in 1950. The Novi was an astonishing machine, not least for the speed with which its main components had been made. We have already seen how quickly the Novi team put its first racing engine together for the 1941 500, and in the winter of 1945/46 Frank Kurtis did a similar job laying out the first new fwd chassis, and Leo Goossen the fwd gearbox, for the new car to replace the makeshift job from 1941. According to Winfield, Leo Goossen and the car's owner, Lewis Welch, 'did in a few months what otherwise would have taken a very long time'. That was the way the new 'Charlatans' worked, although it was commonly believed that Goossen was the brains of the band.

The 500 of 1946 was a very emotive event, coming after the Speedway's closure from 1941, and most spectators were eagerly looking forward to seeing their deserving hero win at long last, most especially after his record-breaking single lap of 134.449 mph and fastest qualifying speed of 133.944 mph, which far outdid Jimmy Snyder's previous best of 130.138 mph from 1939.

Hep was soon thrusting his great powerful roaring car into the lead, and in 71 mins he had travelled 140 miles. After that a nine-minute pit stop showed that he had needed something more than just routine refuelling and re-tyring and, sure enough, its braking had also received considerable attention. This cost Hep a lot of valuable time and, although he regained some ground, it was all to no avail when his car greedily devoured a valve on lap 122.

Along with a number of other Indy drivers, Hep then became involved in the unfortunate ASPAR strike and gave racing a miss through 1947. This meant that by 1948 he had been out of competition for close on two years since his outing with the original Novi, and a lot had happened in the meantime. A second Novi had been built up and the cars were to be driven by former stuntman Cliff Bergere, who had driven in sixteen 500s, and the highly experienced Chester ('Chet') Miller who had already done 13. His best placing had been third in 1938, and his bravery in the following year had earned him much acclaim. This had arisen out of the accident involving Bob Swanson and Floyd Roberts which took place in front of Miller. Without any hesitation he pulled his car off the circuit to avoid running over Swanson who was lying in the way. Miller's injuries kept him away from the racing track for some time and left him with one arm permanently bent.

Bergere then had a falling out with Welch following several practice incidents and a mild crash on his first day with the Novi, at the end of which he pronounced the car unsafe and unceremoniously packed his bags and took his leave. Welch was then only too happy to offer Hep a seat in Bergere's car and, despite having been offered Don Lee's W154 for 1948, the allure of a return to the Novi was too much for him to resist. So he eagerly accepted, enthusing the while about the car to his friend, the distinguished motor racing authority Charles Lytle, as Hep hummed Gus Kahn's:

> Yes Sir! That's my baby!
> No Sir! Don't mean maybe!

. . . with never a thought for the 'maybe'!

Hep had never made any secret of his ambition to see his name on the glittering Borg-Warner Trophy, and even at his age he obviously thought that he was still in with a chance as he looked back on an Indy record of third (1931), fifth (1935), second (1937) and fourth (1941). And, as he could well have found himself thinking: 'So long as they held together, were those Novis not still the fastest cars at the Brickyard and was he himself not still its fastest ever lapper from 1946?' Sadly he saw no darker side, like reactions that might have slowed by a vital fraction of a second since they had last been tested at full stretch by one of the fastest track burners in the world. As it was, he had a comforting old saw to scotch his every doubt: 'Press on regardless!'— 'Take no thought for the morrow!'—'Come what come may!'— 'Doubtless the Lord will provide!'

So Hep arrived for a shake down on Saturday 15 May before getting down to some sterner stuff the next day. At first it all went well enough, with a lap at around 133 mph, that was not far off top pace, but then, suddenly, it all went devastatingly wrong. First, the powerful nose-heavy fwd car skidded sideways in the North East Turn and shot below to the grass infield with Hep giving it a hefty dose of throttle to bring it to heel. Instead, the car promptly spun and flew up towards the outer retaining wall, which it struck violently at an angle. The impact was so great that it forced Hep's goggles and helmet off his head and shook him to and fro in the cockpit (before the days of safety straps) with such violence that his neck was broken.

Reading Eoin Young's *Autocar & Motor* Diary for 5 June 1991, I was struck yet again by the gut-bucket world those old racers of yesteryear lived in, epitomized so well by Eoin's contemporary conversation with the 87-year-old Louie Meyer:

> Those old tanks we drove then . . . you hit the wall and you snapped your
> neck. We didn't have hard helmets, safety harnesses, things like that . . .
> We just raced.'

Mercifully, Hep's whole miserable accident must have been over in a
matter of seconds, although it seemed extended by one of those
eternal, striated walls of silence that accompany disaster. Speedway
Manager Wilbur Shaw gazed on the dismal scene before walking
slowly back to his car and sitting in it, stunned and incredulous, as he
re-lived what he had just seen, before gradually taking it in and beginning to reflect on:

> . . . our many experiences together—as well as our strained relations
> during the ASPAR episode—and I cried for at least five minutes. No
> accident on any track has ever had a more depressing effect on the racing
> fraternity. All of us felt as if we had lost a brother. I don't believe a single
> wheel turned at the Speedway during the remainder of the day and Hep
> remained in our thoughts long after the 1948 race became history.

As so often happens, it was the worst possible time for the Hepburn
family, with Hep's father, aged 83, dying four days after without ever
knowing of his son's death.

The Novi was the very epitome of Power in those times, and it was
ironic that its foremost apostle, Ralph Hepburn, should have died as a
result of trying to power his way out of engulfing disaster. According
to racing veterans who saw it, when the car's front wheels gathered
traction the power-filled Novi took off like a bolt from a gun for the
wall. Such was the price Hep paid for his speed on the day that
heralded the Blight of the Novis.

> In the meantime, in between time,
> (wrote Gus Kahn) Ain't we got . . .

. . . well, certainly not fun after such a high tragedy. But, at least, the
Show would have to go on, and a stalwart character like Dennis
'Duke' Nalon was just the man to shoulder the Novi's burdens at so
critical a time, just as it was to be with another 'Iron Man' called
Graham Hill some 20 years on. The Duke had driven his first 500 in
1938 and, all told, he drove another nine, although he only once
finished high up, but that was when it mattered most on Memorial Day
1948. That day he brought the second of the two Novis home third
after a fastest qualifying average of 131.603 mph. He was not called
'The Iron Duke' for nothing.

The Novis' 1949 showing was more memorable still for him, and it
also involved Rex Mays, as well as some very odd goings-on behind
the scenes. On Memorial Day 1949, and side by side like Cole Porter's
'Babes in the Wood', the two Novis sat proudly on the grid with the
Duke himself on pole position and Mays next to him as they waited for

Wilbur Shaw to give the time honoured call to start. However, few were to know that a short time before that hallowed moment a most extraordinary scene was being enacted inside the sealed hugger-mugger of the locked Novi garage.

At this remarkable last-minute briefing the Novi's 'Governor', Lew Welch, gave his drivers the strictest of orders, on pain of being black-flagged and withdrawn from the race, that whichever car was ahead at the end of the first lap was to stay there and that the trailing car was not to pass its leader for the lead. As if this was not enough, Welch had had his two cars fitted with differing ratios in their three-speed gearboxes, those of Mays being lower than those of Nalon. So it came about that Nalon held an early lead at the 25- and 50-mile marks, with the lower-geared Mays inevitably behind. Thereafter it was not long before Fate upset all Welch's carefully laid stratagems.

On lap 23, about 60 miles into the race, Nalon's rear axle snapped when Mauri Rose, on the track of a possible three-in-a-row win, was in close pursuit of the Novis. One of the shrewdest drivers, if not always the most popular, Rose sized the situation up in a flash and nipped past Nalon before big trouble struck the Novi. By strange coincidence what followed was almost a re-run of Hepburn's 1948 accident with an exploding fuel tank thrown in as well. This quickly caught alight and left a wall of flame eight feet high running across and down the track. The sheer force of the explosion literally blew the seams out of Nalon's 'driving uniform' and gave him extensive burns, which took four very painful months to heal.

Meanwhile, back at base, Welch continued stoutly to deny that Nalon's accident had been caused by axle breakage, despite the clearest photographic evidence to the contrary. Yet, at the same time, this contradictory, 'ornery crittur' of an American saw to it that when the Duke was eventually discharged from hospital he spent several more months getting fully fit at his ranch at Santa Barbara; which was just the rest that Nalon needed. How different from Ferrari's treatment of Niki Lauda (see pages 120/1).

Before the start of that race Duke had been approached by an announcer with a typically fatuous question: 'Had he any message for the crowds?' Duke replied prophetically: 'May God watch over all of us here today', and later he must have found himself echoing an earlier Iron Duke after Waterloo: 'The finger of Providence was upon me and I escaped unhurt.' Nalon preferred to rely on 'the Good Lord [who] helped me get out of the car' — adding:

> I knew from the intense heat, if I was going to get out I had to do so on the left side and get over the outer wall . . . [thinking] . . . This could be it if the sparks ignite the ruptured fuel tank, and I must not breathe the flames. I've got to get out of this thing.

. . . and so he did, though it was damnably close run. But that was the way with Iron Dukes.

Nalon had crashed out on lap 23 after which his companion on the grid, now a very shaken Rex Mays, had had to go on driving past the smouldering wreckage of his friend's car, without knowing his fate until his own Novi succumbed to magneto failure after another 25 laps. Some five months later, Mays died in a dirt race at Del Mar, California, when his car crashed into a barrier and flung him out on to the track into the path of a pursuing car with no hope of an avoidance.

When Nuvolari drove at Long Island in 1936 he had been greatly impressed by Mays' driving, and openly said that he could well have won the race with a more suitable car. By 1937 Mays had the makings of one—an ex-Scuderia Ferrari 3.8-litre 8C Alfa-Romeo, which had been acquired by the wealthy 'Hollywood' Bill White for Mays to drive in the 1937 Vanderbilt Cup. The story goes that the well-known Alfa-Romeo works driver and tester, Attilio Marinoni had stayed on in America for a while after the 1936 Cup to enjoy some traditional American hospitality. Being a polite Italian gentleman, he reciprocated their kindness by passing on much helpful know-how about the tuning of the 8C, which included the replacement of its Rootes blower by a centrifugal unit.

True or not, a contemporary photograph shows Mays seizing a very short initial lead in the 1937 race which he had soon enough to surrender to Caracciola and Rosemeyer. None the less, he still finished third behind Seaman's Mercedes and Rosemeyer's Auto-Union, and ahead of both Farina's V-12 Alfa-Romeo and Delius's Auto-Union after Nuvolari had retired. As a result of this, or so it was said, Mays had later been invited to visit Italy and drive an Alfa-Romeo, although he never actually made the trip, reputedly because he did not have the obligatory dinner suit in his wardrobe!

Brock Yates concludes this intriguing tale:

> Had Mays gone to Italy, he would have been the first American to join the Scuderia [Ferrari] thereby predating the arrival of another Californian, Phil Hill, by almost 20 years.
>
> The Mays Vanderbilt 8C Alfa was last seen in the late 1950s serving as an advertisement outside White's restaurant on Glendale Boulevard in Los Angeles . . .

. . . surely an intriguing thought for a would-be collector!

Mays himself had started his career racing midget cars in 1931 and won the coveted AAA national title in both 1940 and 1941 before spending four years as a ferry pilot during World War II. He had also achieved four pole positions from his ten Indy starts between 1934 and 1949. Although he shared Hep's reputation of being a fast man, and hard to beat, he only finished well twice at Indy with his seconds in 1940/41; his best other finish being seventh in 1947.

The immediate aftermath of World War II produced a stormy period in Indy history when the Teamsters Union and other pressure groups sought to take a hand in 'organizing' the race drivers.

Naturally, all this did was to distance the AAA drivers from the big promoters, although both Mays and Hep played no small part, back stage, in keeping the warring parties from falling too far apart.

For all his experience, Mays's death at the relatively young age of 36 came as a great and terrible shock to his many friends and admirers, for he was a friendly man and it seemed no sort of age for a man of his class to have been a-dying.

The Duke returned to his stamping ground for six more tilts at the Borg-Warner, with Chet Miller as his stable mate in 1950/53. For the first time both cars failed to qualify in 1950, a gloomy portent which was followed by Bud Winfield's sudden death after a road accident that October. But Lew Welch was no quitter and, working from Bud's plans for a wholesale update of the now ageing Novi engine, he pressed on into the new season fortified by enrolling the veteran ace mechanic Jean Marcenac. Their return to the race itself in 1951 was disappointing after their posting second and third in the four-lap qualifying runs, with Nalon also taking pole position and new one and four lap records.

It was, however, better than nothing, as the authors of *Novi* wrote:

> An element of redemption had occurred in 1951 as only the Agajanian car was faster in qualifying. Both Novis were once again in the starting field after their embarrassing absence the previous year. Perhaps in 1952 they could not only retain their high rate of speed, but also demonstrate longevity in the race.

However, a new power called Vukovich had hit the Indy scene in 1952, which left the Novis with the scant consolation of Chet Miller's new qualifying and single lap records, before they both retired early on in the race with supercharger troubles. Miller's one-lap record was posted on 24 May at 139.6 mph, and his four-lap qualifier at 139.034 mph. Both records stood for two years and it was not until 1954 that speeds of over 140 mph were reached, although Miller had achieved a single lap at 140.187 mph during unofficial practice in 1952.

So back they came again in 1953 to do, perhaps even to die. Chet Miller described in 1952 as 'the forty-nine-year-old speedster' and the 'little man of big car racing' had by then driven more competitive laps round the track than any other active driver and 'had put on a stellar performance as he averaged an amazing record breaking 139.034 mph'. Fast!—Faster!!—Fastest!!! went the 'esteem record. Hepburn had started it in 1946 (133.944 mph); in 1951 Nalon upped the mark to 136.494 mph; now Miller had added to the laurels of the Novis' history.' In short, laurels, laurels everywhere save in the all-important Victory Circle, which was just how it turned out for the Novis yet again in 1952 with both cars suffering sheared supercharger drives.

Chet had been thinking about retirement that year, but when he was asked to run again in 1953 he decided to have one more try. So, promptly on the day before the time trials, Chet was out with his Novi, the original one from 1946. It had been rebuilt after Hep's accident in 1948, for, unlike a driver, a car could have as many lives as a cat. As had happened five years before for Hep, the usual shakedown passed off smoothly enough, allowing Chet to put in a lap at 138.46 mph before 'something went wrong', with a loud noise being followed by chilling, eerie stillness. 'Chet Miller had no chance at all, for all the action occurred in the blink of an eye . . . and it was quite obvious that he was beyond medical help. The so-called Novi "jinx" had now claimed a second veteran driver at Indy' and, once again, Duke Nalon was left out on his own to keep the show on the road, while mourning the loss of another close and much loved friend.

Duke just about managed to qualify, in 26th although he had been greeted, all Graham Hill-like, by greatest cheers of all when he went out for his four-lap qualifying run. After spinning into the infield to avoid a driver whose car had broken a wheel and gone out of control, he was awarded 11th place in what was to be his last actual run in the 500.

It was also the end of the road for the original line of Novis, for which it was a case of:

Finish . . . the bright day is done,
And we are for the dark.

. . . though not quite, for the original Miller Ford-Winfield from 1941 still exists. The Chet Miller car is owned privately, with restoration slowly under way, and a third car was presented by Welch to the Indy Museum where it is a static exhibit without an engine. Finally—and praise be to see it!—to judge from recent photographs Duke Nalon looks splendidly alive and well.

So, perhaps at long last, the Blight of the Novis has been lifted and their ghosts laid decently to rest.

Chapter 19
Old Ironsides (aka 'The Fresno Flyer')

William (Bill) Vukovich I

(Born 13 December 1918: Died 30 May 1955 at Indianapolis Speedway when leading the 500 on a potential hat trick)

'The road gets rougher
It's lonelier and tougher'
—*Ira Gershwin: 'The Man That Got Away' (1956)*

The so-called 'Fresno Flyer' was born William Vucerovitch in Alamedo, California in 1919. Like Wilbur Shaw, he barnstormed his way into the world of motor racing through hard menial work in boyhood until World War II brought him work of another kind, maintaining jeeps and trucks. By sheer dint of typically American hard graft he managed to put by enough money to buy a midget racer for after the war, having painted it red all over and christened it 'Old Ironsides'. While Vuki may never have heard of grim 'Old Noll' Cromwell the erstwhile Lord Protector's Puritan soul would surely have rejoiced at Vuky's courage and enterprise as he became, first, midget champion of the West Coast in 1946/47 and national champion in 1950.

In that same year he had his first tilt at an Indy trial with the renowned 'Boyle Special' Maserati, but by 1950 it was well past such youthful heroics, and Vuki sidelined the gallant old warrior before coming back in 1951 with the 'Central Excavating Special', or 'Sled' as it was known. He qualified 20th and the car lasted just 29 laps before bursting its oil tank, which meant that Vuky went home with a bare 750 bucks for his pains.

1951 was the last year in which the great Mauri Rose raced. Like Shaw and Louie Meyer before him, Rose had won two 500s in a row, as well as a third in 1941, when Shaw lost out on that still unrealized first Indy hat trick. In the meantime Vuky's driving had so impressed Rose's sponsor, the millionaire Howard Keck, that he entered his 'Fuel Injection Special' for Vuky to drive in the 1952 500. Ten laps from the end, with the whole of the race at his feet, his 'Special' began to steer oddly and, on lap 192, the end came when he stopped against the North East wall with a broken pivot pin. While Vuky had to sit out what should have been his first winning 500 helplessly on the wall, the Speedway's then medical director, Dr Carlyle B. Bohner, was saying quietly to himself: 'I watched Vuky that day and I think it began to dawn on him that he had licked Indianapolis.' And so he had, for in the ensuing three years no man had ever then come nearer to the magic three-in-row.

1953 produced another Indy heatwave with temperatures of 130°F (55°C) being recorded. One driver, Carl Scarborough, actually died of heat exhaustion, and relief drivers had to be called out for ten of the 23 cars that succeeded in completing at least half of the race. Like with Fangio in the Argentine Grand Prix two years later, a similar touch of 'Old Ironsides' saw Vuky through to win by close on eight miles with no reliefs!

Vuky was a mildly spoken, if sometimes dour and taciturn man, with a dry, mordant wit to match. He was also very determined, and after he lost out on the wall to Troy Ruttman in the closing stages of the1952 500 he was heard to say, no doubt between gritted teeth: 'That man never won an easier one, but you can be damn sure I won't let it happen again next year!' Nor did he; and, come 1954, he was beginning to call a few comic shots like another great American sporting champion, the golfer Walter Hagen, as he twitted a group of rivals the day before the race: 'What are you guys up to? Trying to figure out who's going to finish second tomorrow?' That year he won with a lap in hand, but not before he had survived the challenges of Jack McGrath, Jim Bryan, Troy Ruttman and several others — 'all running as if the devil were close at their heels' — like Vuky himself used to drive.

Indy apart, Vuky raced little, although he did try a run in one of the Carrera Panamericana races in a Lincoln with a terrified co-driver riding shot-gun. Eventually — inevitably — car and road parted company and took to the air, with Vuky taking his hands off the wheel and remarking casually, for all the world as if he were Ayrton Senna having a quiet word with the Almighty: 'OK, then, you drive!'

But Vuky was not always so haphazard. He had put his winnings to good use, buying in petrol stations and investing his money soundly, as well as working regularly himself at one or other of them. Like many a peasant farmer risen to wealth, he still believed that the touch of the master's boot was the best kind of manure in the business!

Accounts vary about his frame of mind as he squared up to the renewed challenge of the hat trick. Some found him calm and unperturbed by the frequent references to its jinx. Others, like Walt Faulkner, reckoned that Vuky had lost much of his bounce through worrying about the feeling that he just HAD 'to win three-in-a-row because everyone had built it up so much'. Faulkner also recalled that, about a week before the race, Vuky had suddenly blurted out, apropos of nothing in particular: 'I don't think I'll finish', before abruptly changing the subject.

Unlike 1953 the weather on race day in 1955 was downright cold, though it seemed to affect Vuky little enough, and he went on wearing his same old mix of T-shirt, white ducks and bowling shoes in contrast to the sweaters and jerkins being donned by most of the drivers.

55 laps into the race, and he was leading by 17 secs, having put in the fastest ever 500 lap (then) at 141.354 mph and it seemed in the bag all over again as he swung through No. 2 Turn to pass three back markers: Rodger Ward, Al Keller and Johnny Boyd, all of whom he had already lapped once. Then, on the instant, Ward's axle broke and the driver lost control. In the ensuing mêlée there was nowhere for Vuky to go, save eternity, as his car hit Boyd's, which in turn had been side-swiped by Keller's, then bounced, spun and bounced again before crashing upside down in flames. Mercifully, if that can ever be the right word, Vuky, pinned in his cockpit, was already dead from a skull fracture. So it was that, for the second time in Indy history, a former winner had died on the track where he had gained his greatest renown, in the way of Floyd Roberts from 1939. Recently, my friend Nigel Roebuck, who shares my addiction to American racing, wrote these words in his 'Fifth Column' for *Autosport*, which make a fitting last word for this rare racer:

> He was a short stocky man not gifted or concerned with social graces, yet possessed of unique magnetism. He made his own rules but was true to them. His son was 11 at the time of his death; now he, the Vukovich who survived racing, grieves again, this time for a son lost . . . Sometimes in the glitz and cynicism of today, we lose sense of things that matter in the world. Like a racing dynasty, struck again.

Chapter 20

The Kid with the Rocking Chair Style

Jim Bryan

(Born 28 January 1927: Died 19 June 1960 at Langhorne Speedway in 100-mile race)

G rant Clarke's lyric sums up Jim Bryan to a 'T' as a:

High falutin', scootin', shootin'
Son of a gun from Arizona
Ragtime cowboy Joe

. . . with the rocking chair touch coming from his habit of swinging in his car as he drove, 'back and forward in the saddle', just like he was on the horses with which he had started—busting broncos—when he was not playing for his school football team. Later he joined the US Air Force as a cadet during World War II before embarking on the sterner stuff of American road and track racing under the eagle eye of ace mechanic, Clint Brawner.

Like Achille Varzi, Jim Bryan was rarely seen without a smoking tube between his lips—the only difference being that his was an unlit cigar. By 1951 he had passed his rookie tests at Indy, and in 1952 he placed as high as sixth, while at the same time continuing to campaign his midget cars very successfully. Once again he caught the eye of Brawner through whom he got the good looking chance to drive Al Dean's new Dean van Lines car for 1954. That year he had to give best to the one and only Vuky, and settle for second after holding the lead for two short periods and driving a characteristically hard and brave race to finish at all, with much of his body cut, battered and bruised, and one foot burned by hot, over-spilling oil. But being Cowboy Jim he still came up smiling.

After that he went on to win three USAC-AAA titles, in 1954 and 1956/57, and, with them, the Trophy of Two Worlds in 1957, for winning overall at Monza and being third at Indy, and again in 1958, when he won Indy and took second at Monza. A very strong record, but a gritty one too for the trail of death and destruction his Indy win had left behind him. Before the 1958 500 some changes had been made in the pit area, which involved abandoning the time honoured 33-on-the-grid formation and having the cars leave the pits one by one before actually forming into their pattern on an opening parade lap, which was to precede the usual pace lap.

Pole position had been wrested by Dick Rathmann from Ed Elisian and Jimmy Reece. Although all three cars were the handiwork of A. J.

Watson, an intense rivalry had been generated between the three drivers, and this, combined with the confusion of the new starting procedures, resulted in Rathmann and Elisian jumping their moving off signals and getting to the first turn ahead of the pace car, with third place man, Reece, fast following suit. During the opening parade lap they realized what had happened and backed right off to enable them to be overtaken by the pace car and the other 30 drivers. Unfortunately the driver of the pace car failed to get the message and continued at a slow pace with the erstwhile leading 3 behind him.

In his Indy history, Al Bloemker described it all as 'the most agonizing exhibition of orderly confusion ever witnessed at the speedway' before they all got themselves sorted into something like their proper order, and the starter, Bill Vanderwater, unfurled his green flag. In a trice the race was on and alight, with Rathmann and Elisian barnstorming their way to Turn No. 3 on their opening race lap with neither man prepared to cede as much as a millimetre, let alone an inch, until Rathmann eventually lifted. By that time it was too late for either of the pacemakers to do anything but pray as they crashed into one another and the concrete wall at almost the same time. Behind them all was pandemonium as Reece braked desperately and Veith rammed Reece from behind, knocking him straight into the path of O'Connor. His car in turn climbed over one of Reece's rear wheels and flew some 50 ft through the air, first landing upside down and then righting itself, while Johnny Parsons, who had started from the second row, collided with Veith.

The third row drivers were luckier. Led by Jim Bryan, they managed to avoid the wreckage before A. J. Foyt did a complete spin to start another set of chain-reaction crashes, as Jerry Unser flew over the wall, fortunately without touching it before coming back to earth on all four wheels, but outside the track. When it was all over:

> O'Connor was dead. Eight of the world's finest racing cars, valued at more than $250,000 dollars were wrecked too badly to continue. Nine more required immediate repairs in the pits before resuming pursuit of the leaders.

Yet the race managed to stagger on under the yellow light for the next 18 laps, with Bryan still leading the pack through the holocaust and eventually winning out after some very close moments. It had been a harrowing experience and, at the end of the race, not even Bryan could raise the ghost of a smile for the cameramen for several minutes: 'It was awful,' he eventually gasped, 'I never saw anything like it. I lived with it for 200 laps.' Not long after he let it be known that he would not be running for a fourth championship, although he did go on to race at Monza a few weeks later, and take part in a few stock car races during the rest of the season.

Following a run of 'Highs' like that on both sides of the Great Pond,

Bryan should have packed his bags, high-tailed it for home and put his feet up for good and all, with the possible exception of that annual trip to the 500, which was always a special case. And that was what he did for a couple of undistinguished years before taking his pitcher of optimism to the well of hope once more and, of all places, to scary old Langhorne, now long since abandoned from 1970—coincidentally, in the same year as haunting Spa-Francorchamps. Like another unpopular circuit, Syracuse, Langhorne was a mile-long dirt track, though differing from most of the conventional 'ovals' in being more truly circular. This meant that the drivers spent the whole race locked into an almost permanent, flat out, opposite-lock slide that gave them not a moment's respite.

For all that, the old cowhand came back for one last round-up with an ever-smiling face, claiming that he was in no way phased by the circuit that even Mario Andretti called 'The Widow Maker'; that he just loved it; and was thrilled to be getting a drive in the Leader Card Special that its Indy driver and second place finisher, Rodger Ward, had turned down. And, for a short time, it all went as merrily as a marriage bell, with second fastest practice time, beaten only by Don Branson, who Andretti reckoned 'the best on dirt there ever has been.'

With the temperature close on 100°F (35°C) Bryan snatched an early lead from the green flag, crossing the line sideways as he broadsided his way to what was euphemistically called 'Turn One' before losing control in the ruts of the 'Puke Hollow', flipped and was suddenly no more.

In best Western tradition, 33-year old Cowboy Jim had died riding hard with his boots on—and before help could reach him. But, at the end of the day, how much of it was worth while and had there ever been any real chance of coming back with the example of Hep so close in the mind?

* * *

INTERLUDE
A Way Back

For sure there had been none for Jim Bryan and it was left to another great American champion of sport, Floyd Paterson, to show the world that there were a few sportsmen who could still find a way back to the top. Ironically, Paterson chose the very day after Bryan's death to do it. In 1956 Rocky Marciano had retired as undefeated heavyweight champion of the world and, in the vacuum, Paterson had beaten Archie Moore for the vacant title in a fifth round knock-out in November of that same year. Thereafter, Paterson defended his title successfully through three contests until he met a mini-Waterloo at the hands of the Swede, Ingemar Johansson, on 26 June 1959. Paterson then knocked Johansson out in the re-match on 20 June 1960 and another old saw from the sporting world had suddenly lost its teeth. It seemed that, after all, there might still be some of 'them' who could make some kind of come-back.

Sixteen years later another very remarkable sportsman was to show us another way—against all the odds, including even that Last Enemy, death itself. Leaving aside Jesus Christ, a traditional smattering of mythical Gods and Demi-Gods and some classical-through-neo-Romantics like Virgil and Dante no traveller has ever emerged from their Avernus or Inferno to tell the tale.

By mid-1976 a new death-and-hell defying champion, Nikolaus Andreas Lauda was 'sittin' on top of the world, just rollin' along, just rollin' along' as victory piled on victory in a breathless succession that had eluded Ferrari since the halcyon days of Ascari in 1952/53. All too soon and suddenly came that Black Sunday of 1 August 1976 that ended Ferrari's new age of miracles and left Lauda at the very gates of death with the last rites and extreme unction being invoked side by side with the sombre undertones of the Gateway to Dante's Inferno: 'Abandon ye all hope who enter!'

In his book *For The Record* Lauda himself says:

> The Priest speaks in Latin, it sounds like a judgement. You can die from extreme unction like that just as you can die from shock. The Priest says nothing kind, never mentions the possibility that I might recover.

But . . .

> on the 4th day I understand that my blood count and lungs are so much better that I shall live.

Could anyone have possibly come any closer to death?

Yet, within 38 days Lauda was back at the wheel of a Grand Prix Ferrari at Monza to the undisguised chagrin of the very man who should have been his chief support—Enzo Ferrari. Here is how Lauda explains this:

> Those days for me were a key experience at Ferrari's; nothing was frank and above board, but underhand. . . . The Old Man never said openly to my face that he didn't want me to drive at Monza, yet afterwards counted it my biggest mistake. Without my early comeback, we could have lost the world championship with style, we should have been so to speak the moral winners, since the man lying in bed was helpless. I lost this chance by coming back so soon!

So what of Lauda, who James Hunt had so narrowly displaced by such a spectacular succession of last-ditch charges? Along with three other drivers, including Carlos Pace and Emerson Fittipaldi, Lauda had made his difficult and controversial decision to pull out at Fuji because of the weather conditions after just one lap, thereby almost certainly turning his back on a second successive world championship and with it the hat trick that would otherwise have been his after 1977. Much has been said, for both good and ill, about that decision, but was his decision really anything more than the reaction of a brave man who suddenly found himself temporarily bereft of anything more to give to an increasingly over-demanding, unforgiving, non-understanding world?

Stranger still, though, was the behaviour of Enzo Ferrari. Instead of giving Lauda all the support and encouragement he could, in the way of Neubauer with Caracciola in 1933/34, all he could bring himself to do was give Lauda the most perfunctory of cold shoulders, as if he himself had been guilty of some sinister crime—like hazarding one of Ferrari's sacred cars. Not that there was anything very new about that, for the uncommendable Commendatore had always behaved in this callous, arbitrary way to all but that very favoured few who seemed to enjoy a 'hot line' of their own to The Deity. All sadly reminiscent of 'Harry and Jack', who we shall meet shortly (see page 141), in Siegfried Sassoon's bitter sweet poem as they trudge up the line to their deaths in World War I.

Yet again one asks: In goodness's name whatever way was this to have treated the man who had both tested and race-driven Ferrari back into the glory years of Ascari and Nuvolari? As 1976 turned out, Lauda had been strung out just that little bit too much to have lasted through the Japanese Grand Prix but, at least, his gallant soul had overcome near-death itself in the manner of his come-back.

Lauda's second championship came the following year and, as some thought, a little fortuitously for the way that he won it with only three Grands Prix firsts to Andretti's four. At the same time, and on a note of some bitterness, he severed his connection with Ferrari once and for all. After two more years racing with Brabham, Lauda pulled the plug out on Grand Prix racing in favour of his new brainchild, Lauda Air. Another three years later, in 1982, he was back again, but now with McLaren, with whom he was to make yet another come-back and win a third world championship in 1984, by just half a point, proving, if nothing else, that one of the marks of a champion was that he should win his races as slowly as possible, like those two old English cricketers from the North who decided to win a vital test match by getting their last wicket runs in singles!

Yet, at the end of his racing days, even the temperate Lauda was to push his luck a little too far by racing into a depressing 1985 when he won only one race, with two lesser places in fourth and fifth. To some it lacked the quality of a champion's last innings, though one should always remember that the great Don Bradman himself had been bowled out first ball on his last test appearance.

None the less, Lauda's had been a great career spread over 12 years, full of remarkable grit and determination for the way that he had overcome both his shaky beginnings and then his near fatal accident. An enigmatic paradox, too, for the way that his erstwhile 'Patron',

Bernie Ecclestone, had seemed so cursorily to have dismissed his (Lauda's) abilities after Carlos Pace's death in early 1977 (see pages 305/6) with the remark that if Pace had lived he would not have needed Lauda anyway!

In all this, both Floyd Paterson and Niki Lauda have made their points about comebacks, and both are happily and actively alive to prove it, while those merry little bells of hell have yet to ring their 'Ting-a-Lings' for The Man Who Came Back Twice.

Chapter 21

A Study in *La Bella Figura*

Luigi Fagioli
(Born 9 June 1968: Died 20 June 1952 in the Monaco sports car Grand Prix)

Giuseppe Farina
*(Born 30 October 1906: Died 30 June 1966 in a road accident near Chambéry en
route to the French Grand Prix)*

Luigi Fagioli and Giuseppe Farina were two intensely proud and competitive Grand Prix drivers who flourished from the thirties to the fifties. Fagioli was the older of the two, having been born in the Abruzzi in 1898, and started serious Grand Prix racing in 1930 with Maserati, whose straight-eight was the outstanding car of the year. Varzi was the team leader and won three races to Fagioli's one. However, 1931 was as bad a year for the Bolognese firm as 1930 had been good, and 1932 was no better with the new monoposto 2.6-litre Alfa-Romeos ruling the roost, although Fagioli drove a spirited race against Nuvolari at Monza to finish just five miles behind in second; the difference being largely determined by pit work.

The new Alfas were withdrawn at the end of the season and went into hibernation until August of 1933 when they re-emerged as part of the Scuderia Ferrari in the hands of Louis Chiron, moving from Bugatti, and Fagioli, having now left Maserati. The result was another Alfa clean sweep, with Chiron and Fagioli each winning three of the remaining important races.

After his very successful three months with Ferrari, following his years in the Maserati wilderness, Fagioli must have thought that his hour had even more truly come when he was invited to join Mercedes-Benz for their Grand Prix return in 1934. With Caracciola still among the walking wounded, Fagioli had every right to think that, as the fastest and fittest driver in his team, he would be given the right to lead and, hopefully, to win as he chose. The reality was to turn out very differently.

Although Fagioli scored two outright wins and a shared third, along with two second places, it was Stuck, for Auto-Union, who had the slightly better record of three outright wins and two seconds, which would have gained him the European Championship had it then existed.

In 1935 a more fully recovered Caracciola won six of the 11 races he contested, compared with Fagioli's three. Fagioli fought his team leader tooth, nail and claw in the French Grand Prix and the Belgian, where the first of the 'Caracciola incidents' occurred. Both Neubauer and Caracciola reckoned that it was his turn to win at Spa. Fagioli thought otherwise and sat furiously on Caracciola's tail for the first part of the race before his scheduled pit stop, when he stormed in and got out of his car, leaving it to von Brauchitsch, who ultimately took second to Rudi.

Fagioli drove on into 1936 when the Mercedes M25E proved a sorry disappointment, and his contract was not renewed for 1937 to enable him to drive the unforgettable W125. Instead he went over to Auto-Union, for whom he made a promising start with fifth at Tripoli, three secs behind Stuck, after being delayed (as he claimed) so much by Caracciola that, after the race, he sought his old adversary out and threatened him with first a wheel hammer and then a knife—or so the stories go. He raced again at Avus three weeks later in a streamlined Auto-Union making fastest practice lap at over 174 mph and leading for some of his 7 lap heat, before his engine blew. Although he also took fourth place in the subsequent Coppa Acerbo, it was the end of the line for the Old Robber, who vanished from the scene for another 13 years before his resurrection into the 'Three Fs' team of 158 Alfas in 1950 with Farina and Fangio.

Despite his bristling attitudes he seldom crashed or blew up his cars, and at the end of his days in 1950/51 he was driving with all his classic fluidity and a smoothness that was still plain to see even in the company of such latter-day artists as Fangio and Farina. His successful Grand Prix come-back found him being invited to take part in the Mille Miglia again, where he won the 1100 class for Osca and was seventh overall in 1951, and a remarkable third overall the following year in a Lancia Aurelia, just one place ahead of his old rival Caracciola, who took fourth in one of the new 300SL Mercedes, behind the winner, the hard driving, hard smoking, hard drinking Giovanni Bracco (Ferrari) and Karl Kling's 300SL which placed second.

It was then rumoured that, as a result of this impressive display, he had been asked to co-drive in the forthcoming Le Mans 24 hour race for Mercedes along with his former arch rival which would have been a sight to see. However, it was not to be for either of them although he did then give Rudi an apology for his violent behaviour towards him at Tripoli in 1937! Caracciola had a serious accident in the sports car race that preceded the Swiss Grand Prix at Berne when a brake locked up, and Fagioli had what turned out to be a fatal accident in the tunnel at Monaco, practising for the sports car event of that same year.

As a driver he was all speed and style; as a man he was all—perhaps too much all—heart, and, in today's idiom, balls. A man of steadfast courage and fierce independence, for whom Pride and Appearance were a religion.

* * *

Farina shared all Fagioli's personal pride, besides demonstrating a style of driving that came to be so much associated with him wherever he raced: the long, laid back, outstretched arm posture that many said was his own creation. Yet who can be sure, bearing in mind that Farina was a protégé of Nuvolari, who had certainly adopted that same style in the mid-thirties, shown off so well by a shot of him in his 1935 monoposto Alfa attacking the Fay hairpin at Monthléry with his left arm fully outstretched at 12 o'clock?

Farina enjoyed a variety of reputations. For Ferrari he was the complete driver: 'a man capable of any performance demanded of him, a man of steel, inside and out, a man who was a racing champion in every sense of the word.' By contrast, Fangio saw him in a very different light:

> . . . all the drivers said that only the Holy Virgin was capable of keeping him on the track, because of the crazy way he used to drive, and that one day the Virgin would get tired of going along behind him.

. . . so, once again, who really knows? In Fangio's book *My Racing Life* there is a splendid Geoffrey Goddard picture showing Farina, again according to Fangio, 'over the limit' in that magnificent British Grand Prix of 1951, and some 20 pages on there is an equally dramatic picture by Federico Kirbus showing Moss dicing just ahead of Fangio in 250Fs, which is gently described as 'a beautiful "pas-de-deux" as they power slide round a corner . . . in their 250F Maseratis', adding: 'In a car like that you could do anything.' No wonder they say that beauty is in the eye of the beholder!

When Nuvolari went over to Auto-Union in 1938, Farina became the leading Italian driver of an Italian car, a supremacy which he unforgettably underlined on the eve of World War II, in late August 1939, at the Swiss Grand Prix with the revamped 158 Alfa-Romeo. That year the Swiss Grand Prix was run off in two 20-lap heats, one for 1.5-litre voiturettes and one for the 3-litre Grand Prix cars with a combined 30-lap final in which the three strong front row contained the best three cars from the Grand Prix heat, then a twosome second row with the best two voiturettes and so on all the way down the grid.

Lang, who was the speedman of 1939, was on pole position with Caracciola next to him, then von Brauchitsch; then, in the second row, Farina with the quicker of the two 158s, then his team mate the redoubtable Clemente Biondetti, winner of four successive Mille Miglie in 1938 and 1948/50. Perhaps the slight drizzle at the start helped the less powerful Alfas, but, choose how, the grandstand spectators gasped audibly as Farina came round on to the second lap in second place overall ahead of everyone but Lang. And so it continued for another six laps before first Caracciola and then gradually Brauchitsch, Müller and Nuvolari got through, leaving Farina to take a remarkable sixth place a lap behind the winner. The next year he won the voiturette Tripoli Grand Prix of 1940 before World War II spread to Italy, and motor racing was suspended for the duration.

Farina next took the field in a 158 at St Cloud in June 1946 alongside Alfa-Romeo's new 'Maestro', Jean-Pierre Wimille, who was to become the No 1 driver of 1946/49. In that race they both retired with transmission failures and gave Raymond Sommer and Maserati one of their rare triumphs over their dominant rivals, who were not to know defeat again until that famous day at Silverstone in July of 1951.

Before the war Farina had been very definitely the top dog at Alfa-Romeo during the 3-litre formula and Jean-Pierre equally definitely the second stringer for all his seniority in terms of Grand Prix experience—which went back to 1930. After the war their status was gradually reversed, which was not at all Farina's idea of *La Bella Figura*. As a result he fell out with Alfa-Romeo, who raced on into 1948 without him. By early 1949 Alfa's three stalwarts from 1946/47— Varzi, Trossi and Wimille—were all dead and Farina's services became sorely needed when they resumed Grand Prix racing in 1950. This was the first season of the newly revived drivers' championship, in which an Alfa-Romeo victory was inevitable and, sure enough, it was the 41-year-old Farina who narrowly won from a 39-year-old Fangio and the veteran Fagioli aged 52.

The next year was Fangio's first title year, but Farina still contrived to make fastest lap both at Silverstone and Monza, where he found himself wrapped in high drama during the closing stages with just a chance of finishing second behind Ascari. At ten laps to go he had to stop to top up a split fuel tank before roaring out hell-bent on clawing the mighty Gonzalez out of second with a fountain of fuel streaking along the road behind him, which one observer likened to 'driving a hand grenade with the pin out'! To have seen him that day driving as he may not have done for years, if ever—'adopting a high speed crouch coming down the 1.25 mile straight past the stands . . . pressing on absolutely regardless—was to have seen a great driver at full stretch, probably well over the limit, fighting near impossible odds. What finer or more soul stirring sight can there be in all Grand Prix racing?

A few weeks later he made a typical lone wolf's descent on Goodwood with a 159 Alfa from 1950 to take part in three short club-type races, two of five laps each, one from scratch and one on handicap, and one for the Goodwood Trophy from scratch over 15 laps (36 miles). Once again the memory can never fade of Farina and his Alfa weaving their way like a great red Barracuda through a shoal of minnows in the handicap race till he had gobbled up all but one—and ultimately catching the greatest of them, the young Stirling Moss, on the last bend of the last of five laps as they came round Woodcote.

I had spent most of the racing with friends including a spell in deck chairs on the Lavant Straight, listening to that marvellous sound, probably for the last time, of a 158 Alfa being driven at absolutely full blast, first in the distance, then growing ever nearer and louder, with the echoing boom of its exhaust and the whine of straight-cut gears, until it finally burst from the confining approaches to St Mary's and hit the wide open spaces of the Lavant Straight. It was like a magnificent orchestra working its way up to the crescendo of a great symphony as it hit the peak of its performance, before departing on its echoing way down to Woodcote and the starting area. A friend asked me what I had thought of the race. How else could I answer but: 'Pure Beethoven?'

Another observer, perched on the top of the control tower had a different tale to tell of 'a tiny object streaking down Lavant, round Woodcote in a long drift and accelerating tremendously out of the corner, damping out the snaking of the car as the full power came whizzing in, and the driver, a colourful snapshot, leaning back in the cockpit of his vermilion car, pale blue shirt sleeves flapping [for that was how they dressed in those days] and an expression of great good humour and enjoyment on the big sunburnt face', which was also then plain for all to see.

After such a wonderful jamboreee it would have been most uncharitable for the Holy Virgin not to have allowed him the very devil of a sleeping out pass for that night!

Of course, there was another side to Farina, that was aloof, hard, arrogant and very much the man on his dignity even to the point of hazarding other drivers who could never relax, even for a moment, for fear he might have to reflect that his great rivals—Wimille, Ascari and Fangio—were all just that little bit better than he. Perhaps, too, his front had to be kept up to conceal the face of an increasingly battle-scarred old Roman legionary as he noticeably approached his mid-40s. Maybe, too, this was the reason why he rarely visited the bedsides of other drivers. Yet, for all that, the man of steel did have a softer side that was highlighted by a story told by Fangio after his crash at Monza in 1952 when he woke to find what at first seemed like Death's Bright Angel standing by him, complete with its wreath, to take him into another world. It was some time before Fangio realized that it was only Farina who had come to see his friend after he had won the race.

Nor can Ascari's habitual domination over every one else during 1952/53, Farina included, have pleased him overly much, even though he did manage one last set of star turns, winning the German Grand Prix of 1953 along with those of Buenos Aires, Naples and Rouen as well as the Nürburgring 1000 kms and the formule libre race at Silverstone in one of Tony Vandervell's great Thinwall Specials.

Unlike Fagioli, who died while he was still on a High in 1952,

Farina's career gradually declined after 1953, although he won at Syracuse in 1954 and took a couple of good places in early 1955. Thereafter he made a couple of fleeting and really rather needless appearances at Indianapolis before retiring into a series of unsuccessful commercial involvements with Jaguar and Alfa-Romeo and a driving school in Turin. In June 1966, the iron man who had survived so many accidents and so many more close shaves that he was said to have spent five years of his life in hospitals met his match in a road accident near Chambéry when the Lotus-Cortina he was driving to the French Grand Prix at Rheims skidded on ice, and not all his ability, never mind the support of the Holy Virgin, could preserve him from death's lurking telegraph pole.

Both Fagioli and Farina were men of learning and achievement—Fagioli as a businessman and accountant; Farina as a lawyer, who became a racing driver and a Doctor of Political Economy, who was also an accomplished skier, footballer, rider, cyclist and cavalry officer. All of which both men cheerfully abandoned to go motor racing. Whatever their faults, they are quite rightly to be numbered among the top five great drivers of their times in the 30s and 40s/50s.

PART 6

A CHEERY OLD CARD, HIS GARIBALDINOS AND GOLDEN BOYS

Chapter 22

A Tragic Tale of Shining Youth and Gathering Shades

Mike Hawthorn
(see pages 28/9)

Peter Collins
(Born 8 November 1931: Died 3 August 1958 during the German Grand Prix on the Nürburgring)

Eugenio Castellotti
(Born 10 October 1930: Died 14 March 1957 practising at Modena)

Luigi Musso
(Born 29 July 1924: Died 6 July 1958 during the French Grand Prix at Rheims)

'Although there were many famous leaders, there were four who seem to be almost symbolic in themselves of the whole saga with its mixture of fantasy, high adventure and tragedy. All were handsome, brilliant and reckless.'
A. G. Macdonnell: Napoleon and his Marshals

The Famous Four of Mike Hawthorn, Peter Collins, Eugenio Castellotti and Luigi Musso in the mid-fifties you might think? But you would be wrong: they were actually all youthful Generals of Napoleonic cavalry in the first decade of the nineteenth century. They could, though, just as well have been our Famous Four for the way they lived their lives in the fast lane, where they died their young and violent deaths. Their French Emperor has no further part to play in this drama, but their neo-Emperor of Maranello from the mid-fifties most certainly has.

Those years found Enzo Ferrari pushing 60, with all his glory days a fast receding memory and facing every kind of trouble—financial, mechanical and driver-wise. The ranks of his old playmates and die-hards were fast being thinned by the greedy inroads of time and death so that, by the end of 1954, only Alberto Ascari remained as a tangible link with his greater days.

The void that this created in every facet of Ferrari's life was very great and not even the up-and-coming young Garibaldinos, Musso and Castellotti, were any real substitute for the likes of Farina, Taruffi, Villoresi, or even Alberto himself, let alone the great, towering figures from the twenties and early/mid-thirties. From this time the whole balance of Ferrari's activity was to undergo a subtle change, symbolized by the arrival at Maranello in late 1952 of Mike Hawthorn, who would soon win his spurs with his awe-inspiring, split-second victory in the French Grand Prix of 1953 over the great Fangio himself. Small wonder that hardened French observers exclaimed audibly as he doffed his helmet at the end of the race: 'Mon Dieu, il est si jeune.'

Certainly every Englishman at Silverstone a fortnight later was willing him to repeat the miracle and especially on his own ground. Ascari was not going to be caught out a second time and won out easily enough in a typically copy-book display, while Hawthorn spun wildly on the third lap as he came out of Woodcote and was lucky to have escaped serious accident. The delay dropped him from fifth to 26th, although he was able to regain his fifth place he finished three laps adrift. Some also said that after the shock of that potentially fatal spin he was never quite the same driver again.

Hawthorn, first, then Collins, Musso and Castellotti, were a quartet of brilliant young men who burst into flower in 1952/55 and died at much the same time in 1957/59. They were a remarkable combination of brave and gifted drivers on the one hand and fun loving young men who believed that time should be seized by the forelock on the other: and, for preference, in the fast lane both on and off the circuit. The result they inspired was inevitably translated into a glamorous, heady cocktail of alcohol, women, song and speed.

In his book *The Fast Ones* Peter Miller recalls:

> People like the effervescent Peter Collins whose co-driver, Mike Hawthorn, was about to take the first stint at the wheel of their Ferrari at Le Mans in 1958, when the other drivers were already standing in their white painted circle across the track waiting for the start (while) Hawthorn was still on the pit counter talking to a pretty girl on the balcony above.
>
> As the seconds ticked away Peter Collins called out to Mike: 'Come on, Mike, blow the car up quickly and let's get back to the boat!'

They might almost have been Sir Henry Segrave playing truant from his last motor race—the Essex six hours sports car race at Brooklands in 1927—when he absconded like a naughty schoolboy during the race and drove off with his wife straight down to Southampton for some outboard boating on the Hamble River: two different but so familiar variations on the song about going on a vacation to get away from it all.

No less in character was it for the 'Ami-Mates' to have stopped, a few weeks later, during their 1-2 Tour d'Honneur, after Collins's fine victory in the British Grand Prix at Silverstone, to enable Mike to take on board a pint of the best from Duncan Hamilton, who was standing at Beckett's, to refresh him on the remainder of their triumphal 'Tour'.

Measured against the Mates, the Garibaldinos, with their proud haughty mien, might sometimes have seemed a tight-lipped, buttoned-up pair. The older of the two, Luigi Musso, came from a high Roman family of sportsmen and diplomats and, like his contemporary the Marquis of Portago, he excelled in shooting, fencing and horseman-ship. He began his career in sports cars at the relatively mature age of 26 and under potentially evil auspices, committing *lèse-majesté* by crashing into a statue of Garibaldi in the 1950 Tour of Sicily! While this incident did not impair either his future prospects or his race, it did leave him woefully short of forward speeds and he was even reported as having had to climb some of the hills on the long circuit in reverse!

By contrast, it seemed as if Mike Hawthorn had been born with a silver spoon in this mouth so simple and effortless was his rise to fame and success. He had started out in 1950 with a couple of his father's pre-war sports Rileys—a 1.5-litre Sprite and an 1100 cc Ulster Imp—with which he won his class at the Brighton Speed Trials that year. Then, in 1951, he took the Sprite to Ireland where he won the handi-cap races for the Ulster and Leinster Trophies and, at the end of the season, the Brooklands Memorial Trophy presented by *Motor Sport*, for his record in British Automobile Racing Club events during the year.

The next year saw him burst upon an astonished world with his single-seater Cooper-Bristol at Goodwood on Easter Monday, after which his name was made and, by the end of the season, in spite of a training accident at Modena, he had been signed on by Ferrari for 1953, the first British driver ever to drive for the Commendatore in a Grand Prix series.

Before Mike Hawthorn opted for his Cooper-Bristol in 1952 he had tried out the 2-litre A-series Connaught during the winter. It was an unsuccessful experiment about which subsequent accounts vary. Chris Nixon's is that Leslie Hawthorn persuaded Rodney Clarke of Con-naught to let Mike have a go in one of his cars and that Mike had then spun the car trying too hard, and had been rejected by both Clarke and Mike Oliver, their development engineer.

The alternative version is that of 'Johnny Johnson', Connaught's Design Draughtsman. By his account Mike drove the car on a dark, cold winter's day at Goodwood, when he went very fast indeed despite the conditions and its being his first experience of a single-seater car and a pre-selector gearbox. Clarke was not pleased especially when Leslie Hawthorn suggested 'we engaged Mike as a mechanic for about £5 per week provided he could drive now and then', and when Ken McAlpine, who was the man with the money, was told of the idea he turned it down flat saying that 'he would not have a mechanic driving one of his cars!'

As it turned out Mike did actually race a works Connaught—and one on loan from McAlpine himself!—in the National Trophy at Turnberry at the end of August 1952, which he won easily enough, even on three cylinders, in the absence of any serious opposition. It was also at this meeting that he got out of the Thinwall Special that he was driving in another race to tell the flustered BRM boys (and when were they not in those days?): 'Take your time lads. They won't start without us!' A similar scene was enacted a year later at Goodwood when it was the Thinwall's turn to throw a mechanical tantrum and for Fangio, now in a BRM, to wave the starter away until order was restored! All such happy carefree days of long ago that would have cost the offending participants an arm and a leg in fines come the reign of Le Roi Balestre!

Next in age, though not necessarily in achievement, was Eugenio Castellotti, who soon became the idol of the Italian crowds as the prospective heir to Nuvolari, Varzi, Farina and Alberto Ascari. He started his substantive career with a privately entered 166S Ferrari in the Mille Miglia of 1950. The following year he was placed 50th overall and sixth in class, and 1952 found him running second overall beyond Pescara before crashing out in the difficult wet conditions on the magic, star-studded road to Rome. In rather kinder weather he finished second to Vittorio Marzotto in the sports car Grand Prix at Monaco after taking time out for a pit stop to slake his thirst with a can of coke, which lost him his lead! Hardly, one might have thought, the wisest path to preferment! However, he persevered and Lancia eventually signed him up to drive their challenging but tricky D50 Grand Prix car in 1955, while he continued to drive for both Ferrari and Lancia in sports car races.

The youngest of the four was Peter Collins. Unlike the others he had started his racing career with the little rear-engined Coopers, first of 500 cc and then, in 1949, of 1100 cc, at the tender age of 17, which made him that little bit younger than even Stirling Moss when he had first gone Coopering.

By 1952 Collins had followed Moss to the heavier and, by then, much too heavy metal of John Heath's HWM along with another lively character, Lance Macklin. Between them, these three dashing young men brought a much needed fillip of teeming life and fun, as well as some pretty solid driving credit, to the Formula 2 scene of 1950/53 before both Moss and Collins departed for higher things. Moss went successively to Maserati, Mercedes, Maserati again, Vanwall and Cooper and now passes from this book's scenario. Collins was signed up by Aston-Martin for sports car racing in 1953 and also by Vandervell to drive his Thinwall Special in the few available formule libre races as a jumping off ground for the Formula 1 Grand Prix Vanwall scheduled for 1954.

By then Collins was beginning to hanker after some rather more solid anchorage and achievement in Grand Prix racing, however much he might be covering himself with glory in the sports car racing of the period. First at Dundrod, where he recovered from a fluffed start to fight his way right through a field that included the 300SLR Mercedes of Fangio and von Trips, briefly to challenge second man, Hawthorn, in his D-Type Jaguar, and the inevitable Stirling Moss, who led for Mercedes. The Aston found the pace too hot, but not before Collins had made his point where it mattered most—under the probing eyes of Alfred Neubauer, who promptly co-opted him to drive with Moss in the forthcoming Targa Florio, where they won a dramatic and thrilling victory that was in great measure the result of Collins's magnificent driving.

Collins had also driven some good races in the Thinwall, and it should be remembered that Vandervell had already played a part in lobbying Hawthorn's talents to Enzo Ferrari at the end of 1952. It is thus reasonable to speculate that Vandervell had also done something similar for Collins in 1954/55: he and perhaps Herr Neubauer as well. Howsoever, it was Collins who was invited to join Ferrari for 1956 in both sports car and Grand Prix races, where he was to remain happily enough until his death.

Castellotti was the last of the four to achieve Grand Prix status and the first to die. In the short time left to him he put up some stout performances for Lancia in 1955 against the renewed might of Mercedes in both the Mille Miglia and the succeeding Grands Prix before his magnificent rain-swept victory in the 1956 Mille Miglia. During 1955 Ascari's D50 had won both at Naples and Turin, while Castellotti had taken fourth at Naples and second at both Pau and Monaco. His last race with the original D50 was at Spa, where he made a gallant appearance in the shattering aftermath of Ascari's death. To uphold the honour of Lancia and as a tribute to Ascari he fought to lead the race, but was soon enough gobbled up by the Mercedes of Fangio and Moss. After that he clung tenaciously on to third place until his tough, gutsy effort ended with a broken gearbox after 16 of the 36 laps.

1956 saw a real change around, with Hawthorn taking Collins' place for what was to be an unhappy spell at BRM, while Collins and Castellotti went off to join Fangio and drive Ferrari's assortment of D50 based cars. The year brought them all mixed fortunes. Collins won two Grands Prix and might well have won at least one more if he had been allowed to keep his seat throughout races in which he was either required, or deliberately chose, to surrender his car to Fangio. Hawthorn and Musso could only net one third place each through the year, and Castellotti was little better served with one second and a shared fourth place to give him fifth ranking in the points table. Fangio, Collins and Moss each won two races in the series, with the split one being shared by Musso and Fangio.

It has sometimes been suggested that Collins's surrender of his car to Fangio in the closing stages of Monza ensured that he won the title at Collins's expense, which is not correct. In 1956 there were seven Grands Prix and a driver could count his best five scores plus one point for every fastest race lap, with points being awarded to the first five finishers: 8-6-4-3-2. In the six Grands Prix to Monza, Fangio had scored 31.5 points from five scoring races/fastest race laps. Had Collins won at Monza, then his score would have gone up to 30, but, as he had failed to score in two races and made no fastest race laps, his 30 points would have represented his optimum score. On the other hand, with 31.5 irreducible points already tucked away in his bag, Fangio could have called it a day on the starting line and still been world champion even if Collins had both won and put in fastest race lap.

During 1952/53 things had run very smoothly for Hawthorn, and much of the troubles that he met later stemmed from the very suddenness and apparent ease of his rise to fame, and the way in which he was able so thoroughly to consolidate it in 1954. In reality it had all been too easy and left him the more ill-equipped to cope with the biting winds of change that began to blow around him after 1954. On the instant, Life was no longer the 'Bowl of Cherries' associated with Miss Maclaine's song any more than he was the laughing child he used to be.

A fire accident, such as the one he had at Syracuse in 1954, can be a horrifying and traumatic enough experience on its own and when it becomes combined with a succession of other problems it can be near catastrophic. Hawthorn had now to face the sudden death, in a motor accident, of a father who meant much to him, the consequent need to look more to the business he had left behind him; the foolish nonsense that was being stirred up by the gutter press about his alleged draft dodging and, as the direful year that was 1955 ground on, the whispers that he had been in some way responsible for the Levegh holocaust at Le Mans.

All in all, it was enough to have broken the strongest and most mature of men, let alone a young, highly strung one of 25, who was increasingly busying himself in a highly charged and hazardous occupation, week-in, week-out. What a far cry it must have seemed from the starry-eyed youngster at the very start of his career gazing wistfully into the brilliant blue sky above Goodwood and wishing to a friendly bystander—'Much rather be doing that' as a flight of auxiliary Meteor jets from nearby Tangmere swept by. As it was he had to be content with being the fastest road racing driver of a day that was ultimately to be the death of him.

At the same Goodwood meeting (in May 1951) a hardened old observer, who had been racing against Hawthorn, had remarked to that same bystander: 'That boy will be world champion one day.'

After this race, in which Hawthorn had gone off the course, he was standing in the paddock when he was called to attend before the stewards. Another providential friend told him that they would ask him what he had done when he left the course, and that he should be sure to tell them that he had looked carefully about him before resuming the circuit. That very question was put to him by Sammy Davis who was presiding, and Mike quickly gave the drill book answer. Davis nodded approvingly and said: 'Good boy!' On that day the charm and openness of the young man, no less than the wise counsel of his elders, won him the hearts of the Stewards with a charm that would, sadly, grow a darker side.

The form book shows that Hawthorn won only one of the ten Grands Prix run in his champion's year of 1958, while taking six second places, five of the ten fastest race laps and four of the ten pole positions compared to Moss's three of each. Of course, with his record of four Grands Prix actually won, Moss had to be the folk hero of the year, yet it has always seemed ironic that, in the same way as Keke Rosberg in 1982, Hawthorn who (again like Rosberg) was one of the fastest and hardest of fighting drivers (albeit on his day) had to win his title almost entirely on second places. Yet that view ignores those pole positions and fastest laps that, for some, represent the truest criterion of a driver's vital ability to go fast when it most matters.

And, thinking of that 'one win' title, would his great rival, Stirling Moss, have had it otherwise at Oporto, when just a word from Moss could have swung the balance completely so as to disqualify Hawthorn and leave Moss in possession of both race and title. They were surely gentlemen as well as rivals in those days.

Two other thoughts about Hawthorn.

First, that on his day he had that rare ability to beat Fangio in straight fight in a way that somehow eluded Moss in Grands Prix.

And second, that both he and Peter Collins might well have been just as mesmerized by Fangio's brilliant drive on the Ring in 1957 as Fangio himself had been. The fact remains, though, that Fangio kept his head better, however great the temptation to let it soar in the clouds—and that the Golden Boys fell into exactly the same error with another wonderfully down-to-earth driver, Tony Brooks, the following year and with tragic results. I somehow doubt, though, if either Brooks or Moss would have let themselves be caught napping in the way of the Mates.

For all its triumph, 1958 was in many ways the bitterest of years for Hawthorn, with the shock and horror of the deaths, in such sharp succession, of his bold team-mate Luigi Musso, and his friend Peter Collins in the two races that sandwiched Collins's win at Silverstone.

And what of that self-same Peter Collins, the young man who had bested Hawthorn in his last completed race? After his wonderful opening year with Ferrari in 1956, nothing seemed to go quite so well for him despite his early wins at Syracuse and Naples in early 1957. So what a joy it was to see him cast off his inky coat of darkness that day at Silverstone, and smile his way through to a splendid last win and, in so doing, to roll time back over the barren 18 months in between as he led the race almost unopposed. If he had not met his tragic end on the Ring a bare two weeks later, who knows but what Hawthorn or, for that matter, Collins himself, might not have gone on to challenge successfully in several more Grands Prix and Hawthorn even taken the title himself before Casablanca?

In that same year Luigi Musso had driven one of the most hair-raising races in the second and last of the Monzanapolis series, setting up the fastest qualifying time in an awe-inspiring drive that involved full opposite lock slides round the rim of the banking as he skated round with inches of daylight showing under the wheels of the big Ferrari. Looking back to that day a couple of months later, one wonders if he had not even then exhausted his dwindling credit balance with that gloomy accountant, Death. Who can say? All we know is that on the afternoon of Sunday, 6 July 1958, Luigi Musso prayed in vain to his Household Gods to take him, yet again, into their safe keeping, and this last of the racing Romans laid down his life in bold pursuit of Hawthorn, determined to show that he was at least the equal if not the outright superior of his British team mates. On that day Roman Pride was to be his undoing.

For all his familiarity with the very fast Rheims triangle, where he had himself won its Grand Prix of 1957, Musso seemed not to have reckoned with Hawthorn's uncanny ability, given the right mood, to lay on bursts of tremendous speed over a really quick circuit. The fast right hand bend after the pits at Rheims was as challenging as Wood-cote at Silverstone (before it was chicanized), the famed kink in the Masta Straight at Spa, the descent to the Nouveau Monde hairpin at Rouen or the pit bend at Berne. These corners were known throughout Europe as ultra-fast, supremely testing and totally unforgiving, so that any driver who would challenge them flat out had to know precisely what he was risking and, perhaps, even to have needed just 'a little bit of Mr Doolittle's bloomin' luck' to see him on his perilous way. On the tenth lap of the French Grand Prix of 1958 Luigi chanced that luck once too often and had it run out on him in an accident that had befallen several less experienced drivers at the same spot.

After his death, stories circulated of high living and gaming debts being his undoing, and tempting him to ferocious feats of faster and faster driving to earn the money he needed to satisfy his pursuing creditors and their sinister attendant Hoods in their shiny suits, who were, almost literally, to hound this highly strung man to an early death. Wherever the truth of all this may lie, his death deprived Italy of its last driver of note and, in an odd sort of way, upset the balance of Grand Prix racing for some considerable time.

His contemporary, Eugenio Castellotti, was a young Milanese with the good luck to inherit a substantial fortune. This enabled him to buy a sports car and grow quickly, perhaps too quickly, into one of the most promising young racing drivers in Italy just when they were becoming increasingly thin on the ground. Such a tall, dashing, debonair young man, with his highly attractive actress lady, Delia Scala, was everything that was to be expected of a leading Italian racing driver of the day, and almost inevitably he had also to be both proud and temperamental.

At least, though, he could drive, as he showed by actually leading the great Moss-Jenkinson-Mercedes combination over the opening 188-mile dash to Ravenna in the 1955 Mille Miglia at an average of 119 mph—and all still on open roads! The next year he went one better and won the great race in a classic drive for Ferrari in the pouring rain, described by Johnny Lurani as 'the model of self-control, style and efficiency'. He started 1957 racing in the Argentine, holding third in his Ferrari behind the Maseratis of Fangio and Behra until three-quarter distance when a hub shaft failed him before taking fifth place in the Buenos Aires Grand Prix, which was to be his last race.

Strangely enough, Behra, with whom he had duelled in the Argentine, was to be peripherally involved in Castellotti's death at Modena on 14 March 1957. Coincidentally, Castellotti had also been at Monza on the day Ascari had died there in 1955. Indeed, Alberto had actually been wearing Castellotti's helmet on that fatal day and Castellotti was to be one of the party who bore Alberto's coffin into the Church of San Carlo al Corso in Milan on the day before the funeral on 28 May 1955. During the last days of his life Castellotti had been enjoying a brief holiday in Florence with La Scala, when it was suddenly interrupted by an urgent summons from Ferrari to return at once to Modena to make sure that Behra, who was testing there, did not break Ferrari's much prized track record. Compared to the threat posed by Behra and, with the so-called 'Honour' of Maranello at stake, the personal convenience of a tired racing driver were of pitifully little consequence to the Commendatore.

So Castellotti set out around 5 am for Modena, which seemed no way to be preparing for the serious and dangerous job of testing a mettlesome, high speed racing car and then driving it fast enough to repel the challenge that would always be mounted by tough competitive drivers like Behra and a well tried 250F. Ferrari's treatment of Castellotti showed yet again how callous and uncaring he could be with his drivers, especially those who lacked the strength to stand up to the old tyrant and tell him what he might do with his precious records!

After a few warming up laps, Castellotti had just signalled that fast work was about to begin when, unaccountably, he seemed to lose control of his car and crashed fatally into a thick concrete wall. At the time this gave rise to the not unusual tales of a dog getting on to the circuit or some fault with the throttle control. Whatever it was mattered little beside the wholly needless death of yet another of Italy's fast shrinking band of top class drivers, leaving behind the memory of a highly spirited young driver with literally years of unfulfilled talent.

Apart from Castellotti's loved one, it was also a deeply saddening occasion for the retiring Luigi Villoresi, who said of the tragedy that the manner of Castellotti's death had broken his long, if sometimes shaky, friendship with Ferrari; adding bitterly: 'For the sake of Ferrari's pride, challenged that day over a cup of coffee in the Biella Club at Modena, was it right to have put in jeopardy the life of a racing driver?'

How could it ever have been?

Racing drivers are sometimes said to have death-wishes, but surely not Castellotti, so full of 'Bella Figura' as he walked proudly past his admirers on the way to the starting line at Monza in 1955, beside his blood-red racing car, sporting his uniform of yellow T-shirt and fading blue slacks that evoked the memory of another even more famous Italian racing driver—Nuvolari himself—who affected the same colours, but with a red wind hat instead of Castellotti's white crash helmet. No, on days like that, the proud, young Eugenio would have had ears for nothing but the plaudits of the crowd and the sound of Italian baroque trumpets ringing in his ears.

On the other hand, Musso could well have had, if not an actual death wish, then at least much to worry him in his last months: not least his own intense and perhaps Ferrari-inspired passion for winning. Might he not have echoed Hamlet's words about life not being worth a pin's fee, or those of another man of great egotistical pride, that John Thomas Brudenell, seventh Earl of Cardigan, who led the Six Hundred down the Valley of Death at Balaclava, remarking to his 2-i-c, Lord George Paget, as he took station at the head of the Light Brigade: 'Well, here goes the last of the Brudenells!' Unlike Luigi Musso, His Lordship emerged unscathed from all the smoke, cannon fire and swords.

Peter Collins's end was no less sad, coming so soon after his popular win at Silverstone. Moss dominated the opening laps of the German Grand Prix, pulling out a staggering lead of 17 secs after three laps before his magneto failed and brought the Ami-Mates and their Dinos back to the front, with Collins leading. However, they reckoned without the speed and fixity of purpose that Tony Brooks carried in his knapsack to the campaign, as he put together another of his 'Syracuse-1955' efforts and reeled in the dashing Dino-men. Laps 8/10 were closely fought, but, by lap 11, Brooks, and his Vanwall, had got through them both and was beginning to open up a lead in his calm, inexorable way. Of course Hawthorn and Collins fought gamely back, but the punch and will-to-win were just not there, and Brooks on his mettle was a very formidable proposition indeed despite his apparent relaxed calmness at the wheel. Then on lap 11, perhaps trying too hard, Collins lost control near the Pflanzgarten, where he left the road and suffered severe head injuries when his car overturned. Like Varzi and Clark, he was a calm driver who crashed seldom, but who still paid with his life for the one that he had.

The effect of Collins's accident on Hawthorn was like that of Marimon's on Gonzalez in 1954. Hawthorn retired on the next lap with reported 'clutch trouble' and was left with the difficult job of picking up the broken pieces of a world championship that had somehow lost all its savour. In a way it was a wonder that as brittle a character as Hawthorn was able to last out that long and gritty season to its end. Yet, somehow, he did, however much his will to win might have faded with the deaths of Musso and Collins in such swift succession, and almost died with that of Lewis-Evans at Casablanca, when he had told team manager, Tavoni, in a whisper that it had been his last race. By that time he had won the world championship by the narrowest margin (in those days) of one point, when it could so easily have gone Moss's way in Portugal.

So, all the while, the shadows had been gathering and a galaxy of bright lights had been gradually extinguished all over the motor racing world in the 22 months that separated the deaths of Eugenio Castellotti on 14 May 1957 and Mike Hawthorn on the Guildford by-pass on 22 January 1959.

But, at the end of the day, when the roll is called and the reckoning taken, how good had they really been? And, had they perhaps not been somewhat over-rated as Grand Prix drivers and, in reality, been better long-distance sports car drivers?

And, had not their lively lifestyles inhibited their consistency by comparison with that of their successors, Clark, Graham Hill, Stewart and Fittipaldi, and their contemporaries Brooks, Moss and Fangio?

And again, with the eye of Hindsight and Overview, was all their 'Great Fun' no more than 'Just one of those crazy Cole Porter things'? — a dashing trip to the moon or a glamorous series of One-Night Stands rather than the enduring quality of a deeper relationship? Or should one take a casual French attitude and dismiss their whole affair lightly as one of 'Autres Temps, Autres Moeurs?' Which this survey of their brief lives seems to imply.

It was Mike Hawthorn who opened the winning score of the four Golden Boys in 1953. Between 1954 and 1958 there were 38 world championship Grands Prix of which Fangio won 16 with one shared; Moss nine with one shared; Brooks three with one shared; Collins three, Hawthorn two and Musso one shared. In addition both Fangio and Hawthorn each won one Grand Prix in 1953 and, in 1959, both Moss and Brooks added two wins to their respective scores. Ignoring 1959, it was Moss who towered over all his contemporaries save Fangio, the dead Ascari and Tony Brooks, leaving Collins and Hawthorn far, far away in equal fourth behind him.

As so often, it is Denis Jenkinson who should have the last word — and, with him, Stirling Moss: 'At the height of his career, around 1955/57, a friend called him a "Golden Boy". To me, he will always be THE Golden Boy of Motor Racing.'

Finally, what of their grim Pupil Master, Enzo Anselmo Ferrari? By the time he reached 60 he had been through three of his main phases since his early days as in indigent, out-of-work ex-serviceman at the end of World War I. From the early through mid-twenties he had been The Fixer, operating largely behind the scenes and, with others, manipulating the strings of power between Fiat and Alfa-Romeo. That period ended effectively with the 2-litre formula after 1925 and was succeeded by his foundation of the Scuderia Ferrari in 1929, which lasted until 1937. Thereafter he continued as Alfa's racing manager until World War II and, after that, at long last he became his own manufacturer and the first real Ferraris began to take part in minor races. Finally, in September of 1948 his first Grand Prix car, the Tipo 125, appeared at Turin and his career as a 'Grande Construttore' had really begun.

There are two ways of looking at Ferrari: the Reverential and the Image-Breaking. Very much to his credit was the way in which he had built up his Scuderia in 1929/37. Not so creditable had been (in concert with others) his poaching of the best brains of Fiat in the years from 1923, even though it ultimately enabled Alfa-Romeo to become a great racing power and Ferrari himself to build up, first, his Scuderia, then the massive success of the Type 158 Alfa-Romeo and, ultimately, his own conquering 375 of 1951 and its many successors.

The title of his autobiography in its English translation, *My Terrible Joys*, is so devilishly apt, for much of it tells the story of a very terrible man, the central fact of whose life seemed death itself. In this he took after those bluff spoken, cheery-breezy, old Clubland-Hero-Type Generals of British fact and fiction who were for ever urging on their gallant young officers to braver feats of derring-do for the 'Honour of Old England'—while reluctantly protesting that they might be sending them to almost certain death! Brave, indeed, for all of them there was the sound of a distant drum—Ferrari included.

Following the death of Ugo Sivocci, while practising the new P1 Alfa-Romeo at Monza in 1923, the works team was withdrawn as a traditional mark of respect, and a similar gesture was accorded to Antonio Ascari at Montlhéry in the French Grand Prix of 1925.

In his Foreword to the English translation of Luigi Orsini and Franco Zagari's *The Scuderia Ferrari: 1929 to 1939*, its joint founder with Ferrari, one Alfredo Caniate, wrote:

> Memories will live for ever in our hearts . . . and more so, for me, of the dear good Gigione Arcangeli, the Lion of Romagna, who sacrificed his life at Monza to this enthusiasm and bravery.

. . . during practice for the Italian Grand Prix of 1931.

Arcangeli's death was the occasion of Mussolini's infamously unfeeling telegram bidding Alfa Romeo/Ferrari to 'Start and Win', with no noble, old fashioned talk about marks of respect.

'He jests at scars that never felt a wound!' says Shakespeare's

Romeo on the way to a tryst with the fair Juliet. Unlike Romeo, Il Duce never cared to be within 50 miles of any battle front. For wholly different reasons, arising from his dislike of flying, Ferrari rarely went to races especially in his later years, preferring to direct his young warriors from afar in their bids to uphold precious Ferrari records, like Castellotti, and the so-called honour of Italy, like Luigi Musso. For both these mettlesome young men these touchstones were to represent the difference between life and death.

The Grands Prix of the fifties and sixties were dangerous and lethal enough without having an ageing Ferrari aping Il Duce with exhortations to bravery from the safety of the horse lines. It calls to mind the bitter sweet comment of Oscar Wilde from the depths of Reading Gaol:

> If this is how Her Majesty treats her convicts she does not deserve to have any at all.

... or the acerbic bitterness of Siegfried Sassoon's War poem *The General* from 1917:

> 'GOOD MORNING, good morning!' the General said
> 'He's a cheery old card,' grunted Harry to Jack
> As they slogged up to Arras with rifle and pack.
> But he did for them both with his plan of attack

Rest long and peacefully: Brave Eugenio Castellotti and Luigi Musso.

PART 7

THE MESSRS MOTOR RACING

Chapter 23

Mr Speedway

Wilbur Shaw

(Born 31 October 1902: Died 30 October 1954 at Decatur, Indiana, in a private airplane accident)

The non-existent but, paradoxically, wholly honorific title of 'Mr Motor Racing' has been enjoyed by a variety of Grand Prix drivers through the years. These two pieces are concerned with the two best known and most famous, both of whom epitomized the pattern and cut of their respective ages to perfection.

* * *

With his stylish 40s and 50s good looks and presence, Wilbur Shaw should have been a natural for the Hollywood part of himself, for preference played, with or without his 76 trombones, by 'Music Man' Robert Preston. Although Shaw and some of his Indy contemporaries are part of Indy movie history, no-one seems to have come up with the idea of a 'Shaw Story'. Probably its nearest contemporary counterpart was the movie *Follow The Sun* from the late 40s, loosely based on the career of the great American golfer, Ben Hogan and played by Rear Admiral Glenn Ford. So Shaw has had to rest content with the fame of being America's 'Mr Motor Racing', or just plain 'Mr Speedway'.

He flourished at Indianapolis from 1924 to 1941 as a driver, and later from 1946 until his death in 1954 as the Speedway's President and General Manager. He did not race again after the 1941 500, and found its revival, five years later, a particularly moving occasion, when for the first time he had to give the time honoured direction: 'Gentlemen, start your engines!', of which he wrote:

> It's difficult to describe the mingled emotions I experienced at that instant . . . a tremendous feeling of satisfaction for my part in making the big show possible again. The record-breaking turnout was particularly gratifying . . . [yet] I was worried about how many of the cars, most of them five to eight years old, would be able to go the distance and make a contest. And almost overshadowing these thoughts was a feeling of envy. . . . I'd have traded places gladly with any of them and paid a bonus to boot for the privilege of [being] . . . in the Maserati which I had crashed

142

while leading the 1941 race, after I had driven it to two of my three Speedway victories . . . [as] . . . I glanced at the pace car and realized that, for one lap at least, I'd be out in front of the pack again. . . .
  The race was on!

If ever the expression 'Press on regardless!' was created for any man, then it most surely was for Wilbur Shaw, whose whole life was dedicated to the American belief that success did not just fall out of trees, but had to be industriously worked for. Thus, in 1916, when he might have been watching the last 500 before the USA entered World War I, he was more concerned with getting a job at the Stutz factory to see him through the summer. The main things he learnt were how to install batteries and chew tobacco—'I didn't feel like a full fledged member of the Stutz organization until (aged 13) I could chew as well as the rest of the men in the plant!' Small surprise that when the USA did enter the 1914–18 war, the 15-year-old Shaw bought himself his first pair of long pants and high-tailed his five foot nothing and hundred pounds weight of body down to the recruiting centre, telling the sergeant: 'Maybe I'm little, but I can lick a lot of the guys you've got in the Marine Corps!' A couple of years before, and a couple of continents away, another young would-be soldier, who later became first a band leader and then a race driver, called Billy Cotton, had been rather more successful in enlisting and finding himself, at much the same age, on the beaches at Gallipoli 'under Johnnie Turk's shelling . . . [wishing] I had never been born.'
  Shaw never got 'Over There'. Instead he built his first racer out of bits and pieces, only to find, like so many other special builders, that he had to take the workshop wall down to get the car out! The Hoosier Motor Speedway was a half-mile course on the outskirts of the Holy City of Indianapolis, and the starter was a fierce character, appropriately called 'Red' Dunning. Red took one look at Shaw's 'Imperial Special' and roared at him to get his old iron off the track. The 18-year-old Shaw gave Dunning several robust pieces of his mind and, before long, they were firm friends for life, with Dunning helping the aspiring Shaw all he could—even letting him call his next racer the 'RED Special'. By the spring of 1924 Shaw had won the National Light Car Championship with the RED and was beginning to rate 'Appearance Money'. 'During the next three years I believe I raced on every mile and half-mile track in Indiana, Illinois and Ohio—except the few that were open only to AAA drivers. That was the life,' wrote Shaw, 'we not only raced on those tracks, we raced to them in the morning and then raced all of the way home at night!'
  By the middle of 1926 Shaw felt he was ready to take the plunge into AAA competition, but not before he had spent an evening listening to the broadcast of the first Dempsey-Tunney title fight. Not that he remembered much about it, except that Tunney won, because there was 'a girl who took my mind completely off the fight and racing and

everything else.' Lacking the experience, no less than the brazen tones of Ethel Merman to tell him 'You're not sick, you're just in love', Shaw got 'sicker and sicker' until he and his blonde Madonna married 'after a whirlwind courtship, which reached hurricane proportions at times,' and spent most of the winter enjoying a Florida honeymoon.

Shaw returned north in the spring of 1927 the happiest guy in the world, and eligible for the 500 into the bargain. A certain Fritz Holliday of the Holliday Steel Company put up the necessary cash, although the car they chose was something of an oddball—the rebuilt 122-cubic-inch Miller that Jimmy Murphy had driven to his death at Syracuse at the end of 1924. Now, with the engine cut down to 91.5 cubic inches by reducing its stroke, this rehash of a racer, complete with its three-year old 'Hex', was being offered to Shaw for his first tilt at the 500: not that he saw it that way for one moment.

> It certainly wasn't the 'hottest' car in the race, by far. But it had four wheels and an engine and that's all I thought I needed . . . [its] music probably wouldn't get any applause at Carnegie Hall. But to me it sounded like a violin and a pipe organ and bagpipe performing together as an accompaniment for the song of the tires on the bricks.

And what did he care about the 'Hex' surrounding 'Murphy's Death Car'? 'In for a penny—in for a pound', was Shaw's thinking as he gleefully accepted his sponsor's naming of the car: 'The Jynx Special'!

Shaw made a slow start, having difficulty at first in focusing on the signals coming from his pit. Gradually he settled down to a rhythm and found himself in seventh place, while taking no end of a physical battering from the hard sprung car and the rough brick surface that made him feel more like 'a punching bag for Jack Dempsey'. For a while, mechanic Louie Meyer relieved an increasingly anxious Shaw until he could stand it no longer and called Louie in. By the end Shaw was having a desperate run at wresting third place from Tony Gulotta, but the speed was just not there and he had to be content with a rookie's fourth place and a cheque for $3,500 at the finish.

The Shaws were expecting their first child in the fall of 1927, but the boy was born prematurely and both mother and son died in childbirth. For Shaw it was the end of a world that had only just started to blossom and it was a long while before he could find a way into it again.

The door was finally unlocked by his re-marriage on 23 March 1929 to Cathleen Stearns—nicknamed 'Boots', after a no less shapely lady from the comic strip of the day: 'Boots and her Buddies'. In its way, it was a mirror of Caracciola's marriage to Baby Hoffmann and, to the end of his days, Shaw himself thought of it as the happiest and most important day of his life.

Yet serious success at Indy continued to elude him after the High of his rookie run from 1927, and one wondered if he had not taken too many liberties with Lady Providence by calling his car the Jynx Special, and not done quite enough to get its 'Hex' exorcized. Whatever the reason, it took him another four long years of tough graft to get into the top ten finishers again—second in 1933. Then he missed out again in 1934 before hitting a good winning run between 1935 and 1940 of 2-8-1-2-1-1, but then, in 1941, his luck backfired on him. When he had a last-minute fire in the garage area of the Speedway, the precious Boyle Special Maserati 8CTF and its spares were saved, but in the confusion one suspect wheel had lost its chalked warning marks— 'OK-Bal-Use Last'. All the other tyres and wheels had been chalk marked simply 'OK-Bal' so the added 'Use Last' made it very much a last resort spare for emergency use only.

By mischance, 'Use Last' got fitted to the Maserati at its second pit stop after 138 of 200 laps and Shaw set out on the last leg of what promised to be a winning race with what he thought was 'a comfortable lead of more than one full lap on everyone in the race, with fresh rubber, plenty of fuel and only 49 laps to go' to a unique finish (for 1941) of four Indy wins and 3 of them in a row. With 49 laps left 'Use Last' gave out and Shaw crashed out of the race into a legacy of pain and plaster until Independence Day.

A question that is often asked is how Shaw's Maserati was so successful at far away Indy and yet the cars were such a flop back home in Europe. The answer lies in the strength of its American personnel and the immense thoroughness with which they prepared the car, combined with the care with which it was driven. And what a team it was, with wealthy 'Boyle Valve Special' businessman Mike Boyle to finance them; the legendary veteran race mechanic and car builder, Cotton Henning, to rework it and make sure that it was really well put together, and the deeply experienced Wilbur Shaw to drive it, whose precept was to take care of the last 100 laps rather than the first 100, and how it paid off.

The team also had one little secret weapon that Henning kept up his sleeve to make sure the engine stayed sweet. The 8CTF had the relatively long stroke of 100 mm (just under 4 ins) and Henning decided to gear the car down to give not more than 6000 rpm instead of the 6300/6500 favoured by the other teams in America and Europe.

Mr Speedway's race records lived long after him, but he himself never raced again, and, with the exception of Mauri Rose in 1947, no driver has come nearer to three-in-a-row than Al Unser who won in 1970/71 and was second in 1972 (after the full 200 laps) to Mark Donohue. Shaw's record of three Indy wins (shared with Louie Meyer from 1928, 1933 and 1936 and Mauri Rose from 1941, 1947 and 1948) was not surpassed until A. J. Foyt achieved his fourth win in 1977.

After a long spell as a senior executive with Firestones until the end of World War II, Shaw went on to play a major part in the revival and improvement of the Speedway beyond its wildest dreams in the immediate post-war years under the wise and temperate Chairmanship of Captain Eddie Rickenbacker's successor, Anton (Tony) Hulman of the Terre Haute Group, who had watched his first 500 at the Brickyard in 1914.

Shaw lived a wonderfully full life, and enjoyed two very happy marriages during a varied career in his chosen worlds of racing and business. He was an American citizen of whom Governor Winthrop would have been very proud for the way in which he had marshalled and deployed his talents to their very best use. Not the least of his accomplishments was as a pilot and flying instructor, which brought him into touch with the movie stars who were taking flying lessons at the time and, ironically, he was to meet his death in an aeroplane disaster while returning from a business flight to Chrysler's new proving grounds at Chelsea, Michigan. The weather on the return journey was dark and overcast and the ground temperature a few degrees below freezing point, so the pilot was granted permission to make an instrument landing. Perhaps the wings were coated with ice, but this must be pure conjecture. What was not at issue was that the plane carried no equipment to correct icing if it did develop. At 19 minutes past 4 o'clock on that cold, darkening afternoon the aircraft with its pilot and two passengers crashed into the ground near Decatur, Indiana. There were no survivors.

Chapter 24

Mr Monaco

Graham Hill

(Born 15 February 1929: Died 29 November 1975 at Arkley, Hertfordshire, in a private airplane accident)

Graham Hill's initiation into motor racing came rather more slowly than Shaw's. He did not even buy his first car until 1953 when he was 24, at an age when Shaw had been a relative veteran not far off driving his first 500, and he did not start in his first race until 1954, when he took second in his heat and fourth in the final in a Formula 3 Cooper.

He first met Colin Chapman, who was to play such a large part in the shaping of his career, at Brands Hatch on August Bank Holiday of that same year. Something about him immediately impressed Chapman, who not only gave Hill a lift back to London and a free dinner, but also decided to take him on as a mechanic, with the possibility of some driving on the side. Hill was never short of what some would have called 'brass', 'neck' or 'bull', and others, more politely, charisma.

During his first years of struggle, in between coming out of the Navy in 1952 and getting his first foot on the rungs of the ladder to success, he was probably better known as an oarsman in the London Rowing Club, whose colours he was always to wear on his racing helmets. For him the two sports had much in common: 'You can't play at rowing, you have to be dedicated. You've got to concentrate, too, and these and many other things which I learnt rowing helped me when I became a racing driver.' It was rowing that brought Hill and his wife, Bette, together. He was coaching the Stuart Ladies Rowing Club on the river Lea, and his Ladies' eight went on to win, successively, the Ladies' Head of the River (twice) and the European Games.

Like the Caracciolas and the Shaws, the Hills made a great team, from—and before—their whistle-stop wedding in London on 13 August 1955. Between them they had just 18 (old) pence in the bank, £5 in Graham's pocket, and what Bette had in her handbag from her secretarial wages, for the reception. They then borrowed a '20-year-old banger' from a friend and honeymooned in 'the grottiest room in the worst hotel in Bognor'. Why Bognor? Because it was near Goodwood, and Graham had the outside ghost of a chance of a spare drive for Team Lotus in the nine-hour race that weekend, although, in the end, all he got was a couple of practice laps.

The first break came in a test day at Brands Hatch at the end of 1955. For Chapman it was just another 'sales day', but for the struggling Hill it was a potential 'Make-or-Break' occasion. Hill's luck was in and, at the end of the day, he got two five-lap runs, taking second f.t.d. Till then Chapman had reckoned him no more than a dour, even truculent mechanic, but now he began to reward Hill with the odd works drive, as did others with their own private entries.

That was to remain very much the story of his fight to get into real motor racing until he joined BRM at the end of 1959. Apart from the experience, Team Lotus had been pretty much of a disaster area and not even the greatest clairvoyant could have discerned that by the end of the next decade he would have become the 'King of Monaco', with three victories in a row from 1963/65 (with two more in 1968/69) and 'Monarch of the Glen' at Watkins, where he took another hat trick in 1963/65.

But, if there was one quality above all others that Graham Hill possessed it was a mixture of True Grit and Old Iron, that exuded a rare spirit of 'Bloody Well Get Up and Go', and of taking life by the scruff of the neck and never letting it get you down.

Hill's Grand Prix career can be slotted conveniently into six parts: the unsuccessful Lotus/BRM run-in from 1958 to 1961, during which he won no race of any significance; the first glory years with BRM from 1962 to 1965, when he won ten Grands Prix, one world championship and three lesser Formula 1 races; the BRM and Lotus 'lows' of 1966/67 when, again, he won nothing, with the glorious exception of Indy in 1966; the Lotus-Cosworth Indian Summer of 1968 to May 1969 when he won four more Grands Prix and a second world championship, before the declining years that followed his win in the *Daily Express* International Trophy in May 1971.

He had managed to survive the first Team Lotus fiasco with some credibility from a period that calls to mind the remark made by a long dead British engineer to Laurence Pomeroy, on lines that I recall Pom quoting: 'Pomeroy, not even JC Himself, working with Holy Tools, could make a go of this car!'

Hill's last Grand Prix for Team Lotus, until 1967, was at Monza in 1959, where his 16 expired with engine failure after one lap and, with that, he gave his Lotus place to Innes Ireland before himself embarking on a long and, ultimately, rewarding spell with BRM. Perhaps ironically, he had chosen to leave Team Lotus just when Chapman was all set to put his troublesome Formula 1 act into order by replacing his disastrous front-engined cars with the rear-engined 18 that would set him firmly on the road to his greatest successes in 1963/65, 1967/72 and 1977/78.

Yet Hill had still some way to go before attaining every driver's ambition—to win his first victory in Formula 1, which he did not achieve until the Easter meeting at Goodwood in 1962. This was the wretched day of the accident which was to close Stirling Moss's racing career. In the meantime, 1960 had been a slow proving year with a new car and team, and 1961 had been dominated by the overall supremacy of the 156 Ferraris punctuated at Monaco and the Ring by the superlative genius of Moss and his Lotus 18. It would all be very different in 1962.

Hill followed up his win at Goodwood with his first Grand Prix victory at Zandvoort, and repeated the performance three more times in a long season through to 29 December. He also took two second places, one fourth and one sixth, which gave him a comfortable enough win both on points and races won from Jim Clark's Lotus. Notably Hill had driven an outstanding race through the rain on the Ring to win a tremendous duel over the last half of the race with that great Ringmaster John Surtees.

1963 and 1965 were very much Clark/Lotus years when Hill had to be content with second ranking in both years, and also in Surtees's championship year of 1964, where he scraped home by one point in the last race of the season. In addition he had won two major Grands Prix three times in a row during 1963/65 at Monaco and Watkins Glen. Nor should one forget that in those days Grand Prix drivers took a great part in sports car and even saloon car racing, as well as in the Tasman winter series. Thus, in 1963 he co-drove a 4-litre Ferrari into third at Sebring's 12-hour race with Pedro Rodriguez, and won the British TT in a GTO Ferrari. In 1964 he won the TT again, as well as the Paris 1000 with Bonnier, with whom he also shared second at Le Mans in a Ferrari 330P, and the New Zealand Grand Prix of 1965.

The much heralded Return of Power in 1966 brought little joy to Graham Hill or his brilliant new team-mate, Jackie Stewart. The new Power-conceived H-16 BRM proved to be a reincarnation of Pom's 'Holy Tool' syndrome, so that BRM were forced to struggle on with the under-powered V-8 from 1965 now enlarged to 2-litres. By the end of 1966 Hill had had more than enough of that situation, and was looking for a change, which suggests that the reason given in one of his books—'after seven years I thought I'd better move in case they painted me over'—was something of an understatement! In any event, there was Graham at the mature age of 38 finding himself almost right back where he had started!

However, the Indy victories of Jim Clark and Graham Hill in 1965/66 had shown that the New Learning had come to stay, however much the old Indy Dugouts might rail—and not least their doyen, A. J. Foyt himself, who tried to claim, for example, that Hill had been responsible for the 11-car pile-up on the first lap. Clark had shown in 1963 and 1965 that one man could do it and, in 1966, Hill had confirmed this belief and, what was more, that it could have been achieved by any one of the three leading British drivers racing that day. And this despite the doubts of the race official who suggested to Graham that he might possibly have not been the winner!

While it might have set the shade of Jules Goux spinning at the thought of milk rather than champagne being the victor's reward, it was Old Iron Graham who gave the last word to that official—and also reputedly to Clark himself when he tried to impugn Hill's victory: 'No way, mate—I drank the milk!' Old Iron knew how to shut the door when necessary! As a matter of interest, the Milk Custom had originated with Louie Meyer from 1928 when he had been paid an endorsing fee of $100 for his drink during the days of Prohibition.

Although the Lotus 49 was an immediate winner in Jim Clark's hands in the Dutch Grand Prix on 4 June 1967 it was Graham Hill who had been responsible for virtually all of its testing, while Clark himself had not even seen the car, let alone driven it, until four days before the race! The whole venture was otherwise entirely new and untried, making Hill's responsibility an awesome one indeed.

Yet, as we shall see on at least two other occasions, he had a marvellous ability for succeeding in difficult circumstances and rescuing a seemingly lost cause. Old Iron was just that kind of man, although he would not have been the man that he was without some streaks of fallibility. For example, the obstinate fact remained that in the nine Grands Prix between 4 June and 22 October of 1967, he had only finished in two Grands Prix, third in the Canadian and second in the American, whereas Clark had won four and taken third and sixth in two others. Nor, at the time, was this writer the only one to wonder if Graham would ever win another Grand Prix for Lotus or anyone else. 1968 was to prove very different for a variety of reasons.

The successive deaths, in early 1968, of Jim Clark at Hockenheim and Mike Spence at Indianapolis came near to breaking Chapman's spirit, and the Team was kept from disintegrating only by Graham's iron will, his flawless example, the strength of his personality and his stout-hearted ability to snatch victory from the jaws of disaster, as he showed in the opening European races at Jarama and Monte Carlo. That done, he found himself having to ward off, and with not overly much support, the massed strength of Jackie Stewart's Matra, the Ferraris of Chris Amon and Ickx, the Lotus 49 of Siffert, the McLarens of Hulme and McLaren, John Surtees's Honda and, when they were on song, the BRMs, Gurney's Eagle and the Brabhams as well.

When they left Monza for the American continent and its last three races Hill led with 30 points, followed by Ickx on 27, Stewart on 26 and Hulme on 24, so it was still anybody's title. Ever the cool hand when the chips were down for the last shoot-out, it was Hill who steadied his aim and hit the target to score the 18 points that mattered most against Ickx's 0, Stewart's 10 and Hulme's 9. Not surprisingly, those who went to Mexico said that they had never seen him drive better. From the ashen tragedy of Clark, and really through the whole of 1968's championship right down to the fiercely contested Mexican Grand Prix at its close, the effort of Team Lotus had been sustained, almost alone, by Graham Hill as if he were Samson himself holding up the pillars of Gaza, in the same way that he had breathed new life and hope into BRM earlier in the decade.

Come 1969 and Hill placed second behind Stewart at Kyalami

before both he and his new team-mate, the dashing Jochen Rindt, had accidents at Montjuich Park that were generally attributed to loss of ground force owing to wing failure. This brought about a total ban on wings at the ensuing Monaco Grand Prix, which Hill won for the fifth time, his car being fitted with a small but permissible rear spoiler. Although he finished the season with a score of 19 points, ranking him seventh, it seemed a travesty of the splendour of 1968, made all the more bitter by his accident at Watkins Glen—so often the scene of some of his greatest triumphs. Towards the end of the race he had spun and stalled his engine, which necessitated a jump start, after which he found he could not re-fasten his seat belts. Unwisely he decided to press on, only to spin again when a tyre deflated, the car overturned and he was thrown out, breaking both legs.

Unbelievably he was back racing again, in a Lotus 49 for Rob Walker, in time for Kyalami five months later and, what was more, finishing in the points yet again (one for sixth), followed by two for fifth in the Spanish Grand Prix. As a result some of the faithful began to wonder if Old Graham might just do it once more and complete his second hat trick at Monaco—in which he failed by four places.

The remaining years before he finally decided to hang up his helmet were happy in the sense that he went on enjoying his racing, but the feeling persisted that he should have been content to remain in his glory and call it a day after he had demonstrated how he could, first, survive yet another serious adversity and, then, win just one more Formula 1 race as he did in May 1971. And how the crowd cheered him to the echo as the Tannoy told us: 'Old Graham's done it again!'

Old Graham eventually quit in 1975, but he continued living life in the busiest, fastest lane, just as if nothing had changed, right down to an outing with the Oxford crew, at stroke of course. Like so many other retired people from all walks of life—'I soon found myself working harder than at any time in my life and it made me wonder what the blazes I had done with the rest of my time!'

All good heroic stuff, yet it had to be conceded that not all of his glittering charisma was as untarnished, nor his remaining time as well spent as it might have been, for a Requiem is also a solemn thing that 'requirest truth in the inward parts' and its 'wisdom understood secretly'. Thus there were some who found his charisma, no less than the quality of his charm and ambassadorship, to have been exaggerated. Indeed, in his book *The Men*, Barrie Gill refers to him as 'the truculent Hill'. More seriously, grave doubts have been cast on the wisdom of his flight on that fatal night of 29 November 1977, in which not only he himself but his entire crew, including the highly talented and promising Tony Brise, perished in the fog over Arkley golf course. Whatever the 'inward part' of the matter, his last minute decision to return that night instead of the following morning was an unmitigated and, probably, needless disaster.

In the way that a racing engine is quickly stilled, Charisma can die on the instant and be forgotten all too easily. For the memory of a man so otherwise great and esteemed that would be no less of a tragedy, like the continued failure of Monaco to honour its erstwhile 'King' with something like a 'Place Graham Hill', in the way, for example, that the little Romanesque town of Vaison-la-Romaine has its Place François Cevert. So, by the same token, why no special Box for his widow and children at 'his' Grand Prix?

PART 8
SOME FAVOURITES OF THE GODS

Chapter 25

Two Young Men in a Hurry

Guy Moll

(Born 1910: Died 15 August 1934 in a racing accident during the Coppa Acerbo, Pescara)

Richard Seaman

(Born 3 February 1913: Died 25 June 1939 in a racing accident while leading the Belgian Grand Prix in heavy rain at Spa-Francorchamps)

Guy Moll and Richard John Beattie Seaman were two young men of the mid-thirties in a hurry to get themselves established in a world that was fast growing increasingly short of time.

Born in 1910, Moll was marginally the older and much the more experienced, finishing third in his first important race, the Marseilles Grand Prix of 1932 when he was beaten only by Raymond Sommer and Tazio Nuvolari himself. High company indeed for a man of his years to have been keeping. Not possible, perhaps, had he not had the advantage of being a protégé of the distinguished Algerian driver, Marcel Lehoux, who had also done much to speed another aspiring driver from North Africa, Jean-Pierre Wimille, on his young way.

Thereafter, Moll prospered well enough through 1933 to be given a place in the Scuderia Ferrari team of 1934. He began well with a surprise win in April at Monaco when Chiron had a Senna-like lapse of concentration on the last lap, which gave the new star his first taste of victory. By some accounts, his success had gone a little to his head by the time he got to Tripoli and, three laps from the end he had to change a tyre, which left him with a frenzied dash to catch up again on Chiron and Varzi in first and second places. Under pressure once again Chiron slid and lost ground, leaving the way open for Moll to challenge Varzi to the finish, almost literally 'Mano-a-Mano'. *The History of the Scuderia Ferrari* describes this real 'down to the wire' finish:

> The first three drivers in a grim-faced, tight lipped group walked together to the dais to be congratulated by Marshal Balbo . . . and beneath the coating of oil and brake dust on their faces the bitterness of that battle could be seen. These were not team-mates, but individuals racing each other in cars that they did not own.

153

Charles Faroux, then the leading French motor journalist, had some sharp things to say in *l'Auto* about 'The Moll Case' after the race. On the other hand, Ferrari, who always had a soft spot for a young Garibaldino in the Nuvolari tradition, avoided comment, preferring to post Moll to the Milan-Laghi Autostrada to try out an ungainly specially bodied P3 in readiness for the forthcoming Avus races. By contrast, Varzi, the victor of Tripoli, was markedly reluctant to drive the car because of its 'nasty vibrations', and had, therefore, to be content with second, behind Moll.

Both Auto-Union and Mercedes brought very full teams to Pescara for the Coppa Acerbo on 15 August 1934 and, as a curtain raiser, the organizers had laid on a short voiturette event for 1100 cc cars over four laps of the great 16-mile road circuit. The race was a walk-over for the K3 MG Magnettes, with Hamilton winning from Cecchini and the newly aspiring Seaman, who wrote to his mother that he was 'quite pleased to be third at Pescara', modestly adding that the second car was 'very special, being much faster than mine, while Hamilton, Straight's No. 1 driver, is much too good a driver for me to compete with yet.'

For Scuderia Ferrari, 15 August was a Black Day. Varzi drove with every ounce of his legendary fire, blowing two cars up in the fury of his attempts to hold back the tide of an advancing new technology that was now beginning to exact a terrible revenge for its whitewashing at Montlhéry. As if Varzi's troubles were not enough, Chiron's P3 was destroyed by fire and, worst of all, Moll wrecked his car in a fatal accident.

As usual, pit stops affected the lead positions around half distance and by the time they had sorted themselves out, Fagioli's Mercedes led by about 50 sec from Moll and Varzi. Like Varzi, Moll had been keeping up a terrific pace throughout the race, with both men consistently lowering the lap record in between stops until, with five laps left (about 80 miles), Fagioli led Moll by 37 secs and Varzi, another 54 secs away. It had been as dramatic and thrilling a race as anyone could have wished, with fortunes constantly and dangerously changing, as one driver after another first seized and then fought desperately to hang on to his precarious lead. By the 16th lap Moll had narrowed the gap to just 29 secs, and if he could maintain that rate of gain he might still win. All round the long circuit the excited home crowd began to scent the possibility of victory for their inspired young hero, who continued to drive, in the words of a contemporary account, 'as though possessed of a kind of madness'.

On the 17th lap Moll lost time that he could so ill afford when he skidded and stalled before the worst happened. Clearing the village of Capelle, Moll caught up with the famous German racing motor cyclist and record-breaker, Ernst Henne, a full lap behind and having his first taste of real Grand Prix racing.

Inevitably, accounts of what actually happened vary. Some say that

Moll was an inexperienced driver 'driving over the top of his head'; some that the inexperienced Henne's driving of his Mercedes 'was known to be wild and suspect'; and some that Moll had got well clear of Henne before his Alfa swerved without warning from the safety of the long straight road ahead to its sudden, violent end.

While Moll had undoubtedly driven some fast and hard races to have risen so rapidly to his fame, there was nothing in his driving before his fatal crash to suggest that he was either dangerously inexperienced or out of his depth. Indeed, the reality was the very opposite, as his growing record of success and achievement from 1932 clearly showed. That he was driving as fast as ever he could on the day was undeniable, but that is surely what top level Grand Prix driving is all about. In the same breath, one wonders why he had been hauled over the coals of French newsprint after Tripoli, for, once again, there was nothing unusual about a mettlesome, young man challenging his more established rivals and, in any case, neither Varzi nor Chiron were exactly novices to be knocked off their length by the first enterprising young shaver who might come along.

At the end of the day, the true rationale of Moll's accident could well have been that of wise old Giovanni Guidotti, for so long Alfa's head tester. By the end of 1933 engine power had so far outstripped chassis design that, with cars like the P3, 'the hardest job was not to get them around the corners, but to keep them on the roads where the straights allowed the cars to reach their maximum speeds.' Therein could lie the true answer to the tragedy of Guy Moll.

That of Dick Seaman shared some of Moll's fatal elements, but by no means all. His substantive career started just as Moll's was running out and lasted through to an equally tragic day in June 1939. Like Moll, Seaman was very much a young man with his way to make in the world, at least until he might either come into his inheritance at 27 or aspire to a well-paid seat in one of the great works teams, which meant Mercedes, Auto-Union or Alfa-Romeo—and very much in that pecking order. In the meantime, whichever way Seaman might turn, he would be faced by the solid bloc of the Berlin–Rome Axis power base and, with it, the improbability of a mere 'Englander' getting a foot in either camp the way the politics of the thirties were emerging.

Neither Time nor Tide were on Seaman's side in a world in which it was not enough just to be good. You also had to be both Noticeable and Noticed, calling to mind the seventeenth century couplet:

> If your talent you would show,
> You must first your trumpet blow.

Seaman's answer was spelt out in his racing colours of stark, dramatic, Black. That, and a deliberate plunge straight in at the deep end of the hurly-burly of continental road racing to gain experience, rather than messing about on the 'nursery slopes' of the English domestic racing of the day. In all this he was very lucky to have met up with another highly competitive and successful young man, Whitney Straight, when they were both Cambridge undergraduates in 1932/33.

From his first successful continental drive at Pescara in August 1934, Seaman quickly showed himself a marked man of note, followed 11 days later by his first outright victory in the 1.5-litre voiturette race on the tricky and demanding Bremgarten circuit at Berne. That win and his subsequent fifth place at Brno brought him to the notice of Nuvolari himself, even though he had finished well behind another young man who was to loom large in Grand Prix history for the next 20 years: the increasingly formidable Dr Giuseppe 'Nino' Farina.

Both men were forceful characters on the up-and-up, and both had good reason to be well-pleased with their opening campaigns in 1934. But, with opposition of Farina's quality, there was no way in which Seaman could afford to stand still, and he had to have an ERA if he was to stand any sort of chance in the voiturette season of 1935. It was rather the story of Mr Pepys's fancy waistcoat: 'God give me means to pay for it!' for Seaman's parents were dead against motor racing as a career, preferring their only son to follow a 'proper' profession which, in those days meant the diplomatic, the law and similar fogeydom, all of which was anathema to a man with Seaman's sporting outdoor tastes. So he set about convincing his mother, and by no means unreasonably, that 'the day would come when I shall have the finest racing cars in the world placed at my disposal. A mechanic will bring it round and all that I shall have to do is drive the car.' And, as ever, Seaman eventually gained both his point and the new ERA that was to begin the consolidation of his 1934 beginnings.

By the end of the year a searching wind of change had begun to suss out the inadequacy of the relatively primitive ERAs, and Seaman was, once again, left looking for a new trumpet to blow if he was to keep up with the newest Maseratis from Italy. In the end he found salvation from that same country in the renowned shape of Giulio Ramponi backed by his own well-tried trust fund, although both he and his great friend, George Monkhouse, had taken a great deal of convincing about Ramponi's plan to resurrect one of the 1.5-litre Delages from 1927 and making it viable and successful. In the end the old Delage enjoyed a wonderful revival and, better still, sent the merry notes of Seaman's trumpet singing into the august ears of Alfred Neubauer and the Daimler Benz AG. So Seaman's dream began to come true, and his prophecy to his mother to be fulfilled.

At noon on 30 January 1933, Adolf Hitler had been sworn in as German Chancellor and, within six months he had engineered the complete Nazification of Germany, and with it his own Dictatorship of a Reich that was newly unified and federalized for the first time in German history. A year later, in June 1934, while the new might of German Grand Prix racing was being deployed at Montlhéry, a very different scene was being enacted within the grim confines of the Stadelheim prison at Munich and the cadet school of Lichterfelde, as

Grand Prix gallery of honour

Top *Lone Ranger: Frank Lockhart in Stutz Black Hawk. His Single-Shot Derringer approach reasoned that 225 mph should have been well within his grasp.* (Neil Eason-Gibson Collection)

Above *Perfect circle: Lockhart's decisive Rookie win from 1926 was followed by his new record of 1927 when he led the whole of the first 90 laps, which was not bettered until 1990 by Emerson Fittipaldi.* (Geoffrey Goddard Collection)

Right *Mr Wonderful crosses the Atlantic: When Mrs Emerson presented the great Vanderbilt Cup to Bernd Rosemeyer on Independence Day, 1937, she told him: 'I think you are just grand and your motor-car is "Wunderbar".'* (Geoffrey Goddard Collection)

Top *The End of a Small Boy's World: You can almost smell the burning rubber as Rosemeyer scorches his way round the right-angled Red Gate Corner at Donington on the way to winning his last race on 2 October 1937.* (Geoffrey Goddard Collection)

Above *Raymond Sommer (right): A Great Fighting Man, whom they also called Coeur de Lion. Here he is with the great Jean-Pierre Wimille at Monaco in May 1948.* (Michael Hewett Collection)

Left *The Chipmunk Trap from May 1948: Wimille seizing an early lead at Monaco in the little 1430 cc Simca-Gordini that would be the death of him in early 1949.* (Author's Collection)

Wet And Dry: Ronnie Peterson and Jochen Rindt. Both Master Car Controllers. (Left) At Monaco opposite the Hotel de Paris (from 1971), and (right) Clermont Ferrand (from 1969), showing just how to corner on the limit in all weathers. (Author's Collection)

Above *Glory Year: Jochen Rindt seems fresh as a daisy after his thrilling last bend win from Jack Brabham at Monaco in 1970.* (Michael Hewett Collection)

Below *The Beloved of Victory: A characteristic view of Alberto Ascari already several lengths ahead of the field, Farina included (No. 16), and a young Mike Hawthorn in his Cooper-Bristol (No. 9) on the extreme right of the grid trying to squeeze through from the second row (he finished third). Silverstone 1952.*

Above *Like Father, Like Son: Antonio Ascari with the six-year-old Alberto by his side in his all-conquering P2 Alfa-Romeo.* (Geoffrey Goddard Collection)

Left *The Special Relationship: A quiet study of an unusually relaxed Colin Chapman, with Jim Clark, The Incomparable, who never looked anything else.* (Geoffrey Goddard Collection)

Below *Versatile as Ever: The Incomparable in the slightly unusual setting of a Lotus 38 in* The Times *Grand Prix at Riverside in October 1964.* (Bob Tronolone)

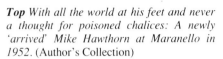

Top With all the world at his feet and never a thought for poisoned chalices: A newly 'arrived' Mike Hawthorn at Maranello in 1952. (Author's Collection)

Above left The Little Dog Who Had His Day: A memoir of Gilles Villeneuve. (Bob Tronolone)

Above right 'The Frowning Providence': Emile Levassor, the man who won the world's first Grande Epreuve. (Montagu Motor Museum Collection)

Right Gloomy Foreboding: Count Eliot Zborowski thoughtfully eyeing his new 60 Mercedes before his fatal run up La Turbie on 1 April 1903. (Quadrant Collection)

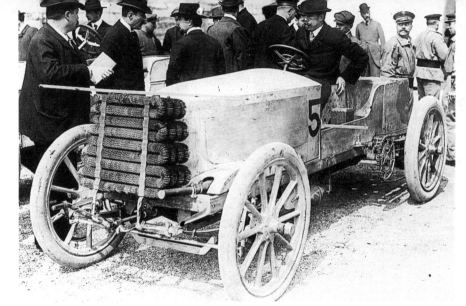

'Just a matter of taking the lead': Both Barrow (top) and Marcel Renault (left) went to the start of the so-called *'Race To Death'* with varying degrees of foreboding that was to haunt Charles Jarrott with *'horrible distinctness'* in the days that followed. By contrast, for Louis Renault (below) it was no more than a *'matter of taking the lead as soon as possible'* and booting it for Bordeaux. (Geoffrey Goddard Collection)

Top and above *The Cyclists and the Deaf French Farmer: The tragedies of both Cesare Giuppone and Paul Zuccarelli went back to the bad old days of practising on the open roads of France with no sentries posted to guard the little side turnings from which all manner of traffic could emerge without warning. In Giuppone's case it was cyclists and in Zuccarelli's a deaf French farmer and his cart. (Geoffrey Goddard Collection)*

Below *'Cran and Élan': Georges Boillot was the epitome of French flamboyance in the years to 1914 and his short career as an air fighter in World War I was all of a piece. Mercedes on the circuit or Fokkers in the sky, it mattered not which, they had to be met with Cran and Élan. (Geoffrey Goddard Collection)*

Top and above 'The friendly, big brown men': Antonio Ascari and Giuseppe Campari 'as they look out on their expanding world of 1924 with all the assured presence and confidence of the bluff, successful North Country businessmen that they were.' (Geoffrey Goddard Collection)

Below A Lucky Win: Campari (with mechanic Attilio Marinoni) just after their win at Lyons in the French Grand Prix of 1924 which was scored very much against the rub of the green at the expense of Ascari (3) who had led for much of the race. (Geoffrey Goddard Collection)

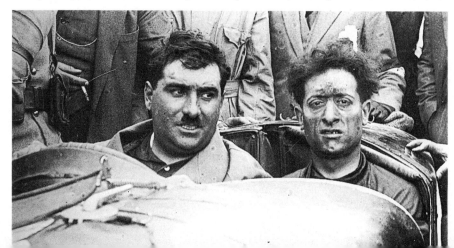

Top and above Last Races of Father and Son: Antonio at Monthléry in 1925 and Alberto at Monaco 30 years later. Note the uncanny similarity of their cornering styles at the two hairpins. (Geoffrey Goddard Collection [Antonio] and John Olliver [Alberto])

Below left 'Pickin' a Chickin!': Borzacchini the Eternal Second, who scored at least a dozen such places in 1931/33. (Geoffrey Goddard Collection)

Below right A Rare Smile from the Man Who Was Led Astray: Unlike his great friend Louis Chiron (left), Varzi was seldom seen to smile. This is one of the rare exceptions. (Geoffrey Goddard Collection)

Above *Yankee Meteor: David Bruce-Brown in heavy disguise with his big Fiat thundering away from the hairpin at Eu down the road back to Dieppe in the French Grand Prix of 1912. (Geoffrey Goddard Collection)*

Below and bottom *Double Winner: Jimmy Murphy made what was then racing history by being the first man to win both the French Grand Prix and the Indy 500, which he achieved in successive years – 1921/22. It was the first time a pole-sitter had also won the 500 and, in addition, his car, the Murphy Special, was the first win for a Miller engine mated to a Duesenberg chassis. (Geoffrey Goddard Collection)*

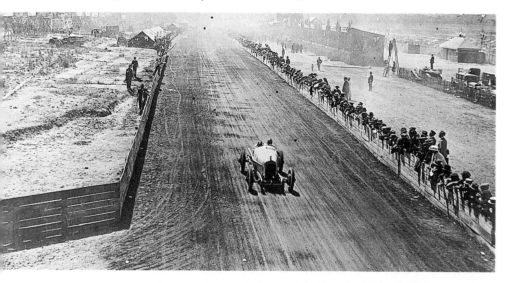

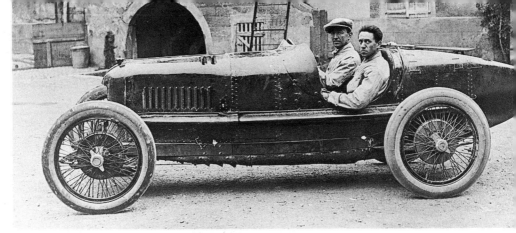

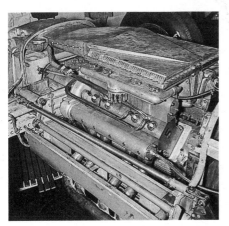

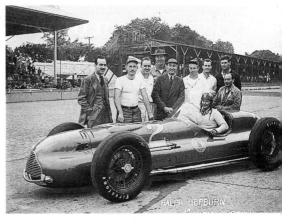

Top *Pietro Bordino, who was also called 'The Red Devil' and 'The Mad Mullah', was the leading Fiat driver of his day in the early to mid-20s and the fastest of his time. He also enlivened the American scene through much of the same period. Here he is in the 1925 2-litre blown Fiat, in which he qualified eighth and finished tenth at Indy. (Geoffrey Goddard Collection)*

Above *'Oh Lord Our Governor, How Excellent is thy name in all the World!' The power plant of Lew Welch's Novi Governor that was driven by Ralph Hepburn in the 1946 500, setting new four-lap qualifying and single lap records, and the car with Hep himself at the wheel. (Geoffrey Goddard Collection)*

Below *Two Great Trackburners: Ralph Hepburn (centre) and Tazio Nuvolari (right) with Harry Miller (left) at Indy in 1938. (Geoffrey Goddard Collection)*

New Qualification Records!
1 Lap --------- 139.600
4 Laps -------- 139.034

Chet Miller
Indianapolis Motor Speedway
1952

Top *Low, Long and Speedy: Rex Mays in the Novi prior to the 1949 500 with Bud Winfield (left) and Nalon (right).* (Geoffrey Goddard Collection)

Above *The Novi's last stand: Chet Miller, who set yet higher one and four lap records in 1952, including an unofficial single lapper at over 140 mph.* (Geoffrey Goddard Collection)

Left *'That man never won an easier one,' growled Bill Vukovich when a pivot pin broke and ended his race with just eight laps left for the outright victory that he had to await for another year. Here the victor, Troy Ruttman (right), then the youngest 500 winner, is comparing his winnings of $61,743.18 with Vuki's $18,693.18 for 17th.* (Geoffrey Goddard Collection)

Top left and right 'Jim Bryan – The Rocking Horse Winner of Monzanapolis'. By finishing third and first and first and second at Monza he emerged as the uncrowned King of the 'Trophy of Two Worlds' races held at the two tracks in 1957/58. The photographs show him receiving the Borg-Warner Trophy and Victory Lane kiss from Shirley MacLaine in 1958 and with his characteristic half smoked cigar in his Belond AP Special. (Geoffrey Goddard Collection)

Above and right 'Abruzzi Robber': Luigi Fagioli, all speed and style at Monaco in 1935 (Michael Hewett Collection) and enjoying the fruits of victory at Silverstone after the British Grand Prix, 1950. (Author's Collection)

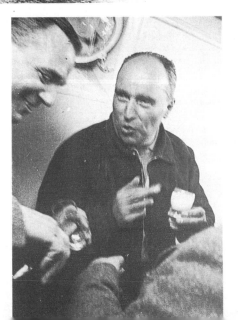

Giuseppe Farina: A Man of Pride: **Above** *After winning the Monaco Grand Prix of 1948 with (left to right) M. Anthony Noghes, President A.C. de Monaco, Princess Ghislaine of Monaco, Prince Rainier and Mme Farina.* (Michael Hewett Collection) **Left** *Fighting the odds and the new found strength of Ferrari in the Grand Prix des Nations at Geneva in July 1950. At the time Farina was third behind Ascari and Fangio. On lap 60 of 68 Villoresi, in the other Ferrari, skidded, crashed and overturned. Farina was unable to avoid the crashed car and damaged his own in the ensuing accident.* (Author's Collection)

Below *'Mon Dieu il est si jeune': Mike Hawthorn after Rheims in 1953, when every Briton at Silverstone a fortnight later was willing him to repeat the miracle on his own home ground.* (Author's Collection)

Right and below *Peter Collins, The Youngest of the Four: (1) Early Promise – (750 cc Cooper-JAP) breaking the course record at the Altcar speed trial in May 1951 and (2) professional fulfilment at the Karüssel hairpin on the Nürburgring in 1958.* (Author's Collection)

Bottom two *Two faces of Luigi Musso: (1) Squaring up to the challenge at Monza in July 1958 with Jim Bryan's Belond AP (No. 1) and Fairman's Jaguar (No. 2). (2) Stroking his way round Thillois to win the Grand Prix de la Marne of 1957 for Ferrari.* (Author's Collection)

Left *Castellotti receiving the plaudits of the crowd as he strides proudly down to the start of the Italian Grand Prix in September 1955 where he finished a very creditable third.* (Author's Collection)

Mr Speedway – Before and After: Indy 1940. **Below** *Wilbur Shaw, qualifying second to Rex Mays's Winfield 'Bowes Seal Fast'.* **Bottom** *After winning the first ever Indy 2-in-a-row ('Boots' is on the left).* (Author's Collection)

Mr Monaco: **Right** *Graham Hill, the family man with daughter at the annual Grand Prix drivers' cricket match at Merstham le Hatch.* (Author's Collection) **Below** *In 1966 Graham joined Jimmy Murphy, Jules Goux and Jim Clark as the fourth driver to have won Indy as well as a Grand Prix.* (Bob Tronolone)

Bottom *Two Young Men in a Hurry: Guy Moll before going out to win the Monaco Grand Prix of 1934 for the Scuderia Ferrari, and Dick Seaman being congratulated by Caracciola after winning the German Grand Prix of 1938.* (Geoffrey Goddard Collection)

Above 'An idle moment's glance' was all the time it took Colin Chapman to see Mike Spence's potential at Monaco in 1963. Here he leads Jo Siffert at Monaco in 1966. (Michael Hewett Collection)

Left and below left Tom Pryce graduated quickly and smoothly during the early 70s in smaller cars like this Royale from 1972 (Author's Collection) before finding an all too brief niche in Formula 1 with Shadow. (Bob Tronolone)

Below The Right Place at the Right Time: François Cevert in 1970 receiving marching orders from Uncle Ken Tyrrell. (Author's Collection)

Top two Peter Revson was a very handsome and gifted all-round driver (Michael Hewett Collection) *with a good record in Grands Prix, Can-Am and Indy. Here he is during the blighted British Grand Prix of 1973* (Geoffrey Goddard Collection) *and just after winning it at Silverstone for McLaren.*

Middle two 'Captain Nice', *as they called Mark Donohue, was a strong performer in Can-Am and Indy racing and he was no slouch in Grand Prix either. Here he is driving Penske's 'Sunoco Special' to victory at Indy in 1972 and obviously very happy with his day's work.* (Bob Tronolone)

Right 'Relaxed and easy-going manner' *was how they sized Mike Spence up as Jim Clark's Indy replacement in 1968.* (Bob Tronolone)

Segrave set great store by smartness of turnout, as witness this shot of him at Brooklands in 1920 beside his ageing little Brescia Bugatti. He was also one of the fastest and smoothest drivers in Europe, setting the fastest lap in the great French Grand Prix of 1924. Here he is shown in pursuit of Count Louis Zborowski's Miller in that event (both Geoffrey Goddard Collection). He is also shown (extreme right) in a happy, laughing mood with his wife (extreme left) who has just succeeded in breaking the traditional champagne bottle across Miss England's bows. (Neil Eason-Gibson Collection)

Top two 'The Whoosh-Bonk Man': Bruce McLaren obviously working very hard indeed to finish third, 1.3 secs ahead of Surtees's Ferrari at Monaco in 1963. (Michael Hewett Collection) In more relaxed mood at Laguna Seca in October 1962. (Bob Tronolone)

Above The Man from over the Sea: Dario Resta (standing behind car) returning to Indy after seven years to drive in the Packard team of 1923. With him are engineer J.G. Vincent, and great Indy drivers Joe Boyer (sitting) and in the car the legendary Ralph de Palma. (Geoffrey Goddard Collection)

Right Robert Benoist (left) – A Very Gallant French Gentleman, and the first driver to win a Grand Slam of a year's Major races since Felice Nazzaro in 1907. (Geoffrey Goddard Collection)

Left Stuart Lewis-Evans, 'A Man Of Promise': posing in his Cooper 500 in March 1954 with John Cooper kneeling on his right and Les Leston on his left, and what a kit of Meccano it all looks nearly 40 years on. But, my, how effective it was! (Author's Collection)

Middle The Beautiful World of Lorenzo Bandini: or so it had seemed to him and Chris Amon as they gazed down on their panoramic view of Monte Carlo on race day. By mid-race Michael Hewett's action shot tells of a harsher reality as the tiring race takes its toll of a driver's strength and reserves. For Bandini these were to come to their end at the chicane on the 82nd of 100 laps of a race that would never again boast its gruelling complement of 1,000 corners. (Michael Hewett Collection)

Below All the accounts speak of Jo Schlesser as a happy man who enjoyed what he was doing even if he never got to the top of the tree. However, Michael Hewett's haunting shot of him in the closing stages of the Holts Trophy race at Crystal Palace makes one wonder as he gazes anxiously through his goggles at his mirrors full of a close pursuing Jackie Oliver. Schlesser tangled with Oliver two laps from the end, and he crashed fatally at Rouen a few weeks later, leaving that wonder sadly unresolved. (Michael Hewett Collection)

Above left and right The 'Obvious and lambent happiness' of Piers and Lady Sarah Courage. (Author's Collection)

Below The indomitable Archie Scott-Brown. Because of his disability Scott-Brown's Formula 1 racing had to be confined to the UK. (Geoffrey Goddard Collection)

Bottom A happy shot of Gunnar Nilsson (left) with Ronnie Peterson (right) in 1977. (Michael Hewett Collection)

Left The Man Who Should Have Stayed In The Pits: Ricardo Rodriguez shortly before his fatal accident in Mexico in November 1962. (Author's Collection)

Below and bottom *Pedro Rodriguez in the pit lane at Brands Hatch and winning the BOAC 1000 km World Championship Sports Car Race on the day they forgot to tell him it was raining! (Author's Collection)*

Right and below Jo Siffert's first great victory – in the British Grand Prix at Brands Hatch in 1968 (Geoffrey Goddard Collection), and all smiles at Questor in 1971. (Bob Tronolone)

Bottom Off to Brooklands 'to take the cement'! Count Louis Zborowski in Chitty-Bang-Bang I outside the portals of Higham (Highland Court), and could he be sporting one of the ancestral cuff-links in his right cuff? (Geoffrey Goddard Collection)

Left and below 'Tiger Tim' Birkin after winning the Irish Grand Prix at Phoenix Park on 6 June 1931, attended by Alfa-Romeo's works engineer/mechanic Attilio Marinoni (Neil Eason-Gibson Collection), *and driving the Team Blower Bentley (No. 18) in the French Grand Prix of 1930 at Pau where he took a remarkable second place. Here he is seen in close pursuit of Count Stanislas Czaykowski in his Type 35C Bugatti, who finished fourth.* (Geoffrey Goddard Collection)

Bottom Count Czaykowski, wearing a white bow tie under his overalls having seemingly just won another race to judge by the attendant flowers on his car. (Geoffrey Goddard Collection)

Opposite page top Two Anxious Looking Aristos: Baron von Trips (Author's Collection) in thoughtful mood and the Marquis of Portago. (Neil Eason-Gibson Collection)

Opposite page middle Jean Behra never won a full Grande Epreuve, and not too many other wins came his way between 1952 and 1959, which must have made his (and Maserati's) Victory at Casablanca in 1957 seem all the sweeter. (Author's Collection)

Right Behra's last race shows him characteristically mixing it on the Avus banking with Count Godin de Beaufort's Porsche (No. 14) in 1959 shortly before Beaufort's crash and his own fatality. (Geoffrey Goddard Collection)

Above and below left Back to Four Wheels?: *Patrick Depailler padding off the Monaco armco with his Seven-League-Booted, Six-Wheeled-Wonder in 1976, when he finished third* (Michael Hewett Collection), *and snapped by Bob Tronolone in more serious mood, perhaps pondering his move from Tyrrell to Ligier, in 1979.*

Below right Four Wheels Good, Two Wheels Better?: *Mike Hailwood's lasting dilemma.* (Geoffrey Goddard Collection)

Top left and right *Avoiding The Tramlines:*
W.G. Williams, the man who was sometimes
three men, appropriately steering a middle
course to win the first Monaco Grand Prix in
1929 (Michael Hewett Collection) and a
portrait from the Geoffrey Goddard
Collection taken at much the same time.

Above *'Single Speech Hamilton': André*
Boillot after winning the ACF's Coupe de la
Commission Sportive in 1927 at Montlhéry
by the narrow margin of 0.4 seconds in a
sleeve-valve Peugeot 176 of 2493 cc at an
average of 63.91 mph. (Geoffrey Goddard
Collection)

Right *The Monaco Grand Prix of 1952 was*
for sports cars only. On lap one Stirling
Moss's Jaguar has already gone through
and Pierre Levegh is following in second
with his perennial Lago-Talbot (No. 68) and
holding off the eventual winner, Marzotto's
Ferrari in third as they fly up the hill from
Ste. Devote. (Michael Hewett Collection)

Top left and right Overall, the calm phlegmatic Louis Rosier was France's most successful driver of the late 40s to early 50s, though by no means the fastest. The two pictures show him in action with his 375 Ferrari at Rouen in 1953, where he is being closely pursued by Harry Schell in his nimble little Gordini 16 (Author's Collection), and in a posed shot at the wheel of his Lago-Talbot. (Guy Griffiths) In passing it seems hard to believe that his Ferrari was the car in which Gonzales had beaten the field at Silverstone two years before.

Above Renaissance Man, 1960s Style: Jo Bonnier in action for BRM in 1960 at Silverstone with a young John Surtees close behind. (Author's Collection)

Left Bernie's Substitute for Lauda: Bernie Ecclestone held Carlos Pace in such high esteem that he would have retained him for 1978 in preference to Lauda himself, although he was saved from being put on his election by Pace's untimely death in early 1977. (Bob Tronolone)

Above *A Hewett study of Didier Pironi from 1980.*

Above right *A dramatic study of Gilles Villeneuve winning the Monaco Grand Prix of 1981 by Michael Hewett.*

Right and below *Two Studies in Determination from 1984: For all his outward gentleness, Elio de Angelis could assume a look of steel, and act the part as well, while in Hewett's action shot he must be literally shaving the armco again at Monaco.* (Michael Hewett Collection)

Top Not Quite Such a Plus-Four Fool: Ernie Triplett (left) about to take a quick squirt down the brickyard with the well-known mechanic, Spider Matlock, in 1933. (Geoffrey Goddard Collection)

Above Happy Warrior: Harry Schell with the BRM 25 in 1958, all lantern jawed, gritting his teeth and going just as hard as ever. (Author's Collection)

Below Count Louis (right) and 'The Moplahs': The Count and his cronies making whoopee in their Palm Beach Caps in the Paddock around Chitty I. (Geoffrey Goddard Collection)

Hitler's revolution embarked on the age-old process of devouring its own children, starting with Roehm and the SA who had played such a part in bringing Hitler to power. For anyone with eyes to see, the whole of Europe would now be running on increasingly borrowed time and, not least, Seaman himself.

In the meanwhile life had to go on, with the Germans scuttling back across the Rhine to lick their Montlhéry wounds and put their tackle in order for their own Grand Prix on 15 July, and with Seaman preparing his K3 Magnette for his first continental race—at Albi on 22 July.

After his elevation to Mercedes Benz following his 1936 voiturette season, Seaman drove in nine races for them in their new and formidable W125. He scored one second, two fourths, two fifths and a seventh, with two retirements and one crash that was not truly his fault. The power gap between that of the Delage (about 170/185 bhp) and the W125 (about 646 bhp from 5660 cc) was enormous, and Seaman had done well to finish with such consistent results. By all standards he should have enjoyed an easier and more successful time in 1938/39 and a good chance of proving himself in the formula's new 3-litre cars. At it turned out, he was allowed just four starts from the nine races of 1938, which he put to pretty useful purpose with a first, second and third and a retirement: he was perhaps unlucky to have dropped into third when he was caught out on the oil slick at Donington, but more of that later. Come 1939 and he had only two starts despite a fastest practice lap at Pau: a retirement in the Eifel before his fatal crash at Spa, when he was leading easily.

But, where did all that leave Seaman in the ultimate reckoning?

First, there was Seaman the ambassador for his country as a stranger in a strange land in 1937/39. At the age of 18 he had been invited to act as an English equerry to the visiting Crown Prince Rupprecht of Bavaria, but when he went to Germany he soon became an important figure in his own right. By the end of 1938 he had met Hitler at the German Motor Show, where he had been impressed by the Führer's electrifying oratory, if not its content, while doubting if Cecil B. de Mille could have done better! By 1939 he clearly felt that he was walking on political eggshells with the massive worsening of the European situation following the successive German annexations of Austria, Czechoslovakia and the Baltic states. Seaman decided to stick it out, largely on the advice of Earl Howe, who was a great support to him at a difficult time. He wrote to Howe:

> I am very glad that your advice takes the form it does, for I have always thought that it would be better for me to remain with Mercedes in spite of political difficulties.

Goodness alone knows what the future would have held for the Seamans if he had lived, and it is idle to speculate on a world that had by then virtually exhausted time in favour of eternity—'To every thing there is a season . . . a time of war . . .' (Eccles. 3:1–8)—while one thinks inevitably of Seaman's love of flying and the imminence of the Battle of Britain, for he and his lovely Erika would surely have returned to England before the world fell apart.

His place in history is no less hard to assess. Of course he was far and away the most successful of the British drivers of his day, and after his win on the Ring in 1938 the *German Automobile Revue* was speaking of him as 'the equal of Lang and Brauchitsch'. His next drive, in the rain at Berne against Caracciola, 'did a great deal to make more certain his position as . . . one of the greatest racing drivers in the world.'

And then came his last race at Spa in 1939, where the weather was so bad that even Caracciola himself left the road for good at La Source on lap nine (of 35), though Seaman plugged relentlessly on, reeling in the cars ahead of him, until he led the whole race. At that point, and with victory almost his to command, he surely had no need to hurry any more, but simply to concentrate on driving steadily to the finish with no fireworks. Yet this was just what he could not do, and one thinks of the day in 1935 when he overdid things while practising at Brno, later admitting to George Monkhouse that:

> . . . there were times . . . when he had the urge to take a corner much too fast . . . [and] . . . found the urge quite irresistible.

His biographer, Prince Chula, added that:

> Dick was anxious to hide this during his lifetime, but now the fact can be revealed, as it has a strong bearing, possibly on the cause of the worst accident of his career.

and, perhaps also because of his two crashes in the Eifelrennen and Peronne in June of 1936.

At Spa it was generally thought that he had taken a previous bend too fast and then found himself on the wrong line for La Source. Yet what destructive devil had driven him to that last excess? For a start he was known to believe that 'when in the lead, you must try to get at least one minute ahead'. Then there was his status with Mercedes. Despite his improved contract for 1939, he still had that vital way to make in a world where money and position were important to him, and where he naturally wanted to show both Mercedes and Neubauer that he was worth a darn sight more than the reserve status meted out to him in 1939. One more thought, that I have long propagated, is that in 1939 he was simply short of racing practice and, at Spa of all places, *and* in the wet: a massive recipe for trouble.

Finally, there was his own driving temperament, highlighted over the years by two very astute and knowledgeable Italians: Ramponi, who had ridden or driven with so many of the great ones, counselling him in Delage days: 'Make you no exaggeration, Mr Seaman!' And Ugolini's description of him, back in 1938: 'Fast, but a trifle too risky!'

For both Guy Moll and Richard Seaman there had, literally, been 'So Little Time' before their worlds fell apart.

Chapter 26
Curious Chance

Mike Spence
(Born 30 December 1936 at Croydon: Died 7 May 1968 during practice for the Indianapolis 500)

By the sheerest of chances the perennially busy Colin Chapman had actually found enough time to snatch an idle moment's glance out of the corner of one eye at a Formula Junior race at Monaco in 1962 and to be so struck by the natural, smooth and relaxed work of a passing driver that he immediately noted him down for possible stardom. That young man was Mike Spence and, by the end of 1963, Chapman was rating his 'discovery' highly enough to give him a Formula 1 drive at Monza. Just 13 laps from the end of the race Spence suffered engine failure when running seventh. In July of the following year, as the result of Peter Arundell's crash, Spence became Jim Clark's recognized second string in the Lotus Formula 1 team. This enabled him to finish the season with two places in the points and to do even better in 1965 before joining Tim Parnell's BRM-based team for the 3-litre formula from 1966.

This new and so-called 'Power Formula' got off to an uncertain start, and Spence did not aspire to a works car until 1967 when, of all cars, it had to be the controversial H-16 BRM—a Grand Design that, like its V-16 predecessor, was to prove a costly fiasco. Yet Spence persevered with the troublesome car through 1967 to gain a hard-earned nine championship points.

The V-12 BRM, which began to appear in late 1967, was a much more competitive and businesslike car. In 1968 it enabled Spence, now teamed up with the hard-driving Pedro Rodriguez, to mount a growing challenge in the two British curtain raisers at Brands Hatch and Silverstone. The Lotus-Cosworth effort had suffered a massive blow in the death of Jim Clark at Hockenheim on 7 April, and not even the redoubtable Graham Hill had much of an answer to either the new Cosworth-powered Gulf-McLarens or the newly competitive BRMs. In both races Spence showed that he was now a potential winner before he ran into mechanical problems. Sadly, these were to be the last races he ever drove in.

At the same time Chapman was faced with the problem of finding a replacement for Jim Clark for the Indy 500, where he had been expected to put in laps at around the 175 mph mark in the STP Lotus-Turbine. Chapman's first choice for a substitute had been Jackie Stewart, but he had put himself out of the running by injuring his wrist in practice for the Formula 2 race at Jarama at the end of April. So, according to Crombac's book, 'Colin invited Spence along.' As he had done at Monaco in 1962, he proved an immediate 'natural' at Indy, and by 4 May he had really shown his hand by posting fastest lap of the year at 164.329 mph.

Three days later, on the 7th, he had improved his performance to a fast and consistent series of laps over the 169 mph mark, with a best one at 169.555 mph, which was within a cat's whisker of Andretti's pole time from 1967 of 169.779 mph. Although Spence was still the rookiest of rookies at the speedway, his 'relaxed and easy-going manner', that had already so attracted Chapman, was being sharply noted by the cognoscenti, no less than his smooth and speedy adaptation to the track. Thus, in that week, Team Lotus had already achieved more than they had in the whole of May 1967, and, with Hill also posting a lap at 169.045 mph, they could afford to put their Indy cars away and fly their drivers off to Jarama for the Spanish Grand Prix on 12 May in the secure knowledge that their triumphant golden argosy to the New World was almost a foregone conclusion. But the snag lay in the 'almost'.

Spence was not just fast and smooth. He was also a very competent test driver and, late on 7th May, he was asked to go out once more and give Greg Weld's companion car a shake-down—a simple enough request that was to have a catastrophic result. Spence had just taken the car up to 163.1 mph when it went out of control and crashed into the wall in the difficult first turn—'difficult' because of the way that it was overshadowed on the outside by two high-tiered grandstands that hampered the view of which way the turn went.

A knowledgeable speedway observer had noted that Spence was running much higher in Weld's car than ever he had in his own, and he saw the 'dust blow under his car when he came into the turn just before the crash and knew he was too far out of the groove to make it through. Then it looked like he saw how fast he was going and knew he'd break loose if he cut too hard and tried to ride it out. . . . By that time it was too late.'

Spence had been travelling at over 125 mph when the car hit the wall broadside on, and spectators said that the right front wheel had appeared to twist back and catch him on the head. He was rushed to hospital, but never recovered consciousness and died some four hours later to begin a calamitous period for the now seemingly doomed turbo cars. The two McLarens entered for Denny Hulme and Bruce himself proved altogether off the pace and never reached the starting line, while the three remaining STP-Lotus turbo cars enjoyed very mixed fortunes. Joe Leonard started from pole position with Graham Hill right by him and Art Pollard back in the middle of row four. Just into the second half of the race, and well placed, Hill's front suspension broke, while both Pollard and Leonard had their fuel pump drives shear when seventh and first, and Leonard with the race almost won for the second year running.

Spence's tragedy came near to breaking Chapman as this extract from Jabby Crombac's book shows:

> Coming as it did so soon after Jimmy's death, this was too much for Colin, and Andrew Ferguson remembers Colin saying to him at the hospital: 'This is it, I quit motor racing. I'm leaving right now—sell the equipment, pay the bills and come home.'
>
> But Andrew knew Colin well enough and decided to proceed as though he had said nothing.
>
> Nobody knows where he went to when he disappeared, but a few days later he was back as though nothing and happened, and never a word was said about Andrew disobeying his instructions.

Now, how right had Chapman been about Spence? While much of the evidence is thin and patchy, everything about Spence's rise from Formula Junior to Formula 1, first in a small way, and gradually expanding, had carried the hallmark of a growing quality so that, at the end, Louis Stanley had felt able to write this brief memorial of his driver:

> A popular unassuming driver of outstanding ability, who in 1968 suddenly matured into a potential World Champion. . . . By his death at Indianapolis, the contemporary motor racing scene was drained of a vital force.

In a survey of 1968 written for *Speedworld International*, I referred to the first appearance 'of the new daemonic Spence' in March's Race of Champions, which is exactly how I remember him for those two brief months to May. On that form and given the right car he had all the makings of a formidable and versatile Grand Prix driver.

Jochen Rindt, however, thought otherwise, judging by this dialogue in Peter Yanso's *Vroom* from 1970:

> To win at Indianapolis is a great thing, but it's not a great driving satisfaction, the car counts too much. I can prove this to you—when Spence went over he went quick immediately. He simply had a good car.

Having seen Spence's last races in Europe I am not sure that I agree with Rindt, who said in the same dialogue that he:

> . . . wouldn't be a racing driver if I had to go racing like in the States because it doesn't attract me. To me that sort of thing is almost like a Roman Tournament, a place for driving around with the horses. It's like a chariot race, like a circus more than an auto race. It's uninteresting.

Somehow I doubt if the Unsers, Fittipaldis, Andrettis, and Mears of this world would agree.

Chapter 27

Sheer Ill Luck

Tom Pryce

(Born 11 June 1949: Died 5 March 1977 in a freak accident during the South African Grand Prix at Kyalami)

Six years later, in 1974, at Silverstone's International Trophy meeting, another promising and freakishly unlucky British driver, Tom Pryce, was making his Formula 1 debut in an unlikely sounding Ford-powered car called a 'Token', whose odd name was derived from a combination of the Christian names of its creators, Tony Vlassopulo and Ken Grob. By mid-May Pryce was qualifying their brainchild 20th out of 31 on the grid at Nivelles, where he lasted for 63 of the 85 laps before a combination of fuel problems and busted front suspension ended his run.

Tom Pryce was born in Ruthin, Denbighshire, on 11 June 1949, the son of a Police Sergeant, and he originally trained as an agricultural engineer. He advanced steadily and unobtrusively through the lesser formulae of the early 70s—Three, Super Vee and Atlantic and Two—before he arrived, just as unobtrusively on the Formula 1 scene at Nivelles in May of 1974. Entrants were restricted for the Monaco Grand Prix a fortnight later so Tom had to be content with a drive in its prestigious Formula 3 event instead, where he gained a resounding victory and was soon being courted by the top brass of Formula 1.

He missed the next two races, making up his mind, before taking 11th place on the grid at Zandvoort in the second string Shadow, four places behind their No. 1, the mercurial Jean-Pierre 'Jumper' Jarier. The start of this race was a disaster for Tom. He was clobbered by James Hunt in the tricky Tarzan hairpin on the first lap and it was just the same at Dijon a fortnight later when he had seized third grid spot 'by using the whole road and sometimes a bit more!', it was said.

After all that trouble he muffed his start and got tangled up with both Carlos Reutemann and Hunt (again), so, at Brands Hatch, he played safe and gridded up beside his fateful opposite, after taking the pre-race prize of 100 bottles of bubbly offered by *The Evening News* for the fastest lap of the first practice session. This time he managed to finish safely enough, though down in eighth after being delayed by a damaged rear suspension mounting, which had also made gear changing difficult. That finish was followed by his first points—a distant sixth on the Ring.

The next year's Race of Champions at Brands Hatch produced a very wet series of practice sessions that left the 'local lad' conspicuously the fastest, a whole second ahead of Scheckter. Race day continued cold and damp with even a short flurry of snowflakes to stir mild echoes of that Pau Grand Prix of 1933, which had been run in a real snowstorm. By 1975 most managers at Brands were more concerned with the more immediate and painful problem of tyre selection between the wets and dries, a perennial problem for racing managers no less than politicians!

After a sharp start from the second row to take a short-lived lead, Ickx was given little further chance to repeat his brilliant wet weather victory of 1974. He was quickly cut down by Scheckter's Tyrrell and then by Pryce, fighting hard to make up for a bad start, and gradually grinding away at Scheckter's advantage, as he equalled Lauda's lap record from 1974. Two laps later, just as Pryce was closing in, the Tyrrell blew up and the young man from Wales was left with an easy home run, during which he equalled his own lap record. It was the happiest of days for Tom and a little crumb of comfort for Shadow after all their disappointments, while none could gainsay the merit of a race that they had wrested from Watson (second), Peterson (third), Ickx (fourth) and Fittipaldi (fifth). Such was the first high point of Pryce's first full season.

Soon after, he enjoyed a dramatic battle at Monaco with Lauda and Peterson from second place on the grid for the lead during the opening laps. Less ferocious than his team-mate, Pryce's style was not without echoes of the young Peterson, all opposite lock and tail hanging out in the breeze: 'Grand Entertainment', *Autosport's* Pete Lyons called it, before adding magisterially: 'the results in terms of lap times have not been there.'

At Ricard a new Pryce appeared: altogether more composed and collected, now recognizing the benefits of an increased smoothness, but still human enough to rue its being 'No fun at all! You feel you're just poodling around when you keep wanting to put the old boot in and get going!' Practice at Silverstone gave this new and distinctly 'undaemonic' Pryce one of his finest hours when he captured a hard-fought pole position from Pace, Lauda and Regazzoni. Unfortunately, he then failed to make use of this opportunity, letting Pace cut across and grab his lead. Pryce hung grimly on and even took a short lead on two occasions before meeting his Waterloo at Becketts, spinning out in a great pool of the stuff. None the less, by the end of the season, he had put together a very respectable tally of eight points for tenth ranking.

Brazil staged the opening race of 1976 and came close to providing a Shadow victory, with Pryce and a magnificent Jarier harrying Lauda for all they were worth. Then it all went wrong on the 34th lap when Hunt lost his oil and somehow, Lauda got through unscathed, while Jarier did not. Pryce just about managed to make it, but eventually had to give best to Depailler by 2.37 secs through being plagued by worn tyres and failing brakes. His resulting third was to be his best place and helped him to equal 11th with Peterson at the end of the year's rankings.

With Jarier giving the opening races of 1977 a miss, Tom found himself No. 1 at Shadow, though the cars were now sadly off the pace. At Kyalami the new Shadows, designated DN8, placed 15th (Pryce) and 20th (Zorzi) on the grid and were well down the field when Zorzi stopped after 21 laps with a dead engine beyond the pits. His trouble was a fuel line that had come adrift and begun to leak, which made the fuel catch mildly alight. This, in turn, inspired two over-zealous marshals to rush across the road with fire extinguishers just as a high speed quartet of Stuck, Pryce, Laffite and Nilsson were approaching at around 150 mph, and fatally hidden in the dead ground between. Stuck and the first marshal were lucky; Pryce and the second one were not. In the impact between them, the second marshal's fire extinguisher hit Pryce and sent his Shadow careering out of control down the straight to the next bend where it left the road. Laffite, following close behind, could not quite avoid the Shadow, although he was lucky enough to escape from the wreckage with nothing more than a few bruises.

For Tom Pryce and that ill-advised marshal there was to be no such luck in another 'freak accident, that underlines the obvious fact that motor racing is a very hazardous sport . . . [calling for] . . . more thoughtful marshalling . . . [to say nothing] . . . of the need for training those who perform vital functions at race meetings to be efficient and to understand the dangers involved, both to drivers and officials.'

All too pitifully easy and obvious enough to say, but something still too imperfectly understood or put into practice at yet another vital time. It was something that should never have happened and, Thank God, the odds are that it no longer would, given today's infinitely higher standards of safety and general organization.

A small piece in a racing Annual of 1974 concluded with the thought that Tom Pryce's season had proved that 'dreams do come true and now Tom can look forward with confidence to a fine future in Formula 1'—always assuming that he had the luck to dodge the fatal arrow that proverbially 'flyeth in the noon-day'.

On 5 March 1977 neither Tom Pryce nor the errant marshal had that kind of luck.

Chapter 28

A New Decade of Gold

François Cevert

(Born 25 February 1939: Died 22 March 1974 practising for the US Grand Prix at Watkins Glen)

Peter Revson

(Born 27 February 1939: Died 22 March 1974 practising at Kyalami, South Africa)

Mark Donohue

(Born 18 March 1937: Died 19 August 1975)

'Hollywood in the 1930s was a melting pot for American slang, and (Johnny) Mercer kept his ears peeled; and when he heard Henry Fonda exclaim "Jeepers Creepers" in his Midwestern twang, Mercer latched on to it.' — *Philip Furia: The Poets of Tin Pan Alley*

A nd the lyric of 'Jeepers, Creepers, Where d'ya get those Peepers' was on its way, though François Cevert was not born or thought of for another decade.

The most striking thing about François was the deep, shimmering blue of his eyes, which seemed to shine through even the darkened visor of his blue crash helmet. Small wonder that Norah Tyrrell could still recall them so clearly when we spoke together of him some 17 years after his death. The whole Tyrrell family had loved him dearly, and expressions like the obvious 'Wonderful Eyes' . . . as well as . . . 'Lovely Person' . . . 'Loved motor racing and would not have given it up for anything' . . . 'Never big-headed' . . . 'Kept the common touch' . . . 'Fun to be with' . . . and 'dedicated to racing' . . . came tumbling out of Ken and Norah's argosy of happier memories. François was a young man 'Beloved of the Gods' if ever there was one; perhaps a counterpart of Elio de Angelis from the next decade, for both men were also gifted musically, as classical pianists of a high order, although François said he could neither whistle nor sing in tune!

Almost throughout his racing career François was to enjoy the legendary Napoleonic touchstone of luck. As one reporter summed him up:

Albert François Cevert may well typify the young driver of the seventies. A bachelor, living in a slick Paris apartment. . . . Tall, lean, and a stand out [sic] snow and water skier. 'Not the sort of driver to be caught with grease under his finger nails' . . . He arrived at these exalted heights

198

with a minimum of experience, a maximum of confidence, and enough ready cash to buy his chances. The money also seemed to be a necessary ingredient for a successful driver of the seventies . . .

. . . as his 'Patron' Ken Tyrrell found out in the early summer of 1973, when François approached him for a rise in 1974. He named a figure which it had taken Jackie Stewart himself 14 Grands Prix and two world championships to attain—and he with just one Grand Prix victory to his credit! Need one add that François got what he wanted, notwithstanding?

Like so many other young men in his position Cevert had first to win a long battle with his father about his racing career. Not unusually, his father wanted him to prepare for a commercial life through studying law, languages and the even more dismal science of economics. Of course, François had other ideas but, like Seaman, he had to fight every millimetre of the way to win his father's grudging agreement about his racing, and wait until he had completed his military service in 1966 and won the 'Volant Shell' prize awarded by the driving school of Magny Cours. This carried with it the prestige needed for the final approval of his father, no less than the right to choose his own Formula 3 car for 1967. His choice of a Renault Alpine was not a good one and a less determined and well-breeched young man might well have lost out. But not François, even that early in his career. With some help from a sponsor he put together the money to buy himself the Tecno for 1968 with which he became French Formula 3 champion and made his early name.

The next year Tecno offered him a works Formula 2 car which enabled him to start in the highly significant German Grand Prix on the Nürburgring where the classes for Formula 1 and Formula 2 were once again to be combined, as they had been in 1967, when the aspiring Jackie Ickx had put in third fastest practice lap overall and challenged the fastest Formula 1 cars until his front suspension broke on lap 12 of 15.

Cevert could not repeat this inspired level of performance in 1969, but he did take second place on the grid behind another golden French hope, Johnny Servoz-Gavin, in a Matra-Ford. Cevert retired on lap ten with crown wheel and pinion failure, outlasting Servoz by three laps. He had better luck at Rheims where he won from a field that included Jackie Stewart himself, which made him a marked man and ensured him a leading place in the Tecno team for 1970.

However, at the end of 1969, Matra had decided to abandon their British Cosworth connection and go 'All French' with their V-12, which the more pragmatic British constructors considered unsuitable—and how right they turned out to be, although the French charge came close to stopping the British dead in their tracks. The 701 March was no substitute for the Matra MS80, which had taken Stewart to his first championship in 1969, and Tyrrell entered 1970 with the cumbersome March, still backed by French Elf sponsorship, and with Servoz as their second string driver. His last race had been in Spain in April, where he had taken fifth place. He then, surprisingly, failed to qualify for Monaco, where he had led from second grid spot the previous year, and by the Belgian Grand Prix he had retired altogether. It transpired later that he had suffered a little known eye injury which blurred and impaired his vision, although at the time, all the Grand Prix world knew was that his retirement left a potential crown lying in the gutter for the taking.

By Zandvoort on 21 June Servoz's place had been filled by François, to some extent because of his good performances with Tecno from 1968, which had not been lost on both Stewart and Tyrrell, though more probably from the wish of his team's Elf sponsors to retain a French driver. In all this François had been supremely lucky in being in just the right series of places at just the right times. As Derek Warwick put it at the end of 1990:

> Its not just a matter of how quick you are but also being in the right place at the right time, being with the right sponsor, when the right vacancy opens up, being the right nationality; all kinds of things . . .

In all of which Lady Luck was the handsome François's ready helpmate.

Unlike, for example, his great mentor Jackie Stewart, François made little initial impression on the Formula 1 scene. Not for him the immediate blistering impact of Stewart himself, Ickx, Emerson Fittipaldi, Scheckter or Villeneuve. Instead his rivals found a new driver who would be brought up by the Tyrrell/Stewart duo in the canon of Alfred Neubauer, a process that did not call for fireworks so much as good old fashioned care, consistency and smoothness, in the belief that, if the talent was really there, the pace would surely follow naturally.

By mid 1971 there were clear signs that Uncle Ken's slow burn approach was bearing fruit as their pupil rode in his master's wheeltracks, for all the world like Stirling Moss and Fangio 16 years earlier. During the year he took second to Stewart at Ricard and the Ring, followed by third at Monza, sixth at Mosport and, finally, that sweetest of all sweet victories, in the final Grand Prix at Watkins Glen, when he stepped into the breach after Stewart's car had lost out with understeering in the early stages. No wonder he crossed the line with both his arms outstretched above his head, shaking them jubilantly as he took Tex Hopkins's extravagantly proffered flag. He had also had another good season in Formula 2 and, as 1971 gave way to 1972, it seemed that his hour might well have come.

However François was not the only brilliant young man who had been looking to come good at the end of 1971, where the Watkins grid had contained several supernumerary entries: Andretti for Ferrari, Donohue for the McLaren and Revson for Tyrrell, of whom Andretti and Donohue opted out in favour of a clashing USAC event, and Revson whose clutch packed up on lap one.

By the fall of 1971 Peter Revson was a mildly cynical, bored 32+, just a few months short of that 33 of which the infinitely more world-weary Lord Byron had written in his Diary [for 22 January 1821]:

Through life's road, so dim and dirty,
I have dragged to three-and-thirty,
What have these years left to me?
Nothing—except thirty-three.

. . . feeling that he had done it all—as, in a sense, he had.

Although money was never a serious problem for Revson, any more than it had been for François, Revson fended rather more notably for himself after he had first run through a gamut of Universities: Cornell for mechanical engineering, Columbia for arts and Hawaii for 'surfing and other pastimes [!] before dallying with advertising for a couple of years, while indulging in some mild club racing. Thereafter he teamed up with an old Cornell lawyer friend, Teddy Mayer, who had in the meanwhile actually qualified. They ran the Revson-Mayer Formula Junior team with Coopers during 1962 and then, in 1963, Revson 'emptied his small bank account, cashed in an accumulation of 21st birthday presents, and sold the little amount of stock required to pay for his college with a fine disregard for the consequences, and departed with his fighting fund of $12,000 to make the big break for Europe.

There he bought a Formula Junior Cooper and an old Thames bread van which he named 'Gilbert' and which he converted into a travelling car transporter and bedroom for himself and his mechanic, Walter Boyd, from California at $50 a week plus keep. Peter, Walter and 'Gilbert' were in business and, by the end of the season they had covered some 16,000 miles, racing all over Europe, winning one big race, and with Peter still having half his war chest in hand. No wonder he looked back on it 'as the time that racing was the sweetest . . . [when] . . . he spoke no foreign language . . . [and] . . . lived like a gipsy . . . with everything an adventure: travelling, ordering in restaurants, going through customs, in the Thames van with Walter. The results of 1963 were mixed, but at least by the end of the season people knew who Peter Revson was.' In just the same way, six to eight years later, the people of Indy and Can-Am would come to know another more mature and powerful Peter Revson.

Like Cevert, Revson also had a British 'Uncle', called Reg Parnell, Britain's first 'Mr Motor Racing' from the earliest post-World War II days. Peter's 1963 doings had not escaped Uncle Reg's notice and he offered him a place in his Formula 1 team for 1964 as a test driver along with two other young, well-heeled, four-wheeled hopefuls: the New Zealander, Chris Amon, and one of the greatest racing motor cyclists of all time, Mike Hailwood, then see-sawing between two wheels and four.

At the end of 1963, with a seventh place in a British Formula 1 race behind him, Revson's future in 1964 should have been well set had Uncle Reg not died during the winter. After that life with son Tim was just not the same. He did, however, manage to get in a couple more Formula 1 races in a Lotus-BRM at the Ring and Monza, where he was still running at the finish. The next year he ran in Europe for an entrepreneur called Ron Harris and won the prestigious Monaco Formula 3 race, not that it seemed to do much for him at the time. Although Harris was paying him £75 a race for Formula 2 events in England and £100 further afield, as well as 40 per cent of the purse, none of it seemed to be getting him anywhere, so he decided to invest in a Brabham BT8 for the new sports car series that autumn in America.

1966 found him teamed up with a lively character called Skip Scott campaigning Ford GT40s, where Revson won the GT class five times, besides winning at Spa, Sebring and Florida and holding the lead before retiring at Daytona, Monza and Le Mans. Revson thought the GT40 one of the great sports cars in history, enthusing over it at the time as 'a very well balanced car. Very easy to drive . . . responded beautifully. . . . Until then I had never driven a sports car that handled quite as well, as forgivingly or as controllably as that one. It stopped well, and for a car of its size and weight, it was very comfortable to drive.' All of which comes as no surprise to anyone who has had the luck to drive one.

Revson continued racing the big sports cars of the day without ever really making a serious break into the Majors' results before 1971. In the meantime he had made good at Indy from 1969, where he had qualified 33rd and last before finishing his underpowered car in fifth in a drive that had echoes of Wilbur Shaw's first Indy drive in 1927 with the similarly underpowered Jynx Special. Like Shaw, his fine drive brought him no rookie honours, largely because his debut had been 'so undemonstrative that he was easily overlooked, particularly by people who didn't know his road racing credentials'. He returned in 1970 with a better car, but it blew after 87 laps and, then, in 1971, came his finest Indy hour with pole position on the grid and second at the finish behind Al Unser Snr. He had also enjoyed by far his best Can-Am series for McLaren with their latest M8E Chevrolet, winning five of the races and taking the Can-Am title.

For 1972 he had hoped to concentrate on Formula 1 and Indy, but this was frustrated by Jackie Stewart's notorious mid-season ulcer, which obliged him to back up Denny Hulme in Can-Am on top of all his other commitments and problems, including Roger Penske's formidable new L & M Porsche team. It was much the same at Indy where he again qualified on the front row only to have his gearbox go after only 22 laps and, at the other lucrative races of Pocono and Ontario, where his cars lasted seven and 81 laps respectively.

In 1972 Tyrrell-Ford was not quite the winner it had been in 1971 so that Stewart and François found themselves second and sixth in the rankings instead of first and third. François's points came from a third at Clermont-Ferrand and two seconds at Nivelles and at Watkins. The American race was notable for the first Formula 1 appearance of the ferocious Jody Scheckter driving an M19 McLaren, where he eventually placed ninth after holding fourth for much of the race until he spun out on a newly damp surface and lost time restarting.

Much more was to be heard of McLaren's 'Baby Bear' in 1973, and not least by Peter Revson, who had excelled himself for McLaren in 1972 by taking fifth in the title rankings, as the just reward for a new-found consistency, which saw him placed second (twice), third (thrice), and fourth and fifth (once each), besides seventh in Belgium. Of course, it did not match Emerson Fittipaldi's champion's card of five wins, two seconds and a third, but it was, none the less, a sterling effort by a man who had been so long absent from Formula 1, and promised very well for 1973 when McLaren's new M23 was expected.

With the new car Revson's continued consistency proved better still in 1973 with another fifth ranking derived from two wins, one second, one third, two fourths and two fifths. This put him one place and 12 points ahead of his team leader, Denny Hulme, and way above Scheckter who, for all his brilliance, had still to open his score. At the same time, as they came up to Watkins Glen and, at the end of the season, François, with fourth ranking and 47 points from his 14 races, had done rather better than Revson in what should have been another season of his admirable consistency. At this point, however, both their golden futures suddenly began to look very different: wide open for Cevert, but fast narrowing for Revson. Cevert's future with Tyrrell still seemed boundless, although he had really still to prove himself convincingly. By contrast, Revson's options were clouding over with uncertainty as his hopes shuttled anxiously between McLaren, Ferrari and Shadow, and he himself went on looking for the right, or indeed any, opening.

First, with McLaren:

> Teddy (Mayer) is really unpredictable. I won the British Grand Prix and Teddy fired me. At Ontario I failed to finish and I wasn't out of the car ten minutes when he told me he wanted to make me an offer! . . . and complimented me on my driving during the previous two months!

And all this at a time when Mayer had already given Scheckter a three-year contract! Surprising?—well, not really if you look ahead to the way Mayer and McLaren messed Villeneuve about in the early autumn 1977 (see page 313).

Back in 1973 it was no wonder that Revson found himself inclining more and more towards the Shadowy newcomers, if only because 'any team that had the determination Shadow seemed to have was sure to get better.' Good enough thinking, perhaps, save that it ignored the possibility of time running out on him in the way that it did on Cevert shortly before midday on 6 October 1973.

By then Revson was fed up with being McLaren's 'Odd pig in the litter', a situation which, perversely, he shared with Scheckter, for whom the future was beginning to seem every bit as doubtful, until Fate decided everything in one stunning blow.

François had damaged his ankles in a crash a fortnight earlier in Canada and they were still bandaged when Watkins practice began. However, this did not stop him making second best time in the first practice session, about 3/4 secs slower than 'maestro' Stewart. The next day François went out determined, as he told Ken Tyrrell: 'To get on pole!' But, as Ken said later: 'It wasn't to be. He just lost it . . . on that part of the circuit where the track went over the entrance road and the guard rail was right up close to the track. The car went between two guard rails and forced them apart.' One wonders, with hindsight, whether he had been one hundred per cent fully fit and strong enough to have hazarded so determined an assault on that dangerous and difficult part of the circuit. But that is something we shall never know.

As it was, at one fell stroke of misfortune, Ken Tyrrell lost his King of 'Gran' Pree', when Stewart's long planned retirement had to be made public, and his Crown Prince on the lethal guard rails of Watkins Glen. In the aftermath, Stewart never raced again; Scheckter went over to fill the first of the blank spaces chez Tyrrell, with fierce little Patrick Depailler as his No. 2, and Revson followed his hunch and signed up with Shadow.

Mark Donohue, whom we left copping out on Watkins Glen in favour of a domestic USAC race at Trenton, New Jersey, united the very remarkable combination of a road and track race driver with that of a technical boffin: like another Andretti or McLaren in the making, he had started out in sports car racing, culminating with Can-Am and Trans-Am, before graduating to Indy in 1969, where he finished seventh with 190 laps covered to become 'Rookie of the Year'. The next year he took a close second behind Al Unser Snr and, two years later, in 1972, he won, made fastest lap and set a race record average of 162.96 mph, which was to last right through to 1984 when Rick Mears raised it marginally to 163.612 mph.

In the autumn of 1970 he and Roger Penske visited England to suss out possible Indy cars for 1971 and Penske fell straight away for the M16A McLaren: 'Build me one!' he said and, in due time, the proto-type was being tested by Denny Hulme and Peter Revson before being passed on to Donohue and Penske. This car became the dark blue and yellow racer sponsored by Penske for Sunoco Oil and driven by Dono-hue. In 1971 he led with it for 61 laps at Indy before his gearbox broke. The car was then rebuilt and won the inaugural Pocono 500 at Michi-gan. Two new cars were then built for Penske's 1972 season, one for Donohue and the other for Gary Bettenhausen. This time Donohue set his long-standing Indy record and the next year he drove his last 500s, classifying 15th at Indy after 92 laps when he retired with piston trouble, and 17th at Pocono after 104 laps, retiring again with piston trouble.

In the meantime he had turned his hand to the world of Formula 1 in the very wet and misty Canadian Grand Prix of 1971 at Mosport, where he drove a works McLaren-Ford into third, which was thought a particularly good effort for a Grand Prix rookie, especially in that kind of weather. Donohue then gave Formula 1 a miss until Penske inveigled him back into the fold to do two races at the end of 1974 in his new Penske-Ford, which he ran on into 1975 with little success. Donohue's last appearance was in practice on the Österreichring, where he crashed heavily and later succumbed to his injuries. Altogether he raced in 14 Grands Prix between 1971 and 1975 from which he salvaged just eight championship points.

Strangely enough, he claimed none of the credit for his many successes in domestic American racing as being down to his Bachelor's degree in mechanical engineering from Brown University in 1959. He used to say that his knowledge of the technical side of racing gave him no sort of advantage either. His college background, no less than the wide variety of the cars that he raced, had made him an object of some suspicion to some of the more hide-bound, stereotyped Indy crowd. But men like Clark, Hill and Donohue himself were difficult to ignore at Indy for very long because of their uncomfortable habit of doing rather well there!

I once heard Donohue described at trackside as 'a Captain Nice if ever there was one', but just what did he achieve among the Mr Nasties? Certainly neither he nor his talented sponsor, Roger Penske, had achieved much from their trips to Europe save to acquire some much needed British-built hardware for their Indy and Can-Am cars, and then to race them very successfully in America. His reputation must, therefore, rest almost entirely on his domestic American record, most particularly at Indy for his long-standing race record from 1972.

Donohue was 38 when he died, but there was nothing otherwise to suggest that, for all his promise and versatility, he would ever have attained the achievements of Andretti or Bruce McLaren. By contrast, at the end of 1973, it was Revson who was being hailed as USA's most versatile driver, who was expected to win at least two Grands Prix in 1974. He certainly had a solid background of success from his five seasons and 30 races in Formula 1 which included two Formula 1 wins in 1973, backed by second and fifth at Indy in 1969/71, including pole position in 1971 from a new qualifying record of 178.696 mph, and a qualifying record at Pocono of 190.648 mph, which stood until 1982 when Rick Mears raised it to 200.983 mph. Although, strictly speaking, Can-Am is no part of Grand Prix racing, Revson was no mean performer there either and, in 1971, he took four firsts, two seconds, one fourth and one seventh in ten races and, the next year, one first, one second, one third and one seventh from nine races, while Cevert also chipped in for 1972 with first, second, third and seventh from nine Can-Am races.

In the final analysis, how good were this new decade's golden lads? With Cevert it was still difficult to judge, even after four seasons, although the unkind thought must persist that if he had had the qualities of a Stewart, Peterson or Fittipaldi from those times, he ought to have been showing them off rather more convincingly than he was by the end of 1973, when just one win could surely not have made a sufficient summer, despite its accompanying ten second places.

As for Revson he had won two Grands Prix with a good back-up of places, and had demonstrated a great deal more ability both to lead and actually win a wide variety of races, be they Grands Prix, Can-Am, USAC or Indy. There was, however, nothing in Shadow's record to suggest that things would have been any different had Revson survived to lead them after his death in yet another miserable guard rail accident in practice before Kyalami in March of 1974.

The title of Revson's biography—Speed With Style—could really have been coined for François as well, for both men were Fast Movers in every sense of the words. With his dark, dashing looks and, above all, his eyes, the ladies must have been dazzled like moths to Cevert's gleaming candle. And if, as the World War II song has it,

> Morale
> Is the gal
> By your side

... then Peter Revson had it with bells on, too, with his 'just good friend', the recently crowned Miss World, Marji Wallace, however, fleeting those joys might be.

PART 9

THE SILKEN TOUCH

Chapter 29

'Sunbeams Scorching All the Day'

Dario Resta
(Born 1884: Died 2 September 1924 at Brooklands track during record attempts with a Grand Prix Sunbeam)

Sir Henry Segrave
(Born 22 September 1896: Died 13 June 1930 during attempt on the World Water Speed Record on Lake Windermere)

'Automobile racing is something one must do consistently or one loses the urge and ability to compete.'—*Dario Resta*

'She'll be alright, Sir, the 13th is my lucky day.'—*Michael Wilcocks, riding engineer with Sir Henry Segrave*

And, come the end of this part, some might say that Resta should never have tempted providence with a come-back, while Segrave should surely have waited just a few days longer until he had enough armoured life jackets for his crew and himself.

As it turned out, Resta's comeback proved fatal to him in September 1924, while a little patience on Segrave's part would have given him the added protection of an armoured jacket and perhaps enabled him to survive the accident to his record boat, Miss England II.

Both men were long serving, dyed-in-the wool men of Sunbeam, whose paths did not cross until the early twenties, although they had both been in America in 1918: Segrave as part of a British Aviation Mission in Washington and Resta, who was still racing on the new speedways, though no longer with the great success of 1915/16.

Segrave was born in 1896 and, like Dick Seaman in later years, he had been fascinated by cars and engines since earliest boyhood, with his father's motor servant, one Wilson, being his favourite human being for letting him drive his father's cars from the age of nine! And what a well-kept bag of secrets that must have been, for Segrave's father never got wind of their exploits till 1936, when the principal actor had been dead for six years! The young Segrave is described as having driven 'many miles without thought of danger, and Wilson being far the more nervous at first!'

Like most of his generation Segrave found himself in action in France by 1915 as a subaltern in the Royal Warwicks. He was badly wounded that May and was not fully recovered till October, when he was posted to the RFC flying school at Upavon. The training of pilots in those days was little longer than their average three week expectancy of life once they got into action. Segrave received his 'wings' on 1 January 1916, having flown a variety of the trainers of those days: Farman Longhorns, BE2Cs and RE5s and 7s, as well as a 'rotten machine the Arroll-Johnston people are turning out'. Curiously enough, Resta had made his Coupe de l'Auto début in a car of that name in 1911 before going to Sunbeam for 1912.

Then, as a result of a flying accident, the recently promoted Captain Segrave was posted to the War Office, complete with a 120 hp Itala, which his father described as 'a devil of a brute'. Towards the end of the year (1916), he met the lady he was soon to marry, a bright young musical comedy actress, Doris Stocker, who had caught the eye of the great impressario, George Edwardes. They were married in October 1917 after Segrave had completed another tour of duty in France. Through all that period he had endured a lot of pain from his injured left foot, which could have been amputated but for the timely intervention of a very skilled surgeon. Even then he was left with what he used to call his permanent 'fatigue gauge', which made him limp at times of overwork or stress, and which cannot have been eased by the big, heavy clutches of those days, not least when it came to racing.

Promoted once again, Major Segrave arrived in America on 18 June 1918, bringing with him his wife and their bulldog, to assist the British Mission in the development of military aviation and training. It had been a perilous crossing, running the gauntlet of the encircling German U-boats before they reached the safety of Halifax. On the way down to Washington Segrave picked up a smart, open 60 hp Apperson in New York and, soon after, on a trip to celebrate their wedding anniversary, his wife introduced him to Bill Brown, brother of the renowned David Bruce-Brown.

By 1918 racing had ground virtually to a halt, even in America, but Segrave's latent enthusiasm for fast motoring was quickly fired by Bill Brown and he soon found his way to the Sheepshead Bay Speedway and gave the Apperson a real outing. At first he wisely took things quietly on the unfamiliar two-mile board track with its steeply banked corners, but presently he found he could work up to over 80 mph, and was actually clocked on one lap at 82. This earned him an engraved plaque to put on the Apperson's dashboard.

After the war Segrave started racing at Brooklands with a Grand Prix Opel from 1914 and, by the end of 1920, he had become something of a 'name' at the track, even attracting the favourable notice of Sunbeam's 'patron', the sardonic Louis Coatalen. A new-found friendship with Kenelm Lee Guinness helped, but Coatalen remained obdurately non-committal about Segrave's Sunbeam prospects for some time before he invited him to drive one of his cars in the forthcoming French Grand Prix of 1921. It mattered not a rush to Segrave that he would have to pay all his expenses for himself, other than his entry fee, or that he would have to foot the bill for any damage he might cause to his patron's precious car, for he also had Coatalen's promise of the possibility of a team place if he could only finish the race.

Guinness had made him competitions manager of his KLG plug business, but Segrave was still going to need much more than just luck if he were ever to achieve his greatest ambition of winning a Grand Prix. Even his friend Guinness was discouraging: 'Good God, man, don't be a damned fool! No British driver has ever finished in the Grand Prix!', which was not strictly true, for by 1914 at least half a dozen British drivers had finished in one or other of the Grands Prix of 1906/08 and 1912/14—particularly if one counted Resta as British.

In fact Resta was Italian, having been born at Livorno in 1884, although some accounts place his birth in Milan in 1882. Of the two I prefer the later date. Resta was the son of a cavalry officer who had decided to emigrate to England in 1886, where he took up studio photography. At the age of 23, Resta took part in the opening meeting at Brooklands on 6 July 1907 and also the well-remembered and emotive closing meeting on the eve of World War I on 3 August 1914. In the earlier event he drove a 1906 Grand Prix Mercedes and would surely have won his race but for a signaller's error. He did rather better in 1914, when he won the Lightning Long Handicap in Louis Coatalen's V-12 Sunbeam.

In between times his first race of international note had been the (French) Grand Prix of 1908 at Dieppe where he drove one of Herbert Austin's 9-litre straight-sixes along with the early racing driver and aeronaut, J. T. C. Moore-Brabazon, later a cabinet minister and Lord Brabazon of Tara, and Warwick Wright, a well-known motor dealer and sportsman. Although these cars suffered the double disadvantage of being over-weight and under-powered, they were at least reliable and enabled 'Brab' and Resta to finish within four mins of one another, in 18th and 19th out of 23 finishers.

Resta reappeared in the Coupe de l'Auto of 1911 in an Arroll-Johnston in which he finished eighth before 1912's 'Little and Large' combination of formule libre and 3-litre cubic capacity cars produced some very interesting racing, wherein the British 'voiturettes' of Sunbeam and Vauxhall figured very prominently. Resta himself finished fourth overall and led the 3-litre class in his Sunbeam at the end of the first day but was pipped to the post by Rigal's Sunbeam for the Coupe at the end of the second day by 75.8 secs, after 14.5 hrs' racing. In 1913 the Grand Prix and the Coupe were run separately. The Sunbeams raced soundly but without distinction, with Resta placing sixth in the Grand Prix and Guinness third in the Coupe. The next year Coatalen had stronger meat in mind and it was no surprise to find him raiding the Peugeot design bank for his 1914 Grand Prix engine. Mercedes took 1-2-3, followed by Goux's 'Peugeot-Peugeot' and what one could call Resta's 'Sunbeam-Peugeot' in fifth and, with that, it was time for everyone to put their mechanical toys away and go to war. . . . Or was it?

As was also to happen in 1939, America opted for a period of neutrality before getting embroiled in World War I and put that time to wonderfully good use by laying the foundations of a new mechanical empire, for the racing of the twenties and beyond that was to be so richly built on by men like the Duesenbergs, the Chevrolets, Harry Miller, Leo Goossen and Fred Offenhauser.

After the Grand Prix of 1914 Resta travelled to America on business and was quickly persuaded to drive Peugeots for the American importers, for whom he achieved spectacular success on road, board and track races, chiefly during 1915 and 1916. The records of American board track racing from 1915 to 1931 show that only a dozen native American drivers scored more championship points than Resta from what was, for him, only a couple of seasons of full-time racing. In addition he was and remains the only non-American driver to have won the coveted AAA Championship (from 1916), the Board Track title from 1915 and the highest winning race purse ($23,000 from the Chicago 500 mile race of 1915). Lastly, of the drivers who started ten or more championship races, the four with the best winning percentages were:

Frank Lockhart	36.3%
Jimmy Murphy	36.0%
DARIO RESTA	31.5%
Louis Chevrolet	31.2%

The lone wolf from over the seas had certainly raced in the impressive best company during his greatest years on the boards.

His record at Indy and in the great road races of 1915/16 was no less impressive. In 1915, over the treacherous 3.84-mile aboriginal street circuit at San Francisco, he led almost throughout in both the Grand Prize and Vanderbilt Cup races and won both from Howdy Wilcox's potent Stutz. He had a harder task at Indy when his 1913 Peugeot came up against the 1914 Mercedes of Ralph de Palma. Both cars made two pit stops in the race, and that of the Mercedes was the smarter, which may have accounted for de Palma's narrow winning margin: that and the steering problems that Resta met with during the last phase of the race, when he had to slow deliberately to ensure placing second once victory seemed beyond hope. As it turned out, he might well have pressed on and snatched a last gasp win from de Palma after his Mercedes broke a con-rod three laps from the end. However, for once, luck—and a considerable degree of skill—rode with de Palma as he coaxed his suffering car over the line still with three-and-a-half minutes to spare.

Resta went on to win the Chicago 500 and its bumper purse in the absence of de Palma, and by October of that year he had a more up-to-date Peugeot from 1914 at his disposal, as did both Johnny Aitken and Howdy Wilcox, two of his greatest rivals. His first appearance with the newer car was at the inauguration of Sheepshead Bay Speedway that October and the occasion is typically described by Russ Catlin in Dick Wallen's colourful and splendid book: *Board Track, Guts, Gold and Glory*:

> Socialite Mrs Orson Kilborn wasted a good bottle of Harkness champagne by smashing it over a retaining wall with the words: 'I christen thee Sheepshead Bay Speedway to the glory of the God of Speed,' and upwards of 12,000 spectators held their collective breaths as Dario Resta and his Peugeot gave them ample reason to. The transplanted Italian with the broad Oxford accent sent his speeding car over the slick surface at an average speed of 108 mph for ten miles in an exhibition run.

Resta, with or without his Oxford accent, did not fare so well in the first race of 350 miles for the Astor Cup, in spite of a record lap of 115.76 mph, as he retired with a broken crank after only 51 of 175 laps. He did better in November, winning the 100-miler for the Harkness Gold Metal but, thereafter, his luck deserted him with three retirements from a variety of mechanical disasters despite a trip to Europe in the winter to replenish his spares and refit his car for its 1916 campaign.

The 500 was cut down to 300 miles, and Resta ran out an easy winner in the continued absence of de Palma's Mercedes. A few weeks later de Palma brought the Merc out of purdah for the Chicago 300, where Resta beat him in a desperate struggle after de Palma was slowed by a plug failure at the very end of the race.

The last big races before America went to war were for the Grand Prize and the Vanderbilt Cup over an 8.4-mile circuit at Santa Monica in November 1916. Resta started well enough by winning the Vanderbilt easily from Earl Cooper's Stutz, but struck ignition trouble after a third of the Grand Prize. Of his main rivals, Aitken had broken a piston on the first lap and Resta's troubles seemed to leave the race securely in Wilcox's hands. However, the end of the season's AAA championship points and its bags of gold were at stake, and this set in train an undignified series of backstairs ploys between Resta and Aitken, who were the nearest challengers for the richly endowed title.

First, Aitken took over Wilcox's Peugeot and then Resta actually tried to buy Cooper's second-placed Stutz for spot cash after having protested, though unsuccessfully, against Aitken's take-over! Eventually Aitken ran out winner on the road by over six minutes from

Cooper, although Resta remained 'Champion' after the AAA's ruling that Wilcox was the legal winner of the race!

Some racing still continued despite America's ultimate entry into World War I, although Resta himself ceased to play any serious part in it after 1916, with his place, and that of his Peugeot, being taken by the Frontenacs, Packards and Duesenbergs from 1917, and soon after, the Millers. The Chevrolet brothers, with their Frontenacs, won every National Championship race in 1917/18, while Resta had to be content with 18th place—in a Frontenac!—and retirement with a broken camshaft housing at Sheepshead Bay in November 1917. The days of Peugeot and, as it seemed, of Resta himself, were over.

By 1923 the wheel had come very much full circle, with Segrave basking in the European limelight as winner of the French Grand Prix for Sunbeam, and Resta still equally in the shadows, whether with Packard in 1923 in America or Sunbeam in Europe, at first in 1922, and later in 1924.

By May 1924 the Sunbeam Grand Prix cars were ready to race, and Resta lost no time in getting his hand in, winning a couple of domestic British hill climbs before taking second place behind Guinness in the voiturette Grand Prix of Geneva. Although the Sunbeams were subsequently proved to be the fastest cars on the course at Lyons in the French Grand Prix, their speed brought them but labour and sorrow because of the faulty magnetos they had fitted on the eve of the race at the behest of their suppliers, Bosch. The high inspiration of Segrave's bravura start soon petered away into a distant fifth behind the new forces of Alfa-Romeo and Delage with his fastest race lap a scant consolation.

Resta's next major race was to have been the Grand Prix of San Sebastian on 25 September, where he, Segrave and Guinness were due to drive the works Sunbeams once again. However, tragedy had intervened a month earlier when Resta blew a rear tyre at over 120 mph while attacking some class records at Brooklands. A rear wheel locked solid and not all of Resta's great skill and experience could save him from the ensuing fatal accident although, happily, his mechanic, Bill Perkins, escaped with burns and cuts. At San Sebastian it was Guinness's turn to meet disaster, skidding in a rut on the muddy surface. Guinness escaped with his life, but his mechanic was killed instantly, while Segrave duly won the race although he was denied a return match at Monza against his great Alfa-Romeo rivals from Lyons. However, *Excelsior* of Bilbao was so impressed with his performance that it prophetically styled him 'El Maestro Completo'.

Segrave went on race driving into 1926 before attacking the World's Land Speed Record (LSR), first in the lumpish 1000 hp Sunbeam and then in its beautiful successor, 'The Golden Arrow', before he turned to the speed boats that were to be the death of him. His first successes on water were with the 8 hp 'Meteorite' in May and June of 1927, but, being Segrave, he was soon after bigger game with, first, the 500 hp

'Miss Alacrity' and then the 930 hp 'Miss England', winning races in Italy, Germany and USA during 1928/29. These included the European Championship of 1929 at Venice, where he also set a new water speed record of 92.8 mph in 'Miss England' to add to 'Golden Arrow's' LSR from March of that year.

1929 was an *Annus Mirabilis* for Segrave, with his dual speed records on land and sea being crowned by his Knighthood on 27 May—for which he arrived 20 minutes late! Happily the bluff, hearty old Monarch had a soft spot for knights like Segrave and Alan Cobham. Before the King administered the honour to Sir Alan he had described it as a 'Real Knighthood' and he was no less gracious to Segrave, even pulling his leg for his lateness in this dialogue: 'You're late, my boy—you're late, you're late!' he joked as Segrave explained that he had been held up by three level crossings only to receive the Royal riposte: 'There you are, you see . . . a speed king—held up by a mere railway train!' After which, the honour conferred, the King invited Segrave into the garden for what was, obviously, a very happy occasion for both men, before he took lunch with the Queen and her Household.

Segrave died at the age of 33 on the 13 June 1930, about two-and-a-half hours after 'Miss England II' crashed, in the sure knowledge that a world record of 98.76 mph had been won and that he had also attained an unofficial 119.8 mph on the third and fatal run. He left behind him the memory of a man of elusive genius and attainment, both physically and elementally always on the move, yet a man with no loose ends about him and not a particle of bone, muscle or brain lying idle, for whom the lines . . .

> Or vie with Segrave, who, with equal skill,
> Wins races, records, board room seats at will.

. . . might well have been his epitaph and, with it all, managing to find the time for a whole heap of good old fashioned fun as well; not just a Completo Maestro, but a Complete Man as well.

Set beside the glittering Segrave, Resta might have seemed a relative nobody at first sight, but in reality he was nothing of the kind. For a start, his sweeping successes in America during 1915/16 had all been achieved in cars that were already past their first youth and operating far from their original French manufactories—rather like the W154 Mercedes-Benz that came to Indy in 1947/49—and with the added disadvantage of being involved in World War I.

Resta himself was a small man with no really commanding features to compare with the burly panache of Georges Boillot, or the muscular beef and cigar toting swagger of Barney Oldfield. Yet he became the first man to outsmart the Americans, and all ends up at their own games and on their own pitches. He had also become adept in the sports of both roller and ice skating, in which he had won championships in London, where he had also proved himself a successful businessman as he was also to do in America.

In 1915, by Peter Helck's account in *The Checkered Flag*, Resta 'had acquired a wife with understanding of the sport and profession, the sister of the late and excellent driver, Spencer Wishart. Like the ladies of the later luminaries [such as Baby Hoffman, Caracciola's well known wife], she held the stop watches and checked the Resta code of regularity.' And no mean code it can have been to judge by the tidal wave of his victories that overwhelmed the American scene of those years.

Viewed in this light, Resta must surely have been an archetypal version of Mario Andretti as the Great All-Rounder of Road, Track, Board and even Dirt: a veritable Man For All Seasons in worlds both old and new.

More than 50 years after Resta's death I came to hear of a Mrs M. Resta living in what was then my home town of Folkestone, but by then the trail had gone cold, although a collector of my acquaintance told me some time later that he had come by a silver racing cup that he had bought from a silversmith and believed to have been among the old lady's relics. A busy life has many drawbacks and I was sorry to have missed the chance of meeting such an interesting survivor of bygone days.

Chapter 30

A Very Gallant French Gentleman

Robert Benoist

(Born 21 March 1895 at Rambouillet, France: Died 12 September 1944 at Buchenwald concentration camp)

If Georges Boillot failed marginally to achieve a Grand Slam of three French Grand Prix victories in three successive years, that great driver's gallant omission was more than made good in 1927 by his successor in French championship, Robert Benoist. Born in Auffargis in 1895, Benoist was working as a mechanic when World War I broke out in 1914, and did not take long to enlist in the French Air Force by 1915. His gentle touch at the controls of any machine, allied to the speed of his reflexes, ensured that he soon became a skilled pilot and, unlike Georges, he survived the war. He then set about making a far greater name for himself as a competition driver, first in rallies, before getting a factory drive with Salmson for a couple of years in voiturette racing. This brought him to the notice of Louis Delage, who snapped him up to drive his new V-12 2-litre Grand Prix car in 1924 alongside the veteran René Thomas, who had won the Indy 500 for Delage ten years before, and another Frenchman, Albert Divo, newly brought over from Louis Coatalen's Sunbeam-Talbot-Darracq group. Both men were an instant success, with Benoist finishing third in the great French Grand prix of 1924 behind Divo and the winner, Campari, with the equally new P2 Alfa-Romeo.

The next year Benoist went one better by winning the French Grand Prix at Montlhéry. Inevitably it was a bitter-sweet victory for so sensitive a man, for its being won at the expense of the tragic death of Antonio Ascari and the consequent withdrawal of the other Alfa-Romeos of Brilli-Peri and Campari. There is little doubt that one of the Alfas would otherwise have won the race. As it was, Benoist's victory was shared with Divo, who had taken over from him for part of the race, but very sportingly returned the wheel to him towards the end of the race to give him the honour of receiving the winner's chequered flag at the finish. After the presentation ceremony, Benoist, like the true gentleman he always was, immediately got back into his racing car and drove, with his team-mate, Louis Wagner, to the scene of Ascari's crash to leave their winners' garlands as a mark of respect for their great competitor.

Benoist drove on through 1926 and 1927 with Delage, whose new 1.5-litre cars proved troublesome and uncomfortable during 1926 before coming into their own, especially for Benoist himself, through 1927 when he won all four of the Grands Prix 'Majors': those of France, Spain, Italy (also European) and Great Britain. At that time, only Felice Nazzaro, in 1907, could boast a comparable record—from the Targa Florio, Kaiserpreis and French Grand Prix races.

Thereafter Benoist's racing career virtually disappeared. Louis Delage had had to give up racing for financial reasons as Grand Prix racing hit another of its doldrums, which left only Bugatti, for whom Benoist drove sporadically and with little success till 1937, when he shared the winning wheel at Le Mans with Jean-Pierre Wimille in a streamlined 3.3-litre Type 57 Bugatti. It was to be the last race of his life and, within 18 months, he had been recalled to the colours for a short spell that ended with the Munich climb-down of 1938 and a brief return to the Bugatti works. Of course this did not last and the outbreak of World War II in 1939 saw Benoist, at the age of 44, back in uniform, but far away from flying again.

After the fall of France he naturally sought to rejoin his unit, but found it was on its way south, and that the roads were blocked by the inevitable trains of refugees fleeing from the pursuing Germans. In those circumstances not even his 57S Bugatti road car was likely to be of much use. Then, to crown it all, he was stopped by a German officer, with obvious designs on the Bugatti, who put both car and driver under armed guard in a military convoy. Although this enabled Benoist to get his car fuelled up, any further escape seemed out of the question with his captor so clearly determined to hang on to his precious war loot!

However, the next morning Benoist had a stroke of luck when the convoy slowed down and he found himself conveniently close to a small side road. A quick drop into bottom gear and a well applied right foot worked wonders and, by the time the astonished Germans realized what had happened, Benoist and his car were to hell and gone over the hills and far away to fight another day.

After that Benoist ultimately joined the Resistance and took over the group that had been led, until his capture by the Germans, by another racing driver, known as 'Williams', whose full name appears on page 290. Benoist was finally caught on 18 June 1944, soon after the D-day landings in Normandy, and taken to the grim Fresnes prison. His biographer and friend, Roger Labric, who was also a racing driver, has told of Benoist's iron fortitude in the face of degradation and torture, coupled with the usual mocking threats and promises of being allowed to see his elderly mother who was by then either under arrest herself or dead. Nothing could be found to break his resolve, not even removal to Buchenwald on 17 August, where he was numbered 13.092 and subjected to further indignity and torture until his execution, along with 32 others, in the dark on 12 September 1944. Accounts of these dates vary slightly. Mine is taken from Labric's biography of Benoist, written/published in August/November 1945. However, the profile of Benoist by Maurice Henry in the 1946 Bois de Boulogne race programme refers to 8 August 1944 as the date of his removal to Buchenwald and to 14 September as that of his death. There had actually been 36 prisoners in his block, four of whom escaped through an exchange of identity papers—two British and two French, one of whom was Yeo-Thomas, known as 'The White Rabbit'. Neither of the two lucky Frenchmen was Robert Benoist.

Benoist, like Boillot, a year before him, had flown above Verdun as a fighter pilot and, in the same way as Louis Renault, he would surely have preferred a fighting end in the sky, like Boillot's from 1916, to execution by the Germans in an underground cell. Boillot and Benoist, and his friend 'Williams' were officers and gentlemen of high courage and patriotic pride, in the mould of Captain Oates, who were not afraid to face an uncompromising fate when their dark hours came.

Barely 12 months later, French motor racing was proudly commemorating the lives of at least two of these three men in a series of three races held in the Bois de Boulogne, for the Coupe Robert Benoist, the Coupe de la Liberation and the Coupe des Prisonniers, with a goodly assembly of Benoist's old friends and rivals, most notably, Raymond Sommer, Louis Gerard and Philippe Etancelin, who led off the line in the third of these races, and Jean-Pierre Wimille who actually won it.

It had to be a very special and moving occasion.

Chapter 31
The Quest for a New Master Driver

Jean-Pierre Wimille

(Born 26 February 1908: Died 28 January 1949 in early morning practice at Buenos Aires)

There had been sporadic attempts to set up different forms of championship in the twenties and, most latterly, in 1931, but it was not until 1935 that a championship with some semblance of system—though, one fears, of little intelligibility to the world at large—was set up. It was styled the European Championship and was won three times by Caracciola (1935, 37/38) and once by each of Rosemeyer (1936) and Lang (1939). Although Grand Prix racing had re-started, however falteringly, in the Bois de Boulogne on 9 September 1945, no move was made to revive the championship of the later thirties until the current system was proposed to the FIA in 1949 by the Marchese Antonio Brivio as a World Championship for drivers. The General Assembly of the FIA were quick to agree and the Italian Automobile Club, whose brainchild it was, felt that they could look forward to a long period of continued Italian domination of the sport. The 'World' tag was always to be a bit of a misnomer, for participation, whether in America by Europeans or vice versa, was always very thinly spread, and the Union of the Two Worlds petered out after 1960 so far as the 'World' Championship was concerned. During the 11 years of its life only Alberto Ascari drove in an Indy 500, in 1952 with a Ferrari, while two Indy drivers raced in Formula 1, Troy Ruttman in the 1958 French Grand Prix, driving a 250F Maserati into tenth place, and Rodger Ward in the 1959 US Grand Prix in a Kurtis-Craft which lasted just twelve laps.

The current championship series has now lasted over 40 years so that any follower of the sport would have to be at least 40 himself to have lived in a time when the World Title was not up for grabs. This in no way obscured the existence of a Master Driver through the period of interregnum between Lang's European title from 1939 and Farina's shining new World one in 1950.

Between 1928 and 1933 the great drivers of the 750 kg period were learning and perfecting their arts, and the foundations of their modern technique of Grand Prix racing were being excavated, if not actually laid, by the five Great Men of those years—Nuvolari, Varzi, Chiron, Caracciola and Fagioli—and then passed on to their acolytes of whom Jean-Pierre Wimille was to prove a very worthy member.

Wimille started out in Grands Prix in 1930. Like Varzi, he soon became recognized as an immaculate, impeccable stylist, who rarely put a wheel wrong and, not surprisingly, the great Fangio himself learnt much from Wimille—and Varzi—when they were in their maturer post-World War II years. Thus Wimille was to remark of Fangio: 'If one day he has a car that is right for his temperament, Fangio will perform miracles.' Tragically, neither he, nor Varzi, lived to see the fulfilment of their view of Fangio or, for that matter, to have driven seriously against him in their native Europe.

Wimille had been born in 1906, and first appeared on a Grand Prix grid in the French Grand Prix at Pau on 21 September 1930. This was not the famous street circuit, but the 9.8-mile Circuit de Morlaas outside the town and was run off in four classes. Jean-Pierre drove a privately entered Type 37A Bugatti and retired after only two laps with supercharger trouble. He persisted with Bugattis through the long and gruelling ten-hour Grand Prix series of 1931 with his best placing a fourth in the Italian 'Major' and eighth on the Ring. All good steady, proving stuff, but little enough copy for his journalist father to write up as yet!

He continued in this vein through 1932, picking up a win at Oran and leading at half distance at Casablanca, before acquiring a Monza Alfa at the end of the year and winning the minor Grand Prix of Lorraine at Nancy. Between 1933 and 1939 most of his races were won either in sports car events or lesser Grands Prix, which was the inevitable lot of any driver, whoever he might be, who could not get a drive with either of the all-powerful German teams or, at worst, Alfa-Romeo. His luck turned in 1938, when he was invited to drive, first, for Bugatti, then Alfa-Romeo and, finally, for Mercedes-Benz in 1939. That last tempting offer came too late in the war-clouded scenes of 1939 and so he had to be content with a last fling for Bugatti before the balloon went up in early September.

Like Robert Benoist he had enlisted in the French Air Force before joining the Resistance after France fell. Thereafter he served in North Africa as a military liaison officer before returning to Paris in time to take part in the highly emotive Bois de Boulogne races of September 1945. Its programme read like a long roll of battle honours: Philippe Etancelin with his faithful old Monza Alfa from the early thirties, in which he had so narrowly failed to win the French Grand Prix in 1933 when Jean-Pierre was still a hard-driving young shaver, with his way still to make in the world; Louis Gerard, with his single seater Maserati, with whom he had fought tooth-and-nail in the 1939 Le Mans '24'; Ernst Friderich, the veteran henchman of Ettore Bugatti from Edwardian days; Delahaye's pre-war stars—Chaboud, Grignard and Villeneuve; 'Coeur de Lion' Sommer himself with his Talbot and the future Maire, Maurice Trintignant, with the family Type 51 Bugatti that he had driven into fifth at Pau in 1938, when Dreyfus had scored his unbelievable win over the Mercedes of Lang and Caracciola. What a wonderful knitting up of old friendships it must have been, despite the sad autumnal tinge brought home by the programme's references to 'Willy Williams, Grand Champion et Grand Resistant' and the titles of the races themselves for the 'Coupes— Robert Benoist, de la Liberation and des Prisonniers.'

With all that, what better driver-car combination could there have been to win the main event than Jean-Pierre and his 4.7-litre Bugatti Monoplace? And, what more typically French ending to the day when Trintignant's trusty old racer 'died' of fuel starvation caused by an over-accumulation of 'Petoulets' (rat droppings) at the bottom of his fuel tank, that had obviously been harbouring generations of such rodents throughout the war? Surely a scene straight from 'Clochemerle' itself, especially when the joke was explained to Jean-Pierre after the race and he nearly died of laughter, before recovering sufficiently to tell Maurice that he was the biggest 'Petoule' of them all, which promptly assured him the nickname 'Petoulet'.

Come 1946, and Jean-Pierre was invited to rejoin Alfa-Romeo, where he remained their leading light until the end of 1948 when they retired for a year. Jean-Pierre had always had a soft spot for the little Simca-Gordini single-seaters of the period and he took an enlarged 1430 cc example down to the Argentine for the annual close season in early 1949. At around 0730 hrs on the morning of Wednesday, 26 January 1949, and in circumstances that have never been fully explained,* any more than those of Alberto Ascari and Jim Clark, he crashed fatally.

In *My Racing Life*, Fangio simply states: 'He went off on the fast Municipal Golf Club Curve. He died some minutes later.' Unlike Norma Varzi, Jean-Pierre's widow 'did not want a large-scale funeral. The wake . . . was attended only by the drivers, race officials and members of the French embassy . . . The European champion's pallbearers were his peers: Villoresi, Ascari, Farina, Fangio, Juan Galvez and the journalist Corrado Filippini.'

The tributes to this great driver were manifold. In his book *The Fast Ones* Peter Miller refers to him, perhaps a little fulsomely, as 'Possibly the greatest driver of all time.' Back in 1937, in *Motoraces*, George Monkhouse wrote: 'So far he has always competed in a much slower car, but even so he has had innumerable seconds and thirds and finished second at the Roosevelt Raceway (to Nuvolari) in 1936 . . . If Continental drivers were awarded marks on the same scale as is used by the BRDC for the Gold Star, then Wimille would have won quite easily. Nuvolari being second and Rosemeyer third (for 1936)!'

Another knowledgeable observer, Edward Eves, put it like this:

> Many experts regarded Wimille as the greatest driver of them all. Certainly he can be regarded as a link between the heroic age of driving

*My own theory on this accident and that of Raymond Sommer is to be found on pages 40/1 under the heading 'The Chipmunk Theory'.

and the modern style. For he had driven against Minoia (in 1931), a veteran of the Edwardian era, and in his final year had inspired Fangio's style, which influences drivers to this day.

What more can one say?

Chapter 32
The 'Whoosh-Bonk' Man

Bruce McLaren
(Born 30 August 1937 in Auckland, New Zealand: Died 2 June 1970 testing a Can-Am McLaren racing car at Goodwood)

Like that of Jim Clark (see pages 53/5) this is essentially a memoir of another Quiet Man and what he achieved in his tragically brief span of life. Bruce McLaren was a virtually self-taught engineer and racing driver, who soon became motor racing's 'Renaissance Man' of the sixties before his death. An all-rounder almost on a par with Mario Andretti, excelling him in some respects, though perhaps not in others, he could design his cars, build them and screw them together, race them and stay one hell of a nice guy at the same time. He owed much of this to his father's early example and teaching from his first days with their Ulster Austin in 1952, in which he took after another gifted, pragmatic engineer/racer called Chapman.

After six proving years divided between his engineering studies and the domestic 'Down Under' motor racing scene, Bruce got the chance of a trip to England under the 'Driver-to-Europe' scheme. Ken Tyrrell has long had the reputation of being an ace talent spotter, although he modestly shrugs it off as something that any fool with half an eye can see for himself, and he soon reached a conclusion about the young Bruce, whom he thought 'would become World Champion because he had the ability to think about it. He wasn't going to be the world's quickest driver, but then the world's quickest driver isn't always World Champion.' However, for once, discerning 'Uncle Ken' was to be proved not wholly right, although Bruce was quick enough to demonstrate his talent from the German Grand Prix of 1958.

From time to time this Grande Épreuve was combined with a separate class for Formula 2 cars, and Bruce made a brilliant start by winning that class just as Ickx was to do some years later in a Formula 2 Matra. He also finished fifth in the overall Grand Prix results and his performance brought him the accolade of a musical ovation from Brands Hatch's singing commentator, John Bolster, to celebrate his 21st birthday on the 30 August.

The next year brought him a works drive from Coopers, and in December of that year (at Sebring), in a full 2.5-litre Cooper-Climax, he became the youngest driver then to have won Formula 1 Grand Prix—by just .06 secs from a similar car driven by Maurice Trintignant for Rob Walker.

Yet racing was never more than a part of Bruce's achievement and he was soon being marked out as a young man with a great future in designing and constructing racing cars, as well as driving them. At the time his closest contemporaries were John Surtees and Jim Clark, who both started their Grand Prix careers with Lotus in 1960 at Monaco (Surtees) and Zandvoort (Clark). To start with, Bruce was the most successful, leading the championship after the first four races and lying equal best with team leader Brabham after five. But then Brabham closed the door with two more winners to take the 1960 title and, after that, it was Clark who established the stranglehold on success in the years to 1965, winning two world championships to Surtees's one and 19 Grands Prix to the three of Surtees and the two of Bruce. At the same time Clark had additionally stolen a march on all of them with his American successes of 1963/65. After that there was little more life at the top in Formula 1 for Bruce until he became his own Cosworth-powered constructor at the beginning of 1968.

In the interim he was cushioned from the effects of the slump in his Grand Prix fortunes by his versatility in other directions and, in particular, his growing ability 'to test drive, to be able to analyse the behaviour of a racing car at competitive track speeds . . . (that came) . . . only from a lot of experience; and experience was something that Bruce had a lot of.' By that time, as man and boy, he had been getting it together since 1949 and the time had come to put it to real practical use.

The 'Whoosh-Bonk' title came, as my old friend Eoin Young has written, from Bruce's enthusiastic assurance of the short time that cars should take to construct: 'You take the suspension off the sports car—WHOOSH!—knock up the chassis and—BONK!—there's the car!' What McLaren engineer Gordon Coppuck described as 'a classic of Bruce's cigarette-package designing. . . .' which neither he nor designer Robin Herd had anything to do with and which: 'Bruce literally designed on scraps of paper and picked out the suspension based on the previous year's sports cars.'

'Bruce knew how the car should be and how it should be laid out,' said Coppuck. 'He was also very good when it came to difficult details on the car. . . . If something looked right, it usually was right, but he [Bruce] always followed this up by saying that if it looked wrong, it was wrong. We (from 1970) will certainly miss Bruce's development on a car. Having taken the car from the drawing office and made it, and then taking it down to Goodwood to test, he could quickly put his finger on any bugs that needed sorting out. He was able to translate these problems to us and communicate well. You could talk to him and understand what he meant, and this communication between the driver and the designer [and this was probably even stronger between him and Tyler Alexander as chief mechanic] was very strong. That, was where I have learned all I know about racing,' concluded Coppuck.

Although the state of racing art is most generally associated with Formula 1 Grand Prix cars, that would have brought little financial joy to the struggling house of McLaren in the sixties. This did not come until Bruce's success in Can-Am racing gave him the chance to become properly established, which was the reason why Bruce himself had originally left Coopers to start his own racing organization.

The sorrow remains that he never lived to see its growth to fruition. Yet, almost in the same breath, you find yourself wondering if there would then have been room for a 'Whoosh-Bonk' man in that future's vastly changed scene, and what Bruce himself would have been making of it all, once shorn of his place as the Supremo who worked by sheer instinct and the seat of his intellectual pants—however grand the scale might have been.

All those thoughts were, of course, way into the future on that June morning in 1970 as Bruce drove down to his beloved Goodwood, full of exciting stories about his trip to America, to test the prototype M8D Can-Am car and then oversee the first McLaren entries at Indy. Eoin Young wrote: 'Bruce had the Can-Am championship in 1967 and 1969 and Denny (Hulme) had filled the gap in 1968. The Can-Am McLarens were unbeatable; they had won all eleven races in the championship the season before, and Bruce was anxious to get back from Indy to test the second car, which he would drive in the 1970 series. The car was ready to run on the Tuesday after the 500, but the fibreglass body had not been completed so it was decided to fit Bruce's car with the body from Denny's for the tests.'

Testing of the new car started at 1045 hrs and Bruce went out for his flying lap an hour-and-a-half later, after a variety of routine adjustments, at 1219 hrs. Three minutes later the car left the road on the main straight and crashed into the protective embankment. The car was wrecked and Bruce was dead. Investigation of the wreckage showed that a section of the tail must have lifted at around 170 mph, 'causing immediate instability and a situation that was beyond human control'.

Thinking back and using that wisdom of hindsight with which we should all be millionaires, might it not perhaps have been wiser to have waited until the new fibreglass body had been completed and fitted to the car that was meant to carry it, before embarking on those ultrahigh speed tests?

One somehow did not associate human error with Bruce, a thought that is borne out by Anthony Curtis's story of being asked, after Bruce's death, which driver he (Curtis) would have felt most safe with in a race, were he able to shrink to the size of a very small mouse and be fitted into a Grand Prix car just for the ride. Back came the unhesitating reply: 'Bruce McLaren'.

And ever since that fatal accident I have continued to experience that well-known sense of total recall of an event that is accompanied by a total suspension of its belief. With some drivers you always feel that the crazy idiot is bound to write himself off some day or other, but with Bruce McLaren (and Jim Clark): no way. They had both always seemed so safe, as well as fast, as to be totally immune from accident or injury, let alone death.

Chapter 33

A Tale of Three Evils: 1958–1973

O f all the myriad evils loosed on mankind by that mischievous young lady, Pandora—False Rumour, Deadly Poison and Cruel Fire form a uniquely hellish trinity. Mercifully, the Grand Prix world has been spared the worst excesses of the first two, but the ravages of fire have more than made up for that.

As long as racing cars remained more or less open to the winds of heaven, their fire risk was containable, but the danger grew with the gradual encapsulation of the driver within an increasingly friable, flammable cocoon of tubes and metal. Sadly, those responsible for the safety of these otherwise improving processes gave little or no thought to the protection of the driver, who remained literally the man in the thick of it all once the riding mechanic had been banished. For him, escape from a fire within those narrow confines became more and more dependent on sheer luck, with little else to help him either inside or outside the car.

For example, although both Seaman and Caracciola lost control of their W154 Mercedes in the rain-swept Belgian Grand Prix of 1939, Rudi was able to step out of his lightly damaged car unscathed, while Seaman found his way blocked by a large tree into which he crashed, fatally, from the flames in which he was trapped.

And so it seemed to go on no matter how many well intentioned people continued to press the question: 'When, oh when, would "They" ever learn?' Of course, the main problem was to identify just who 'They' were and what it was they had to learn before 'They' might be prevailed upon to recognize that there really was a problem. This persisted until the mid-70s to 80s brought in new 'tubs' of unbelievable strength, inboard fire extinguishers, proper flame resistant clothing and breathing tubes for the drivers, better trained and equipped marshals with vastly improved back-up services and a generally greater awareness of the need to protect and preserve human life and limb.

Take some recent examples: in no previous era could Gerhard Berger, Derek Warwick, Johnny Herbert or Martin Donnelly have had the ghost of a chance of recovery let alone survival after their various accidents. Millions of people all over the world, on the circuit or in their homes, must have echoed my own wife's heartfelt plea to Whomsoever for Berger to be saved from the engulfing flames at Imola in 1989. Thanks, above all, to those recent improvements, those pleas were heard, while I just froze and wondered anew how it would all end.

For the five tragic casualties covered in this Part, Stuart Lewis-Evans, Lorenzo Bandini, Jo Schlesser, Piers Courage and Roger Williamson, as for so many others, there had been no such reprieve.

Chapter 34
A Man of Promise

Stuart Lewis-Evans

(Born 20 April 1930: Died 25 October 1958 following a fire accident at the Grand Prix of Casablanca)

If Ifs and Ands were Pots and Pans and monkeys chewed tobacco, that Man of Promise could have won at least one world championship in the years from 1958: a bald and easy claim to make with the wisdom of over 30 years' hindsight, but none the less valid and calling for pause for thought. It would be a bold man who gainsaid the proposition that Stirling Moss was the archetypal Cooperman of all time, driving his own and other 500 cc Formula 3 cars from 9 May 1948 to 2 October 1954, when he took pole position, fastest race lap and first place in one for the last time. In those later Cooper days one of his sternest rivals was that same Man of Promise, Stuart Lewis-Evans, who could sport the distinction of almost beating Stirling into second place in 1954 on, of all places, the Nürburgring. Two years later he was the undoubted king of Formula 3 and struggling for a place with the dying house of Connaught, then tottering on its last financial legs.

Just a year after Tony Brooks's famous victory at Syracuse in 1955, Stuart had his first drive in a Formula 1 car, a Connaught at Goodwood where, after a poor start, he took second in a 15-lapper just 3.4 secs behind the popular Archie Scott-Brown, also in a Connaught and ahead of the Connaughts of Les Leston and Jack Fairman, and Salvadori's 250F Maserati. He went one better at Goodwood in April 1957, winning a 75-miler from Moss's Vanwall and the BRMs of Salvadori and Flockhart. It was to be his one and only Formula 1 win, and gave him the chance of his first drive abroad—at Naples where he held on to second for 20 laps during the middle of the race, eventually retiring 16 laps from the end when a front hub failed. His last race for Connaught, and his first Grande Épreuve, was at Monaco, which he reached thanks not least to a whip-round prior to the race, which raised £500 and gave him fourth place, three laps behind the winning group of Fangio, Brooks and Masten Gregory.

With no more money in the Connaught kitty he was approached quickly enough by Ferrari to drive sports cars, and in a few Grands Prix. In the end he only ever drove one race for them: at Le Mans where he took fifth place behind four Jaguars, leaving one to wonder why on earth Ferrari had ever engaged him for Grands Prix when he already had at least four established leading drivers to call on. By contrast Vanwall found themselves in straits in mid-1957 with both Moss and Brooks temporarily out of action and only Reserves to represent them at the dangerous and difficult Rouen circuit. The race was so totally dominated by Fangio's unforgettable driving that one is apt to overlook Stuart's fine first drive with the unknown Vanwall on an unfamiliar circuit. Again, however, he did not disappoint as he worked his way manfully up to fifth before his car dropped back and ultimately retired through overheating.

If Fangio had collared all the glory at Rouen, the Rheims Grand Prix a week later marked the Realization of the Man of Promise as he took second place on the grid, just 0.2 sec slower than Fangio himself, then still at the very height of his powers. That day the Master Driver was well and truly outshone by the slight figure of Stuart Lewis-Evans, who simply disappeared into the Far Beyond for the first 33 of 61 laps before he had to slow down due to an oil leak spraying his hands and goggles. Despite this handicap he still managed to finish third after which there was no question of any more dallying with Ferrari or anyone else, save Cooper in Formula 2 where, almost as a sideline to his Grand Prix work, he was to dominate the *Autocar* championship during 1958 until the end at Casablanca. No doubt about it: a new star had entered on his course and bagged 400 bottles of the best bubbly for being the first man to lap Rheims at more than 200 kph (124.2 mph) for good measure.

His next finish was in the Pescara Grand Prix celebrating its final revival, and a very gritty one it turned out to be for the new star as he battled his way into fifth after tyre troubles, which nearly caused him to 'lose' his car and at one point forced him off the circuit and to drive 'along the pavement between the fronts of shops and houses and a row of telegraph poles' as he struggled to 'hold' his errant car. But that was Pescara all over, as the benevolent shade of Rosemeyer would doubtless have told him when he reached a better world, and of how he had had a brake seize there in 1935, yet had somehow managed to 'thread' his Auto-Union between the wall of a house and a telegraph pole to regain the road. After the race Dr Porsche measured the gap to be just 6 cm wider than the Auto-Union!

Nothing daunted Stuart went on to Monza where he took pole position and even led between laps 16 and 20 until, once again, his car began to overheat. He ended a cracking good season with second place in the non-title ranking Grand Prix of Morocco, 30.1 secs behind Jean Behra.

Although it was beautifully crafted, the Vanwall was an exacting car that called for meticulous precision from its drivers, for which Moss, Brooks and Stuart himself were all admirably suited. It was certainly not a car to be thrown about like the 250F Maserati.

To understand the Vanwall you had also to know a bit about its creator, who has sometimes been compared to Enzo Ferrari, with whom he certainly had some things in common. Like Ferrari he was tough, determined and autocratic, but there the resemblance stopped. With all that and money at his back, Vandervell was a man who believed in Getting Things Done his way, right down to driving his cars to, and even round, the circuits: in short, everything that the tormented BRM organization had found so difficult to achieve. At the same time he matched this with a deep concern for the welfare of his drivers in a way that was almost unknown to Ferrari, a difference that was highlighted by the solicitous way that he watched Stuart through sickness and health to the day that he died. By the latter part of 1958, Vandervell's courage, strength and understanding was widely appreciated as he reaped the reward of his years of endurance and endeavour both on and off the circuits, where he was so enthusiastically beginning to see off 'those bloody red cars'.

Though somewhat overshadowed by the five outright Vanwall victories of Brooks (three) and Moss (two) up to Casablanca, Stuart still posted some good results for Vanwall during 1958 despite his No. 1 and 2 drivers—and very much in that order—always having the pick of the cars and their major components. Well loved and respected as he most surely was by his team, he cannot always have relished being 'Tail-End Charlie' in an équipe whose cars were sometimes a little short on reliability, ease of handling and general driver amenity. But that was the way of the Vanwall team and nowhere was this more marked than by the 'struggle' for the World Championship by the end of 1958. As it fell out, if Moss was to be 'champion', he had both to win the race and set its fastest lap and, at the same time, ensure that Hawthorn finished no higher than third: a mathematical, artificial result that turned out unhappily for its leading contenders.

For those of my persuasion that championships should be decided basically on a driver's number of outright, unshared wins—a view that I had first advanced in print more than 20 years ago—there should have been nothing for Casablanca to decide save the issue between Vanwall's No. 1 and No. 2 drivers, with no need for any elaborate manoeuvres to ensure that Hawthorn finished ahead of Phil Hill or for Moss to call up the support of either of his team-mates. Simple, clear-cut and, above all, clean. Moss himself recently told Nigel Roebuck that the aftermath of Casablanca was the only time in his active career that he had ever considered giving up racing, for which he gave two reasons. One was that (like me) he objected to the manifest injustice of the world championship system as it then was and, to a great extent, still is. The other will emerge later.

As the race's pattern unfolded, Brooks and Lewis-Evans on the one hand and Phil Hill on the other were all becoming locked into situations that involved giving aid and comfort to their respective team leaders rather than seeking to win the race themselves. Brooks himself has recently told me that, before the race, his car had been fitted with a lower axle ratio, ostensibly to improve acceleration, which, in retrospect, seemed odd on a power circuit like Casablanca. Despite, or maybe because of that low ratio, Brooks made a poor start from the middle of the third row, not that this mattered too much because of his wonderful talent for starting quietly and then working his way up the field. So it was no surprise to find him in third by the 19th lap behind Hill (second) and Moss. Brooks on the warpath was a most formidable opponent, but this time his campaign did not last long and he soon fell back to fourth before retiring, as he recalled to me, with a failed engine out in the country on the 30th lap. One suspects that his lower axle ratio could well have led to his engine over-revving during his pursuit and duel with Hawthorn and that, without that impediment, he could very well have bested both the Ferrari drivers, as he had already done during the year.

As it was, Stuart plugged characteristically on, while his engine was reputedly beginning to show signs of trouble, though seemingly not bad enough for him to stop and investigate. Of course his pit, without today's car-to-base contact, could have had little inkling of the growing gravity of his problem. If one accepts the account of 'Pop' Lewis-Evans, Stuart's position was becoming increasingly hazardous, and if that account was right, then the Vanwall pit had a grim 'Devil's Alternative'/'Catch 22' situation on their hands as to whether or not he should be called in. However, they did nothing and Stuart's engine finally seized 11 laps from home when he lay fifth behind Moss, Hawthorn, Hill and Bonnier, with no real hope of supporting Moss if it came to the crunch. In the ensuing accident his car spun off and crashed hitting a tree, which split its fuel tank and set the car on fire. Stuart scrambled out as best he could in his burning overalls, while three factors combined to make matters worse.

First, that the 1958 cars were running on Avgas petrol which burns at a much greater heat than the alcohol blended fuels in use till the end of 1957; second, that both fire precautions and fire proof clothing were then as scanty as they were primitive, so that before help could reach Stuart he had already been badly burned and, indeed, had been found running about in the opposite direction to the fire-fighters; and third, that he had also inhaled flame.

He was flown back in Vandervell's personal aircraft to East Grinstead where, by coincidence, both his father and older brothers had also had treatment at one time or another. Stuart lingered on for six days before he died on 25 October. For whatsoever reason the Coroner's Inquest did not enquire into the condition and quality of his overalls and not much notice seems to have been taken of their possible shortcomings either then or since: perhaps because Stuart had always been a shy and modest man about whom very little had been published even in the aftermath of his death.

As a child Stuart had suffered from spondylitis and had spent a lot of time in a wheel-chair, which at least enabled him to develop considerable strength in both his arms and shoulders through working its wheels. Although he came to drive a variety of racing cars with great skill, and especially the Vanwalls, his great friend Bernie Ecclestone still remembers carrying buckets of milk about for him whenever they went racing. He developed his skills Coopering against drivers like Stirling Moss and Peter Collins, and through them he ultimately became the ever-improving Grand Prix driver that he was and, no less, the brilliant prospective Formula 2 champion for the last year of his life.

His was a grievous and bitter loss for so many of the people around him, apart from his very close-knit immediate family. For a start, that loss was, in part at least, responsible for Vandervell's premature retirement. It was also the other reason why Stirling Moss himself had then considered giving up racing, for he had been greatly moved by the experience of accompanying Vandervell and the severely injured Lewis-Evans back to England after his accident. Then there was the effect of Stuart's death on Ecclestone himself, who was said 'to have cancelled his plans and turned his back on motor sports for several years': a moment described by Mike Lawrence in *Classic and Sportscar* for July 1991 as 'one of the turning points of post-war motor racing because his [Ecclestone's] influence on the sport has been greater than any other individual's.' But even that does not tell the whole story.

I am far from alone in my belief that had Stuart lived we might well have seen him become world champion. His only possible stumbling block could have been his strength and size, but even that would have been amply taken care of by the changing racing scene in the years from 1959. This, in its turn might equally have encouraged Vandervell himself to stay in the game and persevere with a new and altogether lighter rear-engined Vanwall and make a real 'go' of it with Tony Brooks instead of the half-hearted apologies that appeared in 1959/ 1961. There was also the near certainty that, by then, Stuart would have been booked up by Bernie Ecclestone as the No. 1 in his own Formula 1 Cooper-Climax team.

In the meanwhile, all those old Ifs and Ands have long since disappeared into eternity, leaving our three wise old monkeys still enigmatically chewing their tobacco and closing their eyes, ears and mouths to all forms of evil.

For all that he was slight in build, the memory of Stuart Lewis-Evans still casts the long shadow of a tall man over Grand Prix racing, and not least over the little Kentish church at Charing which contains his memorial tablet.

Chapter 35
A Victim of Rumour

Lorenzo Bandini

(Born 21 October 1935 at Barce, Cyrenaica, N. Africa: Died 10 May 1967 as a result of a fire accident at the Chicane when in second place during the Monaco Grand Prix)

As much as anything else, Lorenzo Bandini was the victim of that Rumour which Virgil called 'of all evils, the most swift'. He was also the victim of a little dose of the Poison Pen with a nightmarish topping of Fire thrown in.

Like several other famous drivers in these pages, Bandini was born in North Africa, at Barce in Cyrenaica, which one associates more with the desert campaigns of the early 40s than with Grand Prix racing. The Bandini family returned to Italy in 1939 shortly before the outbreak of World War II. By 1957 he had decided to quit working on cars and get down to racing them professionally instead. In this he was luckier than his contemporary, Jo Siffert, who had to come up through a much harder school. Bandini shared Siffert's deeply-felt enthusiasms but, being an Italian, he expressed them rather more lyrically as 'like being in love with a beautiful girl and holding one's emotions in check, without being able to explain your feelings to her!'

Bandini owed his early advancement to two men: a certain Signor Freddi, whose daughter he ultimately married and who took him on as an apprentice mechanic at the age of 15 after his father's death, and Mimmo Dei of the Scuderia Centro-Sud in 1960. Initially, however, he was beaten to the Grand Prix post by his friend, contemporary and rival, Giancarlo Baghetti, who was preferred by 'FISA'. Nothing to do with M. Balestre, then or now, but simply by odd coincidence the initials of an association of Italian motor clubs. This body preferred Baghetti for their coveted nomination, and he showed his worth by winning his first race at Syracuse, and then his first Formula 1 Grand Prix at Rheims.

Bandini drove well enough during 1961, and got taken on by Ferrari in 1962 and making a good start by taking third at Monaco. Thereafter, both 1962 and 1963 proved wretched years for both of them, but at least he had made a start. 1964 was altogether better, bringing him fourth place in the title rankings jointly with Richie Ginther of BRM and, best of all, that vitally important first Grand Prix win. Perhaps he was a little lucky in that all the strongest contenders fell by the wayside on the roughly surfaced airfield circuit at Zeltweg, but what did that matter? He had won and the precious result was there for all to see in the record book. The race was also notable for being Rindt's first Grand Prix start, although victory was to take him rather longer to achieve than Bandini. 1965 was another Team Lotus year so that Bandini's best place was second at Monaco, a placing which he repeated in 1966. He followed this up with third at Spa in the new 'Power Formula' where he and Ferrari should have enjoyed a distinct advantage. Yet, at this crucial stage, Ferrari chose to discard John Surtees and then saw his driver, Bandini, lose all his rhythm after a most bitter disappointment at Rheims.

In between these two famous races, a sorry sequence of events involving two of this Part's ingredients—Rumour and Poison—had sadly unfolded themselves. The arrival of John Surtees at Maranello in 1963 had been welcomed by all save a certain Eugenio Dragoni, who had succeeded the popular Romolo Tavoni as Team Manager at the end of Ferrari's successful 1961. An old friend of Ferrari, Dragoni was also fiercely chauvinistic and naturally resented the presence of a British driver, however distinguished, when there was a perfectly good Italian at hand in Lorenzo Bandini to lead the team and, with any luck, become the first Italian to win the world championship since Ascari.

But to return to Bandini at Rheims: for the first time in his life he now found himself on pole position in his 3-litre Ferrari and leading from lap six to lap 32 (out of 48) with increasing ease after Surtees had lost an early lead while a new fuel pump drive was being fitted. At that point Bandini's throttle cable snapped and its replacement took twice as long as Surtees's fuel pump, leaving Bandini to finish a nominal tenth, 11 laps behind in a race that had been his for the taking. The 3-litre Ferraris, which should have been the season's strongest runners had somehow faded away leaving victory to the more homespun Repcos of Jack Brabham and Denny Hulme.

Ferrari missed out on the South African Grand Prix of 1967, but Bandini was out again in a 3-litre Ferrari for Monaco with a new hand, Chris Amon. The two drivers motored down from their hotel on a beautiful Monte Carlo morning and Chris well remembers Bandini stopping the car and standing by it, as he gazed out on the beautiful world of flowers and blue skies spread out beneath him, as if he no longer wanted to be part of the world of sound and fury that would soon be unloosed on the tranquil scene. Magic, Premonition, Foreboding? Call it what you will, there is a saying about the bright day bringing forth the adder and, sure as God made little apples, Fate's adder was lying in wait for Bandini that bright afternoon over quarter of a century ago.

The race itself seemed to be running its course quietly enough until, all of a sudden, after half distance, Bandini started carving great chunks out of Denny Hulme's lead before he seemed to tire and, with 30 of the hot gruelling laps still left, Hulme had restored his 14 second advantage. In those days the race was still run over the traditional 100 laps and, with 18 left, Bandini made a mistake at the chicane, hitting the wooden barriers. His car promptly turned over and caught fire, amid a lethal mixture of wood and, worse still, highly inflammable straw bales.

There could have been little hope for Bandini in the near primitive rescue conditions of those times, and three days later Italy was left to mourn yet another of its leading drivers. I remember well those three seemingly endless, fruitless days when life and death hung in the balance for him, when I found myself thinking of *King Lear* and the lines:

> O let him pass, he hates him
> That would upon the rack of this rough world
> Stretch him out longer.

. . . and, more finally:

> The wonder is he hath endured so long.

. . . while asking myself how that lovely world on which those two young men had gazed so fondly that morning could have changed so suddenly into an island for the damned.

Chapter 36

Nouveau Monde

Jo Schlesser

*(Born 18 May 1928: Died 7 July 1968 in a fire accident on the descent to the Nouveau
Monde hairpin at Rouen on the third lap of the Grand Prix de France)*

Jo Schlesser was born at Liouville (Meuse) in May 1928, and drove in
every kind of sports and racing car between 1952 and 1968 with the
significant exception of the Grande Épreuves, where he made but two
appearances: one in a walking-on rôle in John Frankenheimer's
eponymous film and the other at Rouen on the day that he died. 'A
time to laugh and a time to die' as his pithy French biographer,
Georges Dirand wrote.

Yet you somehow got the feeling that he had been a Grand Prix
driver all his days, living just for the time when he might do it for real,
a 'Jim'll fix it on a grand scale!' Dirand was taken by Jo's rugged
qualities, which he likened to those of the great French mountaineer,
Lionel Terray, not least for the way in which they had both 'left in the
middle of the party' ('Parti au milieu de la Fête'). Schlesser was also a
popular and much-loved figure in every walk of the sport and not least
among the Formula 2 drivers by whom he was fondly known as 'Uncle
Jo'.

Almost throughout the 60s Formula 2 races were contested by significant Grand Prix drivers, even double world champions like Jim
Clark who met his death at just such an event. Thus it was no surprise
to find the popular Crystal Palace circuit of 1.39 miles including in its
programme (for the Holts Trophy) on Whit Monday 10 June 1968,
Grand Prix Drivers like Graham Hill, who would be World Champion
for the second time before the year was out, Jochen Rindt, Piers
Courage, and two Jackies—Ickx and Oliver–Pedro Rodriguez, Henri
Pescarolo, Johnny Servoz-Gavin, Brian Redman and Derek Bell. In
addition there was a lot of rising talent, including Max Mosley—now
the august President of FISA—with a Repco-Brabham-Ford BT23C as
well as the seemingly evergreen Jo Schlesser in a McLaren-Ford M4A.

The race was to be run off in two separate heats of 22 laps each and a
final of 90 laps totalling 125.1 miles/200.5 km to bring it up to the
minimum regulation Formula 2 distance. The heats were won by
Jochen Rindt, a pastmaster at the Palace, and Kurt Ahrens in Repco-
Brabham-Ford BT23Cs, with Oliver finishing fourth in his heat, and
Schlesser seventh in his.

Both Oliver and Schlesser started from the lower end of the grid in
the final, and worked their way through the field, with Oliver leading
Schlesser from lap 11 to lap 70. On the 71st Schlesser managed to

scramble past on the tight little circuit and hold on to his hard-won fourth place until lap 89 when Oliver, with two laps to go, got alongside Schlesser on the pit straight and snatched fourth back along the line into North Tower. Schlesser then appeared to leave his braking too late while running up over Oliver's rear wheel, which ended his race but left Oliver a safe fourth.

Now, none of this would be remarkable without two bizarre coincidences. First, that the two rivals would both be tragically involved in the doom-laden French Grand Prix at Rouen four weeks later; and, second, for a rather remarkable shot taken by photographer Michael Hewett at the Palace Formula 2 race. At the time Oliver was Team Lotus' young lion bucking to win his spurs with Chapman — never the easiest of situations, while Schlesser was a rather older lion about to burden himself with a thoroughly unready car: the new V-8 Honda.

Hewett's picture tells it all. Somehow, somewhere, during lap 71, Schlesser had at last winkled his way past Oliver, but you have only to study Hewett's photo carefully to discern the haunted, careworn, hunted look in Schlesser's face, mouth and eyes to see the pressures of the hour writ large on the unhappy driver. Not for him the comparative relaxation of another Hewett shot in this book showing Bruce McLaren holding off Surtees's (Ferrari) for a split second finish for third place at Monaco in 1963. No doubt about it, Oliver had 'Uncle Joe' well and truly on the gridiron that day and, could Joe have looked into a crystal ball, he might almost have seen the image of the future staring him in the face.

In the run up to that French Grand Prix, I had found myself for once unable to reach the great Rouen circuit in sufficient time for practice due to some tiresome passport irregularity, in England of all places, and when I finally reached the old Hotel de la Poste in the early evening, I found an atmosphere of malaise in sharp contrast to the usual animated pre-Grand Prix scene. The run-up to the French Grand Prix of 1968 had been overshadowed by the deaths of Jim Clark and Mike Spence, who Colin Chapman had replaced in Team Lotus by Jackie Oliver. He had started well by taking fifth place at Spa. Then, after failing to finish at Zandvoort, he hit real trouble during the second day's practice at Rouen when he lost control of his high-foiled Lotus 49 on the fast approach to the pits and demolished the car in a spectacular accident. While he emerged unhurt he was palpably not the flavour of Chapman's weekend. Yet there was worse, much worse, to come two afternoons later on race day.

At the time Honda had just brought out their new Grand Prix car, the air-cooled V-8 RA302, which had given John Surtees scant time to test the car at all, let alone the full and thorough shake-down it needed if it was to be anything like raceworthy at Rouen. Be all that as it might, both Mr Honda and his aspiring new driver were pressing their claims, no less than the sudden influx of new French drivers — Jean-

Pierre Beltoise, Jean-Pierre Jaussaud, Henri Pescarolo and Johnny Servoz-Gavin. So, suddenly, it seemed like 'Now-or-Never-Time' for Jo if he was ever to stand a chance of being France's No. 1 driver.

The FFSA, had become the new organizers of France's classic, now styled the first Grand Prix de France, and had decided not to start the race until 4 pm, by which time the weather had become overcast, creating the usual problems of tyre selection. I had gone down the hill to watch the early part of the race from the area of Nouveau Monde to see how the new power cars coped with the formidable succession of fast downhill bends that had been such a thrilling sight in the days of Ascari and Fangio. All this was preceded by the procession of drivers in custom cars, with Jo himself and, inevitably, Graham Hill getting the biggest 'hand' from the crowd before it was time for the ageing Toto Roche to give the signal for the delayed start.

Jo was next last on the grid and completed his first lap ahead of both Servoz-Gavin and Jo Siffert, who had made a bad start. Schlesser was still maintaining his position into the third lap before disaster struck as he rounded the fast sweep before Nouveau Monde itself. Jo died in the flames after the car had run up the high bank, overturned and exploded, scattering wreckage across the road. In those days races were very rarely stopped, even for incidents like this one, and, from the 'infield' on the opposite side of the road, I could only stand and marvel at the sang-froid of the French marshal, who stood boldly in the middle of the road with his flag poised to warn and guide the dispirited drivers as they picked their sorrowful way through the debris.

Maurice Herzog, who had lost most of his toes on Annapurna in 1950 concluded his book about it with the words: 'There are other Annapurnas in the lives of men'—like there had been for Jo Schlesser throughout 16 years of crowded, happy racing life.

Chapter 37

'The tall chap in a blue helmet'

Piers Courage

(Born 27 May 1942: Died 21 June 1970 in a fire accident at Zandvoort, Holland, during the Dutch Grand Prix)

'. . . with a big grin on his face. And a hell of a good racing driver,' was how his patron, Frank Williams, described the Piers Courage of 1969/70.

I myself remember him well as he and his wife had been in the hotel were we had stayed for the Monaco Grand Prix of 1969. There can be drawbacks in being too much of the cat that walks by itself, though believing that it should keep itself to itself, and I have always regretted not having passed at least some small time of day with the charming and attractive Piers and Lady Sarah Courage. Several things stand out from those crowded days. The smart livery and turnout of the Williams/Brabham BT26; the way that Piers drove it throughout 1969, particularly at Monaco and Watkins Glen and, most striking of all, their air of such obvious and lambent happiness, so well put, again, by Frank Williams:

> I remember one afternoon with them, in Monte Carlo in 1970 . . . sitting in a little cheap café, with everyone stopping to say 'Hello' to them, and I remember thinking that this life was so beautiful and happy for them that it just couldn't go on. I wasn't thinking in terms of his getting killed . . . just that their life was almost too good to be true.

I remembered that thought so well from 1969 and wish even more that I had myself stopped if only just to say 'Hello'.

Piers's 1970 car, the de Tomaso Ford, was nothing like as good and competitive a car as his Brabham from yesteryear, but by mid-season, just when it was beginning to measure up to the pace at Zandvoort, the very worst happened on lap 23 when the Tomaso crashed and caught fire, with no hope, yet again, for the trapped driver. In the meantime the race went on, remorselessly grinding out its tainted tale of laps, with each driver still left in the race having to pass the blazing wreck every time round.

Frank Williams himself was 'devastated' and noted how 'in every respect, life got very tough the next day', not that he had ever actually considered getting out of racing, any more than had Colin Chapman, save, perhaps, for a few anguished days (see page 194). Yet, 'after

Piers died, it was,' for Williams, 'a matter of going racing for different reasons'. Choose how, Monaco seemed a very different place when I went down there the next year—and I had never even met 'the tall chap in the blue helmet'.

Chapter 38

'When will they ever learn? — Perhaps now, at last?'

Roger Williamson

(Born 2 February 1948: Died 29 July 1973 in a fire accident during the early laps of the Dutch Grand Prix at Zandvoort)

B ernard ('Tom') Wheatcroft has long been known as the millionaire property developer, who started out in the aftermath of World War II as a jobbing builder in Leicester with no more than his demob. pay in his pocket. In the years between he has resuscitated dear, departed Donington to a passing semblance of its former self, and created in it the priceless Donington Collection of racing cars. In 1971 he decided to sponsor the fortunes of a young up-and-coming local driver called Roger Williamson, the son of a garage proprietor and former speedway rider, and born in Leicester in 1948. The aspiring Williamson made his way quickly to the top of Kart racing before graduating to real circuit work in 1968. Three years later he and his father found themselves ordering a March Formula 3 with Holbay engine at the Racing Car Show of 1971. His break came later in the year at Monaco when Wheatcroft saw him racing in the pre-final heat and asked him why he had not changed to a new engine for the final. When he explained to Wheatcroft why, he was told to order one at once and charge it to Wheatcroft's account! After that the sky was literally the limit, as Wheatcroft enthused over the way Williamson seemed to go from strength to strength, ultimately winning the top Grovewood award for 1971.

For 1972 the Wheatcroft–Williamson combination decided to continue concentrating on Formula 3 with a GRD to test the temperature of the water, plus the odd foray into Formula 2. As a result he won the Shell Oil and Forward Trust championships of Formula 3, although he did not fare so well in Formula 2. After a few trials in the winter of 1972/73, including Formula 1 BRM, Williamson opted to stay with Wheatcroft and master Formula 2 just as he had already done with Formula 3. The only way to win in Formula 2 was with a March-BMW, and by mid-season Wheatcroft had bought one for him. By that time they were also into Formula 1 with the ex-Jarier 'Rent-a-Drive' March that Wheatcroft had hired for the British and Dutch Grands Prix of 1973. Like most March projects of those days it was to prove an inadequate, ill-starred venture. At Silverstone the March was put out on the second lap by the multiple, Scheckter-inspired pile-up at Wood-cote, and 15 days later Williamson himself was dead.

Williamson had qualified his March about two-thirds down the Zandvoort grid, but had to start at the very back of the dummy grid because of difficulty getting the engine to fire up in the paddock. Five laps into the race he had worked his way up to 13th place (out of 23) and seemed to be going well enough until, on the ninth lap, both he and Purley were seen to be mising at the same time as the dreaded black smoke plume started to rise across the dunes. The unforgivable element in this renewed tragedy was that nobody seemed aware of what had happened, still less to be able to do anything about it, with the brave exception of David Purley, who had stopped immediately by the car and tried to get it turned over on to its wheels, release the trapped driver and get the fire put out: all, be it noted, at the same time and all on his own! The March itself had left the road at 130 mph because of a mechanical failure, before hitting a guard rail at 45 degrees, which promptly collapsed to form itself into a launching pad, projecting the car through the air before it turned over, hit the ground upside down and slid along the road before finally coming to rest.

Since 1972 the Dutch authorities had done much to improve their circuit, yet they had still failed in their equally important duty to provide adequate fire fighting equipment and personnel in the right places and at the right time. The fact that the marshals on the spot were clearly inexperienced, inadequately trained and lacked the necessary fire-proof clothing merely made things worse. Confusion's final masterpiece was provided by the way in which 'this grey race ran to its conclusion', with the spectators little realizing that 'world-wide television was exposing the whole ghastly scene and doing little to help'.

In most respects Williamson's accident was virtually a re-run of Courage's three years earlier, making it deplorably clear that nothing had been done in the meantime. Yet, out of the ashes of 1973, a small measure of improvement began to be discernible, starting with the appointment, by the GPDA/CSI, of the controversial Louis Stanley 'to act as director of circuit safety, ensuring that the fire fighting equipment, techniques, deployment of fire fighters and their level of training are in accordance with the specifications laid down in the report of the 'Jo Siffert Advisory Council'.

Yet when you remember that Siffert's fatal accident had taken place in October 1971, there was little, if any, evidence to show what had actually been done by this solemn body in the intervening 21 months, even though, at long and much needed last, it looked as if some progress might now be made. The day of FISA was still five years away in the future, but in the meantime, perhaps, those indefinite ill-defined 'They' might really be going to get something definite done.

At the same time, Denny Hulme, then President of the GPDA, was expressing the hope that the sport would not lose Tom Wheatcroft's interest and support, especially for his museum and circuit at Donington, while optimistically adding that 'Roger would have been all for that'. So, happily, it has remained even although Tom Wheatcroft himself is no nearer to getting a Formula 1 Grand Prix fixture back for his circuit where it is now well over half a century since the successive victories of Rosemeyer and Nuvolari were celebrated. Yet the memory still happily lingers on.

PART 11
THE HANDICAPPED

Chapter 39
Tales of Fortitude

Alan Stacey
(Born 29 August 1933: Died 19 June 1960 in an accident during the Belgian Grand Prix at Spa-Francorchamps, generally ascribed to his being hit by a bird at speed)

Archie Scott-Brown
(Born 13 May 1927: Died 18 August 1958 at Spa-Francorchamps after losing control of his car in the wet)

Gunnar Nilsson
(Born 20 November 1948: Died 20 October 1978 in Charing Cross Hospital of a fatal cancer, leaving an example of courage and dignity to all)

Grand Prix history is full of stories of drivers, who have overcome the odds and raced on, with little or no regard for pain, injury, accident or money on heroic, if usually isolated, occasions. In the terms of this book my mind turns chiefly to Jimmy Murphy and the French Grand Prix of 1921 (see pages 95/6) and Niki Lauda (see page 120/2). The pieces in this part are concerned with a rather different aspect of bravery that is best called Fortitude and involves the facing up daily to an enduring, and in some cases positively sapping, disability of one kind or another.

Thus, Alan Stacey raced throughout his career with an artificial limb, having lost his right leg below the knee at an early age, while Archie Scott-Brown was born without a right hand and had to manage with a forearm that ended in a notched stump. Yet, somehow, he managed to hold the steering wheel while changing gear. Neither that nor the fact that he also had one leg shorter than the other seemed in any way to inhibit him from going racing with endless verve and gusto. Both these men died as they would have wished, wheel in hand, gallantly fighting their disabilities.

The Fortitude of Gunnar Nilsson, though in its way no less heroic, was on a different plane.

Alan Stacey

Alan Stacey made his Formula 1 début in the British Grand Prix of

1957 in a Lotus 16, sharing the back row with Jack Fairman. Beside him in Team Lotus were Graham Hill with another 16 and Cliff Allison with a 12. Stacey's race lasted 19 laps until he retired with overheating and, after that, he drove no more in Formula 1 until 1959. Neither did he achieve anything in Formula 2 in the meantime. Returning for Team Lotus in 1959 he actually managed to last through the British Grand Prix and finish eighth, several laps behind. Once again his Formula 2 season had proved remarkably barren for both him and Team Lotus as a whole. The truth of the matter was that Chapman had never really wanted to get into Formula 1 at that early stage in his career, when he had more than enough on his plate with Formula 2 and sports car racing, to say nothing of the construction and marketing of his new Elite road car — 'But the drivers were all fired up and Climax were making bigger engines, so away he went.'

The all-new Lotus 18 of 1960 was an instant success in the Argentine Grand Prix and, by Monaco, Stirling Moss had persuaded his patron, Rob Walker, to invest in one for him, with which he immediately obliged by winning the race. By contrast, Team Lotus itself — now consisting of Innes Ireland, John Surtees and Stacey — had a dreadful day, with only Ireland 'finishing' at all in a far away ninth, 44 laps adrift. After that, the prodigals fared rather better at Zandvoort and, while they could do little about Brabham and Moss, who were the class of the field, Ireland and Stacey were at least able to contest third place with becoming vigour and, once Moss dropped back, Stacey raced happily on in second until his transmission packed up after 57 of the 75 laps. For Team Lotus it was a very respectable result.

Next came a more formidable test — the Belgian Grand Prix at Spa-Francorchamps. Although Stacey started on the back row, he had beavered his way up to sixth after 24 of the 36 laps, which put him 'in the points' for the first and only time in his career. By that stage in the meeting there had already been two serious accidents and one fatality.

During Saturday's practice, Moss's Lotus had lost a wheel and Henry Taylor's steering column had broken. Bad enough on its own, in all conscience, but far worse was to follow. On the 19th lap of the race Chris Bristow lost control of his Cooper and crashed fatally and, five laps later, Stacey lost his life in a similar accident. Like Bristow he was thrown from his car and died instantly. The general belief was that Stacey had been struck in the face at speed by a bird and 'Jabby' Crombac's biography of Colin Chapman tells movingly of how:

> Stacey's loss was deeply felt by everyone in the team ... [and how] ... his mechanic Bill Basson, one of the best men in the business, had lost a hand and the two of them had always enjoyed a special relationship. They were tremendously popular with everyone because, despite their particular handicaps, they had risen to the top of their branch in the sport.

And, with that, Spa's sickening weekend of horror had spent itself.

Six years later Jim Clark was to have a similar accident in practice at Rheims, again described by 'Jabby' Crombac: 'whilst going full chat down the long straight. By a sheer miracle and no small amount of skill he was able to keep the car on the road. . . . Colin was very shocked by this incident as he had not forgotten the loss of Alan Stacey from a similar mishap.' Clark was as lucky as Stacey was not and, faced with a similar situation, especially at tricky Spa, even Clark's legendary skills might not have been enough.

Archie Scott-Brown

Jim Clark was one of the great masters of Spa, although he always claimed to dislike it, not least because it was there that he had made his first Continental appearance, in a D-Type Jaguar in 1958, on the day when Archie Scott-Brown had been killed driving a 3.5-litre Lister-Jaguar.

Because of his physical handicaps, Archie had to restrict his racing outside Britain to sports cars only, although he became a well known and respected competitor in the rising tide of domestic British motor races, including Formula 1. After combining his job as a tobacco salesman, based in Cambridge, with an apprenticeship in club racing for some years, he chanced upon a big stroke of luck called Brian Lister. He had been taken by '. . . something in the way I handled the MG [that he then had] and so, despite a certain shortage of essential equipment [as he jokingly described his disabilities] he asked me to drive for him on an all-expenses-paid basis. Of course, I said: "Yes"!'

His first real success came with the 2-litre Lister-Bristol at nearby Snetterton in the 27-mile Curtis Trophy in May 1955. The star of the meeting was Roy Salvadori with the Gilby Engineering 250F Maserati, but, nothing daunted, the aspiring Archie catapulted his 2-seater sports car into a short lead before being overhauled and finally finishing second. By Easter 1956 he was behind the wheel of a works Formula 1 Connaught at Goodwood, with which he first challenged and then led Moss's 250F and Hawthorn's BRM until his brakes tired after 16 laps (of 32) and a piston broke. He continued in this startling form in practice for the Aintree '200' three weeks later, where he grabbed pole position, 2.2 secs faster than Hawthorn's BRM, and led from the start. His run ended after 13 laps and a second bout of piston failure when he was over six seconds in the lead.

His best performance was now to follow in the 175-mile International Trophy race at Silverstone on 5 May. This was the great occasion when, at long last, several up-and-coming British cars and drivers really got among the 'bloody red cars' that riled Vandervell so much, in this case the D50 Lancias of Fangio and Collins. This time Archie had to be content with seventh on the grid, in the second row, and a less commanding role in the race, in which he eventually finished second, 33 secs behind Moss's Vanwall, having beaten all the remaining BRMs, Vanwalls and Connaughts, but, best of all, a brace of Italy's best scarlet runners. His last Formula 1 race of the year was at Brands Hatch for the BRSCC's Formula 1 race event in October 1956, where he won a very popular victory from a good field of Connaughts (including Lewis-Evans) and Salvadori's 250F.

1958 found Archie still racing Connaughts, but now for Bernie Ecclestone, for whom he took sixth in the 100-mile Glover Trophy race at Goodwood, behind team-mate Lewis-Evans in fifth, Cliff Allison's Lotus 12 in fourth, his old rival, Salvadori, now in a Cooper, in third, Brabham in a similar Cooper in second and the winner, Mike Hawthorn's Dino. His last Formula 1 drive was again for Ecclestone in the BARC 200-mile race at Aintree where, in a world that was by then fast changing, he could only finish ninth, behind the Lotus 12s of Allison and Graham Hill and a positive gaggle of Coopers.

Brian Lister had opted for the 3.5-litre class for the 1957 sports car season, dropping a Jaguar engine into his current chassis. Success was immediate, with Archie winning the British Empire Trophy and then eight more of the season's 11 races. Archie then spent the winter 'Down Under', winning the Lady Wigram Trophy with the Lister-Jaguar from a Maserati and Lewis-Evans's Connaught, before being engaged by Briggs Cunningham to co-drive his own newly acquired Lister-Jag. at Sebring with Walter Hansgen. The race was not a success. On the fourth lap Olivier Gendebien drove his Ferrari up the back end of the Lister, coming to rest on Archie's shoulder, with its tyre tread clearly imprinted on his shirt!

What a close call that must have been for Archie and, in hindsight, what a pity he had not called it a day there and then. But that would not have been his way and, instead, he took his Lister-Jag. over to race at Spa on 18 August. It was raining and, just when he was trying that little bit too hard, his car left the road, crashed into the trees and burst into flames. In those days a fire accident usually gave drivers pitifully little to hope for (see Part 10), and they rarely walked away from such an accident. Archie was no more lucky than anyone else.

Gunnar Nilsson

At least, though, Alan Stacey and Archie Scott-Brown had died quickly and with their boots on. Gunnar Nilsson's end was neither. Peter Warr, then of Lotus, had been impressed by what he had seen of the young Swede in the Formula 3 of 1975 and signed him up for Team Lotus from the South African Grand Prix of 1976. It proved to be a very good choice, with Nilsson topping the Lotus points in his first year with a score of 11, which was one better than the disillusioned Peterson, who had swapped Team Lotus for March in the early part of the season.

Team Lotus had been in the doldrums since 1974, but the new Lotus 78 proved a force to be reckoned with, particularly with Mario

Andretti coming back to lead the team in 1977. Nilsson was an excellent No 2, gathering in one win, a third, a fourth and two fifths from his season. His win at Zolder was particularly pleasing, coming as it did after his team leader had spun off in the wet on the first lap. 'Mr Chapman', as Nilsson called him, had briefed his back-up man well:

> . . . if ever Andretti drops out, it is my job to win races so I thought I'd better pull my finger out. I knew that my car was quickest on a wet track, so I concentrated very hard in the wet to keep the car on the circuit and delayed my challenge until the track began to dry, as I assumed it would.

Smart thinking from a newcomer that won him his first Grand Prix by over 14 secs from top of the tree man, Niki Lauda, after he had found things 'very tricky . . . because it was raining at one end of the track and not at the other.'

Then, after Nilsson's two good years proving himself at Team Lotus, Chapman decided to bring back Ronnie Peterson as running mate to Mario Andretti for 1978, with twin No 1 status, but with some very clear ground rules. Either way, the new situation left no room for Nilsson at Team Lotus, who signed up with the then controversial Arrows team and joined up with another figure, who was to become even more controversial before the new year was out: Riccardo Patrese, who had started driving for Arrows in 1977, and opened his score in the last race of that season with a singleton point from the Japanese Grand Prix.

It was to be an ill-fated turn-around for all three men. Both Peterson and Nilsson were dead within the year, and Patrese had been effectively buried by the Grand Prix Establishment. Peterson's story is told later (see pages 44/7) and, as all the world knows, Nilsson had to surrender his contract for 1978 because of the onset of the fatal cancer that would end his young life that October.

Nilsson had been conscious of an increasing pain in his lower abdomen for some time, so much so that he had to give up using the crutch straps of his safety harness during the season. At season's end he had a tumour removed from his groin, and during the rest of the winter the severity of his chemotherapy treatment reduced his body weight by half and, although he was to regain his weight loss, his hair did not regrow. It soon became clear that this was but the beginning of not just a serious, but a positively terminal cancer. Not that this made any difference to his pattern of life. Throughout this grim period he just put up with the increasing pain, intent on seeing his fund for the Charing Cross Hospital to fight cancer properly set up, and insisting on continuing to help others, giving even the most hopeless of cases a will and hope to live.

Shortly before his death Nilsson put out his own personal appeal for his Cancer Treatment Campaign, to which he personally made a substantial contribution. He also paid a moving tribute to the work of the specialists and staff of the New Charing Cross Hospital, revealing for himself that the only reason they may have failed was 'because I went to them for treatment too late'. My own wife had two brushes, of varying seriousness, with this dreadful servant of the grim reaper during the 80s but she emerged as one of the lucky ones. I am sure this was because she was treated with time to spare.

In the previous decade Gunnar Nilsson had not been so swift or so lucky and, in conclusion, we should remind ourselves of his brave, brief life and the moving appeal for his campaign that was made within days of his death by *Motor Sport*.

At the end of the day, the example of his courage and the exemplary way in which he lived through those dreadful days leading up to his death left a rare and indelible example of a wholly different kind of Fortitude.

PART 12

JOSEPH AND THE BROTHERS

Chapter 40

The Mexicans and the Swiss

Pedro Rodriguez

(Born 18 January 1940: Died 11 July 1971 in an unexplained accident during a sports car race at the Norisring, Germany)

Ricardo Rodriguez

(Born 14 February 1942: Died 1 November 1962 at Mexico City in practice for the 1st Mexican Grand Prix)

Joseph (Jo/Seppi) Siffert

(Born 7 July 1936: Died 24 October 1971 during the 'Victory' race at Brands Hatch in an accident thought to have been caused by a broken part)

Surprisingly few racing circuits have been named after famous racing drivers, and the only contemporary example that springs readily to mind is that of The Two Brothers (Los Dos Hernanos) of Mexico City: Pedro and Ricardo Rodriguez.

The younger of the two, Ricardo, was another Grand Prix prodigy, arriving on the Formula 1 scene at the ripe old age of 19½. By that time he had gone through most of the stages of a classic driver's *Cursus Honorum*: Mexican cycling champion at ten; motor cycle champion at 13; auto racing champion at 15 and, at 19, a Ferrari team driver. Of course the brothers were extremely lucky in having one of the wealthiest men in Mexico for a father, which enabled both of them to live well and buy whatever they needed to further their considerable racing ambitions—places with Ferrari included. However, money cannot buy competence, and the brothers had plenty of that as well.

In the 50s, 60s and early 70s many of the leading drivers probably drove in more sports car and lesser races than Grands Prix, and the brothers were certainly no exception. Good results in those events could often provide that vital leg up into a Grand Prix seat, and their good showing in the sports car races of 1961 must have played no small part in Ferrari's North American representative, and triple Le Mans winner, the ubiquitous and seemingly eternal Luigi Chinetti, recommending them to Ferrari as potential Grand Prix drivers, with possibly a sweetener to speed them on their Maranello way. Oddly enough,

Ricardo made his mark before Pedro, who at first opted out of the Grand Prix scene for 1962 in favour of his other business interests.

Ricardo's opening run at Monza verged on the meteoric, even though he was only driving the 65-degree engined Dino 156. He took second place on the grid, 0.8 sec faster than Phil Hill on the second row and just 0.1 sec slower than the current World Championship leader von Trips, widely tipped as the next holder. Trips made a slow start so that the first lap was led by Phil Hill and Ricardo from Clark and Brabham, closely followed by Trips and the Wonderman of 1961, Giancarlo Baghetti, the victor of Syracuse and Rheims.

On the second lap Trips and Clark collided, braking for the Parabolica curve, and left the road with fatal results for Trips and 14 spectators. With ten laps gone Hill still led from Rodriguez, Ginther and Baghetti, but both the flying youngsters retired with broken engines on lap 14, leaving Hill with an easy if saddening victory. The adverse publicity stirred up by Trips's accident made Ferrari give the US Grand Prix at Watkins Glen a miss, which left Ricardo without a drive.

However, he was back again for a fairly full season with Ferrari in 1962, his best result being fourth at Spa in a blanket finish with Phil Hill, who pipped him by just 0.1 sec. Ferrari missed out on the French Grand Prix and sent only Hill to Aintree, which left Ricardo once again without a drive until the Ring, where he achieved his only other finish—a very wet sixth. After that, Ferrari opted out of the ensuing American and South African Grands Prix. 1962 had very definitely not been a Ferrari year, what with mid-season abstentions and the majority of the up-front running being provided by another Hill— Graham, and his BRM coming into their best form—as well as Jim Clark, plus the two singleton wins of McLaren (Cooper) and Gurney (Porsche).

At the end of that unhappy year, on 4 November, the first Mexican Grand Prix was fitted in, as a non-championship event, between the US and South African Grands Prix. Pedro did not enter, but Ricardo did, though much against the wishes of his wife, who he had already told that he would be giving up after just this one more race. So, Ricardo could look forward to fulfilling his pledge and, hopefully, ending his career on a high note on his home ground where he was due to drive a Rob Walker entered Lotus.

He turned in some fast and, as some thought, overly fast laps in practice before stopping and then going out again for that often fatal 'just one more'. Almost inevitably, he crashed violently and fatally. After the accident there emerged the usual differing versions of what had happened, some saying that he had been going too fast to make the fatal turn, others that the Lotus rear suspension had broken. A day of national mourning followed before his burial which, by macabre coincidence, fell on the country's 'Day of the Dead'.

Pedro ultimately deferred his Grand Prix debut until the US Grand

Prix in October 1963, as a third entry for Team Lotus, who already had the World Championship neatly tied up. Prophetically, perhaps, Pedro qualified on the seventh row of a grid which he shared, along with an identical lap time, with his future comrade in arms and great rival, Jo (Seppi) Siffert. At one stage he found himself disputing sixth place with Jo, but he retired on lap 37 with engine trouble, while Jo lasted another 20 laps before falling out with gearbox trouble. In Mexico Pedro was described as 'delighting the crowd with his forceful driving', which soon brought him up from the back of the grid, shared with the young Chris Amon, to ninth place in contention with Graham Hill and Bandini. Pedro retired yet again, this time with broken suspension, while Jo finished ninth.

Pedro drove in only one Grand Prix in 1964, for Ferrari, where he at least finished and won his first championship point for sixth. Once again he came out of retreat for the end of season races in 1965, again with Ferrari, taking fifth at Watkins Glen and seventh in Mexico. In 1966 he became a little more venturesome, contesting the Grands Prix of France and Germany, though retiring in both, before returning to his familiar stamping grounds at Watkins and Mexico for two more retirements.

Though he might not have known it, his long, lean period in the Grand Prix wilderness was about to end when John Cooper offered him a trial run in the big Cooper-Maserati for the South African Grand Prix of 1967. Pedro gridded fourth, 0.1 sec slower than Jim Clark with an H-16-BRM-engined Lotus. The Brabham-Repcos, which had been the top cars of 1966, were confidently expected to win and, with 21 laps left, Hulme seemed to have the race well in hand as he led a local driver, John Love, in a 2.7-litre Cooper-Climax by over a minute, with Pedro about half a minute further behind, followed by Surtees's V-12 Honda.

A lap later and it was all drama and confusion as Hulme had to make a sudden stop to take on more brake fluid, while he watched Love, Pedro (at 24 secs) and Surtees go through before he could get going again. After that the race seemed to settle peacefully down again until, 11 laps from the end, Love had to stop for more fuel. This, at last, let Pedro through into a lead which he never lost in spite of a set of fast balding tyres. Love finished about 26 secs astern, with Surtees third and Hulme eventually fourth. Before the race, precious few would have given Pedro any odds at all, still less Love, yet there they were confounding expectation with first and second!

John Cooper promptly snapped Pedro up for the rest of the season and, although the big, primitive car, with its long-past 'Sell By' dated 3-litre V-12 Maserati engine, was way off the pace, Pedro's bold and sensible driving left him much the most successful of the Cooper-Maserati drivers, besides netting him no less than 15 championship points and equal sixth with Graham Hill. Moreover, if he had not suffered a foot injury in a Formula 2 race at Enna, and missed three races to the Mexican Grand Prix, he would surely have finished higher still in the rankings. As it was, his gutsy attitude enabled him to race in Mexico and finish sixth despite being in considerable pain from injuries that his doctors told him would take a year to heal. How little they knew Pedro!

Not surprisingly, 1968 brought more bidders for his services, including BRM, who had lost Hill to Lotus in 1967 and were about to lose Stewart to Ken Tyrrell's new Grand Prix Team in 1968. In what was then the traditional curtain-raiser at Brands Hatch, Pedro finished second to McLaren in his new Cosworth-powered car, having fair blasted his way through the field after a slow start. In mid-season he had some good runs on the more challenging circuits: at Spa, where he finished second to McLaren, before a series of races run in difficult rain conditions at Zandvoort (third), fastest race lap and a short spell in the lead at Rouen, and sixth on the Ring before winding up the year with third at Mosport (also wet) and fourth in Mexico to give him sixth in the rankings again.

1969 was not a good year for Pedro in Grands Prix, where he drove either privately-entered BRMs or indifferent factory Ferraris. It did, however, enable him to concentrate his mind on long-distance sports car racing at which, with Jo Siffert, he was to become so adept in 1970/71 before their deaths. By 1970 BRM were at last getting their troubled act together again and mounting some really serious challenges, notably on power circuits like Spa, Austria and Monza and, all the more, when Seppi joined Pedro in 1971.

Almost every driver who figures in this book has had a helping hand somewhere down the line, usually from a parent, though often through gritted teeth. While Seppi's father actually took him to his first motor race, there is nothing to show that he ever had any financial help from his parents: there was simply not the money to go round, and from Day One he had to make shift for himself. However, at the age of 12, he had seen a driver called Sommer (see pages 36/41) having a late practice session at Berne, and noted two things which he told his father about on the way home, just as I can remember myself doing with mine after an earlier Swiss Grand Prix in 1939. What struck Seppi so strongly was, first, Sommer's will to attack and, second, the precise way that Raymond Mays changed his gears on each lap. Thus early did Seppi learn two of the great Musts for a racing driver: the boldness of Attack and the coolness of Precision. Solemnly the little boy assured his father:

> When I am grown up I shall go to Confession and Communion in the morning, and in the afternoon I shall drive a racing car . . . and I shall drive like Sommer.

. . . and so he did; and what better exemplar could he have had?

But how was a poor Swiss boy to make his way? Seppi left school at 15 and, first, became a rag merchant. Gradually his tiny business grew thanks to a little bit of luck and an armful of native cheek, allied to a keen nose for a good bargain. After a year he found a more congenial job patching up and selling crashed cars at 40 Swiss centimes an hour, 48 hours a week. Although he had earned more from his rag dealing, he was pleased to find his new work bringing him just that little bit nearer to his real object—cars.

Each year he went on going to Berne to watch every minute of both practice and race, and noted everything that went on. Like Sommer, he also preferred the drivers who pressed on, rather than those who played a waiting game. By 1955, motor cycling had become another passion, and he longed to have a go in competition. His father violently disapproved, threatening to destroy any such machine that might darken his doors! So Seppi had to hold his peace and go on working to qualify as a coach-builder before going off to do his military service.

As if his life had not been full enough with problems, Seppi had had to have an operation when he was six weeks old to correct a malformation of his right foot, which was completely turned inwards and, two years later, with the operation behind him, his right leg was still shorter than his left and also a little thinner. This continuing disability enabled him to bypass some of the more disagreeable aspects of military service and also to work up the second-hand car business that he was now developing on the side. All the time, though, the obstinate problem of raising the money with which to start racing remained, obdurately refusing to go away, let alone solve itself.

Bit by painful bit, he began to make his impression on the world of motor cycle racing from 1957, explaining his early attitudes simply enough:

> I was mad then; I would go flat out from the start no matter what. It wasn't just a race to me, this was my one chance to get there . . . It's no good starting gently if you want to be taken seriously, to make a name. You have to be tough as a beginner so that you can calm down later. . . . When a beginner is killed, people say he was mad, but it's not really true—he was only playing double or quits.

With this kind of 'Fear and Be Slain' approach, Seppi could only go one of two ways and, happily, he survived through to the end of 1959 when he surprised his friends by giving up motor bikes for cars just when he was beginning to make a name for himself. By dint of much hard work and scheming he had put enough money together to make the change although, in some ways, it seemed as if he was going back to that same old world of wondering where the next crust and franc were going to come from.

Jacques Deschenaux, in his biography of Jo Siffert, says that from the start Seppi's driving was both tough and unorthodox . . . 'cutting down his braking distances to the bone, he would charge into each bend on the brink, completely obscuring the correct line. On top of this, his habit of taking the other novices on the inside going into a corner . . . did not go down at all well with the track marshals!' Small wonder that he began to pick up black marks, but so had several other men who became world champions!

On 11 June 1960 Seppi paid 13,000 francs for a Stanguellini FJ Modena racer, which left him with just 11 francs in his pocket! Somehow, he managed to get by, working on his car throughout the night and sleeping rough, while continuing his motor trade activities during the day so that at the end of the year he was able to acquire a Lotus 18. Again he made a good impression, this time by winning a race at Cesanatico, where a certain Franco Lini was heard to say: 'I saw a little Swiss this afternoon whom I don't know at all, but who seemed to me to be going very fast. If I were you, I should watch out for him.' Another classic instance of the right man being in the right place at the right time! Gradually rags were at last starting to turn to riches, and more and more people were going to keep a look out for the rest of this lovable man's outstanding life.

In 1965 he took his next really great leap forward when Rob Walker engaged him to drive his second string Brabham-BRM alongside Jo Bonnier for the season. When considering his options for 1966 Walker found that he could no longer afford to support two cars and drivers, and opted to retain Seppi in preference to Bonnier. A hard but correct choice on Walker's part, not least because his 'driver' had not long since won the Grand Prix at Enna, defeating Jim Clark himself by 0.3 secs and given the Walker team its first major success since Stirling Moss's famous victories from 1961. Seppi's great admirer, Franco Lini, was equally delighted: 'With all those victories you've carried off, you ought to come and live in Sicily—it must be your sort of country!' As for Clark, he could only gasp in amazement: 'Siffert was so broadside that I didn't know whether I ought to take him on the left or the right!'

Seppi had two fairly barren years with Walker's Cooper-Maserati in 1966/67 before his great victory for him in the Lotus 49 at the British Grand Prix of 1968 at Brands Hatch. It had taken Seppi some time to acclimatize himself to what then seemed the formidable 400 bhp of the Cosworth engine and he had had the misfortune to write off his new car in a pre-race shake-down at Brands Hatch in March of that year. To compound misfortune, on the very next day Walker's workshops were completely destroyed by fire, causing great damage to his collection of old cars. Soon enough, however, ranks closed and money was found, but in the meantime there had been one loss that no amount of money in the world could buy back: the life of the incomparable Jim Clark on 7 April 1968. Seppi, along with so many others, was quite overcome: 'He was the greatest of them all,' was all Seppi could find to say—even among his other heroes: Benoit Musy, Raymond Sommer and Stirling Moss.

Lotus had a 49B ready for Seppi and the British Grand Prix at

Brands in July, though they were still fitting things like the driver's seat and the wing mirrors when practice started, leaving Seppi time for only one session. Not that this seemed to matter as the car quickly settled down well and he made a good start in the race ahead of Amon's Ferrari, and just behind the 49s of Graham Hill and Jackie Oliver. Hill broke a half shaft when leading, and Amon managed to nip by Seppi at much the same time. However, he did not stay there long as Seppi re-took him just before Oliver's half shaft also broke, leaving the race between Seppi and a hard pursuing Amon. So Seppi went on to win his first Grande Épreuve and, with it, a sudden realization that he had become a real force to be reckoned with, whether he was driving Grands Prix or high level sports cars.

Seppi had started out in Grands Prix before Pedro Rodriguez, but, oddly enough, their talents had both seemed to come 'on cam' with their new mounts of 1968. By contrast, 1969 brought little good to either of them and then, for 1970, Seppi was faced with the wretched decision about parting company with Rob Walker, who had done so much for him since 1964. His choice lay between the ever-dubious competence of BRM and the unknown quantity that was March, with the latter, importantly, having the promise of financial backing from Porsche. That, and the fact that Seppi wanted a works contract, was enough to incline him to favour March, though this was to bring him little joy through 1970. Happily his friendship with Walker did not suffer, and when Seppi married his Simone in London in May of that year it was his erstwhile patrons who charmingly did him the honours.

On the whole, therefore, it was Pedro who had made the wiser Grand Prix choice for 1970 until Kyalami of 1971 found them in the same teams for both classes of top deck racing, with an uneasy truce reigning between the two firebands of Porsche and BRM. Yet, somehow, as a contemporary report said, it seemed to gell and work:

> The Mexican and the Swiss, whom some people thought of as implacable foes, thus found themselves in the same teams. This rivalry in fact was really more an identity of character: in both men there was the same thoughtful temperament, the will to win regardless of speed. Apart from the odd incidents due to the intolerance of each other on the circuit, [they] got on perfectly well but not for too long; pointed in the same direction their characters were too strongly defined for them ever to be real friends.

And the extent of their co-operation showed in the end of season results, with BRM taking second to Tyrrell in the constructors' rankings, to give them their best showing in years. Sadly it was also soon to be BRM's swansong, for during the second half of 1971 they suffered the twin and mortal blows of the deaths, first of Pedro in July and of Seppi at the end of October.

By mid-season Pedro had taken fourth at Barcelona and second at Zandvoort, which made him fifth equal with Andretti. At that point

Porsche were about to abandon big series sports car racing, and Pedro had naturally started casting around for a drive in 1972. At the end of June he had won his last race for Porsche, on the Österreichring, after a marvellous duel with the Regazzoni's 512 Ferrari, graphically summed up, as ever, by DSJ for *Motor Sport*:

> It was an impressive fighting finish . . . driven for 158 laps of the challenging Österreichring by the quiet and gentle, but oh so rugged Mr Pedro Rodriguez . . . in a truly impressive manner that should really illustrate to everybody what proper motor racing is all about.

How little we knew that after that there would be no more of those inimitable displays of gentle, controlled, fast precision, for ever to be associated with this most gentle and precise of racers, especially on circuits like the Österreichring and his beloved Spa-Francorchamps. A man of stamp if ever there was one—and, no less, of humour and good company, fun and courage that was complemented by a great tranquillity and a becoming sense of dignity, that went so well with his preference for an old and sedate Bentley and the slow measured gait that characterized his walk down to Ste Dévote from the Hotel de Paris on the way to practice at Monaco.

Pedro loved racing almost to a fault, and in a bizarre way his addiction was to be the end of him. Shortly before his death, his great friend, Jo Ramirez, had invited him to dinner to show off his new house, but Pedro had cried off at the last minute because his . . .

> '. . . friend Müller has asked me to drive his Ferrari at the Norisring. I have no racing or anything so do you mind if I do it next week?'
> So I said, 'Yes, no problem.'

Pedro qualified second best and led the race until he met a largely unexplained fatal accident at what was really an unnecessary event for him, but Pedro the man who had to be reminded that it was raining, did not think of racing that way. As his friend Ramirez concluded:

> . . . that's how Pedro was. If anybody offered him a wheelbarrow to race, he would go and race it. He was just a racer all the way.

Six days later as Derek Bell drove one of the JW-Gulf Porsches round Silverstone on an *In Memoriam* lap before the British Grand Prix, the old circuit suddenly seemed to be a very lonely place and, perhaps, for no man more than Seppi Siffert as he sat on the outside edge of the front row of the grid awaiting the starter's flag.

In winning the last Belgian Grand Prix at Spa in 1970, Pedro had pointed the way ahead for BRM, and now their torch had been passed to Seppi to keep the precious flame alight and bring to BRM a touch of Old Iron's genius for recovery from tragedy. Seppi's car did not react well to Silverstone and its vibrations, or to the Ring where he had ignition trouble, but there was simply no gainsaying his flag-to-flag victory in Austria. Then, like as not, he might well have won at Monza if his gearbox had not stuck in fourth around half distance, and after that he wound up his season of Majors with a second at Watkins Glen, to bring him up to equal fourth in the rankings.

The Mexican Grand Prix, scheduled for 24 October, had been cancelled, and the Brands Hatch organizers had the bright idea of filling the vacuum by throwing in a 'World Championship Victory Race' to supplement the programme of races already laid on. By that time Seppi had had a long, harrowing season of no less than 40 races and it was hardly surprising that he was not exactly enchanted at the prospect of a 41st. But he was a man of his word and responded like a true racer by setting a memorable pole position lap that was later equalled by his BRM team-mate, Peter Gethin, the recent victor of Monza.

I remember October 1971 as a particularly beautiful month, both in England and at Watkins Glen, with each day at Brands a very positive pleasure. The Sunday of the race was thus the happiest of days as I drove over, with my teenage children, and all of us keenly looking forward to an entertaining day's racing following the two exciting practice days that had preceded it. Although we had taken a good day's supply of food and drink with us, my daughter simply could not resist stopping to pick up quite the largest lobster I have ever seen from a wayside produce stall, which, need I add, she hung on to as we went our separate ways after we reached the circuit.

The Carnival atmosphere was heightened by the first event for celebrities, for the Jack Brabham Trophy, including the hero of the hour Jackie Stewart, Jack Brabham himself, Colin Chapman and others all in Ford Escort Mexico saloons. Appropriately enough, the donor won the race after a furious ding-dong struggle with Chapman, whose transmission failed when he was leading down the finishing straight on the last lap.

This was followed by a special parade for everyone who had played a part in the sweeping Tyrrell successes through the season, before it was time for The Victory Race itself, which would also include some cars from the then Formula 5000. As happy a day as anyone could have wished, with the possible exception of the obvious lack of form of Stewart himself, who could only make third row on the grid.

After his brilliant form in practice, it was surprising, and perhaps even something of an ill omen, that Seppi muffed his start and got away in only ninth place, which left him with a lot of work to do if he was to win through in the short 40 lap race. However, he beavered vigorously away until, with 14 laps completed, he was up into fourth (at 20 m 07.2), behind only Stewart (Tyrrell at 19 m 59.8), Fittipaldi (at 19 m 54.6) and Gethin (leading at 19 m 54.4) ahead of him.

My last sight of Seppi was of him disappearing fast under the bridge on the 15th lap in pursuit of Stewart, clouded almost immediately by that ever sinister pall of thick, black smoke coiling its way into the sky from the direction of Hawthorn/Hill bend. It was the story of Bandini, Schlesser and Courage all over again, only this time the cars following behind slowed and stopped while the fire was slowly put out and Surtees limped back to his pit with a burst tyre caused by the debris from the first phase of Seppi's accident.

It used to be thought that the BRM had gone out of control when a tyre deflated, but David Tremayne's article in *Motor Sport* of October 1991 has put the solution in a very different and authoritative light, and he has very kindly allowed me to quote from his account:

> What went wrong? 'He had a brush with Ronnie Peterson on the startline,' said former BRM team manager Tim Parnell.
> 'I was there and it was one hell of a bump,' recalls Alan Henry. 'He had all four wheels off on the inside.'
> 'We think that the clash broke the bracket that held the radius arm,' continued Parnell. 'It broke going into Hawthorns.'

and then yet another instance of the bizarre in motor racing as Parnell goes on to tell of one letter he had afterwards

> . . . from a spiritualist who said something broke behind Seppi's left shoulder. And that's exactly what did happen. It was spooky. He hit the bank, the car rolled over in flames and he died through lack of oxygen. His only injury was a fractured ankle.

Mercifully Seppi had already been unconscious before the car caught fire.

As his biographer, Jacques Deschenaux, wrote:

> Help was not very quick in coming, two of the three fire extinguishers at the site of the drama did not work. But, in any case, it was too late. On this day Seppi did not have another chance. He had used up his last ticket.
> 'At a time like this I defy anyone to find any sense in our profession,' declared Jackie Stewart.

Close on 50,000 people attended Seppi's funeral at Fribourg five days later, with his 917 forming part of the cortège, just three months after Derek Bell had commemorated Pedro at Silverstone. For both men racing had been a deeply felt way of life—and death—and neither would have had it otherwise.

For me, 24 October 1971 is still one of the most haunting, unforgettable days. That and the miserable aftermath of the accident as the cars were started up and ground their slow, mournful way back to their pits, like a pack of unhappy hounds being returned prematurely to their kennels after a miserable day's sport.

It seemed a very lonely drive back home—even for someone who hardly knew either Pedro or Seppi.

Chapter 41

Some Nobility and Gentry

Count Louis Vorow Zborowski

(Born 20 February 1895: Died 19 October 1924 in an accident during the Italian Grand Prix at Monza)

Sir Henry Birkin Bt.

(Born 26 July 1896: Died 22 June 1933 at the Countess of Caernarfon's Nursing Home due to blood poisoning attributed to burns received from a hot exhaust pipe during the Tripoli Grand Prix on 7 May 1933)

Count Stanislas Czaykowski

(Died 10 September 1933 at Monza in a fire accident following loss of control of his Bugatti on the wet and greasy circuit)

The Marquis of Portago

(Born 11 October 1928: Died 13 May 1957 from injuries sustained in an accident during the closing stages of the last Mille Miglia)

Count Wolfgang Graf Berghe von Trips

(Born 4 May 1928: Died 10 September 1961 from injuries sustained on the second lap following a collision between his Ferrari and Jim Clark's Lotus)

'The stately homes of England
How beautiful they stand,
They prove the upper classes
Have still the upper hand'—*Noel Coward (aka 'The Master')*

And certainly the characters in this Part lived up to the Master's ideas of aristocratic and gracious living. Count Louis Zborowski was born in 1895 and Sir Henry Birkin Bt. a year later. Count Louis' inheritance enabled him to live in some style, both in New York at 19 West 55th Street, and England at Higham, or Highland Court as it is more recently known, on the outskirts of Canterbury where he stabled a succession of his remarkable racing machines—the 'Chitty, Bang-Bangs' and other interesting cars—during his short and exciting career.

When Henry Birkin (as he then was) came out of the Army he bought a DFP from W. O. Bentley, and had it fitted with an odd-looking, clinker-built, mahogany body, which he raced briefly at Brooklands during 1921. Like Count Louis, Birkin's money was inherited, in this instance through the lace manufactory of Guy Birkin Ltd. His racing career did not really start until 1927, some three years after Louis' death, and he was able, for a time, to maintain a similar lifestyle at two successive estates in Norfolk: Tacolneston Hall and Shadwell Park, where his friends the Segraves had kept Christmas with him in 1929.

Count Louis Vorow Zborowski—the Count's Cuff-links (2)

Count Louis was born on 20 February 1895, and he entered Eton by way of Mr Price's school at Broadstairs in the summer half of 1908 as an Oppidan. Scholarship was never his forte and he found himself in III Form, first in Mr Eggar's House and then in Mr Broke's, with a Mr Hare as his tutor. His position was described as 'very low for a boy of 13' and it was no surprise that he was found 'not up to the work' and departing from Eton after the summer half of 1909. His health kept him out of World War I and not much more was heard of him until, in his own delightful phrase, he 'took the cement' at Easter 1921 with the first of his 'Chitty' cars—a 75 hp chain-driven Mercedes fitted with a 6-cylinder 23-litre Maybach-aero-engine from World War I.

Like most racing men of those days, he drove his car up from Higham on the trade plates of a local firm, Bligh Brothers, in whom he had a financial interest. Chitty would not have won any prizes in a Concours, but that was not what the wily Count had in mind and, while he might not have won any prizes for scholarship at Eton, he quickly saw that a scruffily kept monster might not catch the handicappers' eye so readily as a clean one! He was also abetted by a claque of his madcap friends, who turned up in a variety of large 'Moplah' (see page 332) caps in all manner of loud checks that he had had specially brought in from Palm Beach!

However, much of the Count's scheming went up in smoke when he won Chitty's first two races and later a third, as well as another handicap in his 1914 Lyons Grand Prix Mercedes. The first of these races had been narrowly won from the 5-litre Indianapolis Sunbeam driven by the redoubtable André Boillot (see pages 285/9), from scratch, giving the Count a four second advantage.

While the Count may not have set a fashion in headgear, he certainly had in the monster track racers that were starting to appear and, after that Easter meeting, they soon became all the rage. So it was not long before the Count built a second Chitty, which ran a little in 1921 before being seconded to other exciting duties—like accompanying the Count and his Countess on a North African tour 150 miles into the Sahara desert in full touring trim, supported by his faithful assistant Clive Gallop, with yet another Chitty (III) to carry all the luggage on its platform back. Two more Chittys were in prospect: IV, the Higham Special, which ultimately powered Babs, the Leyland-Thomas on which Parry Thomas was killed attempting the Land Speed Record on 3 March 1927 on Pendine sands, and V which was never actually begun.

However, these great machines were really no more than an eccentric nobleman's playthings and his more serious sporting side was reflected in his collection of 'straight' racing cars, several of which actually raced in Grands Prix or at Indianapolis.

As soon as motor racing settled itself down in the aftermath of World War I, it was only to be expected that Count Eliot's son would busy himself racing, which he did, first at Brooklands and then, more ambitiously, in Europe and America. One of his first cars was a 1914 Grand Prix Mercedes that had come over to England in mid-July of 1914 and stayed for the duration.

Although Lou actually got to Le Mans for the 1921 Grand Prix, it was to find that there was no operational Sunbeam Talbot Darracq (STD) car for him to drive as the one allotted to him had had to be cannibalized for spares for the senior drivers. So he resolved not to be caught napping like that again and to beat the Coatalen system by having cars of his own tailor-made in readiness for the French Grand Prix at Strasbourg in 1922.

He, therefore, despatched his general factotum, Clive Gallop, to France to acquire a Henry engine design for the Aston-Martins that he intended to run. One version of the 'Gallop Purchase' has it that M. Henry himself bisected his line drawing of the straight-eight 3-litre Ballot and gave it to Gallop, no doubt with a suitable bag of gold changing hands; another, that it was M. Gremillon, then head of Peugeot's racing department, who passed on the bisected design and, yet another, that Gremillon himself saw the whole job through for the Count. Whichever way, Count Louis got his very own instant Grands Prix cars, but giving away a vital half litre that they could ill afford. The race was over a distance of 498 miles; Count Louis' car lasted 19 of the 60 laps before his engine failed in tenth place, while Gallop was doing rather better until his car succumbed to engine troubles after 30 laps when he had just taken sixth place.

The little cars did not venture to the Italian Grand Prix at Monza, but Count Louis did manage to place one in second in the 1.5-litre voiturette event for the Penya Rhin Grand Prix at Villafranca in November, ahead of four other finishers, including Segrave's Talbot-Darracq. Initially the Count had actually led the whole race until a puncture after 12 of the 35 laps slowed him down to finish 8 mins 23 secs behind the winner. For a private entrant taking on a well-established works team, it was a distinctly good performance.

Count Louis decided to try his luck in the Indy 500 of 1923 with one of the beautiful SPAD bodied, streamlined, single-seat, unsupercharged Type 30 Bugattis. Alas, their beauty was only skin deep and, compared to the Millers of the day, they were mechanical old hat, although the Prince of Cystria managed to last the whole of the race and finish his car in ninth. Count Louis could only manage 41 of the 200 laps and likened the superiority of the Millers to that of the Fiats at Strasbourg the previous year. It was, thus, no surprise to find the Count returning to Europe armed with one for the Italian and Spanish Grands Prix.

Even at Monza the Indy Millers were outpaced by their lack of road holding and weak transmission and Count Louis' car lasted no more than 15 laps, retiring in fifth. Jimmy Murphy, however, greatly distinguished himself, racing his Miller through the full 497-mile distance to take third place, 5 mins 12.6 secs behind the great Nazzaro's Fiat. Although Miller Automobiles had also entered Murphy and the Count for the Spanish Grand Prix in late October, Murphy did not turn up. Count Louis did, and to much good purpose, for the new banked circuit at Sitges suited both him and the characteristics of his car and he finished second, a mere 56 secs behind Divo's winning Sunbeam, after a very close fight, that had also involved Resta's Sunbeam. Again the Count had led for much of the race and only lost out in the last ten laps due to an unscheduled wheel change.

Unbelievably Count Louis then opted to run his Indy Miller in the 1924 French Grand Prix at Lyons rather than in its natural American habitat, and found his fragile little craft ill-suited to the rough, high roads it had to withstand. His struggle—and that of his mechanic, Sammy Davis—lasted for 16 of the 35 laps before the front axle almost completely parted company with its underslung spring on one side of the car, the pair of them having somehow driven the suffering car for almost the whole of a 14.38-mile lap in that state!

Despite, or maybe because of this gallant display, or even with an eye on the Zborowski fortunes, the stern Louis Coatalen was sufficiently impressed to promise the Count a drive for Sunbeam at Monza in October. However, words had a habit of flying into thin air when Coatalen was around and the Sunbeams were never actually entered. By then, the Count had received the even more tempting offer of a place in the new Mercedes team, alongside Christian Werner, the redoubtable Alfred Neubauer, and Count Masetti, who had just driven a very good race for them in a 4-cylinder Mercedes at San Sebastian, pressing the victorious Sunbeams very strongly.

The race had originally been set for 7 September, but was postponed until 19 October in the hope of attracting some more entries, particularly the new team of straight-eight supercharged Mercedes cars designed by the evergreen Dr Porsche. The cars were still barely raceworthy and, although Masetti offered the briefest of challenges at the start, the four P2 Alfa-Romeos led the main race *en bloc*, followed at an ever increasing distance by the second *bloc*, comprising the four Mercedes.

Accounts of the Count's fatal accident inevitably vary. Some ascribed it to a slide on spilt oil; others say that he was trying too hard in order to make up for time lost. Either way, these particular Mercedes would always enjoy an unhappy reputation for handling. Practice for the race had been observed by a reserve driver from Remagen on the Rhine called Caracciola, for whom 'there were so many things wrong with the cars that even the first string drivers hardly had time for practice!' When offered a relief drive during the race, Caracciola reacted with that good sense that was to remain the hall-mark of his driving, and politely declined! Similarly, Raymond Mays, who drove one of the cars in England in 1927, found its handling no less appalling, and Segrave is said to have warned him sternly against ever driving the car again, although by that time Caracciola himself had won the 1926 German Grand Prix with one of these cars at Avus, but, significantly, not until it had been comprehensively reworked and rebuilt by Christian Werner, with Dr Porsche's approval and, significantly, 'according to his (Werner's) own ideas.' For all who loved Count Louis it was a thousand pities that Werner's good work had not been put in hand and the cars more thoroughly tested before the race.

After the accident there was a three-day long enquiry at Monza, which found that it had been caused by oil that had been dropped on the circuit by one of the dry-sump Alfas, although there were many who still suspected a combination of poor handling and inferior chassis design.

Count Louis' career had been almost as brief as his father's and he had perished in the realization of his ambition to drive a Mercedes in a Grand Prix like his father. While he may not have been at the very top of his class, his was no mean record, put together, as Sammy Davis described it, 'by sheer personal courage and intense enthusiasm . . . not as a professional but for the real love of the game . . . He drove as his father drove, with all his heart and soul, but with his head as well, and the sheer intoxication of it he delighted to show.'

Count Louis was gifted with great wealth, which he used to finance his racing and his other eccentricities: for example the records show that, on 20 May 1925 his English estate was proved at £44,425. He was also a notably generous English gentleman with catholic sporting tastes and it has long pleased me to think that a sporting acquaintance of mine, who used to shoot over the Count's property, continued to use a shooting bag with the Count's distinctive 'Z' marked on it as long as he lived. I can boast but one tenuous but valued link with Higham/ Highland Court: that of applying to the Canterbury Licensing Justices, on behalf of the St Lawrence & Highland Court Cricket Club, for its annual extensions of the permitted hours during the Canterbury

Cricket Week on the lovely St Lawrence cricket ground. Whether or not the Count ever wielded a cricket bat, I do not know, but I like to think he would have approved of my application!

Let his great friend, the late Sammy Davis, have the last word:

> Coming out of the void like that the announcement of Lou's fatal crash was more of a shock than usual, and, still, all these years after I think his absence is felt more than ever. Certainly I have missed him as I never thought I could miss anyone.

Davis was also said to have brought two other curious facts to light. That Count Eliot's accident had been caused by his shirt cuff being caught in the hand throttle and thereby pulling it wide open, and that when Count Louis was killed at Monza he was wearing the very links from that shirt. This provides yet another bizarre coincidence, of the two Zborowskis racing to their deaths in and against Mercedes cars that were both driven by men called Werner.

Sir Henry Birkin Bt.

Sir Henry ('Tim') Birkin was, in every sense, an amateur driver who raced almost entirely for the fun of it and very much in the manner of the Counts Zborowski. Like Count Louis, he epitomized the glamorous, madcap atmosphere of the roaring 20s and early 30s, when he would surely have cut a splendid dash in America, whether on the board tracks or at Indy itself. Instead, he based himself in the English sporting countryside and became the hero of myriad school boys for the brightness of his silk neck-cloths, the panache of his driving and the roar of the cars of the Great Bentley Days.

Birkin's great grandfather had founded his Nottingham lace manufactory in 1827 and today his Company, now called Guy Birkin Ltd, following a merger in 1962, can claim to be the oldest registered lace-making company in the world, and is still vitally involved in the expansion of its trade: efforts that have more than paid off in terms of its share of sales and markets.

Birkin's family's wealth and his Baronetcy were derived from that same industry. Sir Henry was the second son of his father, the second Baronet, Sir Stanley, and a grandson of the first Baronet. Birkin's elder brother died in action in France during World War I and the title ultimately passed to Sir Henry on his father's death in 1931. By bizarre coincidence Birkin's father had also died of blood poisoning.

Henry Ralph Stanley ('Tim') Birkin was born on 26 July 1896 and served in World War I from 1914 right through to 1919, first as a soldier of the line with the 'Robin Hoods' (the 7th Sherwood Foresters) before taking a commission in the 20th Reserve Wing of the Royal Flying Corps, and spent over two years in the Middle East before service in the Royal Warwickshire Regiment. He raced in a desultory sort of way through 1921 and after that took no further part in it until the Essex six-hours race of 1927 at Brooklands in his own 3-litre Bentley. He had married in July 1921, having two daughters born in 1922 and 1926, and was divorced in 1927.

Goodness knows how or indeed where he would be rated as a driver today, for he missed out on the whole of Coatalen's STD years when Segrave made such a name for himself, and only seldom took part in foreign Grands Prix. Yet he has left the legacy of two memorable drives: at Pau in 1930 and Tripoli in 1933. The 1930 Grand Prix of Pau was a distinct odd-ball, run over a 9.8-mile circuit, well away from the familiar town-bound street race.

Bugatti had hoped to run a brace of his new twin-cam 2.3-litre Type 51 cars, but, as so often happened, they were not ready, so Williams, Bouriat, Etancelin, Wimille (in his first French Grand Prix), Lehoux and Count Czaykowski were left to race their lithe Type 35s against, of all things, Birkin's stripped 'Blower' Bentley, weighing in at something like 47 cwt. To counterbalance things at the other end of the scale there was Robert Seneschal's diminutive Grand Prix Delage from 1927.

Luckily for Sir Henry the circuit was open and fast, which enabled him to stay ahead of his lighter rivals, with the exception of Etancelin, who ran out the winner by nearly $3\frac{1}{2}$ minutes. A rather charming touch was provided by the fact of Birkin's car being fitted with a horn, which came in handy when he was trying to overtake an inattentive and perhaps rather bored Louis Chiron, who soon enough pulled over when he saw over two tons of flame-belching green Bentley bearing down upon him. Anyone who has followed or driven such a car through a long dusty summer's day can vouch for its firework displays and Wagnerian sound effects. They truly don't make them like that any more!

Birkin's last drive was his greatest and must have given any British spectators at Tripoli on 7 May 1933 no end of a fillip. The field contained all the great names of the day, save Caracciola and Chiron, but they all had to give best to Birkin and his privately entered Maserati for the first five laps, although this could have been due to the cabalistic manoeuvres of the drivers who were in on 'The Plot'. Choose how, at half-distance he was still second to Nuvolari, and he finally finished third behind both Varzi and Nuvolari after being delayed by poor pit work. While there was nothing to show that he was in anyway implicated or even aware of the Great Tripoli Scandal of 1933 (see pages 81 and 83), Tripoli was to mark him down rather more tragically.

Brock Yates tells a delightful story, in his book *Enzo Ferrari*, of Birkin 'pressing on with Edwardian resolve' and having to do all his own pitwork because Maserati had only sent one mechanic to service both his car and that of Campari, seemingly ignoring the fact that Fagioli was also driving a works Maserati! Interestingly, Yates also refers to Marshal Balbo as starting the race and generally presiding over the whole glittering show, whereas *Auto Italiana* of 20 May 1933 makes it perfectly clear that the race was in fact started by General (as he then was) Badoglio at 1415 hrs precisely, with no mention of the gallant Marshal there or anywhere else. *Motor Sport* of June 1933 also refers to Badoglio, though prematurely promoted to Marshal, starting the race in his capacity of Governor of Tripoli at 'a few minutes after three o'clock'. Accounts surely did vary in those days!

But to return to Sir Henry: assuming Yates's informant to be correct, there are no prizes for guessing who bagged the services of the Maserati mechanic and who was left to enlist 'the aid of a local garageman who turned out to be a hopeless drunk and spent the entire race dozing under a palm tree!' During the race, or even in practice, according to W. O. Bentley, and, perhaps while he was refuelling/wheel changing, 'Tiger Tim' sustained one or more small burn(s) on one or both forearms—for accounts vary between the hot exhaust pipe of the Maserati and cigarette burns. Whatever the cause Birkin characteristically took no notice of these minor hurts until, all too late, those neglected injuries flared up a few weeks later, possibly brought on by a recurrence of wartime malaria from his service in the East. He was admitted to the Countess of Caernarfon's Nursing Home in London, but by then there was no cure for him despite the devoted care of specialists, including his great Bentley-driving friend, Dr J. D. Benjafield (a Consultant Bacteriologist at St Georges Hospital). His condition worsened and he ultimately died on 22 June 1933. With today's drugs he would in all probability have lived to go on enjoying the pleasures of Town and Country which were so much part of his lifestyle, and could well have included being the original of that man who had danced with a girl who had danced with the Prince of Wales, for his second cousin, Lady Freda Dudley Ward, to whom he left virtually all of his remaining estate, had been a long term 'Belle Amie' of that same Prince.

Yet, at the end of the day, what really had remained? What had his hectic life really been all about and, what memorial had he to leave to posterity save for a gravestone in Blakeney Churchyard with its epitaph saluting him as a 'A Racing Motorist of International Fame'; a memorial plaque at Brooklands that was later unveiled by Earl Howe, who called him 'one of the finest fellows who ever lived, whose loss will be felt as much abroad as it will in this country'; and Birkin Way at Tacolneston where he had lived for a short time?

So perhaps it had all happened for the best after all, for the closing years of his life were far from happy, even though they had not seemed to inhibit his zest for motor racing and the country sports that he so much enjoyed, along with motor boating—for preference, at high speed. This was either in the *Ida*, which still exists, or in smaller boats dating back to the earlier days of outboard power. *Ida* was also used on duck shooting expeditions, for which he was a crack shot and a great enthusiast. With this same boat it was also said that he had introduced water-skiing to the Norfolk coast. In addition he owned a schooner variously named *Minnie, Moffie* or *Frothblower.*

The trouble was that country houses and shooting parties for anything up to thirty guns all cost money and, by the end of his days anyway, he was no Barnato who could afford to jog comfortably along at the rate of £800 or £900 a week. His estate papers show this all too clearly. It had also been significant that, whereas he had first bought and then sold the Tacolneston estate, he had only rented Shadwell. A world in which he could no longer be a smart trend-setter, right down to his personally designed dinner jackets, would have had no attraction for him and could only have added to the bouts of depression that were already eating into his life and soul. It had all happened, too, at such a wrong time, coinciding with the shutdown of Bentley Motors and the loss of the essential financial backing that he had been receiving from Dorothy Paget for the 'Blower' cars that gave him so much joy when they were going!

Whether or not he still owned the single-seater at the end of his days, he continued to let it loose from time to time on the Brooklands Outer Circuit for the odd spring meeting, and eventually coaxed a new and final lap record from the old warrior of 137.96 mph during practice for the BARC Easter Meeting of 1932. During the meeting itself he appropriately won the Norfolk Lightning Long Handicap but had to retire from the British Empire Trophy with a cracked cylinder block. The grand old car's swansong came at the August BARC meeting that same year. Although he could not quite surpass his track record, he came perilously close to it on his last lap, at 137.56 mph, when he won a 1/5th sec victory from John Cobb in the 10.5-litre Delage that had once held the Land Speed Record.

Birkin had also been a great supporter of the Blakeney Royal National Lifeboat Institution, of which he had been proud to be its President and, at his funeral, his local crew saw him properly buried there in style with his feet towards the sea he so much loved.

Yet one still remains puzzled—and saddened—by a life whose ending left so much seemingly still undone and the sad, lingering regret that so patriotic a man had had to end his days shopping abroad for his racing cars.

Of course, this was nothing new for a Briton who wanted to go motor racing seriously in the 30s, and it was not to be until the late 50s that the Grand Prix world was forced to recognize the might and talent of British racing drivers and their cars. How 'Tiger Tim' would have relished those days and, remember, he would still have been only 62 in 1958 when Mike Hawthorn became the first British World Champion.

Count Stanislas Czaykowski

Count Czaykowski, who died later in 1933, was one of those middle-European titled gentlemen racers who abounded in the 20s and 30s.

Like all the other characters in this Part, he was a man of means, and chose to divide his time between Paris, where he lived, and Nice, where he had relatives and friends, among whom were Bugatti's 'Ancient', Ernst Friederich, from whom the Count bought most of his many Bugattis, and René Dreyfus, with whom he shared many good times. René has described him as 'an avid golfer, and an avid drinker of "Picon et Citron", a pernod-like drink with syrup of lemon added, which seemed pleasantly harmless until it hit you like a sledgehammer!' The temperate René usually contented himself with nothing more than a couple of snorts. Not so Count Stanislas, for whom it was mother's milk! 'there was no doubt,' writes René, 'he drank too much, but the result was noticeable only in his big red face. He was a completely likeable man always—and a fine driver.'

Count Stanislas started his known racing career with an outright win in the voiturette section of the Grand Prix de Comminges on the St Gaudens Circuit in 1929. He also won his next race, the first and only Circuit d'Esterel Plage in March 1930, once again from a negligible field, before winning from himself alone at Lyon, for fields could be extremely patchy in those days! His 1931 season with a Type 35C Bugatti was much fuller: sixth at Tunis and ninth at Monaco before winning the Casablanca street race with a new Type 51 unlike the 35Cs still being campaigned by the well-seasoned Lehoux and Etancelin. Geneva then brought bad luck, when his car ran into the crowd and a spectator was killed, while the Count was lucky to get away with a painful broken rib. This kept him out for a month, and he celebrated his return with his best result to date: third in the prestigious Marne Grand Prix behind Dreyfus (Maserati) and Lehoux (Type 51), followed by three more second places behind Etancelin and his Monza Alfa.

His friend René was being proved right about the Count's growing ability, and to wind up their season the two friends decided to give the small town of Brignoles a whirl by entering their Bugattis for its 'street race', which the locals billed as the first of its kind to be run in a French town—all 27 miles of it! Now, anyone who has pulled off the Autoroute at the sleepy little Brignoles exit will know how ill-suited the town must have been for the staging of such a race. The chosen circuit traversed two level crossings, and also involved closing the heavily used N7 for the duration of the races organized by the local AC du Var, who had assembled a large field for an ambitious programme for all classes of motor cycles, with or without sidecars, and sports and racing cars. They had even attracted the entry from the Scuderia Ferrari of its renowned veteran driver, Ferdinando Minoia, although he non-started. Goodness alone knows how such a race, involving a major Route Nationale and the French railway system ever got sanctioned in the first place, and it was certainly never repeated; though I reflect fondly on its complexities every time I go down by that route to the Côte d'Azur. Pleasant memories for me and, I hope, for René as well, for that humble little circuit gave him his one and only win in a disastrous season. Count Stanislas could only finish third, 5 seconds behind one J. Lumachi, whose name could well be confused with the Italian 'Lumaca' or Snail, or had the Count already been celebrating the end of the season with a little too much 'Picon' and not quite enough 'Citron' in his aperitif?

Although the Count entered 1932 with a Type 51 Bugatti, he achieved very little with it, even in relatively minor races, like the Grands Prix of Lorraine (second and third), Nimes (third) and Casablanca (fourth). He did, however, bring over a 2-litre Bugatti to race in Class E of the BRDC 500-mile race, Britain's belated answer to the great Indy classic. Needless to say the organizers' attempts to explain the significance of the various lines painted on the track to the Count were quite unavailing, but somehow this did not seem to matter as he was still running in third place at mid-afternoon before his car was withdrawn with smoke pouring from its bonnet.

It was not until he acquired a 4.9-litre Type 54 Bugatti in 1933 that he began scoring some more impressive results. He started by raising the world's 1-hour record at Avus to 132.86 mph, before winning the British Empire Trophy on the Outer Circuit at Brooklands at an average speed of 123.55 mph for the 125-mile distance from Kaye Don's similar car, which the Count found a real handful! Earlier, in May, Varzi in another Type 54, had beaten him by the narrow margin of 1/5th sec at Avus and, later in the year, at Comminges the Type 54 came out for its penultimate run, retiring with tyre troubles after only 14 laps.

Although he is down as entering it for the Italian Grand Prix at Monza, he did not start, preferring to run in the ill-starred Monza Grand Prix that succeeded the major event.

Sure enough, he won his heat in the big car with some ease at an average speed of 113.472 mph, which was marginally slower than Fagioli's fastest race lap in the morning of 115.78 mph. After the calamitous second heat when both Campari and Borzacchini lost their lives (see pages 81/2), the third heat was eventually run off without disaster before the final started. At the end of the first lap the aspiring Whitney Straight led in his Maserati, although the race was thought likely to lie between those old Bugatti rivals, Lehoux and the Count. *Motor Sport*'s correspondent, 'R.H.R', recalled thinking with fatal prescience: 'This will be a fine Bugatti finish, first, second and third if Lehoux and Czaykowski will take things quietly and not race each other to death.': Prophetic words of gloom echoing those of Loraine Barrow to Charles Jarrott on the eve of Paris-Madrid in 1903 (see page 67). And, sure enough, on the eighth lap, Lehoux came around alone and headed for the pits to notify Czaykowski's accident. 'R.H.R.' continues: 'My interest as a journalist promptly lapsed. Campari— Borzacchini—they were just fine drivers to me and my interest was purely academic, but Czaykowski was a friend with the same feelings for his Bugatti as I for mine. His trouble seemed more real to me than that of the others . . . I went back to my hotel without waiting for the finish.'

Czaykowski had skidded on the slippery surface at over 100 mph and left the road to crash and have his petrol tank explode and burst into flames long before any help could be brought to him. In their differing ways and in those very different days, there had been no hope for either the Baronet or the Count, whose last hours had come long before those of Circuit Safety and Medical Support.

The Marquis of Portago

'Only the Brave deserve the Fair'

Alfonso de Portago should have lived in the days when knights jousted for their ladies' silken and other favours. Don Alfonso Cabeza de Vac y Leighton, Carvajal y Are, 13th Conde de la Majorada and 17th Marquis de Portago—but 'Fon' to his friends, for short—was a many sided character besides being the late King Alfonso's godson. For some he was the epitome of young European Renaissance Man: a superb all round sportsman, who excelled in all the manly sports and more besides, for he was also a gentleman with pretensions to culture and learning almost as an afterthought: as you might think, an Elizabethan reborn. Their life, though, was no rest cure: you have only to look at a gallery of Elizabethans, young or old, French, Spanish, English or Italian, to realize from their watchful, haunted faces that there could be other and darker sides to their varied, polymathist natures: a careworn flipside that could be compounded of ceaseless pleasure, permanent debt and almost total irresponsibility, no less than the need to keep up appearances. Perhaps, too, his talents were too thinly spread, for the Marquis was never the greatest of drivers and the grass and fences of Aintree probably suited him better than its concrete perimeter.

So, after accompanying Luigi Chinetti as riding ballast in the Carrera Panamericana of 1953, he bought himself a 3-litre Ferrari, which he and Harry Schell co-drove in the Argentine 1000 of 1954. Harry drove all but four laps of the race, during which short time Fon had contrived to drop the car from second to fifth, but thanks to Harry the 'pair' still managed to finish second. He then bought, in the quick succession that one associates with Mr Toad, a Maserati, which blew up first time out, and an Osca, which he crashed on the Nürburgring.

1955 found him campaigning a 2.5-litre Ferrari 625 with results that can only be described as appalling. Retirement at Turin with 'sump trouble': eighth and last classified finisher at Pau; 'mechanical' retirement after 15 laps at Bordeaux and a broken leg, with no practice time recorded, when he crashed out at Silverstone. Back on circuit in late

September for the Oulton Park Gold Cup, he was well down the practice grid and retired 'after a spin'. Thereafter he took no further part in Grand Prix racing until mid-1956 when he had his first works drive for Ferrari. He lasted 20 laps of the French Grand Prix before his Lancia-Ferrari developed gearbox trouble. Silverstone brought him a little more respectability with what was technically a shared drive to second with Peter Collins, who had taken over Fon's car when his own failed after 64 of the 101 laps. Finally, at Monza, he went out with a puncture after six laps and, on that flat note, his Grand Prix career ended.

Fon is sometimes bracketed with another lively character, Harry Schell (see pages 321/4) although he was nowhere near Harry's class as a driver. In early 1957 *Autocar* reported him as hurrying to St Moritz from sunny Nassau and lowering the 25-year-old Cresta Run record by 0.1 sec from 28.9 sec. When it came to horse racing, he was Europe's leading amateur jockey until his weight started giving him some problems and although he rode in a couple of Nationals, he finished in neither.

He was also highly placed in an Olympic Bob, like Piero Taruffi, who actually won Fon's fatal last Mille Miglia. He was also gifted with an attractively dry sense of humour:

> Fangio said I was his most dangerous rival at that particular race, but I fear he may have been exaggerating!
> . . . there are lots of ways to lose weight—personally I think Rubirosa and Aly Khan have the best way, but I'm married!
> For all my fear, I thought that racing had a charm and I decided to take it up . . .
> When I had it [a broken clutch!] back together, there were 53 nuts and bolts left over, and you know what?—The clutch didn't break at Sebring, the back axle did!
> I'm sure I love life more than the average man does. I want to get something out of every minute. I want no time wasted . . . People say that racing drivers don't care whether they live or not . . . That's nonsense, all nonsense.

In early 1957 there were signs that he was beginning to mellow into something of a race driver. In the Cuban Grand Prix he led a field that included Fangio himself until he had a fuel line break, sending him down to third behind Fangio and Shelby. At Sebring he drove most of his car's 12-hour stint to finish seventh, and at Montlhéry he set a lap record and a track record for GT cars.

Sadly, though, those maturing processes had not sunk fully into his character by 12 May, the day of the 24th Mille Miglia that was to bring a final, irrevocable end to the series that had been pioneered from 1927 by that Famous Four of Count Aymo Maggi, Count Franco Mazzotti, Giovanni Canestrini and Renzo Castagneto.

That fatal race gave a clouded victory to Piero Taruffi, who had been trying to win the great classic for years; bitter disappointment to

Peter Collins, who had led much of the race with his renowed photographer-passenger, Louis Klementaski; violent death to the dashing Marquis, his riding passenger Ed Nelson and eleven others; and no opportunity for his team mate, von Trips to come back the next year and win a race, which some accounts claim he 'gave' to gallant old Taruffi by the odd three mins.

So, at the end, we come back to Mr Toad and Fon's penchant for outward show: a man for whom the swaggering gesture was as irresistible as it was to play the gallant momentarily with the current lady of his choice, instead of playing safe and checking his car's fast wearing tyres. That day, with Linda Christian looming large in his sights, Fon was listening to all the wrong voices for those few, fleeting, fatal moments; voices that were to shut out that day and forever his more tranquil thoughts:

> . . . I want to live to be a very old man . . . [but] . . . no matter how long I live, I won't have time for all the things I want to do. I won't hear all the music . . . read all the books . . . have all the women: I won't be able to do a twentieth of the things I want to do.

If only Fon could have restricted himself to the lazy, self-indulgent activities of mythological Gods like Hermes, the rascally Pan the Priapic, and Bacchus the boozy, and left hard driving characters like Helius, the fiery charioteer of the skies, safely at home in the garage. As for Miss Christian, she outlived both Fon and her handsome screen actor husband, Tyrone Power, who had survived war service with the US Marines before dying the year after Fon at the young age of 44.

Count Wolfgang Graf Berghe von Trips

Although von Trips had also been born into money, as a good German he had literally had to work for it the hard way. The Baron drove in some of the lesser domestic sports car races of the day before graduating to sterner stuff as a reserve for Mercedes-Benz in the direful Le Mans of 1955. He drove for them several more times during the rest of that season, notably in Sweden where his brakes let him down and sent him spinning off, and the Irish Tourist Trophy where he shared third place with Simon in a 300SLR Mercedes behind their two team-mates.

In 1956 he drove his first race for Ferrari in the 1000-mile Swedish sports car Grand Prix. This was a Ferrari team benefit, where he was teamed up with Peter Collins and took second behind the winners, Trintignant and Phil Hill, and ahead of a mini-committee consisting of Hawthorn, de Portago and Duncan Hamilton. In the same year he also won the Berlin Grand Prix for 1500 cc sports cars and, at the end of the year, Ferrari called him to drive one of his D50 Lancia based cars in the Italian Grand Prix.

This first moment of Italian glory was short-lived as he crashed out heavily in practice when his steering broke at high speed in the Curva Grande. The bold Baron was lucky to escape with minor cuts and bruises and, as a matter of Ferrari routine, it was impressed upon him that the accident must have been all his own fault, for it was well-known that Ferraris never broke. However, when the cars of both Musso and Fangio himself suffered similar mishaps during the race, Ferrari changed his tune and took the Baron on 'for the duration' (until his death) with the exception of an abortive season in 1959 with Porsche. Forgetting the 'von Krash-type' jokes at his expense—all a bit reminiscent of James 'Hunt the Shunt' days—which took him a long time to live down, it had been a truly horrendous accident which he had been exceedingly lucky to survive.

By January of 1957 he was back in action for a shared drive in the Argentine, but he achieved little thereafter until September when Monza brought him better luck: third, two laps behind Moss and Fangio. 1958 was little better apart from another third, this time in the French Grand Prix, behind Hawthorn and Moss. Again, too, Monza had a nasty sting in its tail when he ran up the back of Harry Schell's BRM in the Lesmo area on the first lap. Trips's car took off, throwing him out this time, and he was again lucky to escape with only a broken leg.

This had mended by 1959 when he opted for a stint with a home-grown product for a change—a single seat Formula 2 Porsche of 1498 cc that was derived from their RSK sports car. Yet again he did not get very far at Monaco, being eliminated by an oil spill skid on the second lap, which involved him with Cliff Allison's Formula 2 Dino 156 Ferrari and Bruce Halford's Formula 2 Lotus-Climax. The poor Baron was left to rue his ill luck and was heard murmuring sadly to himself: 'I don't even have to be on the Ferrari team to break Ferraris!' Once again Ferrari showed that he did have a gentler, compassionate side to him by restoring the Baron to favour for his last two seasons of 1960/61.

Wisely the Baron and his team-mates put their disastrous 1960 season behind them and embarked on the halcyon season of 1961 marred, solely and totally, by Trips's third and last Monza crash. Until then it had been a mini-golden age for Ferrari with his new 1.5-litre shark-nosed babies running rings round an opposition that was without an engine worth the name—unless it was called Stirling Moss!

Four men dominated 1961: first and foremost it had to be Moss, with his two remarkable victories at Monaco and the rain-soaked Ring. Then it was the turn of Giancarlo Baghetti, the Boy Wonder, who had pipped Bandini for the right to the Italian-styled 'FISA' car, with which he covered himself with glory by winning, first at Syracuse and then at Rheims in the French Grand Prix before coming a little unstuck in the unfamiliar British rain at Aintree. Thus did the two wondermen of 1961 account for three of the Grands Prix, leaving the other three on the European mainland for Trips and Hill to fight out for the championship, race by race, with first one and then the other keeping his nose narrowly in front until they came to Monza.

At that stage Trips led by a bare two points and was widely tipped to win the championship outright by taking first place so long as Phil Hill finished no higher than fourth, which summed up the mathematics of the situation. In terms of outright wins, Trips had two to Hill's singleton, with the two folks heroes, Stirling Moss on two wins and Baghetti on one. The occasion was overshadowed by another gloom-laden echo of Trips's aside to *New York Times* correspondent, Robert Daley, the evening before the race: 'Talking about the thin line between maximum speed and crashing, he [Trips] had said abruptly: "It could happen tomorrow. That's the thing about this business. You never know."'

Trips never saw Daley's article, which appeared in the paper's sporting section at about the hour (because of the time difference) that the engines were being revved up at Monza. Before most New Yorkers had finished their first cups of coffee, Trips was dead.

The accident happened on the second lap when Trips and, of all people, Jim Clark, collided in the braking area for the very fast Parabolica curve. That day it was Clark who stepped from his car unscathed, while Trips's Ferrari flew off the road, again throwing its driver out, before crashing into a fence with spectators behind it. Fourteen people ultimately died, as well as the hapless driver, and several more were injured.

Clark's car was immediately impounded, but Colin Chapman adroitly extracted his driver from the shattered aftermath and flew him straight away back to England in his Piper Comanche. The Italian police were not at all pleased and, although Clark returned to take pole position and win at Monza in both 1962 and 1963, he still had to face a police enquiry about an accident that was, by then, two years old.

Clark later described that enquiry as 'a miserable end to what should have been the most memorable day of my life'—the day on which he clinched his first World Championship. It had been no less upsetting for Phil Hill, the champion with the crown of thorns, and a sorry end for the man who had been born Count/Baron Wolfgang Graf Berghe 'Taffy' von Trips and who had been so delicately poised to win that year's World Championship.

It was almost as if there was a Jinx on German drivers for, not counting Austrians, how many purely German drivers of top quality had there ever been then? Caracciola (from 1926), Lang and Rosemeyer from 1935 and, then, a long nothing and nobody until the advent of the Count-Baron in 1956.

By 1961 he had all but achieved the seeming impossible and was actually leading the championship stakes with 33 points against Hill's 29 when the fatal race began. In the end, Hill's Ferrari lasted through to a victory that gained him the championship but, had he finished any lower than second, Trips would have been the first posthumous champion.

As it was, that grim victory remained in suspense for another nine years, when, by coincidence, it would be won by another German: Jochen Rindt.

PART 14

THREE HIGH FLIERS

'Life is as fleeting as a fire.
You never know how long the
flame will last.'

Chapter 42

'Two Peas in a Pod' and 'Mike the Bike'

Jean Behra
*(Born 16 February 1921 at Nice: Died 1 August 1959 on the Avus Ring when his
Sports Porsche went over the top of the banking)*

Patrick Depailler
*(Born 9 August 1944: Died 1 August 1980 during practice for the German Grand
Prix at Hockenheim, Germany)*

S. M. B. ('Mike') Hailwood MBE, GM
*(Born 2 April 1940: Died 23 March 1981 in a road accident near
Tamworth-in-Arden)*

Although their births were separated by two decades Jean Behra
and Patrick Depailler seemed more like two peas from the same
pod: as French as frites, garlic and Gauloises, lively as crickets, brave
as lions and, as some might add, mad as March hares. Wonderful value
for the spectator, great fun as companions and brimful with those
traditional French qualities of 'cran' and 'élan'. Unmistakable, too, in
their outward appearances, and alike in their passion for racing.
  Neither enjoyed too much luck in their Grand Prix careers, yet both
did enough to carve out their own special niches in both history and in
the hearts of those who saw and knew them in their best years. If their
gallant precursors Levegh and Rosier (see pages 295/302) were the
beaux gendarmes, or the 'vieux moustaches', of their time, then they
were worthily succeeded by Jeannot and Patrick. Depailler won two
World Championship Grands Prix during his six years in Formula 1,
along with one pole position and four fastest race laps and, while
Jeannot never won a full World Championship Grand Prix, he won

nine races of rank during his operational years, 1952/59, including the 1957 Grand Prix of Casablanca, and a fastest race lap.

'Name and Rank; they don't give Numbers to losers', is an old saying that is often as cruel as it is unfair—and, in the main, it was surely so both to Jeannot and Patrick. During 1952/59 Grand Prix racing was dominated by the three Master Drivers of the period—Ascari, Fangio and Moss, and it was very much the same with the leading cars of 1974/80: Lotus, Ferrari, McLaren, and then Lotus again dominated. In either period it was very necessary to have been born in the right bed, and neither of our subjects had that kind of luck. Perhaps, too, they lacked the necessary levels of Character demonstrated by the Master Drivers of those years.

Once they had put World War II behind them, Jean-Pierre Wimille, Louis Chiron, Philippe Etancelin and Seppi Siffert's 'beau idéal', Raymond Sommer, were the cornerstones of French motor racing during the mid-to-late 40s until their successive deaths: Wimille in 1949 and Sommer in 1950, followed by the gradual eclipse of Chiron and Etancelin during the first half of the 50s. With all these departures France seemed all of a sudden to have no great front-line figures to fill the gaps, until Jean Behra abandoned two wheels for four in 1951 and signed up with Gordini at the relatively mature age of 30. His volatile driving and his white helmet, with its distinctive black chequered ring round it, were not long in asserting an unmistakable and welcome touch of Gallic verve.

Sad, then, that Gordini's flame was so ephemeral and his équipe such a losing cause that no amount of 'cran' and 'élan' could compensate for its technical, financial and mechanical shortcomings. Yet, out of all this delusion, the so-called 'Sorcerer' did manage to conjure one Famous Victory for France's new hero—in the Rheims Grand Prix of 1952. Behra seized the lead from the very start and led the three-hour race from beginning to end, even damping the fierce challenge of the 'campionissimo' himself in the opening stages—and there were precious few who could do that in 1952/53. However, enough was enough and, although it would always rank as a wonderful French tour-de-force, worthy of their dear departed 'Coeur de Lion', it was to remain almost alone in its pride until the emergence of the French champions of the 70s and 80s.

In the meantime, Jeannot fought doggedly on for Gordini into 1954, wresting one last dramatic victory for him at Pau over an assortment of 250F and other Maseratis and the 625 Ferraris of all the greats, with the exception of Ascari and Fangio. Eventually, after a stern three-hour duel with the genial Maurice Trintignant through the narrow streets of that most picturesque of towns, and never separated by more than the length of three cricket pitches, Behra finally stormed past after 100 of the 110 laps and stayed there to win by just 0.2 secs.

The Grand Prix scene had been greatly enlivened in that year by the arrival of new cars from Mercedes (the W196), Lancia (D50) and

Maserati (250F), although, at the same time, they were to be the death of Gordini. In the autumn Behra had had an approach from Count Orsi, which he could hardly have refused, and for three happy and fulfilling years he made a very happy and modestly successful home with his new Italian masters. After that, with Maserati a spent force, he went on first to BRM and, then, quite fatally, to Ferrari. Of course he should have stayed with BRM, but the very name of Ferrari has always exercised a strange, snake-like fascination for a long succession of unsettled drivers, with the notable exception of three of Britain's greatest: Stirling Moss, Graham Hill and Jackie Stewart. In the end, the temptation proved too great for Jean Behra and he made his fatal move from BRM at the end of 1958, just when their troublesome car was about to come into its own by winning at Zandvoort. On that memorable day Jo Bonnier won the first Grand Prix victory for BRM and the only one for himself, while Jeannot, wearing his Emperor's splendid new clothes, had to be content with a distant fifth in the best placed Ferrari.

And he did not even have the consolation of Spa to give him a chance of showing what he could do in a fast car over a fast, demanding circuit, which might have made a lot of difference to so many things. As it was, he was finding himself increasingly a stranger in a strange land populated by no less strange people for whom English had suddenly become the 'lingua franca'. This, along with their sheer differences in personality, made him feel more and more the odd man out, with every man's hand turned against him. Like many other rugged, independent people, he was probably not the easiest of colleagues or team drivers, and thus the last person to have found a comfortable billet at Maranello.

All this undercurrent of feeling exploded at Rheims, along with the engine of his Dino Ferrari, to create a fiery incident with of all people, Ferrari's much-liked team manager, Romolo Tavoni. His attack on Tavoni proved the absolute end for Jeannot with Ferrari, who brushed aside all his apologies and promises of good behaviour like so much chaff. He had well and truly shot his bolt and he died a few weeks later on the wet and treacherous banking at Avus very much as he had lived, wheel in hand, fighting the odds against whom and whatsoever, which in this case happened to be a little sports Porsche RSK.

His loss was great, sad and not a little moving, for the tough little Frenchman represented an attitude and a type that went back to the beginnings of motor racing history, not least for the way in which, like any old-time golf Pro., he preferred to have his 'shop' close to the racing cars that were his life and meant so much to him. I like to think of him in several places: like Rheims in 1952, or Pau two years later, but most of all driving the pants off all the Great Ones at Casablanca on 27 October 1957—a full Grande Épreuve if ever there was one, dominated on that day by the Master Drive of a great, big-hearted, little man.

In a wholly different context, how right it was that he should have staged his final tour-de-force at Casablanca with its haunting shades of Rick's Bar which with a little homely adaptation of its theme. 'As Time Goes By', calls up the memory of a man for whom it would always have been:

> ... the same old story,
> A fight for power and glory,
> A case of 'Do or Die'.

Jean Behra had died on 1 August 1959 and, by most bizarre coincidence, his spiritual successor, Patrick Depailler was to die driving a racing car on the same day 21 years later—and again in Germany, though at Hockenheim instead of Avus. In one respect, at least, he was the opposite of Behra, as was put well by Nigel Roebuck in his book *Grand Prix Greats*:

> ... [Patrick] had a vulnerability about him that women found magnetic, and his face, in repose, often had a tragic quality—instantly dispelled by that lopsided grin.

and Bob Tronolone's brilliant print of Patrick tells it all just as emotively as Nigel writes it.

I last saw Patrick Depailler at Brands Hatch on a bright sunny day at Brands Hatch in July 1980 as my wife and I strolled idly down the pit lane—still accessible enough in those days—laughing with Patrick and the almost childish joy that he was taking in his horse-play athwart the handlebars of his bicycle: a much needed touch of harmless foolery to lighten the long seriousness that has characterized so much of Grand Prix practice for close on a couple of decades. Not so Patrick, be it his bicycle, his hang-gliding or his big motor bikes. Like Mr Toad, he was quite irrepressible and, like Peter Rabbit, as often as not, he found himself in hot water!

Patrick got his first major break towards a Formula 1 drive when he won the Monaco Formula 3 race in 1972 after winning the French Formula 3 championship of 1971. The French Grand Prix of 1972 was held on Patrick's home ground at the long-forgotten Clermont-Ferrand circuit, and Ken Tyrrell was sufficiently impressed to give another promising local lad a leg upon his way in the world. He started from the eighth row of the grid and finished 20th, five laps away after a steady drive interrupted by the endemic plague of punctures caused by this rough and demanding circuit. After that he had one more drive for Tyrrell in 1972 at Watkins Glen, where he finished a sound seventh behind Stewart, Cevert, Hulme, Peterson, Ickx and Andretti: good company indeed for a relative newcomer.

After that there was no more Formula 1 for Patrick until the late summer of 1973 brought another invitation from Tyrrell to drive at both Mosport and the Glen. This could have been his real chance, but ...

... ten days before he goes and breaks his leg falling off a motorbike! Later when he was driving full time for me, I had it written into his contract that he had to keep away from dangerous toys.

said an all-forgiving Uncle Ken!

François Cevert was an old rival of Patrick's from their Volant-Shell days of 1967, when François had narrowly beaten him to the top award and, at the end of 1973, he seemed firmly set to inherit Jackie Stewart's No. 1 place chez Tyrrell when his 'master' retired. However, it did not work out like that at all. Immediately before Stewart retired, Cevert was killed at the Glen in a practice accident and, forgetting all Patrick's irresponsibility over his motor bike crash, Ken Tyrrell decided to fill the gap by making Patrick his No. 2 driver for 1974, where he stayed very happily until 1978. During his Tyrrell years he posted two good years' rankings of fourth (1976) and fifth (1978) and won just the one Grande Épreuve: at Monaco in 1978.

At that point Patrick felt the pull of 'Bleue de France' so, whatever the wrench—and great it was—he made his patriotic move to join his fellow countryman, Jacques Laffite, in the French Ligier team. At first the sun seemed to shine on him as never before, with fourth in the Argentine, after running second for much of the race; second in Brazil; fifth at Long Beach; first in Spain; a crash out of the lead in Belgium, and fifth with fastest race lap at Monaco. All this left him third equal in 1979's 'half-time' rankings, ahead of everyone but Scheckter and Villeneuve, who were to finish the year in that same order.

So far, so very good. Then, once again, that fatal combination of Mr Toad and Peter Rabbit reasserted itself as he went merrily a-hang-gliding down the wind, crashed heavily to earth and was painfully grounded for the rest of the season. To put it mildly, it had been a pretty ill-advised escapade and, all the more so, just when he seemed to be locked into a winning team. But taking risks was what Patrick's life was all about, re-echoing what his friend Nigel Roebuck had also written of him:

> Depailler's hobbies were always of the Action Man kind . . . skiing . . . scuba-diving and sailing, and . . . he never lost his love of huge, over-powered motor cycles. He had two heroes, Jacques Anquetil and Eddy Merckx, both five times winners of the Tour de France. 'Le Sport Dur', he would stress. That was where the appeal lay.

Just like Mike Hailwood he demonstrated that it was possible to combine the two facets of fun and work. And how well he showed them off during the first half of 1980, when he carried the fortunes of the once renowned House of Alfa-Romeo: a dedicated professional sorting out their troubles one by one and, even after his death, continuing, as it were from the grave itself, to inspire the young Bruno Giacomelli to go on carrying the torch that Patrick had kindled in those few months for his protégé and his team before it all came to an end on 1 August 1980.

Three things about that accident are crystal clear: first, that it was in no way the driver's fault; second, that once the car was set on its fatal course there was nothing the driver could have done to check it and, third, that the accident was almost bound to be fatal.

That day Patrick had gone out to test his Alfa-Romeo in readiness for the forthcoming German Grand Prix at Hockenheim when the car had crashed heavily and fatally at the fast Ostkurve around 1130 hrs. The car itself was massively damaged and no very clear explanation of the accident has ever emerged. All that is known is that Patrick was half way through the corner and entering the second and tighter part of it when the car went wholly off line and hit a guard rail head on. The absence of any catch-fencing at the fatal time left the outside of this very fast 165 mph corner with no other safety margin except a 30-yard run off and a guard rail! Yet, somehow, so typical of Patrick in everything that he thought and did. In his book you fought, drove and even played hard without, in any way, sacrificing the soft centre you might maintain beneath it all. With him there was no such thing as a half measure. Nick Brittan, his manager over the years, summed Patrick up as a man who:

> . . . loved life. But what he did, he accepted the inevitability of death.

. . . recalling Patrick's own remark to Brittan:

> No, no: the future is for other people.

One last thought that I found particularly touching comes from Eoin Young's 'Diary' in *Autocar & Motor* of January 1992:

> When Patrick's son reached 18 his mother asked what he would like for his birthday. He said . . . a dinner party with the friends of his father who was killed testing in 1980.
> That rather special dinner party took place on Saturday the 7th December.

I cannot think of any more charming or moving occasion.

S. M. B. ('Mike') Hailwood, MBE, GM

> ' "Mike the Bike" Hailwood was . . . quite simply the greatest racing motor cyclist that has ever lived . . .'—*Denis Jenkinson*, Motor Sport *May 1981*

I have always loved the simplicity—sheer, stark and, above all, unchallengeable—of Jenk's moving obit on Mike Hailwood. It has none of the false razzmatazz one has come to associate with some of sport's more febrile commentators and I can only think of one sportsman in his own field, on Hailwood's Olympian level, though he might be the last to latch on to the idea. Just as 'Mike the Bike' was the greatest motor cyclist, so was W. G. Grace the greatest cricketer. However, in Hailwood's case, there was another limb to Jenks' epitaph that could certainly not always be ascribed to W.G., for Jenks went on to add:

. . . not just because of what he won but more importantly because of the way he won.

which tells you so much more about the sheer merit of the man.

That and his rescue of Clay Regazzoni from his blazing BRM in the South African Grand Prix at Kyalami in 1973, for which he was very rightly decorated with the George Medal in a classic instance of Majesty confronting Majesty. I can also still recall his appearance on *This Is Your Life* and the obvious pleasure with which he and Regazzoni greeted one another when 'Regga' came on to the screen.

No less heart-warming was his return to win two more TTs in 1978/ 79 after 11 years absence, when even strong men were overcome by the emotion of the occasion and the magical way in which he still seemed to conjure up miracles of artistry from the recesses of yesteryear. Of a truth time will sometimes run back and fetch an Age of Gold and prove to a sceptical world that Old Troupers do come back, like Floyd Paterson (see pages 120/2) and, more recently, Lester Piggott, making the emotional observer wish that such magic Time-Warps could go on for ever, whoever the 'maestro, might be:

. . . lethal as ever conjured up another magical vision of the past . . . [and] . . . conceded nothing with the passing years . . . [with] . . . the instinctive moves, the strength and the uncanny judgement of pace . . . [still seeming] . . . intact as the champion jockey cajoled his mounts to contrasting triumphs.—*John Karter, The Sunday Times*

Nor were these the only occasions when he had played the 'Come-Back' card successfully. Back in the mid/late-60s his first four-wheeled efforts in Formulas 1 and 2 had proved unsuccessful. His persevering return, first to the newly launched Formula 5000, and then to full Formula 1 in 1971/74, coupled with his winning the Formula 2 European title by nearly 20 points from his nearest challenger in 1962, told a very different story, when he really came into his own, most notably at Monza in both 1971 and 1972. On the first occasion he qualified his old friend John Surtees's TS9 in 17th before astonishing all and sundry by taking the lead on lap 25 and running the rest of the race amid the lead group right through to the thrilling blanket finish when he took fourth with no more than a tenth of a second between the four leaders.

Hailwood improved his place to second in 1972, but that and his

European Formula 2 title of that same year were to remain his best four-wheel racing results, although he still managed to post several not undistinguished misses on the way. He ended his Grand Prix days in 1974 driving a McLaren M23 on the Ring until, lying sixth with two laps to go, his car landed awkwardly at the Pflanzgarten and twitched its way into the guard rail. Although the multiple injuries which he sustained to his right leg and knee were his first of any seriousness, he did not race on four wheels again. However, it did not stop his returning to the Island four years later—on two wheels again—to take on the infinitely longer and more challenging IOM TT course.

Looking at his glittering career, some might say that for all his towering achievements the balls had never bounced quite right for him as they had, for example, in Surtees's career when he won his Formula 1 title in 1964. In hindsight you might also criticize it for being full of lost opportunities, particularly in Formula 1, but had it turned out that way, he might not have been that Mike Hailwood who the whole world looked up to in admiration, and held in high esteem. And without that, the world might have been correspondingly poorer. The road traffic accident in which he and his daughter died in March 1981 was surely loss enough.

Thinking of that accident, I cannot count the times that I have called out to my wife, before nipping down to the fish and chip shop or off-licence in the village, something like 'Back in five minutes', and never given the certainty of my return a second's thought—that is, until Mike Hailwood's accident suddenly gave those simple words a wholly new meaning. I know not if it be coincidence, but the village no longer has either of those two amenities!

When all is said and done, though, what really counted was the bravery and quality of the man, which dovetailed in with the respect and affection that he was accorded by all and sundry in every walk of life. Like another simple man of great courage called Abraham Lincoln, he had become in his passing 'One with the Ages'.

PART 15

Chapter 43

Georges' Younger Brother

André Boillot

(Died 10 June 1932 in an accident near La Châtre Hill Climb)

'Georges Boillot had the reputation of being the most skilful and daring driver in the world. His brother André has shown that he has the same qualities with a recklessness which even his brother did not possess . . .'
— *W. F. Bradley*, Targa Florio.

What, one asks oneself, could André Boillot, who died in 1932, have in common with the likes of Jackie Stewart, Trevor Taylor, John Love, all the way from South Africa, Silvio Moser, Chris Irwin, Roy Pike, Roger Williamson, Henri Pescarolo, François Cevert, Patrick Depailler, Alain Prost, Michele Alboreto, Phillippe Alliot and Jean Alesi?

The answer is to be found on page 98 of the current Michelin Motoring Atlas of France just outside a sleepy little town of 5,142 souls, who come to life, all Rip-van-Winkle-like, once a year for the annual running of the Grand Prix de la Châtre for Formula 3 single-seaters. If you look carefully at the map, you can see the smallest of kinks in the D940 on the outskirts of the town and those magic French words: 'Circuit Auto'—all 1.45 miles of it. Down the years from 1956 the good citizens of La Châtre have continued to run their mini Grand Prix, even expanding it in 1978 from 0.79-miles to its present distance. All the names at the head of this page are those of La Châtre's more famous winners, the only exception being the illustrious Jackie Stewart, who came to the circuit unbeaten in 1964 and went away again with only second place, behind one Eric Offenstadt.

The lot of a younger brother can all too often be thankless and hard and, when the older brother happens to have been the greatest Grand Prix driver of his age with the eyes of the racing world firmly riveted upon him—and Georges Boillot saw admirably to that—it can become as impossible a millstone as walking with two left feet.

It was the achievement of Georges' younger brother André to trump his brother's ace in one glorious hand on a winter's day in November 1919, when, to continue Bradley:

. . . his only hope of victory lay in taking chances which no other man would take; this display was so thrilling that it is to be hoped for his own sake . . . he will not repeat it.

Nor did he.

Like the eighteenth century Member of Parliament for Petersfield, William Gerard Hamilton, who won the nickname of 'Single-' or 'One-Speech' Hamilton from his celebrated three-hour maiden speech in 1755, André Boillot never again repeated his bravura performance. It was as if he had burnt up his entire quota of fire, luck and Mr Bradley's plaudits in eight dramatic hours over the snow-capped, wind- and rain-swept Sicilian mountains.

On that bleak winter's day there was another fiery aspirant with his way to make in the racing world called Antonio Ascari (see page 84) and, anxious not to lose a second to gain his goal, he left the line at great speed and covered the 31 kms between Cerda and Caltavaturo in three minutes less than the great René Thomas in his 5-litre Ballot which he had just driven all the way from Gaillon hill climb on the road: a sobering thought in today's times when even the most insignificant competition cars have to be transported to the least of events! At the time the roads were so bad that, at one point, Thomas had to wait while scaffolding was erected to replace a road which had been washed away!

But for World War I André would have taken his place beside Goux and elder brother Georges in the 2.5-litre Peugeots which had been built for the 1914 Coupe de l'Auto, scheduled for the Circuit d'Auvergne on 23 August. As it was, André's car spent the early part of the war being driven, on military service, by Georges before he enlisted in the Air Force, and then by the Peugeot company as a fast liaison vehicle for executive transport for the rest of the war, before it was shipped out to Indy for the 500 of 1919. By that time the little car had reputedly travelled over 200,000 kms before André actually got to driving it!

The little Peugeot gave at least as good an account of itself at Indy as its 3-litre forebear from 1914, which had finished third, but André's luck was not quite as good as Duray's and, with 195 laps gone, when he seemed set fair to finish at least third, or on some accounts fourth, a tyre burst and the car crashed and turned over, leaving him with a classified 15th place for a consolation prize. Such was the dramatic history of this much travelled little racer that André was to bring to the start of the 1919 Targa Florio.

Now, to revert to Antonio Ascari: his meteor soon burnt itself out when he left the road and fell 30 yards down a ravine where, but for the thousand-fold grace of God, would also have gone André Boillot, who made at least six colourful departures from the circuit during his drive, one of which was later the subject of a Gordon Crosby drawing depicting a miraculous escape from a 200 foot fall. André's final departure was no less memorable.

Thomas had broken down on the last lap and was thus no more a threat, though André was not to know this and pressed on towards the finish only to be confronted by a wall of spectators opposite the Tribunes. Miraculously he had enough brakes to stop in time, but not before the car had spun three times and crashed into the grandstand. Once again the exhausted crew of car and driver rescued the errant car to cross the line—but in reverse, thereby risking disqualification. Ernest Ballot himself, Thomas' patron, is reported as helping to get the crew back into their car for all the world like Lars Porsena and Horatius with his:

> 'God Save him,' quoth Lars Porsena,
> 'And bring him safe to shore,
> For such a gallant feat of arms
> Was never seen before.'

André then had to drive back to the point where he had left the straight and narrow, turn round and re-cross the start/finish line the right way and the race was his. Then, in a final Coup de Theatre, he collapsed over the steering wheel, exclaiming loudly: 'C'est pour la France' and not even the great Georges himself could have capped that line!

André's 'Single-Speech' had lasted 7 hrs 51 mins 1 sec and he had beaten the nearest opposition by over half an hour. There were eight finishers, spread across a gap of over two hours and, although (by some accounts) not classified as a finisher, the first man to start, Enzo Ferrari (CMN), was still on the course at the race's end, while ruefully observing that Count Florio had better get his Targa run off in May another year—and, thereafter, it almost invariably was.

'Single-Speech' raced on for another 13 years, but drove in only two more Grands Prix, both of the ACF, in 1921 and 1929 and in the Indy 500s of 1920 and 1921. His 1921 drives were both for Coatalen in his varied guises, giving him fifth at Le Mans and 20th at Indy and, with that, his career in the Majors was over until the ACF's Grand Prix of 1929.

After 1921 André restricted himself almost entirely to the Coppa/Targa Florio races and the various Categorie de Tourisme events between 1923 and 1927, including the 24-hrs of Belgium and Italy in 1924 and the San Sebastian 12 hrs of 1926, with a succession of sleeve-valve Peugeots. These were good robust sports cars fitted with 3.8/4-litre engines; cars with a top speed of around 105/115 mph, which made them slightly quicker than a good vintage Bentley.

By 1927 André was finding his 4-litres of Peugeot increasingly heavy and more of a handful on the rough, hilly Madonie circuit, with all its twists and turns. His best Florio placings were first in the 1922 Coppa and, sixth, third and fourth with the sleeve-valve cars in 1924, 25 and 27.

He also won the Coupe de la Commission Sportive at Montlhéry in

1927 in a single-seater 2.5-litre sleeve valve Peugeot, and finished second to Williams's Bugatti in the ACF race of 1929. The Coupe was a well supported race, although its result had depended to some extent on fuel consumption, which has never been a satisfactory criterion, and André had been lucky to win in a close run finish. Interestingly the car was not fitted with front wheel brakes. The ACF's 1929 classic took place over the Le Mans road circuit and its entirely domestic field was made up of seven privateers and the works entries of two sleeve-valve Peugeots for André, and Guy Bouriat who became better known as a Bugatti driver, and three Bugattis. Boillot and his old-timer led the race for the first five laps and went on to give the works Bugattis a jolly good run for their money over the rest of the 376 mile distance, with Williams leading André home by 1 min 18.8 secs followed by the second works Bugatti of Count Conelli only another eight seconds behind. Like the Commission Sportive's race from 1927, the Grand Prix had been run on a fuel consumption basis, with each car having a tank with a visible fuel gauge behind the driver.

What mattered, though, was that, in a doldrum period for Grand Prix racing as a whole, the racing had been good and close for the whole of its long distance of $4\frac{1}{2}$ hours, as well as giving the various Cinderellas taking part quite something of a Ball. Once again the Peugeots were the usual 4-cylinder, 4-litre sleeve valves and, at the end of the day, André had been a little unlucky to have lost out in the final stages.

Two curious interventions by André's co-driver one 'Dribus', and his tale is done. The record books show André as the entrant of a sleeve-valve Peugeot to be driven by the anonymous 'Dribus', who is shown as sixth finisher. Finally, the last entry relating to André, for the ten hour French Grand Prix of 1931 shows Henri Stoffel as the entrant of a sleeve-valve Peugeot to be driven by André and the mysterious 'Dribus'. However, their car is marked 'Did Not Attend' and nothing more is heard of the nameless Mr Dribus.

André's last important drive involved breaking the Class F. 24 hr record at Miramas, Provence, on the 1/2 June 1932 in a 1.5-litre 4-cylinder 301C Peugeot. Having completed this unexciting task in dull wet weather, by covering 2650 kms at an average speed of 110.47 kph, he set off for La Châtre to take part in their local hill climb in a rather different kind of Peugeot—a hybrid consisting of their 201X car powered by an unsupercharged Bugatti engine of 1100 cc. On Sunday, 5 June, his car skidded off the road, hit a tree and caught fire. André sustained a fractured skull and other injuries of which he died on the 10th in the nearby hospital of Chateauroux.

He had had a colourful and distinguished war in the French Air Force, winning the Croix de Guerre and the Medaille Militaire, after which he joined Peugeot and became their racing manager at the end of the decade when the veteran Jules Goux retired.

His death made an odd, anticlimatic end to the careers of the Boillot brothers, but, as with so many other things, World War I changed the whole face of motor racing, and for none more than 'Les Automobiles et Cycles Peugeot' and their sparkling, talented 'Charlatans', whom they had begot in the years to 1914.

Chapter 44

A Very Gallant English Gentleman

Captain William Charles Frederick Grover-Williams (aka 'Willie' Williams and others)

(Born 1903: Died 1945 in Sachenhausen concentration camp)

You could be pardoned for thinking that a romantic, exciting sport like Grand Prix racing would be full of fascinating, mysterious characters. Yet the reader of these pages is liable to be sadly disappointed, for Bob Judd's Forrest Evers is no more credible than earlier fictional heroes culled from the 'Clubland Hero' pages of Dornford Yates, Sapper and Leslie Charteris and their dashing subjects: Jonah Mansel, Bulldog Drummond and Simon Templar. Be they Madonnas of today or the Flappers of yesteryear they're all sisters under the skin! Scan these pages as you may, you are unlikely to find anyone to fit the bill with the possible exception of a Man who was sometimes thought of as Two Men, and even he has lost much of his air of mystery now that he has become better and more widely known.

The man, 'Williams', was in fact an Englishman born of English parents in 1903, although he was sometimes variously named and thought by some to be French and by others to be English. He was also said to have lived at some time in the French seaside resort of La Baule and bred dogs at the same time as racing Bugattis in a true blue amateur's desultory sort of way, half the time not arriving for the races he had entered! This actually happened in at least six races out of 13 in 1926/28, although it could well have been that 'Le Patron's' often temperamental cars were no more ready than their driver.

But life was smart and casual in those far-off Elsa-Maxwell-Isadora Duncan-Somerset Maugham days under the bright blue Bugatti-coloured skies of France, Italy and Spain where nothing seemed to matter too much. At least, not until an energetic, go-ahead young man called Anthony Noghes decided to run a street-race through his native Monaco. As Director General of the A.C. de Monaco, he was well enough placed to set up such a venture; he had also been both shrewd and fortunate in securing the early favour of Royalty, in the shape of the House of Grimaldi, and the moneyed backing of the Société des

Bains de Mer, which owned the world-famous Casino. And, with a deficit on the first race of 610 francs, he most surely needed them both! Yet, somehow, his luck held out and enabled him to run eight Grands Prix in successive years from 1929, and put the 'Noghes and Rainier' show well and truly on the map before the Second World War.

So, in April 1929, the little Principality suddenly found itself all bustle, flurry and fuss as it made ready for its great event, the like of which had never been seen—at least in Europe. In truth, however, there was nothing new about a street race any more than one lasting 24 hours. The Americans had long since beaten Europe to both ideas and the Monaco Grand Prix was no more the first of its kind than that of Brignoles had pretended to be in 1930 (see page 269/70).

Ironically, the driver most readily associated with Monaco, the great Louis Chiron, had to miss the first Grand Prix because of its clash with the Indy 500, otherwise its result might have been very different. As it was, the race was to be contested by seven Frenchmen, five Italians, one each from Austria, Germany, Poland and Switzerland, and an expatriate Englishman who both entered and drove as 'Williams' in a Type 35B Bugatti. He was also variously known as W. G. Williams, Willie Williams, even William Grover and, later again, Captain William Grover of the French Resistance but more truly by his heading to this chapter.

'Williams', as I shall call him for the time being, was most active in racing between 1926 and 1933, although he was still taking part in 1936 when he finished ninth at Monaco. By that time he had won four of the more important races of 1929/31: the Monaco and French Grands Prix (1929) and those of Belgium and La Baule (1931). In 1936 he had also been one of a team, with Wimille and Veyron, who set up a new 5000 cc class 24 hr record at Montlhéry at an average of 123.93 mph. René Dreyfus who raced with him during those years and knew him well, still wrote of him in *My Two Lives* as a man with a certain air of mystery of whom it was said that:

> . . . he was a wealthy sportsman—he drove a magnificent town car—others thought that he was one of the livery men who operated from the Place de l'Opera in Paris and hired out his car and his chauffeur services to wealthy clients who wished to travel elegantly. . . . No one knew for sure . . . [just] . . . that he was a charming but very reserved gentleman . . . who came to Friderich's shop frequently whenever he raced in the Nice area.

More recently it was also said that he had been chauffeur to the distinguished Irish-born portrait painter, Sir William Orpen, who lived between 1878 and 1931.

Years later, in his delightful New York restaurant, *Le Chanteclair*, René chanced to meet Williams's brother, a Professor of French, who hold him that his friend was a Captain William Grover, who had been killed by the Germans as a member of the French Resistance and that, one day during the war, his family had received a sad parcel containing his few remaining belongings. The fact of his being bilingual and long resident in France had made him a natural choice for undercover Intelligence work, although he remained as elusive as his personality, save that he had been parachuted into France from England before being ultimately captured by the Germans in 1943. He was subsequently subjected to torture in Sachenhausen Camp and executed a year later, having in the meantime given away nothing and nobody. He had also been associated in his Resistance work with another old friend, Robert Benoist, who was later to take over his work in the cause of Liberation before he too was captured and killed (see pages 216/7) by the Gestapo.

Back in 1929 starting grid places were often determined by ballot and Williams's 35B Bugatti took centre spot in the second row behind Marcel Lehoux and Etancelin. Oddly enough, although he is reported as leading off the line, Lehoux does not appear on the Monaco Club's entry list, though it mattered little as he crashed on the second lap. The main race lay between Williams and the somewhat unlikely entry of Caracciola in an SSK Mercedes, which he drove with characteristic finesse and skill. Unfortunately the combination of its size and the time it took to be refuelled was just too much for Rudi to overcome and, after a spirited series of encounters with Williams, he had ultimately to give best. So Williams ran out winner at 49.83 mph, 1 min 17.8 secs ahead of Bouriano's Bugatti, and 2 m 22.6 secs ahead of Rudi in third place. The winner's time was 3 hrs 56 mins 11 secs, and the first three finishers all completed the full distance of 100 laps and rounded all its famed '1000 corners'. Williams raced several more times at Monaco, but never placed higher than a couple of sevenths in 1932/33 and ninth in 1936.

His life and work were movingly commemorated in the programme of races that took place in the Bois de Boulogne in the autumn of 1945, and the race programme itself carried a photograph and a feature about his career in both Grands Prix and Resistance, though the enigma still remained.

As it turns out, the truth of his life was stranger than the legends that were spun around it in his lifetime, evey by those like René, who had been his friends and contemporaries. 'Williams' had indeed been Sir William Orpen's chauffeur, and Orpen's biographer, Bruce Arnold, tells how on visits to Dieppe:

> The black Rolls Royce would appear silently and smoothly making its way along the esplanade . . . with Orpen's chauffeur always dressed in uniform, with brass buttons carefully polished, and the artist with his model seated behind . . . [The model] would drink grenadine: Orpen, whisky.

Orpen was a remarkably gifted, hard working, portrait and war artist, who also enjoyed a full 'club' life with his friends, a domestic life with his children and a secret emotional life with his several mistresses. He kept them all going, but the strain eventually proved too much . . . and his marriage came to grief . . . he lost friends; he turned to drink and by the age of 52 (in 1931) he was dead.

In the meantime he had decided to make Paris his second home, and ultimately his first. At much the same time he met and fell in love with a ravishingly beautiful 20-year-old from Belgium, Yvonne Aubicq. She became his mistress in late 1917/early 1918, when he was a leading war artist, and the relationship continued until 1928 when they parted unhappily due to the combination of 'the unexpected intervention of yet another woman', (name and identity not disclosed) and the personal deterioration of Orpen himself. Despite it all, though, this remarkable man still managed to go on painting and earning prodigiously until the last year of his life, achieving figures that would compare well with the racing record of Jimmy Murphy (see page 270):

1927	£46394
1928	£45138
1929	£54729
1930	£45086

He was also a highly generous man, and when he and Yvonne parted company he saw to it that she had a handsome settlement, with the Rolls thrown in. With it also came Orpen's chauffeur, William Charles Frederick Grover, which was then the full name of the man who raced as 'Williams'.

In the year of his most memorable victory (at Monaco) 'Grover' married Yvonne at Montrouge (Seine) on 27 November 1929. Their name was later changed to Grover-Williams, which Yvonne kept until her death on 17 December 1973 at the age of 78.

One of her friends tells a story of receiving a telephone call one night during the war from her husband to meet her at a certain place, which, at considerable risk she did, having not seen him for some time—for such opportunities were precious in those fraught times. After his arrest Yvonne continued to act as a courier for his group before she, too, was arrested and imprisoned, like Louis Renault, at Fresnes.

Yvonne was one of the luckier ones, surviving the war, after which she was awarded a British Army widow's pension. She finally settled in Evreux, Normandy, where she went on breeding and showing her Scots terriers, both in France and England where she also had friends, some of whom are still alive and with whom I have recently spoken.

The Grover-Williams marriage had been a very happy one and after the war Yvonne went on hoping against hope that her loved one might still be restored to her. A close friend, both during and after the war, Madame Gladys Garcin, wrote how she had seen Yvonne 'lie on the ground and beat her head on the gravel, weeping for him [her husband]: she never believed he was dead.'

Such is the story of the artist, the chauffeur and the model, culled not least from Bruce Arnold's account of their lives in his delightful book *Orpen—Mirror to an Age* and also from conversation with a few who still knew their charming, lovely Yvonne. When I wrote the fiction that is Part 19 of this book, I had not seen Arnold's book, whose discovery I owe, along with so many other touches in *Requiem*, to my friend, David Venables.

This and the first piece in Part 19 (see pages 325/6) are bizarre examples of the narrow line that can separate the fiction, that is in part based on fact, from the solid fact, that was once thought to be at least part fiction, of this Part's account of the Chauffeur, the Artist and his Model. And, if your taste is for a three-ball, why not throw in 'The Waiter, the Porter and the Upstairs Maid', who are fictitious characters taken from the lyric of that name and brought to life by the mellifluous trombone of Jack Teagarden, the dulcet tones of Bing Crosby and the great voice that was Mary Martin.

Chapter 45
Les Beaux Gendarmes

Pierre Levegh

*(Born 22 December 1905: Died 11 June 1955 at Le Mans during the 24 hr race when
his 300SLR Mercedes-Benz crashed into the crowd opposite the pits)*

Louis Rosier

*(Born 5 November 1905: Died 29 October 1956 in hospital after an accident in the
Coupe de Salon at Montlhéry)*

The real name of the French racing driver who drove for Mors in the
early French races between 1898 and 1901 under the name
'Levegh' was Alfred Velghe and it was he, 'Uncle Alfred', who
created the anagram of his real surname, that 'Levegh', under which
he actually raced. He always drove for Mors and, by the turn of the
century, their combination had become one to be conjured with,
especially when he won the important race, Bordeaux-Perigeux-
Bordeaux in June and the Paris-Toulouse-Paris 'Major' in July 1900,
with FTD at La Turbie from April thrown in for good measure. The
first 'Major' of 1901 was over the traditional Paris-Bordeaux road and,
sure enough, Levegh led as far as Tours, where he ran into gear
troubles. With that, he passes from history, leaving, according to
Jarrott the elusive memory of 'a brilliant driver . . . cool to the degree
of coldness . . . [who drove] . . . like a whirlwind without ever appear-
ing to hurry over anything', with a perfect knowledge of his cars
(always Mors) which he kept 'in a high state of perfection'. He died of
a chill in 1904.

Uncle Alfred left no children of his own, but he did have a sister,
Madame Bouillin/Bouillon, who gave birth to a son in December 1905
in Paris, who she christened Pierre. The man who was later, and
somewhat melodramatically, said to have 'inherited death' grew up
into a skilled mechanic and also something of a 'Le Mans Freak', after
seeing the first Vingt-Quatre Heures in 1923. That and his 'Levegh'
inheritance gave him dreams of driving and even winning the great
classic race that was to become his lodestar. Gradually the aspiring
young man came to be entrusted with cars for testing and, as time went
by, he even attracted the occasional drive in rallies and minor races,
culminating in his driving a Bugatti into eighth place in a three-hour
sports car race at Marseilles in 1937. The next year gave him the
chance to drive a Talbot at both Le Mans and the Antwerp Grand
Prix, although he failed to finish in either race and, in the same year,
he adopted Uncle Alfred's 'Nom de Course' as his own and Pierre
Levegh was born.

Come 1939 and he drove a Talbot into third place in the sports car Grand Prix of Luxembourg behind Wimille's winning Bugatti and Biondetti's 4.5-litre V-12 Alfa-Romeo. It is also said that he finished third in the Antwerp Grand Prix of 1939 behind the Alfa-Romeos of Farina and Sommer, but this is open to doubt as the considerable authority of Roland King-Farlow's tables *Grand Prix Facts and Figures* shows that place to have been occupied by Georges Monneret's Delage. He also placed fifth in the Grand Prix of Comminges and, after that, it was World War II, with Le Mans becoming a fighter base, at first for the Allies and, after the fall of France, for the Luftwaffe, not that it mattered much, for whoever occupied it, the Circuit Permanente and its splendid installations were bound to be the sufferers.

The return of peace brought a gradual revival of motor racing and, although he seems to have missed the Bois de Boulogne meeting in 1945 (see pages 217/221), he was soon enough back in action in 1946 with a Talbot. He continued racing in Grands Prix and lesser races as a very active participant on the fringes of Formula A/Formula 1 from 1946, his last such race being the Albi Grand Prix of 29 May 1955, when he drove a 625 Ferrari into fifth place. In the years between he had driven not just Talbots, but also Delage and Maserati, before returning to Talbot and his last Formula 1 run with the 625. In view of the things that were said about his supposed lack of experience after his last minute failure in 1952 and his fatal accident in 1955 (both at Le Mans) it is both important and fair to his memory that these facts about the length of his experience should be clearly stated.

Levegh had to sit out two more 24s in 1949/50 before his first great chance as a private entrant came in 1951. As often happens at Le Mans, almost all the faster cars gradually fell out, with the exception of the Walker-Whitehead Jaguar XK120C and the Talbot of Meyrat/ Mairesse, who took first and second places ahead of the works modified Aston-Martin of Macklin/Thompson and, then, in fourth the Talbot of Levegh/Marchand.

1952 brought the first serious entry at Le Mans by Mercedes-Benz since Caracciola's lone drive against the massed Bentley Band of 1930, and Rudi himself, with his old rival, Luigi Fagioli, were to have driven one of the new 300SLs. However, a jealous Fate had other ideas, with Fagioli dying after an accident at Monaco (see pages 124/5) and Caracciola being seriously injured in a 300SL at Berne. This left only Lang from the great pre-war days and it was he who kept faith with Mercedes tradition by ultimately sharing the winning wheel after all the faster favourites had bitten the dust, including Levegh's specially prepared Talbot.

After the usual first mad opening rush, the six-cylinder 2.3-litre Simca-Gordini of Manzon/Behra led till just before half distance when, among other problems, it ran out of brakes. Barring accident, this left Levegh in complete command of the race, with a car that had been extremely thoroughly prepared and modified for its long gruelling drive. Levegh was a skilled mechanic/engineer with great experience of Talbots, and when his keen ear picked up an unaccustomed vibration he concluded that he had a broken crankshaft bearing and that his car would need the most delicate handling if it were to last the race, let alone preserve its considerable lead. So he made a calculated risk decision to drive the rest of the race himself rather than risk his co-driver mis-handling the car in its critical state. In its way, his decision was akin to Émile Levassor's decision in 1895 (see page 61) to drive on himself rather than wake his co-driver and it so nearly paid off. The suffering crank broke with about 50 mins to go and Levegh was left to taste the ignominy of both unmerited opprobrium and his own failure.

That, at least, was the account propounded by the renowned W. F. Bradley in *The Autocar* in the wake of Levegh's death in the Le Mans holocaust of 1955. There are other more sensational versions, of varying distaste, but I prefer the measured prose of my honoured friend 'W. F.':

> Not a word passed his lips. The flood of criticism swept over him, leaving him apparently unmoved. Antony Lago presented it (the broken bearing bolt) as the explanation of the failure of his car to win. But of the heroism of the driver, the stubborn determination, the agony he endured hour after hour, not a syllable was revealed.

This was the third successive atttempt by a determined 'Kamikaze' inspired driver to go through the Vingt Quatre Heures single-handed and, not surprisingly, fresh rules were brought in for 1953 prohibiting any repetition with no driver being allowed to drive for more than 80 laps at a stretch or for more than 18 hours overall. That year Levegh himself finished eighth in a shared drive with Pozzi. It was the last 24 he would ever complete.

The 1955 event was doom-laden from the moment that Duncan Hamilton arrived at Le Mans to learn of the death of Sir William Lyons's son in a road accident near Cherbourg. By macabre coincidence two Jaguar wives had just dreamt that Hamilton and his co-driver, Tony Rolt, had been killed at Le Mans. Dining in Rouen that same night, four young Frenchmen had come over to the Hamiltons' table to wish them good luck in the race, adding that they had watched the race from the same place opposite the Jaguar pit for the last three years and asked the Hamiltons to look out for them. That 'looking out' was to be far grimmer than any of those happy diners that night could ever have imagined.

After opening their little window on the sports car racing world in 1952, Mercedes-Benz had re-entered Grand Prix racing in 1954 in the grandest possible way before expanding their enterprise, on that same majestic scale, to take in the major sports car events of 1955 with their 300SLR. They had opened that particular account with a bumper entry in the form book when Stirling Moss and Denis Jenkinson completed their unforgettable drive to victory on 1 May 1955 and their next engagment was scheduled for Le Mans on the 11/12 June. The team selected by Neubauer would comprise Fangio/Moss, Kling/Simon and Fitch/Levegh.

Inevitably, even before the race, there were some wiseacres who wagged their heads and shook their fingers, saying that, on the wrong side of 50, Levegh must be getting a bit long in the tooth and also that he lacked the experience to be driving cars of such high speed that they needed air brakes to slow them down. His Le Mans co-driver later even quoted Levegh himself as telling him:

> This course is too narrow for these fast cars. Each time I go by the pits, I feel hemmed in. . . . I do not like sitting on the left in a racing car. It is difficult enough to see the pit signals in the pit, as narrow as it is. A driver needs to feel comfortable to do his best, and I do not feel comfortable in this car.

Assuming such a conversation ever to have taken place, one's first reaction is one of amazement that, if it really represented Levegh's feelings, he had not at once told Neubauer of them. This certainly did not reflect his 'enchantment' when trying the car out at Hockenheim as reported in *Autosport* a week before the race. Nor does any of this talk accord with either the judgement of Neubauer in choosing him in the first place or the obvious competence which Levegh showed when racing the car. In both day and night practice he had been demonstrably faster than both Kling and Fitch and, as the great Fangio/Hawthorn duel reached its awe-filled climax, he was still only marginally slower than those mighty duellists. The paradoxical thought remains that, if he had not been keeping his end up so well at the time, there would have been no accident and the whole tragedy might well never have taken place.

As it was, at around 1810 hrs that evening he found himself travelling flat out opposite the pits with the road ahead blocked and nowhere for him to go. In the ensuing impact Levegh's car exploded in flames as it flew into the packed enclosure opposite the Jaguar pits, taking with it to their deaths those four carefree young diners, along with another 78 men, women and children to say nothing of the toll of the injured.

The mass hysteria that this appalling tragedy generated brought motor racing to its knees and close to its end. Straight away the French government, who had started it all in the first place, banned road racing out of hand; the Swiss Grand Prix was cancelled, never to be resumed, and even the Germans cancelled their Grand Prix. It was left to the more phlegmatic British and Dutch to see that saner and more measured counsels prevailed, enabling their Grands Prix to be run off without problem or mishap on 19 June and 16 July. By 11 September the Italian Grand Prix had also been held as well as a very full programme of British Formula 2 events.

For all that, the message of Le Mans had still not sunk in, as the next major sports car event at Dundrod in September was to demonstrate with damnable clarity. Dundrod's entry of 49 cars involved a speed differential of around 60 mph, and a driver's differential that comprised, at one end of the scale, the world champion, and, at the other, a bunch of happy, jolly clubmen, all racing over one of the most challenging of the pure road circuits of the day. In short, yet another massive recipe for the disaster that it generated, with three more drivers being killed.

Against that background, the Press Conference Statement put out by Mercedes-Benz on 15 June seems difficult to comprehend:

> We have declared to the competent sporting organizations in our capacity as an old firm which is very experienced in the sport of racing that we shall only participate in such events if the three stipulations:
> (1) Satisfactory conditions of the race course
> (2) The security of the onlookers and
> (3) A strict control of the drivers' discipline appear to us to be strictly safeguarded.

With that statement in mind, and with their hands on their hearts, however in the name of goodness could those worthy men of Mercedes have sanctioned their cars' participation at Dundrod, most especially in the light of Le Mans?

And had poor maligned Pierre Levegh, after all, gone to his fiery end for nothing?

One final thought on his name and its spelling. In Chris Nixon's tour de force of a book *Mon Ami Mate* he states that it was spelt 'Bouillin'. He concludes his Chapter 23, though in a wholly different context, with the words: '(And bring a lawyer.)', which is just what I have done, for my own memory/records do not give the answer. My friend, David Venables, the Official Solicitor, tells me the following story:

> I met Pierre Levegh at Silverstone in 1949. I was wandering around Northampton the night before the International Trophy and I found Levegh and his mechanic in Grose's Garage changing the final drive of the Lago-Talbot so I started talking to him and I was always impressed with how one of these God-like Grand Prix drivers was willing to talk to a 16-year-old speaking very poor schoolboy French. From then on I always took an interest in his happenings. I do remember that on the side of his transporter were the words 'Bouillon-Levegh' and I was puzzled about this at the time and tried to work out what it meant.
>
> Would that the total recall with which one is gifted in one's teens lasted right the way through life.

And now the American chronicler of Indy, Rich Taylor, has written, in 1991, of Pierre Bouillion, which gives us yet another spelling, so wasn't life much easier in earlier centuries when we all spelt our names as the fancy took us?

*   *   *

Louis Rosier's career was slightly shorter than that of Levegh, but very much more successful in both Grands Prix and sports car racing. He won his first Grand Prix at Albi in 1947 and was champion of France in 1949/52.

Neville Cardus, in his autobiography, writes of a cricketer of the 30s 'bowling for hours . . . [who] . . . never ceased bowling in those days; he could have always produced a clinching alibi if ever circumstantial evidence had convicted him of anything: 'What were you doing on 17th July at 4.45 pm?' 'Why, bowling, of course!'

And it was just the same with the honest toil of good, steady, dependable old Louis Rosier. Yet even a Beau Gendarme of France can slip his constabular moorings for the occasional moment of devildom. Thus, in the 1950 Le Mans 24, he set what might well have been the undesirable example of driving through all but 20 minutes of its 24 hours without rest. Indeed those 20 minutes probably stressed him more than the other 23 hours and 40 minutes as he fretted them away in the pits worrying that his son might crash his precious entry! Apart from that little interlude the race had given him little trouble except for a broken rocker arm, which had taken 25 mintues to replace, yet still left him the time to finish, with a 10-minute advantage over the second placed men, Meyrat and Mairesse. Leisured days indeed!

His other great moment of victory was in the Albi Grand Prix of 1953, when sheer steadiness enabled the tortoise to overcome the fleeter hares represented by the might of Ascari's 375 Ferrari, the renowned Thinwall Special Ferrari, driven by the ferocious Farina, and the V-16 BRMs of Fangio, Gonzalez and Wharton. The event was run off in two heats, for Formulae 1 and 2, and a combined final. So Louis hedged his bet by entering for both and winning the Formula 2 heat in his 2-litre '500' Ferrari while placing third in the Formula 1 heat in his 375 Ferrari, before winning the combined final with the bigger car.

The Ferraris of Ascari and Farina did not survive their heat and, while Fangio and Wharton placed first and second in their heat, Fangio retired at half-time in the final with failing brakes, and Wharton crashed out two laps later in a total wreck accident that he was very lucky to survive. All of which left Louis and his newest line in big ambling pads to rumble their comfortable way to his fourth win at Albi by half a minute from Gonzalez's tyre destroying BRM, demonstrating, if nothing else, that the race was not always to the swiftest.

Rosier's blue 375 was and, Glory Be!, still is, reputedly the car in which Gonzalez had overcome the might of Alfa-Romeo in that epic British Grand Prix of 1951 before Ascari drove it to a second successive victory on the Ring 15 days later. A month later found Louis at Rouen-les Essarts in another twilit Formula 1 event, with a field that included Levegh's Lago-Talbot as well as Farina and Hawthorn with a brace of 625 Ferraris on trial for the new Formula 1 of 1954. However, the main attraction was the redoubtable old Rouennais, Philippe Etancelin, and his Talbot. After an indifferent practice session, he put on a wonderfully typical 'Phi-Phi' display in the race itself—and at the age of 57—to finish third behind the two Ferraris and well ahead of Harry Schell's F2 Gordini, Levegh's Talbot and Rosier's 375 Ferrari, which could only manage seventh after losing all its ratios but top: a distinct disadvantage at Rouen with its hairpin and uphill slopes to cope with.

Although this piece is concerned chiefly with Louis Rosier, I am sure that whatever Elysian Field he now shares with his companions in arms must often have thrilled to the memory of Etancelin's last race as he rounded the Nouveau Monde hairpin with 'One wheel in the air . . . [as he] . . . hit the accelerator and let the clutch out so that the car shot up . . . [the hill] . . . pouring rubber smoke . . . [and] . . . drew great cheers from the crowd.'

It was a lovely, colourful and, above all, such a wholly characteristic finale to a long and notable career.

Louis raced on consistently throughout the period 1946/56, initially with the big 4.5-litre Lago-Talbots until Formula 1 was replaced in 1952 by the erstwhile Formula 2, when he switched to a Ferrari 500 (1952/3) and 625 (1954) before acquiring a 250F Maserati. Somehow, though, he seemed out of place in anything but the familiar blue Talbots in which he had enjoyed by far his greatest successes: winning the Belgian Grand Prix of 1949, second place in the Pescara Grand Prix of 1950 and third in the British Grand Prix of 1949 and those of Switzerland and Belgium of 1950. He also won the non-ranking Grands Prix of Holland (1950/51), Bordeaux (1951), Cadours (1952) and Albi 1952/53, besides competing in well over a hundred Grand Prix and sports car events, including, of course, his win at Le Mans in 1950. It was a career that many drivers would have envied.

In October 1956 the annual Paris Coupe de Salon was run on a formule libre basis and was won by F. Godia in a 3-litre Maserati from Duncan Hamilton in a D-Type Jaguar and Jean Behra, perhaps surprisingly, in a Talbot. Hamilton himself had acquired a Lago-Talbot in early 1951 and brought with him a lively touch of the great 'Phi-Phi' to its driving in the ensuing years. Rosier was an old friend and his death in the Coupe caused him deep sorrow, which he has described in his entertaining and aptly named autobiography, *Touch Wood*. Let him, then, take over for what followed after the start:

> We entered the first bend at about 150 mph . . . then suddenly, without any warning [his Ferrari] . . . was sideways across the track, . . . I braked hard and watched him spin round, hit the bank . . . bounce up in the air and then land upside down on the track, bounce up again in front of me, disappear as I passed underneath both car and man, and then land upside down once more. I suppose it was all over in a matter of seconds yet, in my mind's eye, I can still see it all happening as if in slow motion. Bits

and pieces of his car fell all over the track, and I believe Musy's car hit the battery from Rosier's car and that the damage that this did to his steering caused his death.

By about the 7th lap I was in 2nd place behind Musy. Going round the banking I [saw that] quite suddenly Musy had gone ... when his Maserati flew off the banking at speed and fell into the road below. Musy was killed instantly.

Louis Rosier was still alive but there was little hope of his surviving. I was so miserable that I went home without even bothering to take a look at the Paris Motor Show.

Louis died later in the month and as I stood by his grave ... I wondered whether the thrill and excitement of the race was worth while when it so often ended like this.

One thing I am sure of, however, Louis would have been the last person to complain; he knew the possible consequences of his chosen life. Nevertheless, for those of us who knew him, the season had ended on a very sad note.

Chapter 46
Renaissance Man Reborn

Joakim (Jo) Bonnier

(Born 31 March 1930: Died 11 June 1972 in an accident during the Le Mans 24 hr race)

I think of Joakim Bonnier in the same civilized bracket as the elegant Belgian driver, Olivier Gendebien, both dwellers in stately old houses, collectors of beautiful artefacts and paintings, connoisseurs of fine wines and, when they could spare the time, racing drivers of considerable, though perhaps not the very highest, class.

Bonnier had the means and the taste to indulge his fancies, as the son of a renowned teacher of genetics and the scion of a wealthy publishing group—Bonniers, Aktiebolag. After a catholic education spread through Stockholm, Oxford and Paris, he opted out of the family business to take part in motor sport and to spend some years as an officer in the Swedish navy in destroyers.

His first Grand Prix drive was shared with an old hand, the veteran Luigi Villoresi, in a works 250F Maserati in the Italian Grand Prix of 1956, when between them they managed to last just seven laps. Before that, he had entered a 1.5-litre Maserati in the British Grand Prix Formula 2 race at Silverstone, but failed to attend.

The next year, 1957, brought the sniff of a 250F to drive either as a privateer or for the Scuderia Centro Sud, but again with little distinction. His third year was a little luckier with second places, in his own 250F, in the important curtain raiser at Syracuse behind Musso's Dino Ferrari and, in July, at Caen. These limited successes must have attracted some favourable attention, particularly his second place at Caen where BRM were racing. At all events, he was included in their works team with Behra and Schell for the Italian Grand Prix, where his car caught fire, and in the closing race of the year at Casablanca, where he took fourth place behind Phil Hill, the new world champion Mike Hawthorn, and, its folk hero, Stirling Moss.

After that Bonnier stayed with BRM till the end of 1960, winning for them that deeply emotive, first ever Grand Prix victory at Zandvoort in May 1959, to round off a sorry decade of frustrating endeavour, disappointment and disillusion. It was also his own first— and last—win. As one might have expected, the age-old duck took some breaking before it emerged safely from its shell and Jo had to work very hard to ward off the challenge of the Coopers of Masten Gregory, Jack Brabham and Stirling Moss before he finally delivered the goods, by 14.2 secs from Brabham. All in all it was a significant landmark in British motor racing history, to be followed by another 16 in the fourteen seasons to Beltoise's rain-swept victory at Monaco in 1972—or 17, if you count Clark's 1966 win in the H-16 BRM-powered Lotus 43.

In 1961 Bonnier moved over to Porsche with that most gifted, if perennially unlucky of drivers—the American Daniel Sexton Gurney. Unhappily their little cars lacked power and gave Bonnier a sorry series of low places until he left them to take first slot with Rob Walker from 1963. Three years later he had ceded his place to Jo Siffert and was running his own 3-litre Cooper-Maserati in the first two 'Return of Power' seasons. Thereafter, he raced a variety of cars: a McLaren BRM in 1968, when he also had a race in a Honda; a Lotus 49 in which he crashed; and finally, as his 'Desert Island Car', a McLaren-BRM M5A, though sadly with little success until the end of 1971 when he decided that time had come to hang his last Grand Prix car on the wall of his home and concentrate on sports car racing and his work for the GPDA.

This controversial and unhappy body had been formed as long ago as 1961, and Jo had been its first Vice-President and ultimately its President. He was diligent and tireless in the attention that he gave to this thankless task, which, to his credit and that of the sport, he continued to the end of his days. And, perhaps, he should have left it there. Yet his urge to compete was too strong and, there he was at the age of 42 gridding up for yet another Le Mans 24 on the 11 June 1972.

At the start of the race he had enjoyed a few moments of lost glory, holding an early lead, in his Lola T280, for a few of the opening laps before falling away. The end came around 0800 hrs on the Sunday morning as he went to overtake a slower Ferrari on the approach to the 'Indianapolis' corner. He mistimed his manoeuvre, touched the Ferrari and lost control of his car, which flew into the air, threw him out and exploded on impact with the ground.

Jo had enjoyed a wide and long career in both sports and Grand Prix cars, with one unforgettable highlight that, for some, would have made up for everything else. He had also been his country's leading driver for a long time, with a distinguished voice in the counsels of the sport and, above all, he had always been his Own Renaissance Man.

Chapter 47

One of the Greatest 'Must Have Beens'

Carlos Pace

(Born 6 October 1944: Died 18 March 1977 in a commercial flying accident)

When Carlos Pace's light plane fell out of the sky in March 1977 he had driven in 72 Grands Prix from 1972 during which he had won one, taken one pole position and set three fastest race laps. Hardly a record to set the world alight and still less to have caused that ultimate pragmatist, Bernie Ecclestone, to have made his telling and memorable remark about the dispensability of Niki Lauda in the wake of Pace's death.

The autumn of 1971 and the spring of 1972 had seen the advent of three remarkable young racing drivers: Carlos Reutemann, in a non-title ranking event at Brands Hatch in October 1971, with a Brabham BT34, commonly known as the 'Lobster Claw'; Niki Lauda, from the very back of the grid at Buenos Aires in a rent-a-drive March-Ford in January 1972; and the Frank Williams entered March-Ford of Carlos Pace at Kyalami in March.

Reutemann was the most spectacular for the way he took pole position in his first Grande Épreuve at Buenos Aires. Lauda achieved but little throughout the season, his best placing being ninth at Brands Hatch; and Pace had only scored three world championship points so that the best that could be said for him was that his grid placings were generally better.

The perceptive Alan Henry in his penetrating book, *Brabham, the Grand Prix Cars*, describes the aftermath of the news of Pace's death in March 1977 in these words:

> Elegant, stylish, courteous, every inch a racing driver in the story-book idiom, the 32-year-old Brazilian had been one of the team's most loyal and enduring supporters ever since he was recruited almost three years earlier. He had toiled hard with the Brabham-Alfa during its troubled infancy and now seemed on the verge of reaping the harvest of success sown by that early enthusiasm.

to which Ecclestone himself added, in what Henry calls a 'rare and touching personal testimonial from a man not renowned for outgoing sentimentality': 'He was a great driver and a lovely bloke.' More astonishing still was his remark to that author some years later: 'If Pace had lived, I would not have needed Niki Lauda.' Henry concludes: 'It is difficult to imagine a more telling tribute.' And especially from a man like Ecclestone, which makes it so difficult to understand in terms of Pace's results.

Lauda opened his score in 1974, and between then and Kyalami 1977 (Pace's last race) he scored 13 Grand Prix wins and 183.5 championship points. Pace opened his in May 1972 and scored one win and 58 points, over the same period.

Judged by the score-card as a yardstick of success, where can the magic of Pace's record have lain? In the sharp world of Bernie Ecclestone it cannot, surely, have been enough just to be 'a lovely bloke'. In Bernie's world, Success, leave alone Ambition usually called for sterner mettle.

So, could Pace's abilities have really been on the level that both Henry and Ecclestone suggest, and Lauda's dispensability at the end of 1977 be so easy for Ecclestone to have accepted? Or have the issues been blinded in some way by hindsight making an overly generous appraisal of a much-loved and respected man's ability? Given the chance to have proved it, would Pace have been another Lauda?

The score card, with its remorseless emphasis on how things look in cold, flat print, can be the harshest and meanest of judges and it was surely pretty ungenerous to Pace. If one writes off the awfulness of Pace's early struggles of 1972/74 with his Frank Williams/Team Surtees entries, did even his better Brabham years yield any sort of bumper harvest especially when you compare them with those of Lauda over the same period? And whatever would Edward Gibbon, with his views about 'the Candid Severity of History', have said about it all? So, what remains?

I am still disinclined to consign Ecclestone's view to limbo for it seems uncharacteristic for so clear-cut a thinker to have regarded Pace as no more than a mere 'might-have-been', so, somehow, we have got to try to be more perceptive. Perhaps the real answer lies in making a compromise with probability that would allow him to be styled as one of the 'Great Must-Have-Beens'. Nor is this quite so fanciful as it might sound, for there was every sign, at the time of his death, that he had almost psyched a promising car into yielding up its promise, while of his driving ability there had never been any doubt.

Accepting that view, then do not the views of Alan Henry, Bernie Ecclestone and, who knows, even this writer, fall more neatly into place? Or is this element of compromise asking to be confounded by the formidable shade of Colin Chapman rising up, with a loud outburst that I can remember so well: 'I'm not having that, it's a bloody compromise!'

In the meantime the formidable burden of keeping Team Brabham to the fore had passed to the no less elegant and stylish John Watson and the mercurial Hans Joachim Stuck, son of the far-famed Auto-Union driver of the thirties.

Chapter 48
'A Verray Parfit Gentil Knight'

Elio de Angelis

(Born 26 March 1958: Died 15 May 1986 in an accident while testing at Paul Ricard, Provence)

'Only testing, right? So all the safety goes out of the window.'—*Eddie Cheever in conversation*

Carlos Reutemann left Team Lotus at the end of 1979 to join Frank Williams, and during the winter Colin Chapman gave trials to five potentially promising young drivers, only two of whom were ultimately to make any serious mark. One was a gritty Brummie, Nigel Mansell, and the other a wealthy, cultured and sophisticated young Italian, Elio de Angelis. Each man was the precise opposite of the other and both started driving for Chapman in 1980, de Angelis from the beginning of the year, as second stringer to Mario Andretti, and Mansell, as a third man, from the Austrian Grand Prix. Elio was then 21 and Mansell 26.

Elio's path to preferment had been as smooth as Mansell's had been hard. Elio was predominantly both a gentleman and a gentle man, but that in no way dispensed with the need to prove himself on the circuit where money and culture were no longer enough. Indeed, if anything, they only accentuated a need for performance, which Elio was not long in supplying.

His credentials included having been twice Italian Kart Champion and a World title holder by 1975; winner of the Italian National series in 1977 and then, in 1978, an abortive test drive for Ferrari and a somewhat questionably won victory in the important Monaco Formula 3 event, which was very fairly described in Ken Wells's short book on Team Lotus from 1986:

> ... Patrick Gaillard was railroaded by de Angelis in an uncompromising manoeuvre at the Station Hairpin. It may have been Elio's greatest win so far but it was not his finest moment!

... for a would-be Knight could sometimes be very 'Imparfit' and positively 'Un-Gentil' when the winning of his spurs was at stake. Nor was it unknown for him to resort to fisticuffs!

Nothing deterred, he was taken on by Shadow for 1979, then regarded as a distinct back-marker, and Elio did well to qualify 16th (from 25) on the grid and finish seventh in his first Grand Prix—the Argentine. The rest of his year was unspectacular and even included the odd DNQ, but he did come back at the end of the year with fourth place at Watkins Glen, and his first three championship points. Understandably, Shadow were not pleased when he abandoned them after that one year, and his translation to Team Lotus was not accomplished without considerable bitterness and financial cost. Wealth, Style, Sophistication, Scholarship, even concert-piano standard Music, had all to go by the board when a young man had his way to make in a hard and increasingly competitive world. So Elio moved on to what both he and Chapman, to say nothing of Nigel Mansell, confidently hoped would be better things in the new decade.

While Shadow were rapidly on the decline, Team Lotus were not much better off as Andretti soldiered miserably through most of 1980 for Chapman, taking just a single point from the last race of the season, and Mansell nothing from his three races. By contrast, however, Elio took 13 points and seventh place in the rankings from a brilliant second in Brazil—only his second drive in a Lotus—two thirds and a sixth. Even then—and really throughout his career—Elio had the invaluable knack of uniting consistency and perseverance, so that, although Team Lotus were neither the fastest nor the best, they could always bank on Elio keeping his end up by plugging away and making his point. Thus during 1981/82 he took eighth ranking from 14 points and ninth from 23, with Mansell left faint but pursuing in both years. In 1982 Elio won his first Grand Prix—on the demanding Österreichring. It was also the last time that Colin Chapman would throw his time-honoured Cap of Victory into the air, for he died four months and a day later on 16 December 1982

The arrival of turbo-charged Renault engines at Team Lotus in 1983 brought an upsurge in Mansell's fortunes and, for the first time, he bested Elio in the year's rankings: 12th place and ten points beside Elio's 17th and two points. 1984 was Mansell's last year with Team Lotus and it was again Elio who achieved the better results, with a highly consistent 34 points from ten races to set him third in the title rankings. Mansell could only score 13 points to equal the record of his great future rival, Ayrton Senna, in ninth. The next year Senna replaced Mansell at Lotus and Mansell moved to Frank Williams and Honda turbo power.

1985 was Elio's seventh and last full season, in which he won a second Grand Prix on the fast challenging San Marino circuit. This time he placed fifth in the rankings, just two points ahead of Mansell himself, but a significant five behind his new Lotus team-mate, Ayrton Senna, who had emulated Elio in crossing the 'Golden Bridge' to Lotus (from Toleman) at the beginning of the year. At the same time the withdrawal of Team Renault from Formula 1 had left their attractive if unsuccessful crew of Patrick Tambay and Derek Warwick temporarily stranded.

However, time rarely stands still and it was now Elio's turn to be railroaded out by a mightier force. Senna had joined Team Lotus for 1985 on the understanding that he would be joint No. 1 with Elio for the first year and top cat for the second. In his careful, calculating way, Senna wanted some breathing space in which to gather some more know-how and experience of life at the top before assuming full No. 1 status. He achieved this for 1986 at the expense of driving the faithful Elio into the wilderness by insisting that there was no room for two No. 1s in a Team Lotus that might not provide the reliability needed to meet the challenges that 1986 was going to pose. It was really a re-run of the problem that Team Lotus had suffered in 1973, when Chapman had tried to run two fighting cocks called Fittipaldi and Peterson on the same dunghill and merely succeeded in helping Jackie Stewart to 'divide and rule' during his last championship year. By 1985 Senna was far too streetwise to have missed that pitfall! So Elio had to go and, with him, the idea that Derek Warwick might take over the seat that he (Senna) had vacated, for the prospect of Warwick pleased Senna no more than had that of Elio. In the end Senna got his way, and a real No. 2 in Johnny Dumfries.

For Elio his new life with Brabham was like going back to Square One all over again, but being a racer, he just shouldered his pack and got on with the job of being on the grid with his new team-mate, Riccardo Patrese, at Jacarepagua, Brazil on 23 March 1986. Gordon Murray's new 'Low Line' Brabham BT55 was by no means God's Gift to Formula 1 and, although Elio managed to place it eighth, it was certainly not going to repeat his 1985 San Marino victory for him. Nor was Elio himself the greatest enthusiast or exponent of the science, or black art, of testing:

> I think its crazy: all the time the team owners complain about the cost of F1 in this Turbo era—so why do they waste money at these stupid tests at each track? Its like having 30 Grands Prix instead of 16!
>
> What difference would it make if we didn't test everywhere? There are two days of practice before the race, which should be enough. I tell you, it would make no difference: the same guys would still be at the front. Maybe everyone's times would be a second slower. So what?

A line of argument that puts me in mind of the Chapter on Rackets in the Lonsdale Book, where the author makes the point that Rackets, one of the fastest court games in the world with a ball capable of reaching a measured speed of 174.10 mph (Willie Boone's from 1985), is:

> . . . too good a game to be spoilt by turning it into labour and the proper function of all games, amusement and healthy recreation, must be preserved intact.

A lesson somewhere perhaps?

On 15 May 1986, three days after Monaco, the Brabham équipe had gone to Paul Ricard for an official testing session in readiness for the French Grand Prix, so that most teams were present. Testing, at a cost of £800 per day per team was said to include 'full medical facilities', yet there were few marshals present, and none wearing fireproof suits. The nearest fire brigade was at Le Beausset, some eight kilometres away, and the nearest helicopter at Marseilles. And all this at a speed circuit where any accident was almost bound to be a big one. In short, total shambles and a total inability to have learnt the lessons of any of the fire accidents as far back as 1967 and Lorenzo Bandini. The fact that it was 'only' a practice session has no relevance.

Elio was, in no sense, a wild man and the probability is that his accident was caused by losing control after part of the rear wing broke. What is beyond belief is that his death should have been due to lack of oxygen rather than the injuries sustained on impact. It has been estimated that he was trapped in the cockpit for eight minutes, while it was a further half an hour before there was a helicopter available to take him away.

Alan Jones, who was the first driver on the scene after the accident, summed it all up:

> We just couldn't do anything, I never felt so frustrated in my life . . . It was a carbon copy of Roger Williamson's accident [see pages 241/3] at Zandvoort all those years ago. Bloody dreadful . . .

. . . and equally inexcusable—as Nigel Roebuck wrote in his most recent book, *Inside Formula 1*:

> In a sensible world we would eliminate this trekking to every circuit . . . for pre-race practice. If it is to continue, we must ensure that 'race' standards apply to rescue work. When we consider the price of an F1 engine, several of which expire in these sessions, the cost of a helicopter should need no discussion.

Widely recognized as a stylist with the rare ability of nursing a sick car, and a sense of manners and values derived from another age, Elio's was far too fine a flame to have been extinguished so carelessly and uncaringly.

PART 17

A TRAGEDY OF IRRECONCILABLE
DIFFERENCES

Chapter 49

Ferrari's New Wonderman and the Captain Who Hazarded His Ship

Gilles Villeneuve

(see pages 57/8)

Didier Pironi

(Born 26 March 1952: Died 23 August 1987 in a power boat racing accident off the Isle of Wight)

'We are men of the same house who
should have lived in friendship.
It was a small thing to come between us.'—*John Buchan, 'John Burnet of Barns'*

Their tragedy was an enigma of needless differences, for they really *were* men of the same house who *should* have lived in friendship for the full length of their lives, instead of squandering them so hastily and, as it seems a decade later, needlessly. The sadness was that neither man could bring himself to look at it in that light; Gilles was a man of strong persuasion whose 'Yea' was 'Yea' and 'Nay' was 'Nay', while Didier was a man of many ambitions in all of which he had to be 'Top', come hell or high water. And, come the events at Imola on 25 April 1982, failing a miracle, they were set on an inevitable collision course. Put simply, the Ferrari victory at Imola in 1982 was to have been Villeneuve's come the last lap. Villeneuve therefore treated his win as a foregone conclusion, only to have Pironi speed up and snatch 'victory' at the last minute.

* * *

Gilles Villeneuve owed his initial advancement to a rare blend of the sheerest raw talent and the luck to have been taken on board at a crucial time by a shrewd, successful and wealthy Montreal entrepreneur called Gaston Parent. He was prepared to accept Gilles's bland assurance that, in what remained of 1976, he could win the prestigious Molson race at Trois-Rivières to add to the other events he had already won that year. All he needed, he said, was $5000 for a car! And, being Gilles, he was as good as his word. By the end of the season he had totally dominated the Players' Challenge series in Canada, taking pole position and winning all but one race where he simply failed to finish. Most important of all, he had won the Trois-Rivières event in open competition with such drivers as James Hunt, who was to win the world championship that year, Patrick Depailler, Alan Jones, Vittorio Brambilla and the rising Patrick Tambay.

Hunt had done very much the decent thing by blowing Gilles's trumpet loudly in the ears of his main sponsors at McLaren when he got back to England in 1976: 'Look, I've just been beaten by this guy Villeneuve and he's really magic', he told John Hogan, 'you really ought to get hold of him'. His luck held when Teddy Mayer took an early liking to him and, once McLaren and Hunt had achieved their world title status at the end of 1976, they were pressing Gilles to fly over to England and talk turkey for 1977.

Almost inevitably Gilles found the going in 1977's Can-Am racing a lot tougher, not least because of the challenge posed by another future world champion, Keke Rosberg to say nothing of the Wolf-Dallara, which was not exactly God's Gift to Gilles's Can-Am racing that year. However, the week-end of 16 July was to see two highly significant Grand Prix débuts in Silverstone's Celebration of the Queen's Silver Jubilee year: the one of a car with forced induction after a gap of more than a quarter of a century—the yellow liveried Renault RS01 and the other of a no less remarkable Canadian driver in Gilles Villeneuve. The turbo age, which Renault, and their lead driver Jean-Pierre Jabouille ushered in, lasted $11\frac{1}{2}$ years; that of Ferrari's new wonder-man, just under five.

Rather less important in the long term was the 'Eliminatoire' run off on the Thursday preceding that Grand Prix (de l'Europe) to sort out the goats from the sheep, represented by no less than 14 'rookie' entries and a few older stagers. In hindsight it seemed a terribly involved way of establishing the already self-evident promise of Gilles himself with his ageing McLaren M23 and Tambay's new Ensign and, at the end of the day, it had been more a victory for principle and the dubious semblance of a fairer system of play.

The new Renault was an unhappy disappointment with its turbo-charger failing after 17 slow and trouble-haunted laps, and even Vil-leneuve, after his good form in practice (ninth on the race grid), could only achieve a low race placing. In fairness, though, this was hardly the driver's fault as he had been holding seventh place easily enough for the first nine laps before prudently stopping to check the engine's rising temperature, only to find that, like Peter Collins with the first

BRM 25 in 1955, the trouble lay in a faulty gauge! But for this there seemed no reason why he should not have driven through to take fourth behind Gunnar Nilsson instead of 11th, two laps behind the winner. The bald unforgiving entry in the record book gives no real indication of the smoothness, confidence and sheer speed of his driving, that made him deservedly Polymer's 'Man of the Meeting'.

For whatsoever reason, it failed to secure him a place with McLaren, which hurt his 'Yea and Nay' philosophy deeply at the time:

> I could not understand why Mayer changed his mind. I could not work out why I should suffer this backward step.

No more could anyone else, but his anguish was soon enough to turn into unbelievable joy when he received The Call From Maranello, and the rest became history. Ferrari was quick to latch on to Gilles' rich potential:

> When they presented me with this 'Piccolo Canadiense' this miniscule bundle of nerves, I immediately recognized in him the physique of Nuvolari and said to myself, 'let's give him a try.'

So, instead of the red and white of McLaren, Gilles completed his first Grand Prix season in the plain red of Ferrari, crashing out in Japan after finishing 12th on his home ground in Canada's Mosport on 9 October.

It was to be a very different story 364 days later, as he jubilantly told the whole world:

> To win a Grand Prix is something, but to win your first at home is completely unthinkable. I have to thank Mr Ferrari and all the team. It is an enormous satisfaction. This is the happiest day of my life!

During just over three more seasons Gilles was to win five more Major Grands Prix as well as the then important Race of Champions at Brands Hatch. Perhaps not the greatest of records, but, with Gilles, it was rarely what he did so much as The Way He Did It. His distinguished biographer, Gerald Donaldson, has written a truly memorable account of this part of a 'Villeneuve Lap' which is to be found in this book (on pages 57/8).

To my personal regret, I saw all too few of Gilles's races, and only knew him through the world's Press and the table talk of my friends, chiefly Gilles's close friend, Nigel Roebuck. Yet I should not wish to close this account of so remarkable a personality without adding a litttle memory of my own, in which I had chanced to become peripherally involved.

My esteemed colleague, Maurice Hamilton, was recently kind enough to include an extract from my account of 'The Mutton Grand Prix' from September 1947 in his delightful *History of the British*

Grand Prix. The principal contestants in this happy skylark were a gaggle of solid-rear-axled, chain-driven Frazer Nashes and, many years later, in 1979, a similar sort of car chanced to be entered for a short race for Vintage and other old cars at Watkins Glen as a bonus issue for the meeting's entertainment.

A year earlier the car's owner, a Canadian called John Sebert, who was amongst other things a TV director, had been directing a commercial for Fiat at a studio in Toronto with Gilles as spokesman. During one of the inevitable waiting about periods, John's wife Adèle, who was the producer, showed Gilles a photo of John racing his little single-seater 'chain car'. Gilles, a Mr Fear-Nought if ever there was one, took one look at Sebert's fragile craft and told her solemnly: 'That looks very dangerous, you shouldn't let him do that!'

The next year, at Watkins, Gilles actually set eyes on the little car in the presence of both its Canadian owner and its actual constructor, my old, and sadly now late friend, Ron Footit, who had already built and raced a similar car with great success for many years, and was now to drive Sebert's version at Watkins. Unfortunately, due to some quirk of officialdom, Ron was not eligible for the event, but he later graphically described to me Gilles's amazement that anyone could soberly contemplate driving, let alone racing, such a seeming death-trap! But, being Gilles, he was at least interested enough to give the car a look-over, although Mr Ferrari would undoubtedly have drawn the line at his taking it out for a brisk lap or two, unlike Jim Clark, who gave a pre-World War II ERA a never to be forgotten outing during practice for the French Grand Prix at Rouen in 1964. Perhaps fortunately, Patrick Depailler, who was one of the few 'modern' drivers of his age with any time to spare for such 'Golden Oldies', was *hors de combat* in 1979 after his hang-gliding accident, otherwise Ron's little creation might have had another unforgettable outing on a par with Jim Clark's!

* * *

Forgetting the safety aspects that brought old Spa to its inevitable end, the substitutes after 1970, at first Nivelles, and then Zolder were a sorry uninspired let-down. Of course nothing could replace an older glory, yet the more enlightened years from 1983 has seen a very heart-warming restoration of much of Spa's grandeur in a way that would surely have delighted both Gilles Villeneuve and, in fairness, Didier Pironi. In the interim, Zolder had been the setting for both Pironi's first Grand Prix victory, on 4th May 1980 (for Ligier) and the death of Villeneuve himself in practice just over two years later. Gilles's tragedy was a classic instance of a faster driver at the end of practice coming over a blind hill, inevitably in a tearing hurry, going for broke and entering a corner only to be confronted by a slower car, leaving the faster man with literally nowhere to go save eternity. No less did it provide equally classic support for the adoption of something akin to Indy's long-standing practice of having only one car out on the circuit at a time during high speed practice for top grid places. It was also an accident that brought together a whole Pandora's Box of horror: the suddenness and ferocity of the accident itself; the great affection in which its victim was held; his immense reserves of both courage and skill and, perhaps worst of all, the events of the preceding fortnight in which he had been so personally involved and—as a general thought—the whole unhappy atmosphere generated by the long standing feud between FOCA and FISA. No wonder that, in all this acrimony, a man like Villeneuve should have stood out like a shining beacon of hope in a darkening world, exemplified so movingly by Nigel Roebuck's observation:

> Gilles was the one reason for going to Formula One races.

I know the feeling so well.

Yet, in all this, one must not ignore the man who was to become the other principal actor in the ensuing double tragedy. It is impossible to restore the dead to life and enable them to describe 'the What and the Why' of their feelings; and, in their absence, the blanks that they leave behind can only be filled in by consideration of the balance of probabilities—a well enough worn path from my other profession.

I am, therefore, going to start with a bald proposition that I do not recall being previously canvassed: that Gilles certainly, and in all probability Didier too, was in no fit state of mind to have undertaken the serious, hazardous, highly demanding business of driving a Grand Prix car at their levels of speed in the immediate aftermath of Imola. The statements made by such seasoned, understanding observers of Grand Prix racing as Rob Walker, John Blunsden and Peter Windsor, are eloquent testimony to Gilles's state of mind, yet no-one, least of all, that most Ancient of Days, Ferrari himself, seems to have given any thought to whether or not Gilles should have been restrained from racing so soon after. And, let it be remembered that Gilles's crisis had nothing to do with an actual racing accident, after which it was very common practice for an uninjured driver to be sent out on to the circuit again as soon as possible.

But, given two such emotional drivers, with tempers at their Imola flash points, ought not someone to have had the prudence to have called them out. For so many reasons, not the least of which must be Circuit Safety, was there not a case for 'resting' both men for a short time, at least, till higher reason might resume its seat?

So much, then, for the tragedy of Gilles; but, what of Didier? When he left Ligier at the end of 1980 he had expressed happiness at the prospect of 'going to a team where they don't have a No. 1 and a No. 2 driver' and, for their first year through 1981 at Ferrari they seemed happy enough together, although Gilles's Joann always affected to have 'reservations' about Didier, which crystallized when the Villeneuves were not asked to the Pironis' wedding before Imola.

Soon after, and following the Imola affair, Pironi, who was then President of the GPDA, had the unbelievable lack of taste to hail his Imola 'victory' as the 'perfect wedding present!' Yet, for all his jesting, the Gods had still not quite let Pironi off the hook. At the Villeneuve Circuit in June Pironi stalled his car on the grid and was rammed by a young Italian Osella driver, Riccardo Paletti, who died as a result of the accident. In no way was this thoroughly unnerving experience Pironi's fault, and he seemed to recover from it well enough to win the ensuing Dutch Grand Prix, which he then formally dedicated to Gilles's memory before going on to contest the German Grand Prix at Hockenheim. At that stage, with 39 points, he was leading the world championship by nine points from his nearest rival, John Watson, despite his two unavoidable no-scores in Belgium and Canada, all of which left him very confortably placed for the second half of the season.

Then, like Jim Clark and Patrick Depailler on the same circuit, he had a serious accident on the second day's practice. Unlike theirs, it was not fatal, although it was to be the end of his Formula 1 career. Pironi had dominated dry weather practice on the first day, finishing just a second faster than Alain Prost's Renault. The second day produced heavy rain throughout, and not everyone bothered to practise at all with no hope of improving first day times. However, there were some hard men who braved the elements, including, as one might have expected, Didier Pironi, the man with the least to prove. Yet he had to go out in the heavy rain and near nil visibility to do battle with the conditions. His moment of truth came as he approached a spray cloud, which contained a slowing Prost and Daly's Williams about to overtake the Renault. Pironi had not banked on having two cars ahead of him and, as it had been for Gilles exactly three months before, he found himself with nowhere to go. Like Marcel Renault, blinded in his dust-cloud all those years ago (see page 68), he did not realize his danger until it was too late and his impact with Prost turned the Renault all too quickly into a launching pad from which his Ferrari was projected high into the air. Didier suffered appalling leg injuries from which he never recovered sufficiently to resume motor racing, in spite of having 31 operations; although he pluckily managed to continue his other sporting pastime of power boat racing till he crashed fatally off the English coast in 1987.

There were those who said that it was a racer's duty to test himself and his car in all conditions, fair or foul, and that Didier had been entirely right to go out and drive them as hard as he knew. Yet, others like this writer, had their reservations, giving rise to the thought that both Daly and Prost, and perhaps others in the vicinity, had been very lucky not to be more seriously involved in Pironi's accident, making his action in pressing on quite so regardlessly akin to a foolhardy sea-captain hazarding his ship.

Whichever way you looked at their accidents, two of the best drivers of their day had needlessly ended their Grand Prix careers within 3 months of one another.

Gerald Donaldson concluded his Villeneuve saga with these moving words:

> Didier Pironi was genuinely sorry about the controversy following Imola. His home was filled with photos of him and Gilles, and after his death in 1987, his companion (his marriage had earlier ended in divorce), Catherine Goux [coincidentally a famous name through nearly 3 decades of Grand Prix racing], gave birth to twin boys. She named them Didier and Gilles.

So it may be, that in death if not in life, their troubled wheels have finally come full circle at the end of their fraught days and that they have both, somehow, somewhere, brought their fiery steeds and souls to rest.

R.I.P. brave Gilles and Didier.

Chapter 50

Pantaloon and Harlequin

Ernie Triplett

(Born 1906 at Belvedere, California: Died 5 March 1934 in an accident while racing at Imperial Valley Fair, El Centro, California)

Jonkheer Carel Pieter Anthonie Jan Hubertus Godin de Beaufort

(Born 10 April 1934 at Maarsbergen Castle, Holland: Died 3 August 1964 after a practice accident on the Nürburgring)

Harry Schell

(Born 29 June 1921: Died 13 May 1960 in a practice accident at Silverstone)

'But the joys of love are fleeting
For Pierrot and Columbine.' — *Song made popular by 'The Seekers': 1968*

If the Elizabethan theatre-goer of Shakespeare's day loved anything more than his blood and thunder theatricals, it was the little touch of knock-about comedy that wound up the drama and sent the audience out laughing all the way home.

As time went by, this type of act came to be replaced by the Italian-inspired 'Commedia dell' Arte' from the later seventeenth century, with its importation of two new characters. First came the colourful Harlequin: a mixture of childlike ignorance, wit and grace and always in love, always in trouble, easily despairing, easily consoled. Then there was the rival for the affections of the female lead, Columbine, whose name of Pantaloon, was said to be derived from a favourite Saint of the Venetians called San Pantaleone. In the Commedia he was generally played as something of a fool, lean and tall, and inevitably wearing pantaloons.

Two and a half centuries later, not a few of those fool's theatrical characteristics had rubbed off on a Californian character called Ernie Triplett.

Ernie Triplett

In anticipation of Mike Hawthorn, Triplett raced wearing a bow tie, though generally a black one, and, believe it or not, red pantaloons, or 'knickers' as the Americans of the period called them. Triplett's career was as successful as it was colourful and centred on the West Coast between February 1928 and March 1934, interspersed with an annual fling at Indy for the 500 from 1929 through 1933. Although he both qualified and finished in all his five 500s, he never placed higher than seventh in 1931 in the Buckeye Duesenberg Special, which he had previously raced in the 200-mile Board Track race at Altoona in June 1929, finishing fourth.

Altoona had the reputation of being both fast and dangerous and had already seen the deaths of two great Indy men— Howdy Wilcox, the 1919 winner, in the track's opening race in 1923, and Joe Boyer in late 1924, after he had won the 500 that same year. The 1929 Altoona result was a bizarre re-run from that of 1924, with the Indy winner of 1929, Ray Keech, crashing fatally when leading the race after 119 laps. On the 120th lap, a relatively unknown driver, Bob Robinson, was running ninth, 15 laps behind Keech and about to be lapped by him yet again, when his car spun and hit the upper rail. The impact tore 50 or 60 feet of the track's steel retaining band loose, which then sprung across it right in Keech's path, leaving him with nowhere to go. The race was red-flagged with Louis Meyer the winner and Triplett in fourth. Some accounts put Triplett as being close behind Keech, and even challenging for the lead, but I prefer to accept the records in Dick Wallen's beautifully produced and informative book, *Board Track, Guts, Gold & Glory*. It was, of course, perfectly possible that Triplett was running close behind Keech, even though he was nine laps adrift.

That day Pantaloon had probably been lucky in avoiding disaster, but, at least, he showed the proverbial wisdom of the fool in giving up the East Coast and its hazards for the future, and restricting his activities to the more familiar West Coast and Indy scenes.

On his home ground he was a very different person, styled as its 'Enfant Terrible', and anything but the 'Plus Four Fool' that he might have seemed, as he won almost all before him until the arrival of Al Gordon, who became his greatest rival and gradually ousted him from his patch in 1933. Gordon was a stocky, rough, tough guy, who ran a night club and had 'driven outlaw for a year or two' before Art Sparks set him up in a car that was aptly named 'Poison Lil'. Gordon's duels with his plus-four friend soon became the stuff of Californian legend in days when racing was still highly dangerous, primitive stuff, with no restraining belts or roll bars and, sometimes, not even helmets, and bumping and boring very much the in thing.

Eventually Triplett was forced into error and a serious accident, which cost him the AAA West Coast title for 1933. As he recovered, he came to realize that there would always be Al Gordons in his life, who would be just that bit leaner and meaner than jolly old Pantaloon with his fancy ties and red plus-twos.

So it came to the day of the Imperial Valley Fair meeting at El

Centro's mile-long dirt track on 5 March 1934. The track was another widow-maker in the traditions of Langhorne, and had not been very well prepared as Triplett and Gordon fought out what was to be the last of their duels, through the familiar clouds of dirt and dust, while an abandoned car being left unattended on the track made a serious accident become only a matter of time. Presently another car hit the stationary hazard and, despite the courageous efforts of driver and mechanic, they could not clear the way before the battling Gordon-Triplett duo swept on to the crowded scene. Triplett did all he could to avert disaster but died in the attempt, along with the other driver and his mechanic. Gordon's car had also crashed heavily, but 5 March was his lucky day as he got away with no more than a broken nose and minor cuts and bruises. His turn would come at legion Ascot in January 1936 along with his mechanic, the well known Spider Matlock.

A few drivers went on racing from time to time in bow ties, but red knickers vanished for ever with the demise of old Pantaloon and, with him, the revived spirit of 'Commedia dell' Arte' with which he had brought some much needed humour and light heartedness to the harsher realities of board and dirt track racing.

Jonkheer Carel Pieter Anthonie Jan Hubertus Godin de Beaufort

Nobody really succeeded to Triplett's mantle, but, come 1960, who could complain of the simple foolery of Harlequin being revived in the genial Count Carel de Beaufort as he squeezed his ample form into the narrow confines of his vividly coloured little Formula 2 Porsche in which he began his Grand Prix career? And, of course, for a true Dutchman, it had to be Orange.

However, by that time there was rather less room and sympathy for such a happy-go-lucky and, sometimes, overly brash figure as the young Count, who was becoming so palpably a relic from an already fast-departing age. On 1 August 1959 he had survived a trip over the top of the high banking at Avus, which was to be the death of the gallant Jean Behra within the hour. Somewhat insensitively the Count had insisted on being photographed at the scene of the accident that he had so fortuitously survived and, not surprisingly, there were some of an older guard who found his antics not quite so amusing.

However, de Beaufort persevered his way into Formula 1 and, before long, his charm and easy manner made both him and his brightly coloured little racing car an accepted and well liked addition to the Grand Prix scene as he went on to qualify respectably enough in five of his European races through 1961, including a seventh place at Monza. After that both 1962 and 1963 brought him two sixth places to put him, however marginally, into the points, accompanied by the odd

DNQ before 1964 saw the end of his short and colourful career. By that time the little Porsche had become time-expired and only started in one race — appropriately enough on his home ground at Zandvoort, where he qualified next last and went out with engine trouble after only nine laps. He then gave Spa, Rouen and Brands Hatch a miss before coming back on the Ring, where he had a heavy practice crash and died of his injuries two days later.

One of the last of the dwindling band of privateers, he had brought a nostalgic touch of the Colourful and the Different to the sport, that was somehow symbolized by the colour of his car and the fact that he raced in his stockinged feet. He claimed that shoes made it difficult for him to work the pedals and, in the same vein of railery, he used to tell his friends that he might tread on a nail and die of blood poisoning!

At least, though, he had been spared the saucy nicknames that were visited on some other drivers like Hunt and 'the shunt', Andrea 'de Crasheris' and the undignified 'Count von Krash' bestowed on the bold Baron von Trips during his earlier days.

Full of fun, if sadly fleeting, had been the days of the Red Pantaloon and the Orange Harlequin, but odd-balls like them pass this way just once and seldom. Their companion in fooling could be a rather more serious character when he chose to be.

Harry Schell

'Or, like Harry Schell, a driver can love girls, laughs and good living. He was a prudent man. In eleven seasons he never had an accident — nor won a major Grand Prix. He made plenty of money finishing fourth, third and second. "With me, racing is a business", he said, "I don't take chances". And he meant it.

If a driver has this philosophy, it might possibly save him. It did not save Harry. — *Robert Daley, The Cruel Sport*

Harry Schell was the first American to become a full time professional Grand Prix driver after World War II. Although he never won a Grand Prix in his 14-year career from 1946 through 1960, his bold, good humoured and dynamic character left an indelible mark wherever he went.

He was born into motor racing on 29 June 1921 of Franco-Irish parents: Laury and Lucy O'Reilly Schell. Although his mother had driven Bugatti/Salmson cars in some minor races during 1926/29, the Schells did not make any real impact on the motor racing world until the mid-30s with their Ecurie Bleue team of semi-sports Delahayes, before they launched out on their V-12 Grand Prix models and, in 1939, a pair of 3-litre supercharged 8CTF Maseratis. Thus the young Harry found himself en route for Indy in 1940 along with the French Grand Prix drivers, René Dreyfus and René le Begue, who were to drive the Ecurie's Maseratis. Barely 19, Harry did not then rate an

Indy drive and the Maseratis did little good in the race, although Wilbur Shaw's sister car, the so-called 'Boyle Special', won for the second year running.

After that it was 'You're in the Army Now', with not too much of Jane Wyman's 'Kiss Me Slow'! touch for young Harry, who became Corporal Schell, and René Dreyfus who was promoted in the field to the rank of Master Sergeant in the American Army. Although they went their separate ways, their paths continued to cross from time to time. In his book *My Two Lives*, Dreyfus recalls coming across Corporal Schell marching a squad of German prisoners towards a fast approaching wall and becoming so engrossed in his conversation with Dreyfus that he forgot all about his troop of squaddies, who, being good Germans accustomed to obeying all orders, just went right on marching straight into the barracks wall! 'What was Harry doing here anyway?' queried Dreyfus. 'I flunked,' Harry replied, 'I had some problems, I also turned over a tank!'

'Poor Harry,' mused Dreyfus: likeable, devil-may-care hapless Harry—and poor American Army, too, for having to fight a war and manage Harry as well: Harry who had happened to be parading the squad simply because he knew a little German as well as French.

Once out of the army in 1946 Harry lost no time in getting hold of an old Maserati which he took to Indy with his French co-driver, Louis Gerard, who had won the Donington Tourist Trophy of 1938 and come close to winning Le Mans in 1939. Predictably, the ageing car did not survive practice, leaving Harry to make his way back to Europe and a 6CM Maserati for the Grand Prix des Nations at Geneva on 21 July. Ever colourful, Harry's car was painted white with a long blue stripe, with the stars and stripes (upside down!) by the cockpit and the legend 'Ecurie L. O'R. Schell'. Sad to relate he did not even get to the start of his heat on that occasion and, besides opening a bar of his own, in Paris, called 'L'Action Automobile', Harry eventually bought a big 4.5-litre Talbot for sports car and Formula 1 racing, and one of the new Coopers that were fast becoming all the rage. By early 1950 Harry and his brother Philippe were running their own team of 500 and 1100 cc Coopers with considerable success, first winning at Mons. Then in the second heat of the Monaco event. Harry had to settle for second behind a brilliant Moss in the final before swapping his 500 cc engine for an 1100 for the Monaco Grand Prix itself. Although Harry has been dead for over 30 years, it still seems right that a free spirit like his should have been the first (in 1950) to drive one of the Coopers' upstart little mavericks in a full Formula 1 Grande Épreuve, even though their race lasted little more than a single lap as Harry became involved in the eight-in-hand pile up at the chicane on the second. He also got as far as entering one of his Coopers for the leading British hill-climb, Shelsley Walsh, but somehow it got spelt 'Schellsley' in the programme and non-started.

It would be easy to write Harry off as just another plus-four fool, playboying at motor racing, but there was rather more to him than that. In his way he was every bit as hard-working and persevering in his motor racing as, for example, Louis Rosier (see page 300). Indeed, few drivers are more consistently mentioned in the *Sheldon Records of Grand Prix and Voiturette Racing* for that whole busy decade. Moreover, that record contains little or no account of his 'Coopering' fom 1949 or his sports car racing.

Harry's first remotely successful Grand Prix car was an A6GM Maserati from the 1952/53 formula fitted with a full 250F engine for the new Formula 1 from 1954. He immediately put his hybrid into the points with sixth in the Argentine and, once back in Europe, with a pit crew of French film actresses in tow, he took second place in the Rome Grand Prix behind Stirling Moss in an 'entire' 250F. Harry battled on through the season with his hybrid which he had to push home to take seventh place in the German Grand Prix, before taking first place in the second heat at Cadours and third place at Aintree in a privately entered 250F proper.

Harry's six years of hard graft were now about to reap their first real reward, at Barcelona in October 1954, when he took his Maserati into the lead from the front row of the grid, after equalling Hawthorn's best practice time (3rd on the grid). 'Hell Fire Harry' then led for two blistering laps before Ascari stormed past him in the new Lancia D50, with which he led till his clutch went after another six laps. Harry then took up the contest for the lead once again, with Hawthorn and Trintignant for Ferrari, leading on laps 10, 13, 15, 17, 19 and 23 when he spun and later retired. But what a race he had made of it while it lasted and, not surprisingly, it was the take-off point of his career.

After a brief flirtation with both Maserati and Ferrari in early 1955, he became Vanwall's first real standard-bearer in Vandervell's long uphill struggle to get his slow developing British racer into the winner's circle, which he actually achieved in two British domestic races in 1955 at Snetterton and Castle Combe. During 1956 not Moses himself could have fought harder to attain the promised land as Harry fought the Vanwall tooth and nail against the might of Ferrari and Maserati, with his best result, fourth at Spa, and his best drives at Rheims, where he first challenged the red cars and then passed all but one of them on sheer speed, and at Monza, where he actually led them all outright on one glorious lap—the 11th.

That was Harry's last race for Vanwall and, in the end, it was left to the 1957 combination of Stirling Moss and Tony Brooks to make the vital breakthrough, which, more than anyone, Harry had pioneered. By that time (July 1957), Harry had gone on to a mixture of BRM and Maserati, before settling down happily with the British team in 1958–59. His combination at Bourne with BRM and Jean Behra was a particularly happy one that brought together two of Grand Prix's great fighters and funsters and, in retrospect, it was a great pity that they could not have stayed there together for 1959.

Harry had a typically comic adventure, which also involved his old friend, René Dreyfus, in the first US Grand Prix since 1916 when he was driving a Cooper. After practice times were posted, who should be in the front row of the grid but Harry in what was clearly an also-ran car! Romolo Tavoni of Ferrari was scandalized, and threatened to withdraw his cars if this travesty of justice was allowed to continue! Eventually René Dreyfus, who, providentially, happened to be the Race Steward, intervened and Harry, 'grinning like a Cheshire cat . . . said that as a gesture of sportsmanship he would volunteer to give up his rightful place to keep the peace!'

Peacemaker Dreyfus thereupon relayed this to the timekeepers, only to find them taking the inflexible stand of Pontius Pilate: 'What I Have Written, I Have Written!' So, in the end, Tavoni had to climb down and Harry took off from the front row, going out after seven laps with a burned out clutch. As Dreyfus put it: 'Precisely where it was on the back stretch . . . that Harry took the short cut . . . has never been ascertained.' Harry never admitted anything and just grinned mischievously whenever the matter was mentioned in Dreyfus's delightful New York restaurant, *Le Chanteclair*!

Unlike another great funster, Bernd Rosemeyer, Harry was as superstitious about the number 13 as Alberto Ascari or Dick Seaman and, sure enough, it was on Friday 13 May 1960, that greedy Death caught him out in a Cooper doing two things he greatly disliked: driving in the rain and driving in practice. Going through a large puddle at Becketts he spun out backwards into a low brick wall, the accident breaking his neck.

Harry was undoubtedly a greater personality than ever he was a driver, but nobody who saw him take on the full might of Italy in 1956 with that fast but still desperately unproved Vanwall could have failed to appreciate his fighting qualities, any more than they could have missed out on his perennial sense of innocent fun. Yet, for all his outward appearance of devil-may-care and live-for-the-moment, Harry thought of himself as a cautious driver with little desire to kill himself still less anyone else.

His trouble was that he could never quite get his act together, so that it remained an ephemeral passing show of Brilliant Days and correspondingly Awful Months.

* * *

Ernie Triplett, Godin de Beaufort and Harry Schell belonged to the vanished days epitomized by the soldier's song from World War I which has many names and still more versions about:

> . . . going to a Happy Land where everything is bright,
> Where the hangouts grow on bushes and we stay out all night
> . . . And little drops of Haig and Haig come trickling down the rocks.

Chapter 51

The Wages of Sin: a cautionary tale of a tyro, a tycoon and a taxi-dancer

'I've found the subject mentioned in Accounts of Suicides,
O tell me the truth about love.' *W. H. Auden: 'Collected Poems—1927/57'*

'The Goat has rarely got the time
To think concupiscence a crime' *(Unknown)*

'Behind the corpse in the reservoir, behind the ghost on the links,
Behind the lady who dances and the man who madly drinks,
Under the look of fatigue, the attack of migraine and the sigh,
There is always another story, there is more than meets the eye.'
—W. H. Auden: 'The Ascent of F6'

All this happened a long time ago, assuming it ever happened at all, for I only have it from an ageing, embittered racing mechanic late one night when he was well into his second bottle of Pastis. All I can say is that, given the attitudes and characters of those days, it could easily have been true.

'He was bold, he was bad, he was mean' tells all you need to know about the tycoon—or 'Big Bug', as he would have been called in his day. There was little that his money could not buy—save perhaps contentment or happiness.

The tyro was an earnest, hard working young man desperately looking for his Eldorado in the racing success that might set him on the road to fame and fortune.

Both sad enough cases in their vastly different ways. But, saddest of all—and the most genuine in her sadness—was the poor taxi-dancer plying her wretched trade in the 'Pen' for 'Ten-Cents-a-Dance', as a torch song of the day had it.

What quirk of chance could conceivably bring them together and, if it ever did, who knew how they might all end up? As it turned out, very simply.

Bored of an evening, with nothing better to do, the tycoon went out to sample the night-life of the city where he was staying for the current Grand Prix, when his ever-roving eye lighted on a bistro with a dance floor.

The tycoon wanted an attractive woman and the taxi-dancer was all of that. The taxi-dancer wanted to earn money, so what could be more natural than for him to book her for the evening and all the other evenings before the racing came to an end.

The taxi-dancer soon gathered that the tycoon was something pretty big in cars and racing, though he was careful enough not to let her know his name. Of course, she told her boyfriend about the King-Fish she might have netted and how useful he could be with all his connections.

What followed was written in the stars. The taxi-dancer gave up one trade for an even older one, and the boyfriend, who was in any case a very promising young driver, found himself in with a chance of some works drives in the tycoon's team.

The trouble is that nothing lasts, and men like the tycoon can quickly tire of their newest and most ravishing mistress, and the taxi-dancer soon enough found herself being unceremoniously dumped back on the rank with nobody but the lowest dross wanting to spend even 10 cents on damaged goods—for, that was how men thought in those days. And, worse, she had in the meantime fallen heavily for the tycoon.

To crown it all, Death now decided to take a hand at the table. It would be nice to think that it all worked out smoothly, but Death's hands usually pack a hefty punch. The taxi-dancer, seeing nothing left to live for, committed suicide and the boyfriend engineered the tycoon's death at the wheel of his car.

A happy ending for the boyfriend, after all? Not a bit of it, once Death started gradually making inroads into his soul. As time went by, he gave up his racing and then his work and everything else except his Pastis, which he still contrived to beg, borrow or steal.

Such was the down-and-out drop out I had chanced on that night and three days later I read of a man answering his description being run over and killed with an empty bottle of Pastis clutched in his hand.

Death rarely deals his cards out kindly.

Chapter 52

Suicide Pact?

A 30-year old Czech mechanic called Josef Bradzil, living at Press-burg, some 30 miles East of Vienna, arrived to practice at Brno for the Czech Grand Prix of 1934 due to be run on 30 September. He brought with him what was said to have been a new Maserati of the same type as that raced by Nuvolari in the Italian Grand Prix, which would have made it a 3.5-litre, 6C/34. As the detailed Maserati chassis records prepared by Zagari/Orsini do not show the sale of any new 6C/34 around that time either to Bradzil or his purported manager, Marcic, this seems an unlikely story, although the probability is that Bradzil did practice some kind of Maserati there and later die in it.

The story goes that Bradzil bought the car at the Bologna factory with money given to him by this Marcic, who had seemingly borrowed it from his fiancée. For whatever reason the engagment was broken off and the jilted lady angrily demanded the return of her money. Although Bradzil was arrested on the Tuesday before the race, the benevolent Czech authorities obviously regarded imprisonment for debt as lightheartedly as eighteenth/nineteenth century England. So the debtor was released to take part in the first day of practice the next day, on condition that he then went inside again for the rest of the week before being let out again to race on the Sunday! As Harold Nockolds charmingly put it in a subsequent issue of *Motor Sport*: 'It seemed a pity to waste a good car!'

When practice began Bradzil went off at full tilt until he arrived at a sharp corner on the 20-mile circuit at 125 mph, with no possible chance of getting round. The crash was described as:

> ... terrific. The Maserati leaped across a ditch and chopped down two full size trees. In doing so the car itself broke into two pieces. Bradzil was hurled out of the cockpit and killed instantaneously.

If half or quarter of this questionable account be true, it must have been one of the most comprehensive accidents since that of Loraine Barrow in Paris-Madrid, 1903 (see page 69). The Inquest is said to have 'proved that everything pointed to suicide, bearing in mind the speed of the car and the angle of the corner' and concludes that 'Truth and Fiction seem to have nothing on each other when it comes to strangeness.'

Suicide or no? How can one tell after all this time and with so little clear evidence to go on? As Scott Bailey wrote of David Bruce-Brown (see page 94): 'This is a story yet to be fully plumbed,' although such information as there is must raise a general presumption of suicide. Nothing more seems to have been heard of either the mysterious lady of means, who was said to have been Marcic's fiancée, or of Marcic himself. Odd in itself, but nothing like so odd as the fact that the only known account of the tragedy is the one published by *Motor Sport*, when, for example, both George Eyston and Dick Seaman, who drove their K3 Magnettes into third and fifth places in the voiturette race that preceded the Grand Prix, must surely have heard of such an unusual incident. Yet, for example, Chula's biography of Seaman contains no reference to the 'incident', any more than the well illustrated and detailed *History of the Scuderia Ferrari*, who were represented that day by Varzi, Chiron and Comotti; or Maserati, whose car Nuvolari was driving.

How one wishes that some of the photographs of those Brno scenes could speak.

Chapter 53

Some Clubland Heroes of Road and Track

Mark Pepys, sixth Earl of Cottenham, was an amateur racing driver of some ability in the 20s and, come the early 30s he had written a couple of novels with motor racing backgrounds in the Sapper/Dornford Yates vein, and published by Cassell. The earlier one, *All Out*, from 1932 has always seemed to me the better one, although the later *Sicilian Circuit*, from 1933, contains some delightfully arcane period touches, particularly of Mussolini's Italy ('a very good thing') and Bolshevik Russia ('a very dangerous and bad thing').

In the books the stories are written by the Earl as 'Tommy Furness', a semi-retired racing driver with a Hispano-Suiza, a Sunbeam and a sporting Alvis in his motor house and a retinue of servants, although he affects being 'not rich for nowadays: but fairly comfortably off . . . (going) to the National regularly, rearing a few pheasants on the 900 acres of rough shooting which I own near Battle, and spending four months of the year in Scotland. Of course, I never miss a big motor race when I can help it, when I stay at the "Rivolitz" where I am waited on by Henri, doyen of head waiters, René, the rubicund chef, and Gaston the wine waiter.' And it is just the same when the gastronomic scene shifts to England with stewards more dignified and benign than archdeacons to decant the best '08 or pop two bottles of the Pommery '19 over silver and candlelight or a spot of 'Light Port' after luncheon. Never mind having money, today I should very happily settle for being just 'not rich' by Tommy's depressed post-World War I standards!

Needless to say, Tommy and his friend, Strut, who is the top driver in Europe, both have ravishing ladies to match, one a delectable English rose and the other a dark French beauty. Altogether the noble Earl and his entourage emerge as more credible than the heroes of Yates and Sapper, and their ladies strike as more realistic for all their frills and fall-lalls. While today we live in an age of ultra-explicit sex, Tommy contrives to make his heroines remarkably implicit over sex, which can be so much more fun.

Cottenham's first book centred round a mad millionaire with a penchant for robbery on a grand scale. Of course he only planned and financed it, being content to leave the dirty work to underlings, one of whom was a French Grand Prix driver, Maurice Martel, who had obviously fallen on hard times.

He was given the job, first, of nicking a Holbein belonging to one of Tommy's shooting chums, and then a necklace from an American millionairess's suite in the Hotel 'Rivolitz'. All these high jinks, and plenty of others besides, were to take place during the run up to the French Grand Prix at Montbleau (Montlhéry) in which, of course, Martel was driving. Of course, Tommy and his circle were mortified to find that a member of 'the totem' should have 'gone off the rails' and let the side down. However, being good sportsmen and English gentlemen, they found a way to forgive and forget poor Maurice once he 'paid his debt to society' by making a good end, crashing his car and committing suicide during the race, though naturally, not before he had jettisoned his faithful riding mechanic and left him safely at the pits.

To return, then, to our heroes. When they were not clubbing, socializing, motor racing or huntin', shootin' and fishin', they managed to find time to embark on other deeds of derring-do, rounding up stolen Holbeins or other highly valuables in between rescuing trapped capitalist businessmen from the Lubianka prison with the aid and blessing of an approving Clubland Colonel, who happened also to be the Head of the CID.

Chapter 54

'Ciccio' and 'Fatty': another Echo of Clubland

Giovanni Canestrini was one of the four founders of the Mille Miglia from 1927 and a very great motor racing writer, who was writing into the 50s, when Alberto Ascari had grown into the great champion that he became. After Alberto's death, Canestrini wrote one of the many memorials to him. He greatly admired Alberto but would never call him by his familiar nickname 'Ciccio' [an English apposite would be 'Fatty']. As Canestrini himself said:

> I never called him 'Ciccio' — it pleased neither him nor me — especially to call a World Champion, representing our country by such a name — a pet-name so popular, which among other things contrasted strongly with his character and style . . .
> . . . But Gigi always called him Alberto.

. . . as indeed befitted so great a champion.

By one of those odd coincidences that fill *Grand Prix Requiem* the lead character, who is obviously something of a Segrave 'look-alike', is given just a surname. He is simply called 'Fatty' by all and sundry to the puzzlement of the French lady he was to marry at the end of the first novel, who asked Tom:

> 'Why does everyone call Mr Strut, Fatty? He's not fat at all!'
> 'Because,' [Tom] replied truthfully, 'he was horribly fat at school.'
> 'What a reason!' she sniffed, haughtily. 'Men are extraordinary creatures.'

By chance I re-read Kevin Desmond and Cottenham at much the same time, while going through this book and was immediately struck by the quirk of coincidence that seemed to link Ascari, the great champion of fact, with Strut, his counterpart in the fiction of an earlier age. I had never twigged this particular coincidence before, still less thought of adding to it the further conjunction of fatality by Furness/Cottenham's race being at 'Montbleau', surely Montlhéry where Alberto's father had died.

Chapter 55

Count Louis and the Moplahs

Re-reading the Zborowski pieces in William Boddy's erudite *History of Brooklands* struck some odd reminiscent chords in its references to the Count's claque who used to watch him 'take the cement' clad in large, loud check caps which they had, improbably, imported from Palm Beach. But could I place what I was looking for? Could I Heck—except that it also involved large, open motor cars and picaresque adventures in far away places. But the penny still obstinately refused to drop until I came on the story of the Count's expedition 160-odd miles into the Sahara, with his wife and close on 20 litres of a road-equipped Chitty II.

My search was at an end, for its object was the scene in John Buchan's otherwise plain tale of a coup d'etat in an anonymous South American state that began with the arrival of a group of strangely clad young Americans and their even more outlandish looking ladies: 'Pretty little savages with heads like mops,' a more sober member of the party remarked, 'I've christened them the Moplahs,' before they departed on a series of long excursions in large touring cars and disappeared 200 miles into a forbidden valley of desert and high peaks.

A typical Count Louis adventure if ever there was one, but John Buchan did not usually give his young heroes and particularly heroines so much licence to spread their frivolous wings, while I wondered if, somehow, the future Deputy Chairman of Reuters, Member of Parliament and Governor-General of Canada might just have dallied for a passing hour in the Count's enchanted circle at Brooklands in the early 20s and acquired a few ideas for the Moplahs to put on to paper when the *The Courts of the Morning* came to be written in the last years of the 20s.

It would not have been in the least out of character for a man of such broad culture and wide reading, and there is at least one car chase from the 30s, involving a Bentley and a Stutz, in one of his other novels to keep the Moplahs company.

Chapter 56

The Bishop and His Suffragan: a Frivolous Flight of Fancy

There is very little fiction between these covers save for some sections of this Part, but, while I have certainly neither imagined nor invented it, the story has gained some credence that Pierre Levegh was sometimes known as 'The Bishop', allegedly because of his long, solemn face. For a start, this just simply does not add up as any 'mug shot' of its subject amply demonstrates, and I can only think that this flight of fancy must have originated in the phonetic pronunciation of Levegh's adopted surname as 'Le-Veck' close to l'Évêque, which translated into English is 'the Bishop'.

A small sadness in a way because the idea of our Beaux Gendarmes (see page 95) rumbling round their 'diocese', as Bishop and Suffragan, in their ambling pad of a Talbot is not without its humour, however phoney the derivation.

Chapter 57

The Stuff of Dreams

L et us end by taking a short walk with Tommy Furness and Strut as
they stroll round Count Louis' 'cement' on a fine summer's night
reminiscing:

> 'You know,' announced Fatty suddenly, 'this old place is full of
> memories.'
> 'Meaning . . .,' I prompted.
> 'I mean, Tommy, that I often feel the old drivers are somewhere about.
> You know, the ones that made motor racing in the old days.'

. . . a feeling I know so well from years of walking or driving over
circuits where high level motor racing has been going on for a long
time, like Spa, Monza, the deserted road from Paris to Bordeaux on
an early summer morning, the ghostly buildings of the Rheims-Gueux
triangle or the Nürburgring. Really the list is almost endless and with
them:

> 'Our revels now are ended . . . and
> Are melted into air, into thin air:
>
> . . . And, like this insubstantial pageant faded,
> Leave not a rack behind. . . .
> —*William Shakespeare, The Tempest*

Bibliography

60 Ans de Competition Automobile en Belgique, 1896/1956
500 Miles to Go, Al Bloemker (Muller)
1000 bhp Grand Prix Cars, The, Ian Bamsey (Haynes)
A Racing Driver's World, Caracciola (Cassell)
A Record of Grand Prix and Voiturette Motor Racing: Vols 1 & 2, and 5 & 6, Paul Sheldon and others
All Out, Mark Pepys, 6th Earl of Cottenham (Cassell)
Annapurna, Maurice Herzog (Jonathan Cape)
Auto-Union V-16 supercharged (Haynes)
Automobile Connoisseurs Vol. 3
Autosport File: Lotus
Autosport File: Williams, various authors (Temple Press)
Board Track, Guts, Gold and Glory, Dick Wallen
Boxing Companion, The, ed. Denzil Batchelor (Eyre & Spottiswoode)
Brabham: The Grand Prix Cars, Alan Henry (Hazleton Publishing)
British Grand Prix 1926/7 and 1948 to date, Maurice Hamilton (Crowood)
Champion Book of World Championship Facts and Figures, The, Mike Kettlewell
Checkered Flag, The, Peter Helck (Scribners)
Cinquante Ans de Competition Automobiles (Automobiles Peugeot)
Classic Racing Cars, Nye & Goddard (Haynes)
Classic Twin-Cam Engine, The, Griffith Borgeson (Dalton Watson)
Clubland Heroes, Richard Usborne (Barrie & Jenkins, London)
Colin Chapman: The Man and His Cars, Gerard ('Jabby') Crombac (Patrick Stephens)
Complete History of Grand Prix Motor Racing, The, Adriano Cimarosti (MRP Bateman)
Cooper Cars, Doug Nye (Osprey)
Count Maggi's Mille Miglia, Peter Miller (Alan Sutton/St Martins Press)
Courts of the Morning, The, John Buchan (Hodder & Stoughton)
Cruel Sport, The, Robert Daley (S.V.)
Der Kraftfahrsport im Neuen Deutschland (1934)
Devil Behind Them, The, John Bentley (Angus & Robertson)
Dick Seaman: Racing Motorist, HRH Prince Chula Chakrabongse of Siam (G. T. Foulis)
Drivers' Profiles: Jochen Rindt, Alan Henry (Hazleton)
Enzo Ferrari: The Man and the Machine, Brock Yates (Doubleday)
Ettore Bugatti, W. F. Bradley (Motor Racing Publications)
Evolution of the Racing Car, The, Laurence Pomeroy (Wm Kimber)
Famous Racing Cars, Doug Nye (Patrick Stephens)
Fast Ones, The, Peter Miller (Stanley Paul)

Fastest Men on Earth, The, Paul Clifton (Herbert Jenkins)
Fifty Famous Motor Races, Alan Henry (Patrick Stephens)
Formula One, Bob Judd (Pan)
Gentlemen, Start Your Engines, Wilbur Shaw (The Bodley Head)
Gilles Villeneuve, Gerald Donaldson (Motor Racing Publications)
Golden Age of the American Racing Car, The, Griffith Borgeson
  (Norton)
Graham, Graham Hill with Neil Ewart (Hutchinson/Stanley Paul)
Grand Prix 10, 1969, Louis T. Stanley (Allen)
Grand Prix 1950/80 in 3 vols, Mike Lang (Haynes)
Grand Prix Car 1906/39, The, Laurence Pomeroy (Temple Press)
Grand Prix Cars 1945/65, Mike Lawrence (Aston)
Grand Prix Data Book, David Hayhoe (Haynes)
Grand Prix Drivers, Herman Lang (G. T. Foulis)
Grand Prix Drivers, The (Hazelton Publishing)
Grand Prix Greats, Nigel Roebuck (Patrick Stephens)
Grand Prix People, Gerald Donaldson (Motor Racing Publications)
Grand Prix Racing 1906/14 (T.A.S.O. Mathieson)
Grand Prix Racing, Facts and Figures (3rd edn) Geo. Monkhouse &
  Roland King-Farlow (G. T. Foulis)
Grand Prix Report—Auto-Union, 1934/9
Grand Prix, Barré Lyndon (John Miles)
Great Auto Races, Peter Helck (Abrams)
Great Motor Sport of the Thirties, John Dugdale (Wilton House
  Gentry)
Great Racing Drivers, Doug Nye (Hamlyn)
Great Racing Drivers, ed. David Hodges (Temple Press)
Great Savannah Races, The, Julian K. Quattlebaum M.D. (University
  of Georgia Press)
Hamlyn Encylopaedia of Grand Prix Racing, The (David Hodges)
History of Brooklands Motor Course 1906/40, The, W. Boddy
  (Grenville Publishing)
History of the Grand Prix Car 1966/85, Doug Nye (Hazleton)
History of the Scuderia Ferrari, The, Orsini & Zagari (Osprey)
History of the Swiss Grand Prix, René Hafeli (Benteli)
I Did It My Way, Billy Cotton (Harrap)
Il Diavolo Rosso Corre Ancora, Pino Fondi (Edizione Librairie Siciliane)
Indy, Rich Taylor (St Martins Press)
Indy: Race & Ritual, Terry Reed (Presidio Press)
Inside Formula 1, Nigel Roebuck (Patrick Stephens)
Jo Schlesser: Une Histoire d'Homme, George Dirand (Editions
  Sport-Auto)
Jo Siffert, Jacques Deschenaux (Wm Kimber)
John P. Marquand: An American Life, Millicent Ball (Atlantic/Little
  Brown)
Kampf um Meter und Sekunden, Manfred von Brauchitsch (Verlag der
  Nation)

L'Echo de Mai, Paris 24 May 1903
La Favalosa Targa Florio, Giovanni Canestrini
La Grandiose et Meurtrière Course, Paris-Madrid, Jean Robert Dulier (Paul Coty, Paris)
La Mort dans mon contrat—A life of François Cevert, Jean-Claude Halle (Flammarion)
Land Speed Record, The, Peter J. R. Holthusen (Guild Publishing, London)
Lonely Road, Nevil Shute (Pan)
Lonsdale Book of Rackets etc., The, Aberdare and others (Seeley Service)
Louis Renault: Patron Absolu, Gilbert Hatry (Editions Lafourcade, Paris)
Man with Two Shadows, The, Kevin Desmond (Proteus)
Manner, Kurven und Rekorde, Buttner/Feez (Frackh'sche Verlagshandlung, Stuttgart)
Mario Andretti: World Champion (Hamlyn)
Mask of Dimitrioz: The, Eric Ambler (Hodder & Stoughton Ltd/ Fontana Books)
McLaren: The GP, Can-Am and Indy Cars, Doug Nye (Hazleton)
McLaren: The Man, the Cars and the Team, Eoin S. Young (Bond Parkhurst)
Mein Mann der Rennfahrer, Elly Rosemeyer-Beinhorn (Im Deutschen Verlag, Berlin)
Men at the Wheel, Peter Miller (Batsford)
Men, The, Barrie Gill (Leslie Frewin)
Mercedes-Benz GP Racing 1934/55, Geo. Monkhouse (White Mouse Editions)
Mercedes-Benz, Karl Ludvigsen (Bond Parkhurst)
Mille Miglia 1927/57, Giovanni Lurani (Edita, Lausanne)
Mon Ami Mate, Chris Nixon (Transport Bookman)
Monaco Grand Prix: Portrait of a Pageant, Craig Brown and Len Newman (Motor Racing Publications)
Monza 1922/72 (SIAS, Milan)
Motor Car, The, 1765–1914, Anthony Bird (Batsford)
Motor Racing with Mercedes-Benz 1937, Geo. Monkhouse (Newnes)
Motor Racing, S. C. H. David (Iliffe)
Motor Sport Year Books, The, 1972/5
Motoraces, Geo. Monkhouse (Newnes)
Motoring Sport, Stück & Bürggaller (G. T. Foulis)
My Father Mr Mercedes, Guy Jellinek Mercedes (G. T. Foulis)
My Motoring Reminiscences, S. F. Edge
My Racing Life, Juan Manuel Fangio (Patrick Stephens)
My Two Lives, René Dreyfus (Aztec Corporation)
Nuvolari, Cesare de Agostini (S & K)
Nuvolari, Count G. Lurani (Sports Car Press)
Parry Thomas, Hugh Tours (Batsford)

Poets of Tin Pan Alley, The, Philip Furia (Oxford)
Power & Glory, William E. Court, Vols 1 & 2 (Patrick Stephens)
Power & Speed, various authors (Temple Press, 1938)
Race Drivers, Benno Muller
Racing Fifteen-Hundreds, The, David Venables (Transport Bookman)
Racing the Silver Arrows, Chris Nixon (Osprey)
Racing Voiturettes, E. K. H. Karslake (Motor Racing Publications)
Record of Motor Racing, The, Gerald Rose (Motor Racing Publications)
Renault 1898/1966 ed. Pierre Tisnes
Renault de Billancourt, Saint Loup (Amiot Dumont, Paris)
Renault Frères: Their Contribution to the Early History of Automobilism, Edgar N. Duffield
Renault: l'Empire de Billancourt, Jacques Borge & Nicolas Viasnoff (E. P. A., Paris)
Robert Benoist: Champion du Monde, Roger Labric (Edicta, Paris)
Romantic Story of Motor Racing, The, Campbell (Hutchinson)
Rosemeyer, Elly Beinhorn & Chris Nixon (Transport Bookman)
Sicilian Circuit, Mark Pepys, 6th Earl of Cottenham (Cassell)
Sir Henry Segrave, Cyril Posthumus (Batsford)
So Little Time, John P. Marquand (Robert Hale)
Speed Was My Life, Alfred Neubauer (Barrie & Rockliff)
Speed With Style, Peter Revson & Leon Mandel (Wm Kimber)
Sport and the Law, Edward Grayson (Butterworth)
Stirling Moss: My Cars, My Career, Stirling Moss with Doug Nye (Patrick Stephens)
Stories of the Road, Henry N. Manney III (Bond Parkhurst)
Targa Florio, W. F. Bradley (G. T. Foulis)
Ten Years of Motor and Motor Racing, Charles Jarrott
Three-Pointed Star, David Scott-Moncreiff and others (Cassell)
To Draw a Long Line, C. E. 'Johnny' Johnson (Bookmarque Publishing)
Touch Wood, Duncan Hamilton (Barrie & Rockliff)
TT 1907/89, Nick Harris (Hazleton Publishing)
Una Curva Cieca—Life of Achille Varzi (Giorgio Nada Editore)
Vroom!, Peter Manso (Pitman)
W. O. Bentley: autobiography (Hutchinson)
Winners, ed. Brian Laban (Orbis)
World's Greatest Motor Competitions: Le Mans, The, Ian Bamsey (Batsford)
World's Greatest Motor Competitions: The Mille Miglia, Mike Lawrence (Batsford)

Index